KEELY AND HIS DISCOVERIES

John Stuart Mill, in order to protect science, carried empiricism to its extreme sceptical consequences, and thereby cut the ground from under the feet of all science.—PROFESSOR OTTO PFLEIDERER, D.D.

The word of our God shall stand for ever.—ISA. xl. 8.

Imagination is wholly taken captive by the stupendous revelation of the God-force which modern conceptions of the Cosmos furnish. Through the whole universe beats the one life-force, that is God, controlling every molecule in the petal of a daisy, in the meteoric ring of Saturn, in the remotest nebula that outskirts space, as though that molecule were the universe. In each molecule and atom God lives and moves and has His being, thereby sustaining theirs.... Prophet after prophet cries, and psalmist after psalmist sings, that so indeed he has found it; that therein is the divine sonship of man, therein the assurance of eternal life.—REV. R. A. ARMSTRONG.

The living man with his interior consciousness of self and individuality is on two planes of nature at once, as a ship is in two media at once, half in the water and half in the air. To manage your ship successfully you must take cognizance of the laws governing each of those media. To deal successfully with your human being you must understand his physiology no doubt, but you must equally understand his psychology, and something of the collateral phenomena of nature in those regions or planes to which the phenomena of the psychic man belong.—A. P. SINNETT.

The splendid generalizations of our physicists and our naturalists, have had for me an enthralling and entrancing interest. I find as I look out on the world, in the light of all this new knowledge, a pressure of God upon consciousness everywhere; and if this physical force which is God, moves through, sustains, communes, with each smallest physical atom of the whole, much more must that conscious energy which is God, move through, sustain, commune with, these conscious atoms, these several monads, which are you and I, and our friend, and our brother far away. The even flow of the divine force through every material atom, which is the supreme revelation of physical science in our time, itself leads irresistibly on to the suggestion of the constant flow of spiritual energy in actual communion with every spiritual monad that there is. It becomes but a question of opening the eyes of the soul, unstopping the ears of the inward spirit, to see and hear the God who in us also surely lives and moves and has His being, thereby sustaining ours. As the physical atom is physically touched and held and thrilled by God, it is what we should expect that the conscious monad, no less should be consciously touched and held and thrilled by Him.—REV. R. A. ARMSTRONG.

KEELY AND HIS DISCOVERIES

by

MRS. BLOOMFIELD MOORE

Fredonia Books
Amsterdam, The Netherlands

Keely and His Discoveries

by
Mrs. Bloomfield Moore

ISBN: 1-58963-613-9

Copyright © 2001 by Fredonia Books

Reprinted from the original edition

Fredonia Books
Amsterdam, the Netherlands
http://www.fredoniabooks.com

All rights reserved, including the right to reproduce this book, or portions thereof, in any form.

DEDICATED

TO

JAMES DEWAR, M.A., LL.D., F.R.S., M.R.I

FULLERIAN PROFESSOR OF CHEMISTRY, R.I.
JACKSON PROFESSOR, UNIVERSITY OF CAMBRIDGE,

IN ADMIRATION OF HIS DISTINGUISHED SERVICES

FOR SCIENCE,

AND IN GRATEFUL ACKNOWLEDGMENT OF HIS

PROLONGED AND STEADFAST INTEREST

IN KEELY'S WORK OF EVOLUTION.

12, GREAT STANHOPE STREET, MAYFAIR,
   16th May, 1893.

> "Euroclydon driveth us—where?
>   On quicksands and shoals of the sea,
> On rocks that wait hungry to tear
>   And devour with tigerish glee.
>
> "But lo! where we land tempest-tost
>   Is the work that has waited our hand;—
> Not one step of that life shall be lost
>   Whose way an All-seeing hath planned."

We never know through what divine mysteries of compensation the Great Father of the Universe may be carrying out His sublime plans.—MISS MURDOCH.

Enthusiasm is the genius of sincerity, and Truth accomplishes no victory without it.—BULWER LYTTON.

Science is bound by the everlasting law of honour to face every problem fearlessly.—LORD KELVIN.

For my part, I too much value the pursuit of truth and the discovery of any new fact in nature, to avoid inquiry because it appears to clash with prevailing opinions.—WM. CROOKES, F.R.S.

The secret of success is constancy to purpose.—LORD BEACONSFIELD.

> The simple peasant who observes a fact
> And from a fact deduces principles,
> Adds social treasure to the public wealth.
>
> . . . . . .
>
> Facts are the basis of Philosophy.
> Philosophy is the harmony of facts
> Seen in their right relations.—*Lyrics of a Golden Age.*

CONTENTS.   *Page*

PREFACE.—By the Rev. John Andrew xi

INTRODUCTION xv

CHAPTER I.
1872—1882.
INTRODUCTORY 1

CHAPTER II.
1882—1886.
ETHER THE TRUE PROTOPLASM, AN EPITOME OF MACVICAR'S SKETCH
OF A PHILOSOPHY 11

CHAPTER III.
1885—1887.
THE NATURE OF KEELY'S PROBLEMS 30

CHAPTER IV.
1887.
SYMPATHETIC VIBRATORY FORCE 41

CHAPTER V.
ETHERIC VIBRATION.—THE KEY FORCE 54

CHAPTER VI.
THE FOUNTAIN HEAD OF FORCE 65

CHAPTER VII.
THE KEY TO THE PROBLEMS.—KEELY'S SECRETS 72

CHAPTER VIII.
1888.
HELPERS ON THE ROAD, AND HINDERERS 101

Contents.

CHAPTER IX.
1889—1890.
KEELY SUPPORTED BY EMINENT MEN OF SCIENCE.—AERIAL NAVIGATION 113

CHAPTER X.
1881—1891.
THE KEELY MOTOR BUBBLE.—MACVICAR'S LOGICAL ANALYSIS . 129

CHAPTER XI.
1890.
VIBRATORY SYMPATHETIC AND POLAR FLOWS.—KEELY'S CONTRIBUTIONS TO SCIENCE 145

CHAPTER XII.
VIBRATORY PHYSICS.—TRUE SCIENCE 167

CHAPTER XIII.
"MORE SCIENCE" 186

CHAPTER XIV.
VIBRATORY PHYSICS.—THE CONNECTING LINK BETWEEN MIND AND MATTER 206

CHAPTER XV.
THE PHILOSOPHY OF HISTORY.—KEELY THE FOUNDER OF A SYSTEM 229

CHAPTER XVI.
1891.
AN APPEAL IN BEHALF OF THE CONTINUANCE OF KEELY'S RESEARCHES 238

CHAPTER XVII.
1891.
MORE OF KEELY'S THEORIES.—HIS TRADUCERS EXPOSED . . 265

CHAPTER XVIII.
A PIONEER IN AN UNKNOWN REALM 285

CHAPTER XIX.
LATENT FORCE IN INTERSTITIAL SPACES.—ELECTRO-MAGNETIC RADIATION.—MOLECULAR DISSOCIATION. BY JOHN ERNST WORRELL KEELY 298

Contents.

CHAPTER XX.
1892.

PROGRESSIVE SCIENCE.—KEELY'S PRESENT POSITION.—A REVIEW OF THE SITUATION 319

CHAPTER XXI.

FAITH BY SCIENCE: THE DAWN OF A NEW ORDER OF THINGS . 332

CONCLUSION.

KEELY'S PHYSICAL PHILOSOPHY.—By Professor D. G. Brinton, M.D., of the University of Pennsylvania 358

APPENDIX I. 365

APPENDIX II. 368

APPENDIX III. 370

VERSES 373

PREFACE.

By the REV. JOHN ANDREW, *of Belfast.*

"WAIT ON THE LORD."

WHEN the Almighty is taking men into His deeper confidence as to His Creation ways, and how His ways may be taken advantage of for man's service and benefit, the gifted one through whom such revealing is being made should not be hurried by the common bustle of the world, but should be protected in the privacy where the Creator and he are closeted together in the giving and receiving which is thus transpiring.

Scientific patience is, in all such cases, imperative. When the gifted one is bustled by the world, as Mr. Keely has been, his inspiration is disturbed and his advance hindered. If the first inkling of some great revealing thus in progress should promise some mighty find for the material advantage of mankind, there is naturally a quickened desire to gain possession; but if in such an event impatience should impel the seer, ere his far-visioned sight has reached the end, deplorable delay may be the result.

This is the thing which has happened in the case which this little volume comes forth to relate and explain. It is not intended to unfold the systematic methods of the gifted genius concerning whom it speaks; that will come, in his own words, in due time. The aim of this volume is to show the course of events in relation to his researches; and to open the mystery of how it came about that he should have been so much misunderstood and hindered. It tells how he, in the dim dawn of initial inspiration, first glimpsed and touched THE Power which is about to be given to the possession of mankind for the supply of wants, and the relief of toil. How he struggled and wrestled like the patriarch of old who said, "I will not let Thee go, except Thou bless me." How men of the world, seeing the struggle and estimating the power, said, "Make haste and harness this power to our machinery, and we shall pay you." How, in his need of means, he was tempted and fell; making an attempt to harness to machinery a power whose very form and kind he had not yet been given to discern. And then, when this too hasty attempt had failed, how the disappointed world laughed and mocked, and fumed, and called him an impostor.

This volume seeks to explain this KEELY MYSTERY; and to show that although a mistake was made, it was only a passing mistake. The mistake has been rectified; and the seer, now in possession of peace and privacy, has fully sighted the power, and is making progress in bringing it into subjugation.

He has been interviewed by competent men, men of enlarged scientific vision; and in the protection of their esteem, and by the liberal pecuniary aid of one who has made scientific interests an object of sacred solicitude, Mr. Keely is likely to succeed in opening to the world another of the stores which the Almighty Creator and Preserver, ever provident of His children's needs, has prepared in reserve against the time of their necessity. We may theorize, but God alone knows the means by which the regeneration of mankind, and the establishment of the kingdom of righteousness and peace shall come about. The All-merciful has a purpose and plan of His own. The power which Mr. Keely is dealing with belongs to the ways and means of the evolution of civilization and material providence; and it will depend on how men make use of it how far it may clear or block the way of this planet's highest weal. The power, however, which Mr. Keely is dealing with lies so close to the spiritual realm of things, and brings us so near to the point at which the Almighty is in immediate touch of His Creation in His unceasing upholding of it, that all Christian men might be expected to take a deep interest in researches which promise so much. It may reasonably be hoped that this volume may promote this interest, and turn the attention to coming events which are casting more than shadows before. With this hope we commend it to the reading of the wise. Those who delight in yellow-covered literature may pass it by; it contains no plot for the excitement of such.

INTRODUCTION.

Ex Vivo Omnia.

We stand before the dawning of a new day in science and humanity, —a new discovery, surpassing any that has been hitherto made; which promises to afford us a key to some of the most recondite secrets of nature, and to open up to our view a new world.—Dr. HUFELAND.

THE error of our century in questions of research seems to have been in the persistent investigation of the phenomena of matter (or material organization) as the sole province of physics, regarding psychical research as lying outside. The term physics is derived from a Greek word signifying "nature." Nature does not limit herself to matter and mechanism. The phenomena of spirit are as much a part of Nature as are those of matter. The psychological theories of our physicists display a decided leaning towards materialism, disregarding the manifestations of the vital principle,—the *vis motrix*,—and refusing to investigate beyond the limits which they have imposed upon themselves, and which, if accepted by all, would take us back to the belief of the pagans, as echoed by Voltaire:

> Est-ce-là ce rayon de l'Essence Suprême
> Que l'on nous peint si lumineux?
> Est-ce-là cet Esprit survivant à nous-même?
> Il nait avec nos sens, croît, s'affaiblit comme eux:
> Hélas! il périra de même.

Sympathetic philosophy teaches that the various phenomena of the human constitution cannot be properly comprehended and explained without observing the distinction between the physical and material, and the moral and spiritual nature of man. It demonstrates incontrovertibly the separate existence and independent activity of the soul of man, and that the spirit governs the body instead of being governed by the body. As Spenser has said,—

> For of the soul the body form doth take;
> For soul is form, and doth the body make.

Huxley tells us that science prospers exactly in proportion as it is religious, and that religion flourishes in exact proportion to the scientific depth and firmness of its basis. "Civilization, society, and morals," says Figuier, "are like a string of beads, whose fastening is the belief in the immortality of the soul. Break the fastening and the beads are scattered."

Now, as Nature nowhere exhibits to our visual perceptions a soul acting without a body, and as we do not know in what manner the spiritual faculties are united to the organization, psychology is compelled to investigate the operations of the intellect as if they were performed altogether independently of the body; whereas they are only manifested, in the ordinary state of existence, through the intermediate agency of the corporeal organs.

The accumulation of psychological facts and speculations which characterize this age appears to have made little or no permanent impression upon the minds of our scientists and our philosophers. Bishop Berkeley asks, "Have not Fatalism and Sadducism gained ground during the general passion for the corpuscularian and mechanical philosophy which hath prevailed?" Buffon, in writing of the sympathy, or relation, which exists throughout the whole animal economy, said, "Let us, with the ancients, call this singular correspondence of the different parts of the body a sympathy, or, with the moderns consider it as an unknown relation in the action of the nervous system, we cannot too carefully observe its effects, if we wish to perfect the theory of medicine." Colquhoun, commenting upon Buffon's statement, says that far too little attention has been paid to the spiritual nature of man,—to the effects of those immaterial and invisible influences *which, analogous to the chemical and electrical agents, are the true springs of our organization*, continually producing changes internally which are externally perceived as the marked effects of unseen causes, and which cannot be explained upon the principles of any law of mechanism.

These unseen causes are now made clear to us by the truths which Vibratory Physics and Sympathetic Philosophy demonstrate and sustain. The prophecy of Dr. Hufeland (made in connection with an account of certain phenomena arising from the unchangeable laws of sympathetic association) is soon to be fulfilled, and the door thrown open to "a new world" of research. Professor Rücker in his papers on "Molecular Forces," William Crookes in his lecture on "The Genesis of Elements," Norman Lockyer in his book on "The Chemistry of the Sun,"—all these scientists have approached so near to this hitherto bolted, double-barred and locked portal that the wonder is not so much that they have approached as that, drawing so near, they have not passed within.

Professor Rücker, in his papers (read before the Royal Institution of Great Britain) explaining the attractive and repulsive action of molecules, found himself obliged to apologize to scientists for suggesting the possibility of an intelligence by which alone he could explain certain phenomena unaccounted for by science; but do we not find proof in ourselves that the action of molecules is an intelligent action? for we must admit the individuality of the molecules in our organisms, in order to understand how it is that nourishment maintains life. Try as we may to account for the action of aliment upon the system, all is resolved into the fact that there must be some intelligent force at work. Do we ourselves disunite and intermingle, by myriad channels, in order to rejoin and replace a molecule which awaits this aid? We must either affirm that it is so, that we place them where we think they are needed, or that it is the molecules that find a place of themselves. We know that we are occupied in other ways which demand all our thoughts. It must, therefore, be that these molecules find their own place. Admit this, and we accord life and intelligence to them. If we reason that it is our nerves which appropriate substances that they need for the maintenance of their energy and their harmonious action, we then concede to the nerves what we deny to the molecules. Or, if we think it more natural to attribute this power to the viscera,—the stomach, for example,—we only change the thesis.

It will be said that it is pantheism to assert that matter, under all the forms which it presents, is only groups of aggregates of sympathetic molecules, of a substance unalterable in its individualities; a thinking, acting substance. Let us not deny what we are unable to explain. God is all that *is*, without everything that *is* being individually God. Etheric force has been compared to the trunk of a tree, the roots of which rest in Infinity. The branches of the tree correspond to the various modifications of this one force,—heat, light, electricity, and its close companion force, magnetism. It is held in suspension in our atmosphere. It exists throughout the universe. Actual science not admitting a void, then all things must touch one another. To touch is to be but one by contiguity, or there would be between one thing and another something which might be termed space, or nothing. Now, as nothing cannot exist, there must be something between "the atomic triplets" which are, according to the Keely theory, found in each molecule. This something in the molecule he affirms to be "the universal fluid," or molecular ether. One thing touching another, all must therefore be all in all, and through all, by the sensitive combination of all the molecules in the universe, as is demonstrated by electricity, galvanism, the loadstone, etc. If we account for the intelligent action of molecules by attributing it to what has been variously called "the universal fluid," "the electric fluid," "the galvanic fluid," "the nervous fluid," "the magnetic fluid," it will only be substituting one name for another; it is still some part or other of the organization which discerns and joins to itself a portion of one of the fluids referred to, or one of these fluids which discerns and mingles with the material molecules; it is still the life of the part, the life of the molecule, life individualized in all and through all.

Admitting, then, that there is a universal fluid, it must exist in and through all things. If void does not exist, everything is full; if all is full, everything is in contact; if everything is in contact, the whole influences and is influenced because all is life; and life is movement, because movement is a continual disunion and union of all the molecules which compose the whole. The ancient philosophers admitted all this. Under the different names of "macrocosm," "microcosm," "corpuscles," "emanations," "attraction," "repulsion," "sympathy," and "antipathy,"—all names which are only one,—their various propositions were merely the product of inductions influenced by *their modes of observing*, as the deductions of scientists are influenced in our day.

Balzac tells us that everything here below is the product of an ethereal substance, the common basis of various phenomena, known under the inappropriate names of electricity, heat, light, galvanic and magnetic fluid, etc., and that the universality of its transmutations constitutes what is vulgarly called matter. We cannot take up a book on physics (written with *true* scientific knowledge) in which we do not find evidence that its author acknowledges that there is, correctly speaking, but one force in nature. Radcliffe tells us that what is called electricity is only a one-sided aspect of a law which, when fully revealed, will be found to rule over organic as well as inorganic nature—a law to which the discoveries of science and the teachings of philosophy alike bear testimony,—a law which does not entomb life in matter, but which transfigures matter with a life which, when traced to its source, will prove only to be the effluence of the Divine life.

Macvicar teaches that the nearer we ascend to the fountain-head of being and of action, the more magical must everything inevitably become; for that fountain head is pure volition. And pure volition, as a cause is precisely what is meant by magic; for by magic is meant a mode of producing a phenomenon without mechanical appliances,—that is, without that seeming continuity of resisting parts and that leverage which satisfy our muscular sense and our imagination and bring the phenomenon into the category of what we call "the natural;" that is, the sphere of the elastic, the gravitating,—the sphere into which the *vis inertiæ* is alone admitted.

There is in Professor Crookes's "Genesis of the Elements" an hypothesis of great interest,—a projectment of philosophical truth which brings him nearer than any known living scientist to the ground held by Keely. Davy defines hypothesis as the scaffolding of science, useful to build up true knowledge, but capable of being put up or taken down at pleasure, without injuring the edifice of philosophy. When we find men in different parts of the world constructing the same kind of scaffolding, we may feel fairly sure that they have an edifice to build. The scaffolding may prove to be insecure, but it can be flung away and another constructed. It is the edifice that is all-important,—the philosophy not the hypotheses. The science of learning, says Professor Lesley, and the science of knowledge are not quite identical; and learning has too often, in the case of individuals, overwhelmed and smothered to death knowledge. It is a familiar fact that great discoveries come at long intervals, brought by specially-commissioned and highly-endowed messengers; while a perpetual procession of humble servants of nature arrive with gifts of lesser moment, but equally genuine, curious, and interesting novelties. From what unknown land does all this wealth of information come? who are these bearers of it? and who intrusted each with his particular burden, which he carries aloft as if it deserved exclusive admiration? Why do those who bring the best things walk so seriously and modestly along as if they were in the performance of a sacred duty, for which they scarcely esteem themselves worthy?

The Bishop of Carlisle, in his paper on "The Uniformity of Nature," suggests the answer to all who are prepared to approach the abyss which has hitherto divided physical science from spiritual science,—an abyss which is soon to be illumined by the sunlight of demonstration and spanned by the bridge of knowledge. To quote from the paper of the Bishop of Carlisle, "There are matters of the highest moment which manifestly do lie outside the domain of physical science. The possibility of the continuance of human existence in a spiritual form after the termination of physical life is, beyond contradiction, one of the grandest and most momentous of possibilities, but in the nature of things it lies outside physics. Yet there is nothing absolutely absurd, nothing which contradicts any human instinct, in the supposition of such possibility; consequently, the student of physical science, even if he cannot find time or inclination to look into such matters himself, may well have patience with those who can. And he may easily afford to be generous: the field of physical science is grand enough for any ambition, and there is room enough in the wide world both for physical and for psychical research."

But does psychical research lie outside the domain of physical science? What is the supernatural but the higher workings of laws which we call natural, as far as we have been able to investigate them? Is not the supernatural, then, just as legitimate a subject of consideration, for the truly scientific mind, as is the natural? If it explain, satisfactorily, phenomena which cannot be otherwise explained, there is no good reason why its aid should not be invoked by men of science. The truth is, that the ordinary course of nature is one continued miracle, one continued manifestation of the Divine mind. "Everything which is, is thought," says Amiel, "but not conscious and individual thought. Everything is a symbol of a symbol; and a symbol of what?—of mind. We are hemmed round with mystery, and the greatest mysteries are contained in what we see, and do, every day."

Keely affirms, with other philosophers, that there is only one unique substance, and that this substance is the Divine spirit, the spirit of life, and that this spirit of life is God, who fills everything with His thoughts; disjoining and grouping together these multitudes of thoughts in different bodies called atmospheres, fluids, matters, animal, vegetable, and mineral forms.

Herbert Spencer says that amid the mysteries that become the more mysterious the more they are thought about, there will remain the one absolute certainty, that we are ever in the presence of an infinite and an eternal energy, from which all things proceed. Macvicar foreshadowed the teachings of this new philosophy when he wrote, "All motion in the universe is rhythmical. This is seen in the forward and backward movement of the pendulum, the ebb and the flow of the tides, the succession of day and night, the systolic and and disastolic action of the heart, and in the inspiration and expiration of the lungs. Our breathing is a double motion of universal æther, an active and a reactive movement. This androgyne principle, with its dual motion, is the breath of God in man." The writings of the ancients teem with these ideas, which have been handed down to us from generation to generation, and are now flashing their light, like torches in the darkness, upon mysteries too long regarded as "lying outside the domains of physical science."

Twenty years ago Macvicar wrote his "Sketch of a Philosophy," in which he advanced the above views, with other views now maintained and demonstrated by Keely, who during these twenty years, without knowing Macvicar's views, or of his existence even, has been engaged in that "dead-work which cannot be delegated," the result of which is not learning, but knowledge; for learning, says Lessing, is only our knowledge of the experience of others; knowledge is our own. This burden of dead-work, writes Lesley, every great discoverer has had to carry for years and years, unknown to the world at large, before the world was electrified by his appearance as its genius. Without it, there can be no discovery of what is rightly called a scientific truth. Every advancement in science comes from this "dead-work," and creates, of its own nature, an improvement in the condition of the race; putting, as it does, the multitudes of human society on a fairer and friendlier footing with one another. And during these twenty years of "dead-work" the discoverer of etheric force has pursued the even tenor of his way, under circumstances which show him to be a giant in intellectual greatness, insensible to paltry, hostile criticism, patient under opposition, dead to all temptations of self-interest, calmly superior to the misjudgments of the short-sighted and ignoble; noble means as indispensable to him as noble ends; fame and riches less important than his honour; his joys arising from the accomplishment of his work and the love and the sympathy of the few who have comprehended him! "Only the noble-hearted can understand the noble-hearted." Keely's chief ambition has been to utilize the force he discovered; not for his own aggrandizement, but to bless the lives of his fellow-men. He has scaled the rocks which barricade earth from heaven, and he knows that the fire which he has brought down with him is divine.

This so-called secret is an open secret, which, after it is known, may be read everywhere,—in the revolution of the planets as well as in the crystallization of minerals and in the growth of a flower.

Introduction. xxiii

"But why does not Keely share his knowledge with others?" "Why does he not proclaim his secret to the world?" are questions that are often asked. Keely has no secret to proclaim to the world. Not until the aerial ship is in operation will *the world* be able to comprehend the nature of Keely's discoveries. When the distinguished physicist, Professor Dewar, of the Royal Institution of Great Britain, goes to America this summer, he will be instructed by Mr. Keely in his dissociation processes. Every man who has passed the mere threshold of science ought to be aware that it is quite possible to be in possession of a series of facts long before he is capable of giving a rational and satisfactory explanation of them—in short, before he is enabled to discover their causes even. This "dead-work" has occupied many years of Keely's life; and only within the last five years has he reached that degree of perfection which warranted the erection of a scaffolding for the construction of the true edifice of philosophy.

We have only to recall the wonderful discoveries which have been made in modern times, relative to the properties of heat, of electricity, of galvanism, etc., in order to acknowledge that had any man ventured to anticipate the powers and uses of the steam-engine, the voltaic pile, the electrical battery, or of any other of those mighty instruments by means of which the mind of man has acquired so vast a dominion over the world of matter, he would probably have been considered a visionary; and had he been able to exhibit the effects of any of these instruments, before the principles which regulate their action had become generally known to philosophers, they would in all likelihood have been attributed to fraud or to juggling. Herein lies the secret of Keely's delay. His work is not yet completed to that point where he can cease experimenting and publish the results of his "dead work" to the world.

"When will he be ready?" is a question often asked; but it is one that God only can answer, as to the year and day. It now seems as if the time were near at hand,—within this very year; but not even Keely himself can fix the date, until he has finished his present course of experiments, his "graduation" of his twenty-seventh and last group of depolar disks, for effecting change and interchange with polar force.

"But what are his hypotheses? and what the tenets of his new philosophy?" His hypotheses are as antithetic to existing hypotheses in chemistry as the Newtonian system, at its first publication, was antithetic to the vortices of Descartes. The philosophy is not of his creation; nor is it a new philosophy. It is as old as the universe. Its tenets are unpopular, heterodox tenets, but their grandeur, when compared with prevailing theories, will cause the latter to appear like the soap-bubbles that Sir William Drummond said the grown-up children of science amuse themselves with; whilst the honest vulgar stand gazing in stupid admiration, dignifying these learned vagaries with the name of science. It is the sole edifice of true philosophy, the corner-stone of which was laid at Creation, when God said, "Let there be light; and there was light." The scaffolding which our modern Prometheus has built is not the airy fabric of delusion, nor the baser fabric of a fraud, as has been so often asserted. It has been built plank by plank, upon firm ground, and every plank is of pure gold, as will be seen in due time.

It has been justly said that we have no ground for assuming that we have approached a limit in the field of discovery, or for claiming finality in our interpretations of Nature. We have, as yet, only lifted one corner of the curtain, enabling us to peep at some of the machinery by which her operations are effected, while much more remains concealed; and we know little of the marvels which in course of time may be made clear to us.

Earnest minds in all ages and in all countries have arrived at the same inferences which Keely has reached in his researches,—viz., that the one intelligent force in nature is not a mere mathematical dynamism in space and time, but a true Power existing in its type and fulness,—deity. You may say that such an inference belongs to religion, not to science, but you cannot divorce the two. No systematic distinction between philosophical, religious, and scientific ideas can be maintained. All the three run into one another with the most perfect legitimacy. Their dissociation can be effected only by art, their divorce only by violence. Great as is the revolution in mechanics which is to take place through this discovery, it has an equally important bearing on all questions connected with psychical research. Once demonstrated, we shall hear no more of the brain secreting thought, as the liver secretes bile. The laws of " rythmical harmony," of " assimilation," of "sympathetic association," will be found governing all things, in the glorious heavens above us, down to the least atom upon our earth. Leibnitz's assertion, that "perceptivity and its correlative perceptibility are coextensive with the whole sphere of individualized being," will be accounted for without depriving us of a Creator. "The music of the spheres" will be proved a reality, instead of a figure of speech. St. Paul's words, "In Him we live, and move, and have our being," will be better understood. The power of mind over matter will be incontrovertibly demonstrated.

" The requirement of every demonstration is that it shall give sufficient proof of the truth it asserts." This Keely is prepared to give,—mechanical demonstration; and should he really have discovered the fundamental creative law, which he long since divined must exist, proving that the universal ether which permeates all molecules is the tangible link between God and man, connecting the infinite with the finite,—that it is the true protoplasm, or mother element of everything,—we may look for a philosophy which will explain all unexplained phenomena and reconcile the conflicting opinions of scientists.

The great law of sympathetic association, once understood, will become known as it is,—viz., as the governing medium of the universe. Herein lies the secret, the revelation of which will usher in the spiritual age foretold by the Prophets of the Old Testament and the Apostles of the New Testament. Inspiration is not confined to prophets and apostles and poets : the man of science, the writer, all who reach out after the Infinite, receive their measure of inspiration according to their capacity. We need a new revelation to turn back " the tidal wave of materialism " which has rolled in upon the scientific world, as much as Moses needed one when he sought to penetrate the mysteries of the Creation; and our revelation is near at hand,—a revelation which will change the statical " I am " into the dynamical "I will,"—a revelation which, while teaching us to look from Nature up to Nature's God, will reveal to us our own powers as "children of God," as "heirs of immortality."

"Knowledge," said Lord Beaconsfield, "is like the mystic ladder in the Patriarch's dream. Its base rests on the primeval earth—its crest is lost in the shadowy splendour of the empyrean; while the great authors who, for traditionary ages, have held the chain of science and philosophy, of poesy and erudition, are the angels ascending and descending the sacred scale, maintaining, as it were, the communication between man and heaven."

This beautiful imagery holds within it that seed of truth, which is said to exist in the wildest fable; for, although all great discoveries, pertaining to the material world, have been made gradually, with much starting on the wrong track, much false deduction and much worthless result, spiritual truths can be revealed to man in no other way than by that spiritual influence which maintains communication between the terrestrial and the celestial, or the material and the spiritual. "Truth is attained through immediate intuition," say the Aryan teachers; but only by those who have educated their sixth sense; as will be seen in Mr. Sinclair's new work, "Vera Vita; or, the Philosophy of Sympathy." While the imaginative scientist is puzzling himself about new natural forces and the apparent suspension of old and hitherto invariable laws, Sinclair, in his writings, shows us that it is because we do not recognize the elements of nature that their influences remain mysterious to us.

Mr. Sinclair is as firm in his belief as is Mr. Keely that this element is the great connecting link between the Creator and the created, and that it is capable of rendering more marvellous services to man than all the discovered uses of electricity.

The coincidences in the theories of these two philosophers are the more remarkable, inasmuch as Mr. Sinclair's have their origin, as set forth in his book "A New Creed," in metaphysics; while "Keely's wide and far-reaching philosophy" (to quote the words of a distinguished physicist)

Introduction. xxvii

"has a physical genesis, and has been developed by long years of patient and persistent research." But it is an undisputed fact that, in countries far distant from each other, different men have fallen into the same lines of research; and have made correspondent discoveries, at the same time, without having had any communication with each other; and never has there been a time when so many were testing all things that appear to give proof of the super-sensual element in man. There is a very general impression all over the world, says Marie Correlli, that the time is ripe for a clearer revelation of God and "the hidden things of God" than we have ever had before.

All persons who are interested in Keely's discoveries and the nature of the unknown element discovered by Keely and Sinclair, will find in the writings of the latter a more lucid explanation of sympathetic association than Keely himself has ever been able to give in writing. The title of this remarkable book would have been more wisely chosen had its author called it "A New Element and a New Order of Things." The Rev. Philip Schaff, D.D., says of creeds :—"The Bible is the word of God to man : the Creed is the answer of man to God. The Bible is the book to be explained and applied; the Creed is the Church's understanding and summary of the Bible." It is in this light that Mr. Sinclair's new creed, human and humane, should be read.

There is no conductivity in the ether lines, writes Sinclair, for selfish desires and motives; for they are not of the soul, but are only sounds of the lips (or wishes of the material part of us), so that the established connecting-rod between the living soul and the source of life is insulated from desires that are not begotten in sympathy, and they at once run to earth. Where there is no connection there can be no communion. Without the natural sympathetic etheric connection between the source of life and the soul, there can be no communication. "A New Creed," like the sympathetic etheric philosophy of Keely, reveals the connecting link between the finite and the Infinite, and teaches us that the primal law of evolution and of progress is slowly but surely preparing our race for the time when Christianity will be something more than a mere profession, and "the brotherhood of humanity" will no longer be the meaningless phrase that it now is. We are led to see, by this pure philosophy, that "our solar system is a type of a healthy social system; that in it each one affects, binds, controls, sustains, helps, makes free each other; that no star lives for itself alone;" that man was not made to mourn, and that our sufferings arise from our ignorance of the laws governing the innate motive power within us.

The times are not degenerate! Men's faith
   Mounts higher than of old. No crumbling creed
   Can take from the immortal soul its need
Of something greater than itself. The wraith
   Of dead belief we cherished in our youth,
   Fades but to let us welcome new born truth.
Man may not worship at the ancient shrine,
   Prone on his face, in self-accusing scorn.
   That night is passed; he hails a fairer morn,
And knows himself a something half divine!
   No humble worm whose heritage is sin,
But part of God—he feels the Christ within!
No fierce Jehovah with a frowning mien
   He worships. Nay, through love, and not through fear,
   He seeks the truth, and *finds its source is near!*
He feels and owns the power of things unseen,
   Where once he scoffed. *God's great primeval plan*
   Is fast unfolding in the soul of man.—ELLA W. WILCOX.

KEELY AND HIS DISCOVERIES.

CHAPTER I.

1872 TO 1882.

INTRODUCTORY.

 Within the half-century the hypothetical ether has amply vindicated its novel claim to take its place as a mysterious entity side by side with matter and energy among the ultimate components of the objective universe. . . . Modern science sets before our eyes the comprehensive and glorious idea of a cosmos which is one and the same throughout, in sun and star and world and atom, in light and heat and life and mechanism, in herb and tree and man and animal, in body, soul, and spirit, mind and matter.—GRANT ALLEN on *Evolution*.

 The man who can demonstrate the existence of an unsuspected and unknown force has a right, in the absence of demonstrative proof to the contrary, to form his own theory of its origin, and to make it the basis of his own system. Keely is looking at physical phenomena and their explanations from a point of view so different from that of the inductive school, that we hardly know how to combine the two, or show their bearings upon each other. For myself, I think now, as I thought and said in my address, that the absolutely exclusive position, taken up by Huxley, Tyndall, and the so-called Material School, is ludicrously indefensible; and that we should be as perfectly open to evidence in any direction, as we were 2000 years ago.—THE REV. H. W. WATSON, D.Sc., F.R.S.

So many men of learning are now holding Dr. Watson's views that the time seems to have arrived, in which the theories of Keely will receive, from those who are competent to judge of their value, the attention that they deserve. Before entering upon their merits, or setting them down for others to judge of their worth, the way must be prepared by showing the claims which they possess from their correspondence with some of the most advanced ideas of the present day, as well as with the teachings of the wisest men in past centuries.

 The mode which is the least laborious to accomplish this

end, is by collecting what has been written and printed, which bears upon, and elucidates this subject.

It is now very generally known that Mr. Keely, while pursuing a line of experiment in vibrations, "accidentally" as Edison would say, made his discovery of an energy, the origin of which was unknown to himself; and six years passed, in experiment, before he was able to repeat its production at will. In the meantime he had exhausted his resources and willingly accepted the proposal of men, who, after witnessing the operation of the energy that he was able to show with this unknown force, offered to organize a company to furnish him with the means to construct an engine to use this force as the motive power, anticipating immediate success.

But discovery is one thing, invention quite another thing, and the years rolled on without Mr. Keely's being able to fulfil his promises. In 1882, which was about ten years after the company was formed, an action at law was brought against him for non-fulfilment of his contract. The *Evening Bulletin* of March 30th of that year thus explains, truthfully, the position.

THE KEELY MOTOR.

A STATEMENT FROM ONE OF THE INVENTOR'S STOCKHOLDERS.

"*To the Editor of the Evening Bulletin*: In your issue of last Tuesday appears an article which deserves attention, and also calls for some explanation upon that very much misunderstood question of the Keely motor. From some cause not easy to learn, there seems to be a tendency to keep only one side of that subject before the public.

"Being one of the unfortunates of the Keely motor speculation, interest has led me to investigate not only the invention and the man who has everything to do with it, but also the management of the company, which is equally important to those who put their money into the enterprise as an investment. Permit me, therefore, to state a few of the facts which, if known, would very much change some of the popular views now held.

"There are perhaps a thousand stockholders in the Keely Motor Company. The mass of these, like myself, are not the prosecutors in this case against Mr. Keely. We do not believe that Mr. Keely can be forced to divulge any valuable secrets if he possesses them. We do not believe that a case in court is calculated to prolong the inventor's life, or render it more safe from the accidents to which he is exposed. We do not believe that these proceedings are likely to increase his good will towards the company. *Some* of us know that by purchasing Keely motor stock, we have not thereby put our money into the invention, nor has Mr. Keely had the benefit of it. We also know that some, if not all, of the parties to this prosecution, especially those who are most vehement in its favour under the pretence of protecting the common stockholders, are selfish to the last degree, while for themselves they have the least cause to complain. Their official records show an utter disregard of the interests of stockholders or the rights of the inventor: while the success of the invention is to them a secondary consideration. It is they, and not the inventor, who have drummed up the customers, and recommended and sold the stock. They, and not he, are answerable to the purchasers. If Mr. Keely is guilty of deception, they are to say the least equally so. Look at a few statements:

"When the Keely Motor Company was started, in 1874, its organizers received their stock without paying for it. About three-fourths of the whole amount were thus given away by Mr. Keely. He retained about one-seventh, and was cheated out of a good portion of that before he had gone far. Only 400 shares out of 20,000 were retained in the treasury, and that but a short time; for these recipients of the " dead-head stock " made hasty havoc of the market by a rapid unloading of their shares and pocketing the proceeds. So the poor little 400 shares of treasury stock brought only the minimum price to afford temporary relief to a distressed company.

" The bankrupt condition of this incipient corporation threatened it with a cessation of existence, unless somebody came to the rescue, for the 'originals,' who had received a harvest by the sale of their 'free stock,' would not now give a dollar to save the concern. They were all fixed, but what of the innocent stockholders who had purchased this stock ?

They should not be allowed to suffer, as they must if the company went out. So Mr. Keely came to the rescue, and consented to the following scheme, which was prepared by schemers, as the sequel proved. He had two inventions besides the motor, and they could be handled to advantage in this emergency. These Mr. Keely assigned to the company, and the stock was increased from 20,000 to 100,000 shares. The 80,000 new shares were to be divided equally: 40,000 to pay for the inventions, and 40,000 went to the company *without one dollar of pay.* So, Mr. Keely received no money in this transaction; and of the 40,000 shares which he should have received, not 5000 ever reached him; fraudulent claims having captured the rest while in the hands of the 'trustee.' Of the 5000 shares also, much had been obligated in advance by the inventor to carry forward the work which otherwise must have been delayed, so that he had less than 1000 shares left when all claims were settled. This grand act is called the 'consolidation,' which took place in 1879, and since which all moneys raised by the company have come from the sale of shares out of this 40,000, which Mr. Keely then gave to the company. By some mysterious operations in the 'management' this 'Treasury Stock' has shrunk away very rapidly, bringing at times only a fraction of the price which other stocks of the same kind were selling for in the market, while the little cash which it has brought has only in part been used by Mr. Keely, and that has been served out to him in a sparing way, which would be shameful even if he had not furnished it all to begin with. The company now owe to Mr. Keely fifty thousand dollars loaned outright in its early history. To this indebtedness considerable has since been added. The public statements that Mr. Keely has been supplied with large amounts of money from the company are untrue, while it is true that of those who are regarded as his dupes a half dozen or more have made on an average at least $50,000 each from the 'enterprise.' The money with which Mr. Keely capitalized the company, in the first place, was obtained from the sale of territorial rights to men who have formed other companies for the purpose.

"If Mr. Keely deserves prosecution by any parties, it is those

Introductory.

who bought these rights, and not the ring who now control the company with stock which has cost them nothing.

"If anybody deserves to be sued by the stockholders it is these very persons who recommended and sold them the stock, and have taken the benefit of it, and who at the same time are responsible for the miserable management which has caused detention of the work, distress in the company, depreciation in the stock and dissatisfaction among stockholders.

"ONE."

The further history of "The Keely Motor Bubble" will be given later on, but it is the position in earlier years, that we must first deal with, to get a clear comprehension of the causes of the delays which again and again shattered the hopes of the sanguine investors just when they were the most buoyant, from an apparent increased control of the mysterious force Keely was handling. Further quotations from the press will best show the light in which Keely's work was regarded by those who considered themselves competent to pass judgment upon him and his efforts. The *Daily News* in Philadelphia, on May 25th, 1886, contained a most sensible editorial, with the heading

WHAT HAS KEELY DISCOVERED?

"For a number of years Mr. John W. Keely, of this city, and various associates have occupied the attention of the public to a greater or less extent, from time to time. The claim on behalf of Mr. Keely is that he has discovered a new motive power, so far transcending all previous achievements in this direction, as to overturn most of the universally recognized conclusions regarding dynamics. Of course such a claim was sure to be met with derision, and the derision was sure of continuance until silenced by the most thorough practical demonstration.

"Discussion of the matter has not seemed profitable in the absence of such a demonstration; but now it seems proper to note an apparently new status of Mr. Keely's affairs, as shown by some experiments conducted last Saturday in the presence of a number of visitors. Some, at least, of these visitors were qualified for critical observation, and the noteworthy fact is that Mr. Keely was able to produce, under their close inspection, a dynamic result which none of them pretended to account for by any known law of physics, outside of that which Mr. Keely claims as the base of his operation. He evolved, almost instantaneously, according to the united report of those who were present, a substance having an elastic energy varying from 10,000 to 20,000 pounds per square inch, and instantly discharged or liberated it into the atmosphere, without the evolution of heat in its production, or of cold on its sudden liberation. These phenomena alone would seem to establish that the substance he is dealing with is one not hitherto known to science.

"It seems rather frivolous to dismiss this matter with the supposition that trained specialists are to be hoodwinked by concealed springs, buried pipes for the introduction of compressed air and the like. Surely such gentlemen ought very easily to determine at once whether the surroundings and conditions of the experiments were such as to favour any kind of legerdemain; and if they found them so, it is strange that they should spend some hours in investigating that which has been asserted to be 'a transparent humbug.'

"The appearances are that Mr. Keely has at least removed his enterprise from the domain of ridicule to that of respectful investigation, and this, after all, is great progress."

On Wednesday, July 28th, 1886, the *Public Ledger* had a leader headed,

LET US HAVE SOME ACTUAL USEFUL WORK.

"With regard to the occasional revivals of the Keely motor, whether annual, semi-annual, or biennial, as they have come along in the last ten or a dozen years, the *Ledger* has paid but little attention to them for a long time; and possibly this last display last week might have been allowed to take the same unnoticed course, but that the "whizz" of the big sphere seems to have been so rapid, and the racket so stunning, as to more greatly puzzle those present at the exhibition than on any former occasion. The matter for a long time has presented itself to us in but two aspects mainly. First, there was large public interest in the asserted development of physical force by new and very strange means—very interesting if there really was a probability of a new device or new means of developing power that could be harnessed and made to do useful work; and second, so far as the matter took the form of exploiting a private enterprise or stimulating a boom for a private speculation, there was but very limited interest for the public. In this latter aspect it was almost exclusively an affair between Mr. Keely and the stockholders of his company, who felt willing to back their faith in the substantiality of his invention or discovery, by investing their money in the company's stock. This was no affair for a public journal to meddle in, unless some imposture was designed that might affect the general public.

"That is the way the *Ledger* has regarded the matter for several years; and, as during that period it seemed to be almost exclusively a private matter of little public interest, we have had little or no concern with it. Of course the *Ledger* stood ready all the time, as it stands now ready, to welcome anything that promises to be useful or of advantage in any way as an addition to the mechanical or other working facilities of our day. That Mr. Keely might have a clue to such an addition we did not dispute on the mere ground that it was new or strange, or because experts pronounced it impossible; for many stranger things have happened. Mankind, even those who are illumined by the highest human knowledge and intelligence, do not yet know all that is to be known, as we are reminded almost every day by the strides of scientific and mechanical progress. We would rather have found Mr. Keely less inclined to be mysterious; we could have wished him to have been less disposed to talk in terms that sound very like meaningless jargon to most well-informed persons; but still we did not think it proper, or fair, or wise, to reject his claims on these grounds, but have simply let them rest in abeyance, so far as the *Ledger* is concerned, because behind all this, and behind many more such essays, is the possibility that the success of some one of them may solve the problem of what is to be done when the world's supply of fuel, whether in form of wood, or coal, or peat, or gas, is either practically exhausted or to be got at only at a cost that would largely preclude its use. Mr. Keely, we say, may have a clue to that, as also may some one of those who are experimenting with the several manifestations of electric or magnetic force.

"What we would have had Mr. Keely do, and, until he does it, his operations have but little practical value in the sight of the *Ledger*, would have been to harness his motor to do some useful work, to gear it by cogwheel or by belt and pulley, or by some other mechanical device, to a main shaft that has driving lathes, or planers, or other machines—something that was doing actual useful work, day in and day out, as other machines do. Of machines that will manifest great pressure on a gauge, of contrivances that have enormous lifting power, of explosives that demonstrate stupendous force, the appliances of science and the mechanic arts have large numbers, and they are handier and more manageable than any Mr. Keely has shown. These are not to the point—except, perhaps, to persons endowed with large faith. The machine that will do actual, useful, large work, by a manipulation of new energy, or by a display of energy by new and manageable means, this or these are the things the public and the *Ledger* will be glad to hail."

At this time Mr. Keely had not reached that stage in his researches when he could carry out the suggestions made by the able writer of the *Ledger* leader; and if our discoverer of an unknown force had not been known to some persons "endowed with large faith" in his discovery, it would have been lost to the world. An anonymous writer has said the idea that living nature is not a collection of dead-heads, never seems to have struck the non-progressivists. The thing that is has been, and the thing that is will continue to be; this is the sum and substance of the doctrine they profess. They commit the mistake of supposing they live in a finished planet when in reality they exist on an orb that has relatively just begun to live. The time allowed us for observation and study of nature and of ourselves, is limited in a marked degree.

Just when we are beginning to know how to read the book, we are forced to close its pages because the intellectual eyesight finds itself within the trammels of age. All we can do is to make a hit here, and a hit there, and to hand on our little bit of intelligence to those who come after us, in the hope that they also will keep their eyes and ears open, and, in like manner, hand on a cumulative store of knowledge to their heirs and successors. During the brief span of a man's existence, then, it is difficult for him to prove much progress either in himself or in his surroundings. The eternal hills seem the same to him when the light of life dies out, as when first his eyes beheld their outlines. Stern, uncompromising, apparently immutable, the hills remain to him the type of all that is fixed, all that is unchangeable around. Yet this is not the story of science. Tennyson, who is always true to nature, says :—

> " The hills are shadows, and they flow
> From form to form, and nothing stands ;
> They melt like mists, the solid lands ;
> Like clouds they shape themselves and go."
> *In Memoriam*, cxxiii., 2nd Stanza.

This is good poetry ; better still, it is good science.

The Himalayas, big and grand as they are, must represent mountains whose rise was a thing of a very "recent" date, geologically speaking. This is proved, because we see rocks belonging to a relatively recent age, appearing as part and parcel of their lofty peaks. Very different is the case with the hills and mountains of, say, north-western Scotland. There you come upon peaks of an age well-nigh coëval with the world's earliest settling down to a steady, solid, and respectable existence. The Scottish hills are the old, the very old, aristocrats of the cosmical circle ; the Himalayas, Alps, and the rest, are the new race whose origin goes not further back than a generation, as it were.

Yet, about the oldest of the mountains there is nothing which is absolutely enduring. Equally with the newer hills, geological progress and action are written on the face of their history. The hills are only phases of cosmical arrangement; they are here in the to-day of the world ; they may be gone in the world's to-morrow. Before Science had learned to lisp this, the prophetic word of men moved by the Holy Ghost had said: "Of old Thou hast laid the foundations of the earth, and the heavens are the work of Thy hands. They shall perish, but Thou remainest; yea, all of them shall wax old like a garment, and as a vesture shalt Thou change them and they shall be changed." The world is neither perfect nor finished in a geological sense, any more than it is perfect in an ethical sense. It is full of progressive action everywhere, and, to quote from another author, "our planet and our solar system are but as the small dust of the balance in the colossal scale of the worlds that are."

Had there been no one to read the future in the light of the past, among those who witnessed the production of the force discovered by Keely in 1872, he could not have continued his researches, as he has done during these intervening years, from lack of the funds necessary to carry them on. But there were men who knew the worth of the discovery, and who, sanguine as to almost immediate results, did something more than stand idly "ready to welcome" them when produced. They furnished the money with which Keely laboured year after year, and encouraged him to persevere, when without such aid he might have been forced to abandon his researches for want of the necessaries of life. During this period, Keely's discovery was only thought of in reference to its commercial value, and for a decade he made no progress: but, after his researches led up to the conviction that he was on the road to another and infinitely more important discovery, namely, the source of life and the connecting link between intelligent will and matter, his progress has been almost uninterrupted. His ambition is not only to give a costless motive power to the world, but to make clear to men of science the path he is exploring.

CHAPTER II.

1882 TO 1886.

ETHER THE TRUE PROTOPLASM, AN EPITOME OF MACVICAR'S SKETCH OF A PHILOSOPHY.

All that has been predicted of atoms, their attractions and repulsions, according to the primary laws of their being, only becomes intelligible when we assume the presence of mind.—SIR JOHN F. W. HERSCHELL (1865).

It is in no small degree reassuring to find that we are not chained to inert matter, but to the living energies of its forms. . . . This leads us to the inference, long suspected, that all matter, as well as the ethereal medium itself consists ultimately of one and the same primordial element.—COL. A. T. FRASER, *Darkness and Light in the Land of Egypt.*

FOR ten years Keely's demonstrations were confined to the liberation, at will, of the energy he had "stumbled over" while experimenting on vibrations in 1872; and his efforts were put forth for the construction of "the perfect engine," which he had promised to The Keely Motor Company. He made the mistake of pursuing his researches on the line of *invention* instead of *discovery*. All his thoughts were concentrated in this direction up to the year 1882. Engine after engine was abandoned and sold as old metal, in his repeated failures to construct one that would keep up the rotary motion of the ether that was necessary to hold it in any structure. Explosion after explosion occurred, sometimes harmless to him, at other times laying him up for weeks at a time.

Two more years were lost in efforts to devise an automatic arrangement, which should enable the machine, invented by Keely for liberating the energy, to be handled by any operator, and it was not until 1884 that steady progress was seen, from year to year, as the result of his enlarged researches. When Keely was asked, at this time, how long he thought it would be before he would have the engine he was then at work upon ready to patent, he illustrated his situation by an anecdote: "A man fell down, one dark night, into a mine; catching a rope in his descent, he clung to it until morning. With the first glimpse of daylight, he saw that had he let go his hold of the rope he would have had but a few inches to fall. I am precisely in the situation of that man. I do not know how near success may be, nor yet how far off it is."

August 5th, 1885, the *New York Home Journal* announced that Keely had imprisoned the ether; and, as was then wrongly supposed, that the unknown force was the ether itself; not the medium of the force, as it is now known to be. The late George Perry, who was then editor of that journal, heralded the announcement with these comments:—
"No object seems to be too high or remote for human endeavour. It is not strange that some of these attempts should stagger the faith of all but the boldest imaginations. A notable example of this class is the famous etheric motor invented by Keely, of Philadelphia, and the subject of a communication which we print below from a well-known American lady in Italy. The inventor claims to have found a new force, one that entirely transcends those that have been hitherto appropriated for human use. Heat, steam, electricity, magnetism are but crude antetypes of this new discovery. It is essentially the creator of these forces. It is scarcely less than the 'primum mobile.'

Indeed in reading the exposition of its potentialities one can hardly help doubting whether the concrete matter of our earth is not too weak and volatile to contain, restrain, and direct this vast cosmic energy except in infinitesimal proportions. How shall iron and steel stand before the power which builds up and clasps the very atoms of their mass? Where shall the inventor look for 'safety discs' to stay his new-found force, when every substance within his reach is but a residuum of the activity of this identical principle? How shall strength of materials avail against the power that gives, and indeed is, strength of materials? This, however, is but a metaphysical doubt, and as the invention has already demonstrated its practical efficiency on a small scale, there is a presumption that it may be extended to the higher degrees. At all events, whether the force can or cannot be harnessed to do the daily work of the world, the discovery is one that will mark an epoch in the progress of science and give the inventor and his patrons a meed of immortality. Granted they are but poets building a lofty cosmical rhyme, their work shall have not the less an enduring honour."

The New Force—Etheric Vapour.

The discoverer of a hitherto unknown force in nature which, when certain inventions are perfected, will create a revolution in science, as well as in mechanics, has for many years concentrated his mind upon gaining supreme control over one of nature's greatest and grandest forces. Or, more correctly speaking, in efforts to control and apply to mechanics one of the various manifestations of the one force in nature.

" The force which binds the atoms, which controls secreting glands,
 Is the same that guides the planets, acting by divine commands."

The hypothetical ether conceived of by scientists, to account for the transmission of light, is not hypothetical to this discoverer. He knows its nature and its power. By the operation of an instrument of his own invention, he can release it at will from the suspension in which it is always held in our atmosphere. It is so liberated, by an almost instantaneous process of intense vibratory action, and passed through a tube the opening of which is no larger than a pin's head, furnishing sufficient power to run a one hundred horse-power engine. The importance of this discovery cannot be conceived; its limit seems boundless; its value cannot be put in figures. Step by step, with a patient perseverance which one day the world will honour, this man of genius has made his researches, fighting with and overcoming difficulties which seemed insurmountable, during years in which no disinterested hands were extended to aid him, no encouraging words of appreciation bestowed upon him by the scientists whom he vainly tried to interest in his experiments; assailed by calumnies, which, emanating from those who should have been the first to extend aid, have over and over pierced his noble heart like poisoned arrows.

History will not forget that, in the nineteenth century, the story of Prometheus found a counterpart, and that the greatest man of the age, seeking to scale the heavens to bring down blessings for mankind, met with Prometheus's reward from the vultures of calumny who, up to the present moment, have not spared their talons upon him.

The dangerous conditions attending the introductory features of the development of etheric vapour are not yet entirely overcome; but this throws no shadow of a doubt as to the inventor's eventual success in the minds of those who know the magnitude of the difficulties he has already mastered.

O. W. Babcock, in an American journal says of this discovery, " Human comprehension is inadequate to grasp its possibilities or power, for prosperity and for peace. It includes all that relates mechanically to travel, manufacture, mining, engineering and warfare. The discoverer has entered a new world, and although an unexplored wilderness of untold wealth lies beyond, he is treading firmly its border, which daily widens as with ever-increasing interest he pursues his explorations. He has passed the dreary realm where scientists are groping. His researches are made in the open field of elemental force where gravity, inertia, cohesion, momentum are disturbed in their haunts and diverted to use; where, from the unity of origin, emanates infinite energy in its diversified forms," and to this I would add—where he, the discoverer, is able to look from nature up to nature's God, understanding and explaining, as no mortal ever before understood and explained, how simple is the way in which God "works His wonders to perform."

A compilation of Macvicar's "Sketch of a Philosophy," entitled "Ether the true Protoplasm," was sent to Mr. Keely; and shortly after, Mrs. Hughes' book on the evolution of tones and colours. Mr. Keely will himself, in his theoretical *exposé* make known the manner in which he was led, by the writings of Dr. Macvicar and Mrs. Hughes, into the knowledge which raised the veil that had before hidden from him the operations of Nature with this " the most powerful and most general of all her forces;" operations which will explain all that is now mysterious to us in the workings of gravity.

The question has been asked whether science, having destroyed faith, has supplied us with anything better. But has science destroyed faith? Certainly not. There would be no such thing as counterfeit coin were it not for the existence of sterling gold. True science has its counterfeit, and it is due to spurious science that the bulwarks of religious faith have been besieged; but they are not destroyed. Drummond says that it will be the splendid task of the future theology to disclose to scepticism the naturalness of the supernatural.

The pure Philosophy which true science seems about to reveal discloses not a universe of dead matter, but a universe alive from its core to its outermost extremity, and animated by mind and means, to which matter, perfectly organized, is absolutely subservient. It illuminates mysteries of nature which have only been partially revealed to us, and lifts the veil which has hitherto shrouded in darkness still greater mysteries involved in this universal power, which keeps and sustains all systems of worlds in their relation towards each and all. More and more clearly shall we be led by true science to see that the universe "is founded upon a distinct idea," and that the harmony of this distinct idea is manifested in all of God's works. Sir Isaac Newton, in his "Fundamental Principles of Natural Philosophy," calls the great magnetic agent "the soul of the world," and says, "all senses are excited by this spirit, and through it the animals move their limbs; but these things cannot be explained in few words, and we have not yet sufficient experience to determine fully the laws by which this universal spirit operates." Centuries may pass before these laws will be "fully understood"; but Etheric Philosophy casts a plummet into depths that have never been sounded, and reveals this "unparticled substance," "the cosmic matter," "the primal stuff" "the celestial ocean of universal ether," as the true protoplasm, and the medium by which mind shapes matter and gives it all its properties. It teaches us that, through it, we are *connected in sympathy* with all other souls and with all the objects of nature, even, to the stars and all the heavenly bodies. But even though we do not understand the laws which control its operations, we find therein a legitimate field of research. It is surely more legitimate for science to ascribe failures in such researches to our still existing ignorance of that which we may possibly know in time than to set such laws down as unknowable. " Thought in its spontaneity has the run of the universe, and there should be no bar to discovery." Our only hope, says Macvicar, lies in the universality of the cosmical laws and the ultimate homogeneity of created substances, or reality.

In stating some of the various hypotheses which have been put forward by Macvicar, more as a sketch than as a new system of philosophy, it is not necessary to make any comments. If the scaffolding be good the edifice will appear in time. If worthless, no edifice can be constructed. Therefore, it must be remembered that it is only with the scaffolding that we have to do at present. If it has been left for our age to demonstrate the truth or the falsity of certain deductions made in past ages—if we arrive at a partial knowledge, even, of truths which ancient wisdom saw with dim vision, we must never forget that our century has had the benefit of the light reflected down the stream of time. Macvicar's " Sketch of a Philosophy " was published in 1868. He said that his ideas would not be acceptable, or even intelligible, to an age when the popular demand is for very light reading; when science is marvellously content with the attainments which it has already made; and when, " as to the method of science we are told, with more and more confidence every day, that all we can do for the discovery of realities is to go out of doors, leaving ' the inner man ' all alone, and to compare the odour of the present with the smell of the past, and then, turning our noses towards the future, to follow them wherever they may lead us." He continues, Sensation, we are taught, is the alone architect of all trustworthy knowledge; the author both as to form and substance of all that is belief-worthy. No such thing as intuition, we are told; reason merely a habit, rising from the long-continued use of the organism. This looking only to mechanism is as much the plague and sorrow of our times as it was when Macvicar complained of it as divorcing science from philosophy. Philosophic wisdom, says Willcox, is a structure built up of all knowledges—grand and sublime: *permanent*, not of the present nor the past. Science holds, in its relation to philosophy, the same position that theology sustains to religion. " En dehors de toutes les sciences spéciales et au-dessus d'elles, il y' a lieu à une science plus haute et plus générale, et, c'est ce qu' on appèle philosophie."—(Paul Janet, *Revue des Deux Mondes*.)

Of what nature are the ideas which Macvicar was so sure would be unpopular? In compiling from his writings, such are selected as seem to be the best, toward elucidating the mysteries which lie in the operation of the laws governing the universal ether, so far as his hypotheses carried him. If matter without form preceded the creation of vitality, "it is only when the principle of life had been given," says Charpignon, "that the intrinsic properties of atoms were compelled, by the law of affinities, to form individualities; which, from that moment, becoming a centre of action, were enabled to act as modifying causes of the principle of life, and assimilate themselves to it, according to the ends of their creation." Here is a conjecture, to start with, that it will be well to remember; for, as in the hypotheses of Macvicar and the demonstrations of Keely, the law of assimilation is made the pivot upon which all turns, " providing at once for the free and the forced, at once for mind and for matter, and placing them in a scientific relationship to one another." This law Macvicar calls the "cosmical law," because to it alone, ever operating under the eye and fulfilling the design of the great Creator who is always and in all places immanent to His creation, an appeal is ever made. By this law a far greater number of the phemomena of nature and the laboratory can be explained than have been otherwise explained by scores of laws which are frankly admitted to be empirical. Surely this is no slight claim for this law to be studied, with a view to its acceptance or rejection. To repeat, this law is to the effect that every individualized object tends to assimilate itself to itself, in successive moments of its existence, and all objects to assimilate one another. The ground of it is, that the simple and pure substance of creation, has for its special function to manifest the Creator; and consequently to assimilate itself to His will and attributes, in so far as the finite can assimilate itself to the Infinite. Hence it is, in its own nature, wholly plastic or devoid of fixed innate properties, and wholly assimilative, both with respect to its own portions or parts and to surrounding objects, as well as to its position in space, and, in so far as it is capable, to the mind of the Creator. Thus, there immediately awake, in the material elements, individuality and the properties of sphericity, elasticity, and inertia, along with a tendency to be assimilated as to place, or, as it is commonly called, reciprocal attraction. Hence, in the first place, the construction in the ether, or realm of light, of groups of ethereal elements, generating material elements. Hence, secondly, a tendency in the material elements, when previously distributed in space, to form into groups, in which their ethereal atmospheres may become completely confluent; while their material nuclei, being possessed of a more powerful individuality than ethereal elements, come into juxtaposition merely, thus constituting molecules. By legitimate deductions from cosmical law, the forms and structures of these molecules must always be as symmetrical as the reaction of their own constituent particles, and that of their surroundings, will allow. The law of assimilation gives the same results as mathematics in determining the forms of systems of equal, and similar, elastic and reciprocally attractive spherical forces, or centres of force, when they have settled in a state of equilibrium; proving these forms to be symmetrical in the highest degree. Here, however, Macvicar and Keely differ, in hypothesis, as to the structure of the ultimate material element; but this difference does not affect "the scaffolding" of pure philosophy, in which everything that is cognizable has its own place, is on a solid basis, is harmonious with its surroundings, and is explained and justified by them:—raising chemistry to the level and bringing it within the sphere of mechanics; investing its objects, at the same time, with all the distinctness of the objects of other branches of natural science.

Because the chemist in his laboratory cannot succeed in decomposing certain substances, it has been inferred that they are essentially undecomposable, simple and untransformable; and on this hypothesis the whole science of mineralogy proceeds. But when it is considered that all of these chemical atoms, before they have come into the chemist's hands, have been securely consolidated and mineralized, so as to be able to withstand the ordeal of the volcano and the central heat, compared with which the most powerful analytic agencies of the laboratory are but a mimicry, is it for a moment to be supposed, although their internal structure were still molecular, that they would break down in the chemist's hands? Surely, all his containing vessels, which are but things of human art, must go to pieces before them.

The present prevailing theory of development contradicts one half by the other half. It extends the doctrine of development and transmutation to species which happen to be visible to such eyes as we have; it denies it to such as happen to be invisible to us. If all animals and plants have been obtained by the secular synthesis of transformed monera, and the differentiation of the organs composing them—thus giving in the last analysis one form and kind of protoplasm as the root of all; the pursuit of the same line of thought—the same theory, applied to the atoms of the chemist, with their various properties and atomic weights, gives, as the common ground of all, a single material element; each chemical atom being a structure composed of this material element, but so stable as to be indecomposable in the laboratory. Let this be granted, as asserted by Macvicar in 1868, and by Keely now, and the theory of evolution, whatever may be the case as to its cogency, at least possesses a scientific form. It is no longer a conception which breaks down midway between its first and its last terms. But letting science, in this respect, stand for the present as it is, and supposing the seventy recognized elements of the laboratory (which do not include the twenty or more new elements recently said to have been discovered by Krüss and Nilson in certain rare Scandinavian minerals) or rather, perhaps, some very high multiple of their number to constitute that cosmic gas from which the solar system has been evolved, the theory of development shows itself to be as imperfect on the great scale, and in point of extent, as it is in point of homogeneity in its intimate material. Macvicar continues—Beyond that cosmic gas there certainly is the ether, a medium which no longer can be ignored in any physical theory of nature. What, then, is the relation of the cosmic gas to the ether? Evolutionists do not answer this question, but Macvicar seeks to render the whole system of thought homogeneous, and to show that, just as all organisms are the synthetic developments of one kind of moneron, and all chemical atoms and molecules the synthetic development of one kind of material element, so is the material element a synthetic development of ethereal elements. These also are Mr. Keely's views; but neither Macvicar nor Keely rest in the conception of a congeries of particles which are wholly blind and devoid of feeling and thought, diffused throughout all space, believing such particles to be the first of things. "Reason, if it is to enjoy intellectual repose, can have it only in finding, beyond and above all things else, a unity, a power, intelligence, personality—in one word, God. This is the only legitimate haven of a theory of development: sending back the tide of materialism and pantheism which has swept its mire over our age into the ebb again; as, after having reached the full, it has so often done already, before the constitutional instincts or inspirations of humanity, with which speculative minds may, indeed, dally for a generation but which are ultimately inexorable." Macvicar maintains with Keely that from God, as the Author of all, nature may be reached with those very features which it is seen to possess; that it is essential to every philosophy, which is or shall be in harmony with intelligence, that it shall be based upon a unity; that no philosophy possesses all the claims to intellectual regard which it may possibly have, unless that unity be an intelligent Being; that to suppose thought and feeling to wake up for the first time in that which was previously blind and dead from all eternity, is nothing short of absurd to those who are led by the evidence of design, to look from nature up to nature's God, in whom all nature lives and moves and has its being.

While the protoplasm of the biologist is a substance which is more or less opaque or visible, the protoplasm now conceived of as the material of the whole creation in its first state, when development is to begin, must, on the contrary, be altogether homogeneous and invisible. But none the less is it entitled to the name of protoplasm; nay, it alone must be justly entitled to that name, for it is the first of created things, and, being the product of an Almighty Being, it must be altogether plastic in His hands. It can have no constitution of its own derived from itself; but must, so far as the finite can, with respect to the infinite, reflect, represent, embody, show forth His attributes and being. Still, there is limitation to this. Certain properties and demands with regard to that which exists, with limited extension, in space, are inexorable. Macvicar reasons that with such limitations the primal substance of creation must be fully obedient or assimilated to the Creator—not in a transient manner, but permanently; and that in its nature the primal substance, the true protoplasm, must be an assimilative substance. Granting that this protoplasm be partitioned into individualities, he makes the deduction that each and all of these individualized beings and things would, up to the full measure of their capacity, not only tend to assimilate themselves to the ever-present Being to whom they owe their own being, but they would tend also to assimilate themselves each to itself, with respect both to space and time; as also that they would all tend to assimilate one another. Taking this as the cosmical mode of action, or law, and on the strength of this law alone, without invoking the aid of any other law, he attempts to explain *all* those phenomena to which the physicist, the chemist, and the biologist usually address themselves. Illustrating the manner in which this law applies itself to phenomena, he gives as the first products of this law the perpetuation of an original mode of existence, and the establishment of permanence of properties under certain restrictions; the ground of the remarkable persistency and permanence of well-constituted species;

a general harmony and homology throughout all creation: proceeding to illustrate its action on the mental or spiritual world; accounting for perception, remembrance, reasoning, imagining, judging, and upon all our other modes of mental activity, as operations of the cosmical law of assimilation.

In the world of physics he gives, as illustrations of this same law of assimilation, attraction, inertia, elasticity, heredity, reversion, symmetry culminating in sphericity or symmetrical cellularity, chemical and electrical action; especially in voltaic action the influence and the persistence of this law is most remarkably displayed. By the way of familiar illustration, he takes the original voltaic cell, and without attempting to explain how one solid, copper or platinum, comes to be less assimilable to a liquid than another, such as zinc, he shows that just what we are to expect, from this law of assimilation, takes place—viz., that at the zinc there tends to form a stratum of oxygen, and that, at the platinum, there tends to form a stratum of hydrogen. Pursuing the old view as to the cause of the state of tension induced in the dilute sulphuric acid, the continuous decomposition of the water, the solidifying action of the zinc surface, he confines his attention to the current of force instituted by the oxygen; advancing the idea that this is not merely force in general, of which all that is to be considered is its quantity and direction; but force, of which the form of its elements or their formative power is also to be considered; —that formative power being representative or productive of oxygen. To the objection that such a conception is occult and mysterious, he asks if it is more occult and mysterious than what is implied and confessed to be hid under the term electricity, or in the phenomena of heredity, or than anything else which is adduced as a cause of a particular phenomenon. The cosmical law of assimilation explains all these phenomena, and, without any special hypothesis, is precisely what is wanted, in order to render natural knowledge as a whole accessible to the student: something which puts him in possession, from the first, of a master-thought, which, if he carry it along with him, will present all nature as a harmony;

explaining all that stands in need of explanation. Macvicar continues :—

If it be asked how possibly out of one law, and such a one, there could arise anything like that endless variety which nature displays, the answer is, that the law operates between two limits, poles, or points of assimilation, which are entirely dissimilar, and by two processes simultaneously, analysis and synthesis, which are the opposites of each other. Hence it comes to pass that actual nature is a web, in which unity and multiplicity, identity and difference, are everywhere interwoven, and in such harmony that nature is everywhere beautiful.

It is not necessary here to repeat the illustrations by which Macvicar seeks to demonstrate that existence is force—self-manifesting, or spontaneously radiant, so to speak, into that which is idea, if there be a recipient of ideas, or a percipient of ideas; or, more generally, a percipient within the sphere of its action. He does not prescribe any limits, in space, as to the extent of this self-manifesting power. Thus, it is one of the most certain facts in physics that every atom of this planet, nay, every atom of the planet Neptune, whose distance from the sun is thirty times as great as our distance, manifests itself to every atom of this planet—not, indeed, as a percept, but as the subject and the object of attraction or motion. Nay, by the aid of the ether, which is the grand medium whereby the self-manifesting power of being is enabled to take effect at a distance when no other being is interposed, the fixed stars manifest themselves at our planet, though their distances be inconceivably great. Distant objects acting like all objects assimilatively, assimilate the intervening ether and the optic apparatus to themselves, and thus render themselves perceptible. This they do, indeed, only under great limitation, imposed by the laws of inertia or motion in space, to which the ether is subject—limitation which, in man, it requires self-teaching and experience to remove, so that he may perceive the object in its true forms and dimensions. But this is only man's peculiarity, in consequence of his organic defects at birth. The chick, the day it leaves the egg, can run up with equal precision to a crumb of bread, or to an ant's egg at a distance. And so with all species whose myo-neuro-cerebral system functions perfectly from their birth. At his best, the embodied mind in man sees objects only in perspective. But the nature of this self-manifesting power need not be dwelt upon, since it is only the existence of this power that is insisted upon. How far beyond the visible and tangible parts of the body, the spirit, as a power exerting some kind of action or other, extends, Macvicar thinks cannot be determined. No doubt, every force has a centre of action; but as to the full extent in space of a unit of natural force, as an agent of one kind or another, no limits can be assigned. Who shall tell us the boundary in the outward of that power which says "I will," "I feel," "I see"? Its modes of acting mechanically are, no doubt, limited to the extent of the investing organism. Nay, in order to their extending even so far, it is necessary that the unity of the organism be maintained by the healthy integrity of the nervous system. In that case consciousness claims all the organism as its domain; and not only when the organism is entire does it refer any pain that arises to the region that is hurt, but after a limb has been amputated, and when it exists only as a phantom, consciousness still feels towards it as if it were still the old reality. Such is the effect of habit, or present assimilation to previous practice.

Our cosmical law, the law of assimilation, must determine, if not the nature, at least the mode of action of this force—this self-manifesting power—for plainly this action must be assimilative. And that it is so, when giving rise to perception, is clearly and distinctly seen; for what is the perceiving of an object, but the mind, as a percipient, assimilating itself to that object? and what is the percept or remembrance of the object, which remains in the mind but the idea—that is, the assimilated symbol of the object, which, however, in consequence of the intrusion in the perception of the mind's own activity, and of other previously acquired ideas, as also the perceptive image is often very defective as a representation of the reality perceived? We may say that this self-manifesting power, which is thus the characteristic of all that exists, is the agency provided whereby the cosmical law of assimilation shall be realized, though the intimate nature of that agency remains, as now, wholly inscrutable. Nor can it be said to be physical until it is embodied in the ether. In that case, it is rhythmical, or undulatory, and formally representative of the object whence it emanates. But it is enough to know that the most intimate and ultimate property—the characteristic, in short, of that which exists—is self-manifesting power. Now, the existence of a self-manifesting power in an object implies that the object is itself a power or force, or an aggregate of such. This is enough for the purposes of philosophy and science, and we only deceive ourselves when we suppose that we can think of anything that exists and which is not at the same time a force or power. . . .

Of most things that exist, if not of all, let us say that they are capable of existing in either of two states—the dynamical or the statical—and that, when viewed as dynamical, they are *forces* or *powers ;* when viewed as statical, they are *substances*. When we exhaust or think away the properties of existence, the last which vanishes is self-manifesting power in the object which exists, this property being such that when it vanishes so does the object to which existence was awarded. In the science of the day it is maintained by our most popular authors and lecturers that the "physical forces"—taken in the singular number, physical force—is the last word, the ultimate principle. The physical forces are represented as all that there is for God, whereas they are but as *the fingers* of God.

The idea of antecedent design, either in reference to nature as a whole, or in reference to any object in particular, is dropped as unscientific, or repudiated as unsound ; in short, a reference to the physical forces, is the last word permitted in any treatise, if that treatise is to be admitted as possessing a scientific character. Or, if there be one word more, it is only the "correlation" of those same physical forces, and their "conservation," or persistence eternally in the same amount of energy in the universe. In their own place and within their own sphere, these are physical truths, which are of the greatest value. The former is a wholesome relapse into the old philosophy of nature. The latter is also a return to a view which is more sound than that which was popular before the doctrine of conservation was resuscitated.

Descartes' opinion, that there was a conservation of motion in the universe, was demonstrated by Newton to be a mistake. Leibnitz adjusted the truth between these great men, showing that it was not motion, but the possibility or means of motion—in one word, energy—that was conserved in the universe.

The doctrine of the conservation of energy amounts to nothing more than this, that inasmuch as every ultimate atom of matter is perfectly elastic, so is the whole universe of atoms perfectly elastic. Hence it is a doctrine which cannot be legitimately extended beyond the merely material sphere; except on the assumption that matter is the only reality, and that there is no such thing as a spiritual world at all—an assumption which, however often it has been made, serves only to awaken a prevailing voice to the contrary, and the firm vote of a large majority to the effect that mind exists as well as matter.

Taking the law of assimilation as the cosmical law, together with self-manifesting power as the characteristic of being, we reach a primary classification of created objects, which corresponds with that which is known as mind and matter—or rather let us say mind and that which is not mind; for there is ground for the apprehension that mind and matter do not include all that exists; and that, along with matter, ether ought to be considered as something intimately related to matter indeed, but yet not just matter. When the elements of the ethereal medium are regarded as truly and simply material, however small and light they may be, the elasticity and pressure which must be assigned to that medium in order to admit of the velocity of light, are altogether out of the harmony of things, and wholly incredible, especially when confronted with the phenomena and the theory of astronomy. Thus, to justify the velocity of light on the same principles as those of sound, in various material media, the ethereal pressure must be 122,400,000,000 times greater than that of the atmosphere—which is incredible, says Macvicar.

But what as to mind? To find what shall be called mind, let us suppose an individualized object which is not an isolated object, or a universe to itself, but a member in a system;

then, in obedience to what has been stated, that object must be at once self-manifesting and impressed by the other objects around it, and, in being so impressed, assimilated to them more or less. . . . Admitting the self-manifesting power to be sensitive, percipient, or conscious, then quantity or intensity of substance or power in a monad is the condition requisite for feeling and thought. And thus, by an immediate co-ordination of our fundamental ideas of self-manifesting power and assimilative action, more or less, we reach a distinct conception of mind viewed in relation with that which is not mind. By this deduction, the primeval created substance, the true protoplasm is still supposed to be homogeneous, animated by its assimilation to the everlasting, the Infinite.

This protoplasm is partitioned in varying degrees so that there are in creation some individualized or separate objects or forces consisting of so small an amount or such weakness of substance that they are wholly fixed and merely perceptible, while there are others consisting of so much more that they are free in their inner life, and have power to perceive themselves also—not, indeed, in the centres of their being, and as unimpressed and without ideas, but as members in a system, impressed or assimilated by other objects, and so having ideas, with power to look in this direction or that, and to act accordingly.

Such, then, according to Macvicar, is the nature of mind or spirit. It is a being so constituted as to be at once in possession of ideas, and so far fixed; and also in possession of undetermined life or activity, and so far free. These are, as it were, the opposite poles of its being, and the conditions of its activity. If either is wanting, the other vanishes. Without something fixed in the mind, some object of thought or feeling, there can be no thinking or feeling. Without something unfixed there can be nothing to think or to feel with, much less can there be any thinking or feeling of self—that is, self-consciousness. But, grant this condition in the individual, and add the law of assimilation, operating first from God above, thus giving reason and conscience, on the higher aspect of our being; and, secondly, from nature around, thus giving observation and instincts harmonious with our situation in the system of the universe, and then human nature emerges.

But human nature plainly belongs to the last day of the work of creation rather than the first, where we are now. In man, to all appearance, the organism is the mother and nurse of the spirit. And though the assimilative action of the mind upon the body becomes normally, at least, stronger and stronger as life advances, so long as the organ retains all its perfection, yet at first the assimilative action of the body upon the mind is almost everything. The infant, the child, is little else but the victim of sensation—that is, of assimilations in its mind, effected by the force of external nature, including the organism itself. But as the mind, through the sustained action towards the focus of the myo-neuro-cerebral system, which is in the brain, gains quantity or intensity—in one word, energy—it becomes more independent and free, and more able to react out of itself upon the organism in any direction of which it makes choice. . . .

Hitherto, Macvicar has proceeded analytically, or from the one to the many; now, synthetically, from multiplicity to unity:— he continues:—As to the matter in hand, we may say, shortly, that a world of substances becoming multiple and diffuse, and at last merging into ethereal elements, being now given as the product of the law of assimilation in reference to the *immensity* of the Creator, the same law, when viewed in reference to the *unity* of the Creator, leads us to infer a process of quite a contrary character. It leads us to expect to find the ethereal elements tending to construct unities of greater energy than themselves. Then, if all cosmical action is cyclical, matter, when existing free in the ether, must ultimately tend to dissolve into pure ether again; for, if the law of creation is as a cycle, in which, after development and as its fruit, the last term gives the first, then has he grounds for his conjecture that complication in structure is necessary to the segregation of nervous matter, and the construction of a "myo-neuro-cerebral system"; and that ether and matter, after developing a molecular economy, as the mother and nurse of a soul or monad of a higher order than the merely material element, through or by this organism, complete the cycle of the economy of the material nature, and eventually touch upon the spiritual world again and contribute to it. Whether this inference is correct or not, it presents a noble hypothesis for consideration, and one which should command attention at a time when the writings of John Worrell Keely, the discoverer of "etheric force," and the inventor of vibratory machinery for the utilization of this force in mechanics, are about to be given to the world, supporting as they do, some of "the unwelcome views" advanced by Macvicar a quarter of a century ago. Although Macvicar and Keely differ in their theories of molecular morphology, they agree entirely in calling the cosmical law of sympathetic association or assimilation the watchword and the law of creation. This true protoplasm, the ether, which Macvicar postulated, Keely claims to have proved "a reality": making use of the ether, which he liberates by vibratory machinery, as the medium of a motive power, which he calls "sympathetic negative attraction."

CHAPTER III.

THE NATURE OF KEELY'S PROBLEMS.

1885 TO 1887.

> Too few the helpers on the road,
> Too heavy burdens in the load.
>
> When a movement is willed a current is sent forth from the brain.
> SIR JAMES CRICHTON BROWNE.

IN November 1884, Mr. Keely obtained a standard for progressive research in the success of an experiment, which he had tried many times before, without arriving at the result that his theories had led him to expect. One of those present, at the time that this test was made, afterwards wrote to Mr. Keely, to obtain an explanation of the dynamic force which had been witnessed, causing a small globe to rotate when two persons had taken hold of the rod together, with a firm grasp; one of whom was standing on a circular sheet of metal, from which piano wires stretched toward the globe, near enough to touch one of the plates of glass which insulated the ball. Mr. Keely replied, "I cannot describe it other than the receptive concussion of the two forces, positive and negative, coming together, seeking their coincidents and thus producing rotation by harmonious waves, not streams. You ask if sound waves had anything to do with the motion of the globe? Nothing; the introductory settings are entirely different. The ball ceased to rotate when I took your left hand in my right hand, while with our other hands holding the iron rod resting on the metal plate, because the receptive flows became independent of the circular chord of resonation as set up mechanically.

The Nature of Keely's Problems.

The power of rotation comes on the positive; and the power of negation breaks it up." . . .

Encouraged by this confirmation of his theories, Keely pursued his researches with renewed vigour. At this time he wrote, "I am straining every nerve to accomplish certain matters in a given time, working from twelve to fourteen hours daily. Although in my illness I have had some peaceful hours in thinking over the fascinating points associated with the researches to which I am devoting my life, I have also had some very stormy ones in reviewing the many unjust insinuations and denouncements that have been heaped upon me by the ignorant and the base-hearted. My one desire has been the acquisition of knowledge; and, no matter how great the impediment thrown in my path, I will work without ceasing to attain my end. After struggling for over seventeen years, allowing scientists to examine my machinery in the most thorough manner, and to make the most sensitive tests, denunciations have multiplied against me. One charge is that I use sodium in my mercury, in the vacuum test. I have thought that I would never again make any effort to prove that I am honest; but I am working in a new lead, and for the satisfaction of the few friends that I have I propose to show my introductory evolutions, in proof of the negatization of an etheric substance to produce vacuum. The mercury may be delivered to me by an expert: I will operate from an open mercury bath: using the most perfect mercury gauge obtainable, attached to the same sphere that the column is operated from. Professor Rogers, the highest authority we have, saw the operation of inducing these etheric vacuums and pronounced the result wonderful. He said that the scientific world would go down on its knees, if I produced only one pound of vacuum under the conditions named. I showed from one to fourteen lbs. during the evolutions. . . . As soon as I have been able to combine all the positive and negative forces of etheric vibration in the triple vibratory sphere-engine that I am now at work upon, in short, as soon as I have completed a perfect, patentable machine, then my labours will cease on the Motor line; and after my patents are taken out, I will devote the remainder of my life to *Aerial Navigation,* for I have the only true system to make it an entire success in the vibratory lift and the vibratory push-process."

It will be seen that, at this stage, Keely had no idea of giving up the engine; and was still as confident of ultimate success as in the beginning. There is no doubt that, had not the time arrived when the directing power of Providence led him away in quite another direction from the line that he was then working upon, his system for Aerial Navigation would have been lost to this century. "The heart of man deviseth his way, but the Lord directs his steps."

About this time Keely met with an accident. Under date *March 22nd,* he wrote, "It has been impossible for me to write, my right hand and arm were so severely strained, but I have not been idle. I have had time for reflection, and I have been setting up a key to explain vibratory rotation. I have also a plan for a device to be attached to the Liberator as an indicator to show when the neutral centre is free from its intensification while operating. In this way the dangerous influences will be avoided which present themselves on the extension of the vibratory waves that operate the gun. All the introductory details of the present engine are as perfect as is possible for the first lead. It is in the form of a sphere, about thirty inches in diameter and weighs 800 lbs. Yesterday saw the pure, positive action of my new Liberator. Mr. Collier and his brother George were present, and witnessed thirty expulsions, made by myself; after which I had them produce the vapour, by imitating my manipulations; which they were unable to do with the old generator. They were very much delighted. To say that the last three weeks have been trying ones, is using very mild language to express what I have suffered from accidents, disappointments, etc., etc. I have been frozen in at my workshop; and all things seemed to go wrong; but my present successes are as an anchor, which I thank God for, who, in His bountiful goodness, has carried me into a port of safety over tempestuous seas." Again, under various dates, Keely wrote:—
"Unbounded success has crowned my new departure. I am now preparing new features that are necessary as adjuncts

to denote the true condition, as regards safety in my different vibratory operations." "Without the aid sent me from on high there would have been nothing left of the discovery mechanically; nor would there now be a single foot-hold on which hope could rest for a completion of the Keely Motor enterprise." . . . " I had an accident to one of my registers this morning. It burst with a tremendous report, shaking things up in a lively way, but no other damage was done beyond that to the register."

" The draughts are nearly completed for the compound vibratory engine, and next week the work will be commenced and pushed forward with all possible speed. This is the machine for continuous operation. The Liberator is as perfect as is possible ; and, if the outside adjuncts are in proper sympathy, my struggles will soon be at an end." . . . " All things are verging into a condition of perfection through the aid that I have received, but for which the science of vibratory etheric force would, as far as my researches are concerned, have been lost to the world. I feel that the world is waiting for this force ; that this advance in science is necessary to keep the proper equilibrium in our age of progress." . . . .

"There are moments in which I feel that I can measure the very stars, which shine like Edens in planetary space; fit abodes for beings who have made it the study of their lives on earth to create peace and happiness for all around them. Is nature a mystery ? No, God is in nature. I do not believe in the line, ' God moves in a mysterious way His wonders to perform.' In my estimation, He moves in a very plain and simple way, if we will open, our hearts to the understanding of His way. To the man who cannot appreciate the workings of nature, chemically and otherwise, God's ways may appear mysterious ; but when he comes to know nature's works he will find simplicity itself in its highest order of expression.

" Could I have one wish, as to science, gratified, I would ask to live long enough to be able to appreciate even but one etheric variation in planetary evolution. It might take fifty thousand years to attain this knowledge, but what is that period of time when compared with the cycles that have passed away since this earth existed? Yes, in one sense, 'God does move in a mysterious way His wonders to perform.'" . . . .

"The whirlpool of science has indeed engulphed me in its fascinating vortex." . . .

"*May 20th.*—Yesterday was a day of trials and disappointments. It seemed as if nothing would work right. After labouring six hours to set my safety process, the first operation of the Liberator tore the caps all to pieces. I replaced them by a set of duplicates, and set the Liberator down to the low octaves, when everything worked to a charm. Night was approaching, and I left the workshop to get something to eat, returning about eight o'clock to re-conduct experiments, in order to discover if possible the cause of the sudden and most unexpected intensification. I followed up with great care the progressive lines until I reached the tenth octave, and then liberated a score of times, yet no variation on liberator. Next, I made an attachment to my safety arrangement, and also to my strongest resonator, to experiment on vibratory rotation with my shell; when, within two minutes, it attained a frightful velocity: then I suddenly retracted to the negative, bringing the velocity down from about 1500 per minute to 150. The operation was magnificent, lasting sixty-four minutes, when a second intensification took place, demolishing two safety-shells and one vibratory indicator. I was perfectly dumfounded, and unable to account for such a phenomenon. It was then near midnight, but I had made up my mind not to discontinue until I had solved the mystery. After an hour's reflection, I set up a new position on the resonating wave plates in the forty resonating circuit on the base of liberator; and got a result which for purity of uniformity surpassed all experiments that I have ever made. I believe I have now struck the root of this difficulty, and that I shall be able to master it; and obtain continuity of action with perfect rotation."

"*June 1st,* 1885.—I am in a perfect sea of mental and physical strain, intensified in anticipation of the near approach of final and complete success, and bombarded from all points of the compass by demands and inquiries; yet, in my researches, months pass as minutes. The immense mental and physical

The Nature of Keely's Problems. 35

strain of the past few weeks, the struggles and disappointments have almost broken me up. Until the reaction took place, which followed my success, I could never have conceived the possibility of my becoming so reduced in strength as I am now. My labours in the future will be of a much milder character; but, before I again commence them, I must have a few days more of recuperation. I was so absorbed in my researches that I forgot my duty to myself, as regards the requirements of health, and I am now paying the penalty. It has been misery to me to have absorbed so much more time and capital than I anticipated; and without the heaven-sent aid which I have received the world would have lost sight of me for ever." . . . .

"In view of the unjust comments in certain journals, I intend to withdraw entirely from all contact with newspaper men, to give no more exhibitions after the one which closes the series, and to devote all my time and energies to bringing my models into a patentable condition. It is said that the New York reporters intended to denounce me before witnessing my last experiments. Certainly utter ignorance of my philosophy was displayed in their articles, but they were like the viper biting on the file, and only hurt themselves: for men who possess but a moderate degree of scientific knowledge have denounced them, in turn, as the most ignorant men they had ever come in contact with. They stated that I started with a power estimated at over one million pounds pressure to the square inch on the head of my liberator, a sheer absurdity. The rock I am standing on can no more be moved by a whirlwind of such attacks than the atmospheric disturbance of equilibrium emanating from a butterfly's wing in motion could blow down the rock of Gibraltar. I enclose a newspaper cutting: it was written by an engineer who has interested himself sufficiently in my work to be able to thoroughly understand my position." . . .

" *July* 15*th*.—My researches teach me that electricity is but a certain condensed form of atomic vibration, a form showing only the introductory features which precede the etheric vibratory condition. It is a modulated force so conditioned, in its more modest flows, as to be susceptible of benefit to all organisms. Though destructive to a great degree in its explosive positions, it is the medium by which the whole system of organic nature is permeated beneficially; transfusing certain forms of inert matter with life-giving principles. It is to a certain degree an effluence of divinity; but only as the branch is to the tree. We have to go far beyond this condition to reach the pure etheric one, or the body of the tree. The Vibratory Etheric tree has many branches, and electricity is but one of them. Though it is a medium by which the operations of vital forces are performed, it cannot in my opinion be considered the soul of matter." . . .

"My safety arrangements (governors and indicators) for liberating are not working well; but I am labouring to attain perfection on these devices, and I hope soon to have them all right." . . .

"I have extraordinary powers, it is true, and I must use them to the best advantage; for I know they are the gift of the Almighty, who will, I feel sure, carry me to the end of the work which He has given me to accomplish." . . .

"I am positive that this year will terminate my struggles. My work is all progressing satisfactorily, and I am pushing everything forward as rapidly as possible." . . .

August 5th.—Mr. Keely wrote to one of his friends,—"I have met with an accident to the Liberator. I was experimenting on the third order of intensification, when the rotation on the circuit was thrown down in the compound resonating chamber, which, by the instantaneous multiplication of the volume induced thereby, caused an explosion bursting the metal casing which enclosed the forty resonators, completely dismantling the Liberator. The shock took my senses from me for a few moments, but I was not even scratched this time. A part of the wall was torn away, and resonators and vibrators were thrown all over the room. The neighbourhood was quite lively for a time, but I quieted all fears by telling the frightened ones that I was only experimenting. I allowed everything to remain until Dr. Woods and Mr. Collier had seen the effect of the explosion."

The orders of intensification for accelerating dissociation would not be understood by any explanations that could be

The Nature of Keely's Problems.

made, if unaccompanied by the demonstrations witnessed by the late Professor Leidy, Dr. Brinton, and others.

When the ether flows from a tube, its negative centre represents molecular sub-division, carrying interstitially (or between its molecules) the lowest order of liberated ozone. This is the first order of ozone and is wonderfully refreshing and vitalizing to those who breathe it. The second order, or atomic separation, releases a much higher grade of ozone; in fact, too pure for inhalation, as it produces insensibility. The third order, or etheric, is the one that has been (though attended with much danger to the operator) utilized by Keely in his carbon register to produce the circuit of high vibration that breaks up the molecular magnetism which is recognized as cohesion.

The acceleration of these orders is governed by the introductory impulse on a certain combination of vibratory chords, arranged for this purpose in the instrument, with which Keely dissociates the elements of water; and which he calls a liberator.

In molecular dissociation one fork of 620 is used, setting the chords on the first octave.

In atomic separation, two forks: one of 620 and one of 630 per second; setting the chords on the second octave.

In the etheric three forks: one of 620, one of 630, and one of 12,000, setting the chords on the third octave.

Keely's Three Systems.

My first system is the one which requires introductory mediums of differential gravities, air and water, to induce disturbance of equilibrium on the liberation of vapour, which only reached the inter-atomic position and was held there by the submersion of the molecular and atomic leads in the 'generator' I then used. It was impossible with these mediums to go beyond the atomic with this instrument; and I could not dispense with the water until my liberator was invented, nor reach the maximum of the full line of vibration. My first system embraces liberator engine and gun.

"My second system of dissociation I consider complete, as far as the liberation of the ether is concerned, but not sufficiently complete, as yet, in its devices for indicating and governing the vibratory etheric circuit, to make it a safe medium.

"My third system embraces aerial and sub-marine navigation. The experimental sphere intended to test the combination of the positive and negative rotation is nearly completed.

... "I have done everything that I could do to demonstrate the integrity of my inventions, and I will never again allow my devices to be submitted to examinations; not that I am afraid they will be stolen, but I do not wish to have the construction of my improved mechanical devices known until my patents are taken out. Nor will I ever again make a statement, specifying the time when certain work will be finished. If I thought to-morrow would end all my struggles on this system, I would not say so. I have been a great sufferer from my inability to keep my promises, fully believing in my power to keep them, and now I must and will prove that all is right before I promise.

... "The work on the vibratory engine is progressing rapidly. I spend an hour or two every day at the shop where my work is being done, examining every part of it critically as it is being put together. The safety arrangements which I am having attached to my liberator will greatly improve it. Its operation will now be conducted with a gum bulb instead of a violin bow, the pressure of which gives the introductory chord of impulse that vitalizes the whole machine. The chords will all be set in progressive sympathy from the first octave to the fortieth. ...

"I have been writing out some of my theories as to sound and odour. These two subjects have intensified me considerably of late, on account of the peculiar position they occupy in their lines of sub-division; as also the peculiar laws that govern them in their dissemination. I see the time approaching when I will be able to write up my system of the true philosophy of nature's grandest force, and have at my control the proper apparatus to analyze and demonstrate all *the progressive links of transmittive sympathy from the crude molecular to the high etheric.*" ...

The Nature of Keely's Problems.

"*December* 17*th*, 1885.—The setting up of the circles for computing the different lines of etheric chords, in setting the vibratory conditions for continuity, requires close study. I feel convinced that a perfect solution of my difficulties will follow when this part of the work has been completed; and that, before many weeks have passed, a revelation will be unfolded that will startle the world; a revelation, so simple in its character, that the physicists will stand aghast, and perhaps feel humiliated by the nature of their efforts in the past to solve certain problems. . . . I find my chief trouble in chording up the masses of the different parts composing the negative centres. The negative centre is included in the one-third volume of shell or sphere, starting from the neutral axis or point of suspension. This point of suspension only becomes perfect when the rotation is established on the sphere. One hundred revolutions per minute is all the velocity required to neutralize the gravity of the central third with the velocity of the vibratory circuit at one hundred thousand per second. Taking all matters into consideration associated with the mechanical part of the enterprise, the month of January ought to find all completed, ready for sympathetic graduation. But I fear to be too sanguine when I remember the loss of time and the interferences from exhibitions to which I have been subjected in the past. I feel more and more the great importance of devoting all my energies to the great task that Divine Power has ordained me to perform." . . .

At the close of the year 1885, everything seemed to promise full and complete success during the coming year. Mr. Charles Collier, the patent lawyer, shared Keely's confidence in the near completion of his " struggles." The stockholders were enthusiastic, and the stockbrokers were on the *qui vive*, anticipating a great rise in the shares of The Keely Motor Company. Mr. Collier had written in August to Major Ricarde-Seaver [1] : "The Bank of England is not more

---

[1] This electrician took the first box of stored electricity from Paris to Sir William Thomson (now Lord Kelvin) in Edinburgh ; and as early as in 1884 he had convinced himself that Keely had grounds for his claims as a discoverer of an unknown force in nature.

solid than is our enterprise. My belief is that the present year will see us through, patents and all."

The journals had ceased to ridicule, and some of them were giving serious attention to the possibilities lying hidden in the discovery of an unknown force. In 1886, Mr. William Walsh, editor of "Lippincott's Magazine," accepted a paper on the subject, publishing it in the September number. It was entitled *Keely's Etheric Force*.

This was the first article accepted by any Philadelphia editor, setting forth Keely's claims on the public for the patience and protection which the discoverer of a force in nature needs, while researching the unknown laws that govern its operation. Up to this time Keely had been held responsible for the errors made in the premature organization of a Keely Motor Company, and the selling of stock before there was anything to give in return for the money paid in by investors.

CHAPTER IV.

SYMPATHETIC VIBRATORY FORCE, 1887.

The teleological view was opposed to the mechanical, which regarded the universe as a collocation of mere facts without any further significance. The mechanical view looked backward to the antecedents of a phenomenon, and explained things by reducing them to their lowest terms; the teleological or philosophical view looked forward to the end or purpose which was being realized, which was the reason of the whole development, and in the deepest sense its cause. Mechanical explanation was an infinite progress, which could ultimately explain nothing; in the last resort, *causæ efficientes pendent a finalibus.* In defining the nature of the end which it thus asserted, philosophy had to wage unsparing battle against the naturalistic tendencies of our time. —(*From a Review of Professor Seth's address delivered in Glasgow in* 1891.)

IN 1887, a series of articles appeared in *The British Mercantile Gazette*, then edited by Mr. Arthur Goddard. The June number devoted more than eight columns to the progress and present position of the discoverer of Etheric Force.

To the Editor of the *British Mercantile Gazette.*

SIR,—Dr. Ziermann, a German writer, has said that a great deal of sound sense and moral courage are required to introduce ideas which will only be recognised as truth after the lapse of time. He adds, " Nay, even to recognize their truth will require more understanding than falls to the share of most men." The day will come, I think, when your action in giving the pages of your journal to quotations from Mr. Keely's papers on Etheric Physics and Etheric Philosophy, will make known your claim to this ' understanding.' In the meantime, you have, by your appreciation of his labours and your sympathy in his trials, extended that assistance to the discoverer of this newly-known force in Nature which is more powerful than any other agent in inspiring to renewed efforts; after ridicule and calumny, long continued, have done their worst towards depressing the vital centres of nerve-force. When Mr. Keely has made known the law of sympathetic association to the world, the full meaning of the words "sympathy," "help," "consolation," will be better understood than they are now. The most important discoveries, the most difficult problems of research, the most arduous scientific labours have been achieved by men who have battled with persecution and contempt at every step of their progress; enduring all, as he has done, with patience; in the full assurance that the glorious truths entrusted to him to reveal will, in the end, be proclaimed for the advancement of the race. "The nobler the soul," writes Ouida, "the more sensitive it is to the blows of injustice." Cicero tells us that praise stimulates great souls into greater exertions; and Plutarch said that souls are sensitive to sympathy, to praise, and to blame, in exact proportions to the fineness of their fibre. Mr. Keely proves this truth by actual tests, as will be seen in time, to the satisfaction of all investigators.

Every branch of science, every doctrine of extensive application, has had its alphabet, its rudiments, its grammar; indeed, at each fresh step in the path of discovery, the researcher has to work out by experiments the unknown laws which govern his discovery. Ignorant himself, he builds up his knowledge upon a foundation which, uncertain as it must be at first, becomes as secure as that of Gibraltar rocks when, one by one, he has removed the misshapen stones of error, and replaced them with the hewn granite blocks of truth. To attempt to introduce scientists, without any previous preparation, to any new system, no matter how solid its foundation, would be like giving a book published in Greek to a man to read who had never before seen its characters. We do not expect a complicated problem in the higher mathematical analysis to be solved by one who is ignorant of the elementary rules of arithmetic. Just as futile would it be to expect scientists to comprehend the laws of etheric physics and etheric philosophy at one glance.

'There are some secrets which, who knows not now,
Must, ere he reach them, climb the heapy Alps
Of science, and devote long years to toil.'

Norman Lockyer, in his 'Chemistry of the Sun,' writes of molecules that 'one feels as if dealing with something that is more like a mental than a physical attribute—a sort of expression of free will on the part of the molecules.' Herein lies one of the secrets of Mr. Keely's so-called 'compound secret.' Again, Mr. Lockyer writes: 'The law which connects radiation with absorption, and at once enables us to read the riddle set by the sun and stars, is, then, simply the law of sympathetic vibration.' This is the very corner-stone of Mr. Keely's philosophy—yes, even of his discovery.

It has been said that all great men who have lived, or who now live, have been indebted for their knowledge to teachers or to books; but all progress depends upon the use made of such knowledge when acquired. In order to bear fruit, knowledge must be increased by reflection, and by placing the mind in that attitude which brings into play the powers of intuition; or, rather, placing it in the receptive state which admits of the in-flowing of what is called inspiration.

Molecular vibration is Keely's legitimate field of research. In this field his discovery was made, many years since; but it is only now, within this year, that he has reached any approach to a solution of the stupendous problems which have arisen barring and baffling all progress, at times, towards the complete subjugation and control of the force that he had discovered. Again and again has he invited the attention of scientists to his discovery, from the commencement of his researches; but the few scientists who condescended to accept his invitations were so ignorant of the mysteries which they sought to investigate—of 'the alphabet and rudiments' of etheric physics—that they found it easier to accuse him of jugglery and of fraud than to account for the phenomena that they witnessed. They addressed their report to a public even more ignorant than themselves, if such a thing could be possible, with the result of preventing other scientists, who would have better understood the experiments, from examining into Keely's claims, as the discoverer of an unknown force. A system of doctrine can be legitimately refuted only upon its own principles, viz., by disproving its facts, and invalidating the principles deduced from them. It is, then, the facts, and not the opinions of the ignorant or the prejudiced, which are of chief importance here, as in all other questions of moment.

All those men who have witnessed the production of etheric force and its application experimentally, during the exhibitions given at various times, have, if capable of understanding such a marvellous discovery as Keely has made, agreed to a man in bearing testimony, at the time, that no known force could have produced such results under the same conditions.

It is now three years since Keely invited certain English men of science (experimenting in the same field where his explorations commenced) to examine his Liberator; which was dismantled for the purpose, and all its parts assembled for examination before being put together for the production of etheric force, when these men refused to visit his workshop, and it has been said that a Professor of the University of Pennsylvania prevented the investigation by his assertion that compressed air is the force used by Keely with which to dupe his audiences. A schoolboy's knowledge of the change of temperature always accompanying the compression of air would prevent such an assertion from being made by anyone who had witnessed the operation of the Liberator in the production and storage of etheric force, during which there is not the slightest change of temperature. Had these English scientists, with their knowledge of acoustics, been present on the occasion referred to, no such groundless assertion would have possessed any influence with either; and the world of science would have sooner known and acknowledged the nature and the worth of this great discovery.

Roget says that if we are to reason at all, we can reason only upon the principle that for every effect there must exist a corresponding cause; or, in other words, that there is an established and invariable order of sequence among the changes which take place in the universe. The bar to all further reasoning lies in the fact that there are men who, admitting all the phenomena we behold are the effects of certain causes, still say that these causes are utterly unknown to us, and that their discovery is wholly beyond the reach of our faculties. Those who urge this do not seem to be aware that its general application in every sense would shake the foundation of every kind of knowledge—even that which we regard as built upon the most solid basis. Of causation it is agreed that we know nothing; all that we do know is that one event succeeds another with undeviating constancy; and what do we know of magnetism, electricity, galvanism, but such facts as have been elicited by the labours of experimental enquirers, and the laws which have been deduced from their generalization? Would it be considered a sufficient reason for the absolute rejection of any of these facts—or a whole class of facts—that we are still ignorant of the principle upon which they depend, and that such knowledge is beyond our reach? Facts are every day believed, upon observation, or upon testimony, which we should be exceedingly puzzled to account for, if called upon to do so. Every man who has passed the mere threshold of science ought to be aware that it is quite possible to be in possession of a series of facts, long before he is capable of giving a rational and satisfactory explanation of them; in short, before he is enabled to discover their causes. Also that he must classify his facts and construct hypotheses before he can impart his experimental position to others. Many things which were, for a long time, treated as fabulous and incredible have been proved, in our age, to be authentic facts, as soon as the evidence in support of them was duly subjected to the crucible of scientific investigation. Take, for example, Professor Dewar's researches in the cause, or origin, of meteoric stones. Fortunately for his branches of research and experiment, he is possessed of that philosophical spirit and energy which enables him to divest himself of all prejudice, and, in constructing his theories, to welcome the evidence of truth from whatever quarter it approaches. More than two thousand years elapsed between the first record of the phenomenon, by Anaxagoras, and Mr. Howard's observations in 1802, during which time the fact was disputed most strenuously by many, while, in our time, Professor

Dewar's explanations of the same, upon intelligible and satisfactory principles, have confirmed the statements made centuries ago. How few the years, in comparison, since Keely's grand discovery first broke upon his own mind, which he has devoted to experiment, to invention, to the classification of facts, and the building up of hypotheses, before reaching the goal of his desires. Men will marvel at the shortness of the period when all that he has accomplished is made known. The delays which have occurred in bringing before the world the actual discovery of this primal force, from which all the forces of nature spring, have been in part occasioned by the want of that sympathy and appreciation which Keely would have received from his fellow-men, had scientists believed him to be honest in his claims. He would not then have been left in the merciless hands of "a ring," which gave or withheld financial aid according as he could be "thumbscrewed," into giving exhibitions for speculative ends on the part of "the ring." These costly days of delay are now a thing of the past. Keely's programme of work for the remainder of the year embraces such exhibitions of his progress as can be given without interfering with this programme.

Coleridge says in "Table Talk,"—"I have seen what I am certain I would not have believed on your telling; and in all reason, therefore, I can neither expect nor wish that you should believe on mine." It is of all tasks the most difficult to procure any favourable reception for doctrines which are objectionable only because they are deemed to be incompatible with preconceived notions. It does not answer to disturb the calmness of views now held by our most eminent physicists, who seem to expect that nature will always accommodate her operations to their preconceived notions of possibility, and adapt her phenomena to their arbitrary systems of philosophy. We are all familiar with the anecdote of the wise Indian potentate who imagined that his informant was imposing upon his credulity when giving him an accurate description of the steam-engine. Now what would be thought of that philosopher who, in attempting to communicate an adequate idea of the operation of the steam-engine, should content himself with a mere description of its mechanism—of its wheels and levers, and cylinders and pistons—keeping entirely out of view the moving power—the steam; and ridiculing all investigation into the nature, application, and phenomena of this power. Yet this is exactly what microscopic observers of the animal economy call "absurd and useless inquiry." The true springs of our organization are not these muscles, these arteries, these nerves, which are described and experimented upon with so much care and exactness. They are hidden springs, the action of which are as miracles to those who have vainly tried to account for the motion of the muscles at the command of the will; for the power of vision, which places the human eye in intimate and immediate connection with the soul—dependent as they are upon unknown laws, assigned them by the great, omniscient and omnipotent Being by whom they were originally created, and Who is the one source of all power.

Although in our present ordinary state of existence we are permitted to see only "as through a glass darkly," ignorant of many of the powers and processes of nature, as well as of the causes to which they are to be ascribed, we are not, therefore, entitled to set limits to her operations, and to say to her, " Hitherto shalt thou go, and no further!" We must not presume, says Glanvill, to assign bounds to the exercise of the power of the Almighty, nor are these operations and that power to be controlled by the arbitrary theories and capricious fancies of man. We are surrounded by the incredible—the seemingly miraculous. Who would not ask for demonstration when told that a gnat's wing, in its ordinary flight, beats many hundred times in a second? But what is this, when compared to the astonishing truths which modern optical inquiries reveal—such as teach us that the sensation of violet light affects our eyes 707 millions of millions of times per second in order to effect that sensation?

How strangely must they estimate nature, how highly must they value their own conceits, who deny the possibility of any cause of any effect, merely because it is incomprehensible. In fact, what do men comprehend? What do they know of causes? When Newton said that gravitation held the world together, he assigned no reason why the heavenly bodies do not fly off from each other into infinite space. The discoverer of etheric force is able to give the reasons for, and the explanations of, the laws involved in all that he asserts; or, rather, all that he propounds; for, with the true humility of wisdom, he asserts nothing. Newton at first thought that he had discovered in electricity the ether which he asserted pervades all nature, until, by repeated experiments, he became convinced of the insufficiency of that principle to explain the phenomena. Other philosophers have speculated upon magnetism in the same way, and upon the similarity between magnetism and electricity. Mr. Keely's experiments show that the two are, in part, antagonistic, and that both are but modifications of the one force in nature. There have been some physiologists who have maintained that the nerves are merely the conductors of some fluid from the brain and spinal cord to the different parts of the body, and that this circulating fluid is capable of an external expansion, which takes place with such energy as to form an atmosphere, or sphere of activity, similar to that of electrical bodies. Dr. Roget observes that the velocity with which the nerves subservient to sensation transmit the impressions they receive at one extremity, along their whole course, exceeds all measurement, and can be compared only to that of electricity passing along a conducting wire. A comparison with gravity would have been nearer the truth, though no computation ever has been made, or ever can be made, between the flight of gravity and of electricity, so infinitely swifter is the former.

Béclard almost completely demonstrated the truth of Roget's hypothesis concerning the action of "the nervous fluid" by cutting a nerve of considerable size, adjoining a muscle, which induced paralysis in this part. Perceiving the contractile action reappear, when he approached the two ends of the nerve to the distance of three lines, he became convinced that an imponderable substance, a fluid of some kind, traversed the interval of separation, in order to restore the muscular action. By another experiment he demonstrated its striking analogy to galvanic electricity. The late Professor Keil, of Jena, also made some very interesting experiments of the same character, one of which tends to demonstrate the susceptibility of the nervous system to the magnetic influence, and the efficacy of the magnet in the cure of certain infirmities. It was communicated by him to a meeting of the Royal Society of London more than fifty years since. If we are justified, then, in assuming the existence of this nervous fluid, writes Colquhoun, in 1836, whether secreted by, or merely conducted by the nerves, and of its analogy to the other known, active, and imponderable fluids, and of its capability of external expansion, as in the case of electricity, it does not appear to be a very violent or unwarrantable proceeding to extend the hypothesis a little further, and to infer that it is also capable of being transmitted or directed outwards, either involuntarily or by the volition of one individual, with such energy as to produce certain real and perceptible effects upon the organism of another, in a manner analogous to what is known to occur in the case of the torpedo the gymnotus-electricus, etc.

Should it be that Mr. Keely's compound secret includes any explanation of this operation of will-force, showing that it may be cultivated, in common with the other powers which God has given us, we shall then recover some of the knowledge lost out of the world, or retained only in gipsy tribes and among Indian adepts.

The effects of the law of sympathetic association, which Mr. Keely demonstrates as the governing medium of the universe, find illustrations in inanimate nature. What else is the influence which one string of a lute has upon a string of another lute when a stroke upon it causes a proportionable motion and sound in the sympathizing consort, which is distant from it, and not perceptibly touched? It has been found that, in a watchmaker's shop, the timepieces, or clocks, connected with the same wall or shelf, have such a sympathetic effect in keeping time, that they stop those which beat in irregular time; and, if any are at rest, set those going which beat accurately. Norman Lockyer deals with the law of sympathetic association as follows:—" While in the giving out of light *we are dealing with molecular vibration taking place so energetically as to give rise to luminous radiation,* absorption phenomena afford no evidence of this motion of the molecules *when their vibrations are far less violent."* . . . " The molecules are so apt to vibrate *each in its own period* that they will take up vibrations from light which is passing among them, *provided always that the light thus passing among them contains the proper vibrations."* . . . "Let us try to get a mental image of what goes on. There is an experiment in the world of sound which will help us." . . . "Take two large tuning-forks, mounted on sounding-boxes, and *tuned to exact unison.* One of the forks is set in active vibration by means of a fiddle-bow, and then brought near to the other one, the open mouths presented to each other. After a few moments, if the fork originally sounded is damped to stop its sound, it will be found that the other fork has taken up the vibration, and is sounding distinctly. *If the two forks are not in unison, no amount of bowing of the one will have the slightest effect in producing sound from the other.*"

Although physicists know that this extraordinary influence exists between inanimate objects as a class, they look upon the human organism as little more than a machine, taking small interest in researches which evince the dominion of mind over matter. Keely's experimental research in this province has shown him that it is neither the electric nor the magnetic flow, but the etheric, which sends its current along our nerves; that the electric or the magnetic bears an infinitely small ratio to that of an etheric flow, both as to velocity and tenuity; that true coincidents can exist between any mediums—cartilage to steel, steel to wood, wood to stone, and stone to cartilage; that the same influence (sympathetic association) which governs all the solids holds the same governing influence over all liquids; and again, from liquid to solid, embracing the three kingdoms, animal, vegetable and mineral; that the action of mind over matter thoroughly substantiates these incontrovertible laws of sympathetic etheric influence; that the only true medium which exists in nature is the sympathetic flow emanating from the normal human brain, governing correctly the graduating and setting-up of the true sympathetic vibratory positions in machinery necessary to success; that these flows come in on the order of the fifth and seventh positions of atomic subdivision, compound ether a resultant of this subdivision; that, if metallic mediums are brought under the influence of this sympathetic flow they become organisms which carry the same influence with them that the human brain does over living physical positions—that the composition of the metallic and of the physical are one and the same thing, although the molecular arrangement of the physical may be entirely opposite to the metallic on their aggregations; that the harmonious chords induced by sympathetic positive vibration permeate the molecules in each, notwithstanding, and bring about the perfect equation of any differentiation that may exist—in one, the same as in the other—and thus they become one and the same medium [1] for sympathetic transmission; that the etheric flow is of a tenuity coincident to the condition governing the seventh subdivision of matter—a condition of subtlety that readily and instantaneously permeates all forms of aggregated matter, from air to solid hammered steel—the velocity of the permeation being the same with the one as with the other; that the tenuity of the etheric flow is so infinitely fine that any magnifying glass, the power of which would enlarge the smallest grain of sand to the size of the sun, brought to bear upon it, would not make it visible to us; that light, traversing at the speed of 200,000 miles per second a distance requiring a thousand centuries to reach, would be traversed by the etheric flow in an indefinite fragment of a second.

These are some of the problems which Mr. Keely has had to solve before he could adapt his vibratory machinery to the etheric flow. The true conditions for transmitting it sympathetically through a differential wire of platinum and silver have now been attained, after eight years of intense study and elaborate experiment. The introductory indications began to show themselves about two years ago, but the inter-

---

[1] The stretching of a catgut chord over a resonator set to the chord of B flat is precisely the same in its resultant issue as the steel wire set over the same resonator.

missions on transmission were so frequent and so great as to discourage Mr. Keely from further research on this line. Then came one of those "inspirations" which men call "accident," revealing to him "the true conditions" necessary to produce a sympathetic flow, free of differentiation, proving conclusively the truth of his theory of the law governing the atomic triplets in their association. Differentiation, by compound negative vibration of their neutral centres, causes antagonism, and thus the great attractive power that aggregates them becomes one of dispersion or expansion, accompanied by immense velocity of rotation, which carries its influence through the whole volume of air, 230 cubic inches contained in sphere, within its $33\frac{1}{3}$ chord of its circle of coincidence. By this wire of platinum and silver the current of force is now passed to run the vibratory disk, thus altogether upsetting the "compressed air" theory of Professor Barker, Dr. Hall, and others of less note.

"In setting the conditions of molecular sympathetic transmission by wire," writes Keely, "the same law calls for the harmonious adjustment of the thirds, to produce a non-intermittent flow of sympathy. Intermission means failure here. That differential molecular volume is required, in two different mediums of molecular density, to destroy differentiation of sympathetic flow, seems at first sight to controvert the very law established by the great Creator, which constitutes harmony—a paradoxical position which has heretofore misled physicists who have propounded and set forth most erroneous doctrines, because they have accepted the introductory conditions, discarding their sympathetic surroundings. The volume of the neutral centre of the earth is of no more magnitude than the one of a molecule: the sympathetic condition of one can be reached in the same time as the other by its coincident chord."

Thus it will be seen what difficulties Keely has encountered in his persevering efforts to use the etheric flow in vibratory machinery. One by one he has conquered each, attaining the transmission of the etheric current in the same manner as the electric current, with this one notable difference—that, in order to show insulation to the sceptical, he passes the etheric current through blocks of glass in running his vibratory devices.

When Keely's system is finished, then, and not until then, all that is involved in his discovery will be made known to the world.

NOTE.

Five years after this paper on Etheric force was written, Dr. Henry Wood, of Boston, wrote an article, which appeared in *The Arena* of October, 1891, having the title *Healing through Mind*. Dr. Wood says: "Truth may be considered as a rounded unit. Truths have various and unequal values, but each has its peculiar place, and if it be missing or distorted, the loss is not only local but general. Unity is made up of variety, and therein is completeness. Any honest search after truth is profitable, for thereby is made manifest the kingdom of the real. . . .

"We forget that immaterial forces rule not only the invisible but the visible universe. Matter, whether in the vegetable, animal, or human organism, is moulded, shaped, and its quality determined by unseen forces back of and higher than itself. We rely upon the drug, because we can feel, taste, see, and smell it. We are colour-blind to invisible potency of a higher order, and practically conclude that it is nonexistent."—*Healing through Mind*.

CHAPTER V.

ETHERIC VIBRATION. THE KEY FORCE.

Discovery is not invention.—EDISON.

SCIENCE has been compared to a stately and wide-spreading tree, stretching outward and upward its ever-growing boughs. As yet mankind has reached only to its lowermost branches, too often satisfied with the dead calyxes which have fallen from it to the ground, after serving their uses for the protection of the vital germs of truth. The seed of the next advance in science can only germinate as the dry husk decays, within which its potentiality was secretly developed.

For upwards of ten centuries false portions of the philosophy of Aristotle enslaved the minds of civilized Europe, only, at last, to perish and pass away like withered leaves.

The most perfect system of philosophy must always be that which can reconcile and bring together the greatest number of facts that can come within the sphere of the subject. In this consists the sole glory of Newton, whose discovery rests upon no higher order of proof. In the words of Dr. Chalmers, "Authority scowled upon this discovery, taste was disgusted by it, and fashion was ashamed of it. All the beauteous speculation of former days was cruelly broken up by this new announcement of the better philosophy, and scattered like the fragments of an aerial vision, over which the past generations of the world had been slumbering in profound and pleasing reverie."

Thus we see that time is no sure test of a doctrine, nor ages of ignorance any standard by which to measure a system. Facts can have a value only when properly represented and demonstrated by proof. Velpeau said nothing can lie like a fact. Sir Humphry Davy asserted that no one thing had so much checked the progress of philosophy as the confidence of teachers in delivering dogmas as facts, which it would be presumptuous to question. This reveals the spirit which made the crude physics of Aristotle the natural philosophy of Europe.

The philosophy of vibratory rotation, which is yet to be propounded to the world, reveals the identity of facts which seem dissimilar, binding together into a system the most unconnected and unlike results of experience, apparently. John Worrell Keely, the discoverer of an unknown force and the propounder of a pure philosophy, learned at an early stage of his researches not to accept dogmas as truths, finding it safer to trust to that "inner light" which has guided him than to wander after the *ignes-fatui* of a false system. He has been like a traveller exploring an unknown zone in the shade of night, losing his way at times, but ever keeping before him the gleam of breaking day which dawned upon him at the start. Scientists have kept aloof from him, or, after superficial examinations, have branded him as "a modern Cagliostro," "a wizard," "a magician," and "a fraud." Calumnies he never stoops to answer, for he knows that when his last problem is solved to his own satisfaction his discovery and his inventions will defend him in trumpet tones around our globe. Buchanan says, "Who would expect a society of learned men, the special cultivators and guardians of science, as they claim to be, to know as much of the wonderful philosophy now developing as those who have no artificial reputation to risk in expressing an opinion, no false and inflated conceptions of dignity and stability to hold them back, and who stand ready to march on from truth to truth as fast and far as experimental demonstration can lead them?"

Johnson tells us that the first care of the builder of a new system is to demolish the fabrics that are standing. But the cobwebs of age cannot be disturbed without rousing the bats, to whom daylight is death.

When has Nature ever whispered her secrets but for the advancement of our race on that royal road which leads to the subjugation of the power she reveals? But not until the inspiration of thought has done its work in applying the power to mechanics, can the tyrant thus encountered be transformed into the slave.

So was it with steam, so has it been with electricity, and so will it be with vibratory force. All experience shows that the steady progress of the patient study of what are termed Nature's laws does not attract public attention until there are some practical results. Professor Tyndall has said that the men who go close to the mouth of Nature and listen to her communications leave the discoveries they make for the benefit of posterity to be developed by practical men. The invention of vibratory machinery for the liberation and the operation in mechanics of sympathetic force is an instance where practical application of the discovery may be made by the discoverer. After years of experiments with this force, what does the public know of its nature? Nothing; for as yet no practical results have been obtained. Here is a power sustaining the same relations to electricity that the trunk of a tree does to its branches,—the discovery of which heralds to the scientific world possibilities affecting motive industries, such as should command the attention of all men; and yet it is known only as a theme for jest and ridicule and reproach! And why is this? Partly from the mismanagement of a prematurely-organized Keely Motor Company, and partly because men competent to judge for themselves have preferred to take the opinion of others not competent, instead of investigating each for himself.

Attempts to interest scientists in the marvellous mechanism by which etheric force is evolved from the atmosphere have failed, even as Galileo failed at Padua to persuade the principal professor of philosophy there to look at the moon and planets through his glasses. The professor pertinaciously refused, as wrote Galileo to his friend Kepler. Mankind hate truth, said Lady Mary Montague: she should have said, mankind hate new truths. The most simple and rational advances in medical science have been received with scorn and derision, or with stupid censure. Harvey was nicknamed "the circulator"[1] after his discovery of the circulation of the

[1] In Latin "circulator" means "quack."

blood,—which discovery was ridiculed by his colleagues and compeers. The same reception awaited Jenner's introduction of vaccination.

The revelation of new truths is compared to the upheaval of rocks which reveal deeply-hidden strata. Stolid conservatism dislikes and avoids such facts, because they involve new thinking and disturb old theories. The leaden weight of scepticism drags down the minds of many, paralyzing their power of reasoning upon facts which reveal truth, from another standpoint than their own, with new simplicity and grandeur in the divine laws of the universe. Others there are, embracing the majority of mankind, according to Hazlitt, who stick to an opinion that they have long supported, and that *supports* them. But whenever a discovery or invention has made its way so well by itself as to achieve reputation, most people assert that they always believed in it from the first; and so will it be with Keely's inventions, in time.

In our day so rapidly are anticipations realized and sanguine hopes converted into existing facts, one wonderful discovery followed by another, that it is strange to find men possessing any breadth of intellect rejecting truths from hearsay, instead of examining all things and holding fast to the truth. The laws of sympathetic association need only to be demonstrated and understood to carry conviction of their truth with them. They control our world and everything in it, from matter to spirit. They control all the systems of worlds in the universe; *for they are the laws which Kepler predicted would in this century be revealed to man.* The divine element is shown by these laws to be like the sun behind the clouds,—the source of all light, though itself unseen.

Already the existence of this unknown force is as well established as was the expansive power of steam in the days when the world looked on and laughed at Rumsey and Fitch and Fulton while they were constructing their steamboats. Even when they were used for inland navigation, men of science declared ocean navigation by steam impracticable, up to the very hour of its consummation. In like manner with electricity, scientists declared an ocean telegraph impossible, asserting that the current strong enough to bear messages would melt the wires. Nothing could be more unpopular than railways were at their start. In England, Stephenson's were called "nuisances," and false prophets arose then (as now with Keely's inventions) to foretell their failure. It was predicted that they would soon be abandoned, and, if not given up, that they would starve the poor, destroy canal interests, crush thousands in fearful accidents, and cover the land with horror.

When I say that the existence of this force is *established*, I do not mean that it is established by a favourable verdict from public opinion,—which, as Douglas Jerrold said, is but the average stupidity of mankind, and which is always steadily and persistently opposed to great and revolutionary discoveries. Establishment consists in convincing men competent to judge that the effects produced by etheric force could not be caused by any known force. And it is now years since such a verdict was first given, substantiated repeatedly since, by the testimony of men as incapable of fraud or collusion as is the discoverer himself.

Newton, in discovering the existence of a force which we call gravity, did not pursue his investigations sufficiently far to proclaim a power which neutralizes or overcomes gravity, the existence of which Keely demonstrates in his vibratory-lift experiments.

But it is one thing to discover a force in nature, and quite another thing to control it. It is one thing to lasso a wild horse, and quite another thing to subdue the animal, harness it, bridle it, and get the curb-bit in the mouth.

Keely has lassoed his wild horse; he has harnessed it and bridled it; and when he has the bit in its place, this force will take its stand with steam and electricity, asking nothing, and giving more than science ever before conferred on the human race.

The *Home Journal* of October 20th, 1886, contained a paper which possesses some interest as having been written at the time Mr. Keely was using what he called a "Liberator," which enabled him to dispense with the use of water; but he was obliged to return to his former method soon after.

Etheric Vibration.

The late editor of the New York *Home Journal*, noticing the preceding paper, which appeared in *Lippincott's Magazine*, asks:—" But is not this new force too mighty to be managed by mere earthly instruments, such as iron, copper, or lead? It is the key force, the one that presided over the creation of these very metals, and can it reasonably be expected to be caged and fettered by them? Can the bubble withstand the onset of the wave, of which it is a mere drift?"

When lightning was first drawn from the clouds by Franklin, did it occur to any man living to predict that electricity (which Keely defines as a certain form of atomic vibration) could be stored, to use at will as a motive power? If atomic vibration can be made to serve the purposes of mechanics, why not etheric vibration?

But let Keely answer for himself. Some years since he wrote as follows:—" In analyzing theoretically the mechanical standard necessary for a solution of the philosophy of 'Etheric Vibration,' and the systematic mechanism to produce a rotating circle of etheric force, I must admit that the phenomenon, as presented to myself, by seeming accident, after almost a lifetime of study, still partially holds itself to my understanding as paradoxical. After constructing many mechanical devices in my vain attempts to come more closely to what I term a radiaphonic vibratory position, with microphonic adjustments, I have only been able to reach a few true and standard positions, which I can satisfactorily analyze. There is but one principle underlying all, and this principle is the key to the problem."

Keely continues with an explanation of the mechanism of his generator, which he invented and constructed for the multiplication of vibrations, under the disturbance of equilibrium by mediums of different specific gravities—air as one, water as the other. He has since abandoned the generator for a vibratory machine which he calls a "liberator," in which no water is used to develop the force: the disturbance of the equilibrium being effected by a medium thoroughly vibratory in its character. The vapour which Keely produces from this liberator is perfectly free from all humidity, thus giving it a tenuity which he had never been able to reach before, and of a character most desirable for the perfect and high lines of action. In the various improvements which Keely has made in his mechanism, feeling his way in the dark as it were, he sometimes speaks of having "stupidly stumbled over them," of "seeming accident," or "seeming chance," where another would call it "inspiration." "Providence sends chance, and man moulds it to his own design." The improvement upon the generator was conceived by Keely during his desperate struggles to effect a simultaneous action between the molecular and atomic leads—an action that was absolutely essential for the full line of continuation. This shorter and simpler way of reaching his desired end was suggested, in part, to him by a quotation from some one of our scientific writings, made in a letter that he received. I am not sure about this quotation, but I think it was: "Nature works with dual force, but at rest she is a unit."

"In the image of God made He man," and in the image of man Keely has constructed his liberator. Not literally, but, as his vibrophone (for collecting the waves of sound and making each wave distinct from the other in tone when the "wave-plate" is struck after the sound has died away) is constructed after the human ear, so his liberator corresponds in its parts to the human head.

But to return to the question asked in the *Home Journal*. "Can this subtle force reasonably be expected to be caged and fettered by mere earthly instruments?" This is the answer, as given by Keely himself: "You ask my opinion regarding my ultimate success in the practical use of etheric force. My faith is unbounded by doubts. The successful result is as positive as the revolutions of our globe, and comes under the great law which governs all nature's highest and grandest and most sensitive operations."

Since Keely wrote the above lines he has had time to get discouraged, if he could know discouragement; but

Etheric Vibration. 61

he has conquered too many of the stupendous problems, which barricaded his way in the past, not to feel equally sanguine now of eventual success in his last problem, viz. the attaining of continuity of action, which at the present time seems all but within his grasp.

Some of his views may prove of interest at a time when his achievements are beginning to be a little better understood. Gravity he defines as transmittive inter-etheric force under immense etheric vibration. He continues :—The action of the mind itself is a vibratory etheric evolution, controlling the physical, its negative power being depreciatory in its effects, and its positive influence elevating.

The idea of getting a power as tenuous as this under such control as to make it useful in mechanics is scouted by all physicists. And no wonder that it is so. But when the character of the velocity of etheric force, even in a molecule, is understood, the mind that comprehends it must succumb to its philosophy. To move suddenly a square inch of air, at the velocity of this vibratory circuit, on full line of graduation, and at a vibration only of 2,750,000 per second, would require a force at least of twenty-five times that of gunpowder. Taking the expansive force of gunpowder at 21,000 lbs. per square inch, it would be 525,000 lbs. per square inch. This is incomprehensible. The explosion of nitroglycerine, which has two and a half times less vibrations per second, when placed on the surface of a solid rock, will tear up the rock before disturbing the equilibrium of the air above it. The disturbance takes place after the explosion. To induce an action on a weight of only twenty grains, the weight of a small bird-shot, with a range of motion of but one inch, giving it an action of one million per second, would require the actual force of two and a half tons per second; or, in other words, ten-horse power per minute. Etheric vibration would move tons at the same velocity when submitted to the vibratory circuit. Thus, the finer the substance the greater the power and the velocity under such vibration.

The vapour from the liberator, registered at 20,000 pounds per square inch, has a range of atomic motion of 1333⅓ the diameter of the atmospheric molecule, with constant rotary vibratory action. At 10,000 pounds, 666⅔; at 5000, 333⅓; at 2500, 166⅔; at 1250, 83⅓; at 625, 41⅔. The higher the range of atomic motion the greater is its tenuity, and the range is according to the registered pressure. This rule cannot be applied to any other vapour or gas at present known to scientists. The very evolution on the negative shows a vacuum of a much higher order than was ever produced before, thus confounding, to perfect blindness, all theories that have been brought to bear upon the situation, in its analysis. The highest vacuum known is 17 999999-1000000 pounds, or not quite 30 inches; but by this process etheric vacuums have been repeatedly produced of 50 to 57 inches; ranging down to 30 inches, or 57 pounds. All operations of nature have for their sensitizing centres of introductory action, triple vacuum evolutions. These evolutions are centred in what I call atomic triple revolutions, highly radiaphonic in their character, and thoroughly independent of all outside forces in their spheres of action. In fact, no conceivable power, however great, can break up their independent centres. So infinitely minute are they in their position that, within a circle that would enclose the smallest grain of sand, hundreds of billions of them perform, with infinite mathematical precision, their continuous vibratory revolution of inconceivable velocity.

These triple centres are the very foundation of the universe, and the great Creator has, in His majestic designs, fixed them indissolubly in their position. Mathematically considered, the respective and relative motion of these atomic triplets, gravitating to and revolving around each other, is about one and one-third of their circumference. The problem of this action, when reduced to a mathematical analysis (presupposing taking it as the quadrature of the circle) would baffle the highest order of mathematical science known to bring it to a numerical equation.

The requirement of every demonstration is that it shall give sufficient proof of the truth it asserts. Any demonstration which does less than this cannot be relied upon, and no demonstration ever made has done more than this. We ought to know that the possibilities of success are in proportion as the means applied are adequate or inadequate for the purpose; and, as different principles exist in various forms of matter, it is quite impossible to demonstrate every truth by the same means or the same principles. I look upon it as the prejudice of ignorance which exacts that every demonstration shall be given by a prescribed rule of science, as if the science of the present were thoroughly conversant with every principle that exists in nature. The majority of physicists exact this, though some of them know that these means are entirely inadequate. Every revolving body is impressed by nature with certain laws making it susceptible of the operation of force which, being applied, impels motion. These laws may all be expressed under the general term, "Forces," which, though various in their nature, possess an equalizing power; controlling each other (as in the case of the atomic triplets) in such a way that neither can predominate beyond a certain limit. Consequently, these bodies can never approach nearer each other than a fixed point: nor recede from each other beyond another certain point. Hence, these forces are, at some mean point, made perfectly equal, and therefore may be considered as but one force; therefore as but one element. It matters not that other and disturbing forces exist outside or inside the space these bodies revolve in, because if this force must be considered as acting uniformly—applying itself to each of these bodies in a way to produce a perfect equation on all, it is as if this outside force were non-existing.

The true study of the Deity by man being in the observation of His marvellous works, the discovery of a fundamental, creative law of as wide and comprehensive grasp as would make this etheric vapour a tangible link between God and man would enable us to realize, in a measure, the actual existing working qualities of God Himself (speaking most reverentially) as he would those of a fellow-man. Such a link would constitute a base or superstructure of recognition, praise, worship and imitation, such as seems to underlie the whole Biblical structure as a foundation.—*Keely*.

Dr. Macvicar, in his theories of the bearing of the cosmical law of assimilation on molecular action, says: "During this retreat of matter into ether in single material elements or units of weight, the molecules and masses from which such vaporization into the common vapour of matter is going on, may be expected to be phosphorescent."

This surmise Keely has, over and over, demonstrated, as a fact; also showing how gravitation operates as a lever: etheric wave motion: concentration under vibratory concussion: and negative vacuous tenuity.

Mrs. F. J. Hughes, writing upon "Tones and Colours," advances theories of her own, which correspond with those demonstrated by Keely. She writes, in a private letter: "I firmly believe that exactly the same laws as those which develop sound keep the heavenly bodies in their order. You can even trace the poles in sound. My great desire is for some philosophical mind to take up my views, as entirely gained from the Scriptures; and I am certain that they will be found to be the laws developing every natural science throughout the universe."

Thus men and women in various parts of the world who still hold to their belief in and worship of God, are "standing on ground which is truly scientific, having nothing to fear from the progress of thought, in so far as it is entitled to the name of scientific—nay, are in a position to lead the way in all that can be justly so called."

CHAPTER VI.

THE FOUNTAIN HEAD OF FORCE.

Those who occupy themselves with the mysteries of molecular vibration bear the victorious wreaths of successful discovery, and show that every atom teems with wonders not less incomprehensible than those of the vast and bright far-off suns.—REYNOLDS.

The famous Keely motor, which has been hovering on the horizon of success for a decade, is but an attempt to repeat in an engine of metal the play of forces which goes on at the inmost focus of life, the human will, or in the cosmic spaces occupied only by the ultimate atoms. The engineer with his mallet shooting the cannon-ball by means of a few light taps on a receiver of depolarized atoms of water is only re-enacting the *rôle* of the will when with subtle blows it sets the nerve aura in vibration, and this goes on multiplying in force and sweep of muscle until the ball is thrown from the hand with a power proportionate to the one-man machinery. The inventor Keely seeks a more effective machinery; a combination of thousands of will-forces in a single arm, as it were. But he keeps the same vibrating principle, and the power in both cases is psychical. That is, in its last analysis.—GEORGE PERRY.

One eternal and immutable law embraces all things and all times.—CICERO.

When the truth is made known, it will unwarp the complications of man's manufacture; and show everything in nature to be very simple.—DAVID SINCLAIR, author of *A New Creed*.—Digby, Long & Co.

A GRADUAL change seems to be taking place in the minds of the well-informed in reference to the discoverer of, and experimenter with, etheric force—John Worrell Keely—which will in time remove the burden of accusations from him to those who are responsible for the load which he has had to carry.

Those who know the most of Mr. Keely's philosophy, and

of his inventions to apply this new force to mechanics, are the most sanguine as to his ultimate success. They say he is great enough in soul, wise enough in mind, and sublime enough in courage to overcome all difficulties, and to stand at last before the world as the greatest discoverer and inventor in the world :—that the hour demanded his coming—that he was not born for his great work before his appointed time. They predict that he will, with the hammer of science, demolish the idols of science; that the demonstration of the truth of his system will humble the pride of those scientists who are materialists, by revealing some of the mysteries which lie behind the world of matter; proving that physical disintegration affects only the mode, and not the existence, of individual consciousness.

The discovery of vibratory etheric force, even though never utilized in mechanics, brings us upon the bridge which divides physical science from spiritual science, and opens up domains the grandeur and glory of which eye hath not seen, ear hath not heard, nor hath it entered into the mind of man to conceive. The few who understand the nature and the extent of Keely's vast researches say that he is about to give a new philosophy to the world, which will upset all other systems; they say that he knows what force is; and that he seeks to know what impels and fixes the neutral centre, which attracts to itself countless correlations of matter, until it becomes a world; that he is approaching the origin of life, of memory, and of death; and more, that he knows how ignorant he still is: possessing the humility of a little child who knows nothing of science. Such a philosopher deserves the appreciation and the encouragement of all who hold Truth as the one thing most worth living for—and dying for, if need be.

What is etheric force? the inquirer asks. It is the soul of nature. It is the primal force from which all the forces of nature spring.

Fichte writes: "The will is the living principle of the world of spirit, as motion is of the world of sense. I stand between two opposite worlds; the one visible, in which the act alone avails; the other invisible and incomprehensible, acted on only by the will. *I am an effective force in both these worlds."*

Newton said that this subtle ether penetrates through all, even the hardest bodies, and is concealed in their substance. Through the strength and activity of this spirit, bodies attract each other, and adhere together when brought into contact. In it, and by it, distance is annihilated, and all objects touch each other. Through this "life spirit" light also flows, and is refracted and reflected, and warms bodies. Through it we are connected in sympathy with all other souls, and all the objects of nature, even to all the heavenly bodies. The word ether is from "$αἴθω$," to light up or kindle. According to Pythagoras and all the oldest philosophers, it was viewed as a divine luminous principle or substance, which permeates all things, and, at the same time, contains all things. They called it the astral light. The Germans call it the "Weltgeist," the breath of the Father, the Holy Ghost, the life-principle.

The sheet-anchor of Keely's philosophy is, in the words of Hooker, one power, ever present, ever ruling, neglecting not the least, not quailing before the greatest : the lowest not excluded from its care, nor the highest exempted from its dominion. A power that presents itself to us as a force : the one force in nature, thrilling to its deepest heart, and flowing forth responsive to every call. A power which does all things, and assumes all forms ; which has been called electricity in the storm, heat in the fire, magnetism in the iron bar, light in the taper, but ever one grand reality, one all-embracing law. Cosmical law at the fountain-head, suggesting that, as the Creator Himself is only one in substance, so also, primarily, will the creation be, to which He awards existence. The extreme simplicity of this deduction, made as it is in the face of all the variety and multiplicity of individualized objects that there are in the universe, seems to involve many difficulties. But, as Macvicar writes, different beings, whether classes or individuals, are known to us, not by any difference in their substance, but only by differences in their attributes. And since being or substance, and power or potentiality, differ from each other only in conception, only as the statical differs from the dynamical, it is reasonable, nay, in the circumstances it is alone legitimate, to suppose that it is not in virtue of some absolute difference in substance (for none appears), but only from differences in the quantity or intensity of substance or power in the individual, and from the variety of their build, that different individuals display such different potentialities or endowments as they do display; and come to be justly classified as they are into various orders of beings. *Inasmuch as the Author of all is Himself a Spiritual Being, cosmical law leads us to expect that the type of created being shall be spirit also.* Nor can Being in any object be so attenuated or so far removed from Him who filleth all in all, but it must surely retain an aura of the spiritual nature. This, then, is the corner-stone of Keely's philosophy—one power; one law; order and method reigning throughout creation; spirit controlling matter; as the divine order and law of creation, that the spiritual should govern the material,—that the whole realm of matter should be under the dominion of the world of spirit.

When Keely's discovery has been made known to scientists, a new field of research will be opened up in the realm of Philosophy, where all eternal, physical, and metaphysical truths are correlated; for Philosophy has been well defined by Willcox as the science of that human thought which contains all human knowledges. He who possesses the structure of philosophic wisdom built up of all knowledges—grand and sublime—has a mental abode wherein to dwell which other men have not. Dr. Macvicar says:—" The nearer we ascend to the fountain-head of being and of action, the more magical must everything inevitably become, for that fountain-head is pure volition. And pure volition, as a cause, is precisely what is meant by magic; for by magic is merely meant a mode of producing a phenomenon without mechanical appliances—that is, without that seeming continuity of resisting parts and that leverage which satisfy our muscular sense and our imagination, and bring the phenomenon into the category of what we call ' the natural '—that is, the sphere of the elastic, the gravitating, the sphere into which the *vis inertiæ* is alone admitted." In Keely's philosophy, as in Dr. Macvicar's "Sketch of a Philosophy," the economy of creation is not regarded as a theory of development all in one direction, which is the popular supposition, but as a cycle in which, after development and as its fruit, the last term gives again the first. Herein is found the link by which the law of continuity is maintained throughout, and the cycle of things is made to be complete:—the link which is missing in the popular science of the day, with this very serious consequence, that, to keep the break out of sight, the entire doctrine of spirit and the spiritual world is ignored or denied altogether.

Joseph Cook affirms that, "as science progresses, it draws nearer in all its forms to the proof of the spiritual origin of force—that is, of the *divine immanence in natural law*. God was not transiently present in nature—that is, in a mere creative moment; nor has He now left the world in a state of orphanage, bereft of a deific influence and care, but He is *immanent* in nature, as the Apostle Paul affirmed: *In Him we live, and are moved, and have our being;* as certainly as the unborn infant's life is that of the mother, so it is divinely true that somehow God's life includes ours."

The philosophy of Keely sets forth the universal ether (denied by scientists in the last century to suit their views of the celestial spaces, which they declared to be a vacuum) as the medium by which our lives are included in God's life; demonstrating how it is that we live because He lives, and shall live as long as He exists: how our being is comprised in His, so that if we could suppose the divine life to come to an end, ours would terminate with it as surely—to compare great things with small—as a stream would cease to flow when its fountain is dried up; teaching that our existence may be distinct, but never separate from His, and that in the hidden depth of the soul there is somewhere a point where our individual being comes in contact with God, and is identified with the infinite life.

"If extreme vicissitudes of belief on the part of men of science are evidence of uncertainty, it may be affirmed that, of all kinds of knowledge, none is more uncertain than science." The existence of the universal ether is now affirmed again, and must be affirmed, as one of the most elementary facts in physical science. Sir J. F. Herschel asserts that, supposing the ether to be analogous to other elastic media, an amount of it equal in quantity of matter to that which is contained in a cubic inch of air (which weighs about one-third of a grain), if enclosed in a cube of one inch in the side, would exert a bursting power of upwards of seventeen billions of pounds on each side of the cube, while common air exerts only fifteen pounds. It should not, therefore, be surprising to those who have witnessed the manifestations of etheric force, as exhibited by Keely in producing a pressure ranging from 8000 to 30,000 pounds to the square inch, when modern scientists support Herschel's views, as they do, unhesitatingly; rather should they be surprised at the marvellous perseverance which has kept Keely, in the face of every discouragement, true to his inspired mission; conquering every difficulty, surmounting every obstacle, and turning his mistakes into stepping-stones which have helped him to attain the goal he has, from the start, aimed at reaching—viz. the *utilizing in mechanics of the power he discovered many years ago*. Before the grandeur and glory of such an attainment, all things had to give way. Like a General who sees the fortress looming up in the distance which he must take to complete his victory, his horse's hoofs trampling the dead and dying in his path, so has this discoverer and inventor been unmindful of all that lay between him and his goal. Taking for the key-note of his experiments, in applying inter-molecular vapour to the running of an engine, that all the movements of elastic elements are rhythmical, he has had problems to solve which needed the full measure of inspiration he has received before he could attain that degree of success which he has now reached.

Mr. Keely realizes the full extent of the difficulties which he yet has to contend with in obtaining continuity of action, though, with his sanguine temperament, anticipating near and complete success. To quote from his writings:—" The mathematics of vibratory etheric science, both pure and applied, require long and arduous research. It seems to me that no man's life is sufficient, with the most intense application, to cover more than the introductory branch. The theory of elliptic functions, the calculus of probabilities, are but as pigmies in comparison to a science which requires the utmost tension of the human mind to grasp. But let us wait patiently for the light that will come—that is even now dawning."

> All we can dream of loveliness within,
> All ever hoped for by a will intense,
> This shall one day be palpable to sense,
> And earth at last become to heaven akin.

These four lines, from Robert Browning's sonnet on Keely's discoveries, read like an inspired insight into that "Age of Harmony," which interpreters of scripture prophecies anticipate the twentieth century will usher into our world; recalling Shakespeare's seeming knowledge, before Harvey's discovery even, of the circulation of the blood. "All truth is inspired."

CHAPTER VII.

THE KEY TO THE PROBLEMS. KEELY'S SECRETS.

Causa latet, vis est notissima.—*Proverb.*

(*The cause is hidden, the power is most apparent.*)

Electricity is in principle as material as water; so it appears, and Mr. Carl Hering has expressed the fact with much of clearness and force. He says, "It is a well-known fact that the quantity of electricity measured in coulombs never is generated, never is consumed, and never does grow less, excepting leakage. The current flowing out of a lamp is exactly the same in quantity as that going into it; the same is true of motors and of generators, showing that electricity of itself is neither consumed while doing work nor is it generated. After doing work in a lamp or motor, it comes out in precisely the same quantity as it entered. A battery is not able to generate quantity or coulombs of electricity; all it is able to do is to take the quantity which pours in at one pole, and sends out at the other pole with an increased pressure. Electricity, therefore, is not merely force (or a form of energy), but matter. It is precisely analogous to water in a water circuit. . . .—*The Court Journal.*

THE theory of Aristotle concerning heat, viz. that it is a condition of matter, together with the dicta of Locke, Davy, Rumford, and Tyndall, have been consigned of late by many to the tomb of exploded theories, and are replaced by those of Lavoisier and Black, which make caloric an actual substance. The Rev. J. J. Smith, M.A., D.D., tells us that the only way the great problem of the universe can ever be scientifically solved is by studying, and arriving at just conclusions with regard to, the true nature and character of force. He maintains, in his paper upon "The Unity and Origin of Force," that, as it is the great organizer of matter, it must not only be superior to it, but also must have been prior, as it existed before organization commenced, and immanent always. Newton, who scoffed at Epicurus's idea that "gravitation is essential and inherent in matter," asserted that gravity must be caused by an agent acting, constantly, according to certain laws. Heat, gravity, light, electricity, magnetism, chemical affinities, are all different phases of the primal force discovered by Keely, and all these forces, it is said, can be obtained from a single ray of sunlight. " The evidence of unity or oneness even between the physical, vital, mental, and spiritual is seen in the light of this law of correlation," says Smith. " A great portion of our muscles contract and relax in obedience to our wills, thereby proving that the mental force can be, and is, in every such instance actually converted into the muscular or the physical." Keely demonstrates the truth of this assertion, claiming that *" all forces are indestructible, immaterial, and homogeneous entities, having their origin and unity in one great intelligent personal will force."*

The Duke of Argyll says :—" We know nothing of the ultimate seat of force. Science, in the modern doctrine of conservation of energy, and the convertibility of forces, is already getting something like a firm hold of the idea that all kinds of forces are but forms or manifestations of some one central force, issuing from some one fountain-head of power." It is Keely's province to prove to materialists—to the world—that this one fountain-head is none other than the Omnipotent and all-pervading Will-Force of the Almighty, " which upholds, guides, and governs, not only our world, but the entire universe. This important truth is destined to shiver the tottering fabric of materialism into fragments at no distant day."

Professor George Bush writes :—" The progress of scientific research, at the present day, has distinguished itself not less by the wideness of the field over which its triumphs have spread, than by the soundness and certainty of the inductions by which it is sustained. It is equally indisputable that we are approximating *the true philosophy* which underlies the enlarged and enlarging spiritual experiences and phenomena of the current age. *That this philosophy, when reached, will conduct us into the realm of the spiritual as the true region of causes*, and disclose new and unthought-of relations between the world of matter and of mind, is doubtless a very reasonable anticipation, and one that even now is widely, though vaguely, entertained."

The Egyptians worshipped Ra, their name for the sun, and Ammon, the emblem of a mysterious power concealed from human perception. The Supreme Being is the grand central spiritual sun, the source and centre of all life, " whose revelation is traced in imperishable figures of universal harmony on the face of Cosmos." " The outward visible world is but the clothing of the invisible," wrote Coleridge. " The whole world process, in its content," says von Hartmann, "is only a logical process; but in its existence a continued act of will." Lilly continues, " That is what physical law means. Reason and Will are inseparably united in the universe, as they are in idea. If we will anything, it is for some reason. In contemplating the structure of the universe, we cannot resist the conclusion that the whole is founded upon a distinct idea."

Keely demonstrates the harmony of this " distinct idea " throughout creation, and shows us that " the sun is the visible effluence and agent, earthward, of the Being without whose prior design and decree there would be no order and no systematic rule on earth," as well as that in " the universal ether " we find the link between mind and matter. " There is more of heaven than of earth, in all terrestrial things; more of spirit than of matter in what are termed material laws." Lange, with prophetic tongue, says that this age of materialism may prove to be but the stillness before the storm which bursts from unknown gulfs to give a new shape to the world. Inch by inch, step by step, physical science has marched towards its desired goal—the verge of physical nature, says Alcott. When it was thought that the verge was reached, that the mysteries which lay beyond were for ever barred to mortals by the iron gate of death, then the discoveries of Faraday, Edison, and Crookes pushed further away the chasm which separates the confessedly knowable from the fancied unknowable, and whole domains previously undreamt of were suddenly exposed to view. Not long since, Canon Wilberforce asked Keely what would become of his discovery and his inventions in case of his death before they became of commercial value to the public. Keely replied that he had written thousands of pages, which he hoped would, in such an event, be mastered by some mind capable of pursuing his researches to practical ends; but in the opinion of the writer, there is no man living who is fitted for this work.

Diogenes of Apollonia identified the reason that regulated the world with the original substance, air. Keely teaches that "the original substance" is ether, *not* air; and that the world is regulated through this ether by its Creator. There are many molecules which contain no air—not one molecule that does not contain the one true "original substance," ether.

Up to 1888 Keely was still pursuing the wrong line of research, still trying to construct an engine which could hold the ether in "a rotating circle of etheric force;" still ignorant of the impossibility of ever reaching commercial success on that line. It was the end of the year before he could be brought to entirely abandon his "perfect engine;" and to confine himself to researches, which he had been pursuing in connection with his repeated failures on the commercial line, to gain more knowledge of the laws which govern the operation of the force that, like a "Will-o'-the-wisp," seemed to delight in leading him astray.

Up to this time his researching devices had been principally of his own construction; but from the time that he devoted himself to the line of research, marked out for him to follow, he was supplied with the best instruments that opticians could make for him after the models or designs which he furnished. If, from 1882 to 1888, he walked with giant strides along the borders of the domain that he had entered, from 1888 to the present time he has made the same progress beyond its borders. From the hour in which he grasped "the key to the problem," the "principle underlying all," the dawn of "a new order of things," broke upon his vision, and he was no longer left at the mercy of the genii whom he had aroused.

In July, 1888, the T.P.S. published the succeeding paper, which had a wide circulation.

KEELY'S SECRETS. 1888.

Part I.

Science is to know things.—HERODOTUS.

Knowledge is developed by experience from innate ideas.—PLATO.

Truth is not attained through reflection, but through immediate intuition. We neither originate thought nor its form.—ARYAN TEACHINGS.

It may be said that if all things come from only one cause or internal source, acting within itself, then motion and matter must be fundamentally and essentially one and the same, and we may look upon matter as being latent force and upon force as being free matter.—FRANZ HARTMANN, M.D.

JOHN WORRELL KEELY—the discoverer of compound interetheric force, as the result of more than twenty years of persistent effort to apply this force to the operation of machinery has, at last, been enabled to produce partial continuity of motion in his engine; but, up to this time, he has not so mastered this subtle force as to control reversions. The development of his various discoveries has been one uninterrupted work of evolution, reaching, within the last year, he thinks, the sphere of perfect vibratory sympathy, both theoretically and practically. The proof of this is found in the fact that he now transmits vibrations along a wire, connected at one end with the vibratory machine which is the source of power, and at its other end with the engine or cannon, as the case may be, which is operated by such vibratory power. Until recently, comparatively speaking, Keely stored force, as he generated it, in a receiver; and experiments were made by him in the presence of thousands, at various times, for the purpose of testing the operations of this force, liberated in the presence of his audience and stored up in this small receiver. The editor of the *Scientific Arena* thus describes what took place at one of these exhibitions, when he was present:—
"The confined vapour was passed through one of the small flexible tubes to a steel cylinder on another table, in which a vertical piston was fitted so that its upper end bore against

The Key to the Problems. 77

the underside of a powerful, weighted lever. The superficial area of this piston was equal to one-half of a square inch, and it acted as a movable fulcrum placed close to the hinged end of the short arm of this lever, whose weight alone required a pressure of 1500 pounds to the square inch against the piston to lift it.

"After testing the pressure by several small weights, added to that of the lever itself, in order to determine how much power had already been accumulated in the receiver, the maximum test was made by placing an iron weight of 580 pounds, by means of a differential pulley, on the extreme end of the long arm of the lever. To lift this weight, without that of the lever supporting it, would require a pressure against the piston of 18,900 pounds to the square inch, counting the difference in the length of the two arms and the area of the piston, which we, as well as several others present, accurately calculated. When all was ready, and the crowded gathering had formed as well as possible to see the test, Keely turned the valve-wheel leading from the receiver to the flexible tube, and through it into the steel cylinder beneath the piston, and simultaneously with the motion of his hand the weighted lever shot up against its stop, a distance of several inches, as if the great mass of iron had been only cork. Then, in order to assure ourselves of the full 25,000 pounds to the square inch claimed, we added most of our weight to the arm of the lever without forcing the piston back again.

"After repeating this experiment till all expressed themselves satisfied, Keely diverted his etheric gas to the exciting work of firing a cannon, into which he placed a leaden bullet about an inch in diameter. He conveyed the force from the receiver by the same kind of flexible copper tube, attaching one end of it to the breech of the gun. When all was again in readiness he gave a quick turn to the inlet valve, and a report like that of a small cannon followed, the ball passing through an inch board and flattening itself out to about three inches in diameter, showing the marvellous power and instantaneous action of this strange vapour."

The difficulty encountered by Keely in his old generator of etheric force grew out of the fact, in part, that the vaporic power produced was so humid that he could not, when he attempted to utilize it, obtain its theoretical value in work. This difficulty has been entirely overcome by dispensing with the water which he used in liberating etheric force, by his old generator; and, by this departure, he has attained a success beyond that which was anticipated by himself, when he abandoned his original line of experiment.[1]

Ignorant, indeed, of the nature of Keely's work must those men be who accuse him of "abandoning his base" or "principle," each time that he discovers his mistakes :— using them as stepping-stones to approach nearer and still nearer to his goal. Reproaching him, even, for keeping his own counsel, until certainty of success rendered it prudent for him to make known that he had changed his field of experiment from positive attraction to negative attraction.

Equally ignorant are those, who would wrench by force his secrets from him before the time is ripe for their disclosure. Let us suppose that Faraday, when he discovered radiant matter in 1816, had formed a "Faraday Phospho-Genetic Radiant Company," to enable him to experiment: fully cognizant of all that Crookes has since discovered, and had taken for his base in experimenting the principle involved in Crookes's discovery. Not succeeding at first, we will suppose that the Company became clamorous for returns, and demanded that his secret principle should be made public. Had he been driven into making it known, who would have credited what Crookes is now able to prove? The effect would have been upon the Faraday Company the same as if a balloon were punctured just as it was soaring heavenward. The same with the Keely Motor Company, had Keely obeyed the order of the Court in 1882, and made his marvellous secret public. It would have collapsed. Therefore, he has maintained his secret in the interests of the stockholders of the Keely Motor Company with a firmness worthy of a Christian martyr. The one person to whom alone Keely then disclosed

---

[1] Keely was obliged to return to his former method soon after, for in overcoming one difficulty he found a more obstinate one to contend with.

it thought him under a delusion, until he had demonstrated its soundness.

Charles B. Collier, Keely's patent lawyer, writes as follows, concerning the difficulties attendant upon "the supposed duty" of his client's imparting his "secrets," as ordered by the Court to do, some time since :—

"If to-day, for the first time in your lives, you saw a harp, attuned and being played upon, and the science of music was unknown to you, you would hardly expect, without considerable time and study, to be able to reproduce the harp, attune its strings in proper relation to each other, and to play upon it so as to produce the harmonies which you had listened to. Mr. Keely's work is analogous to the illustration which I have presented, inasmuch as he is dealing with the subject of sound, or acoustics, but in a much more involved form than as applied simply for the production of harmonies for the delight of the ear. Mr. Keely's engine is analogous to the mechanism of the human ear, in the respect that it is a structure operated upon, and its motion induced by vibration; and to the end of securing and attaining, in and by it, uniformity or regularity of motion, there must be perfect unison, or synchronism, as between it and his structure which is the prime source of vibration. To attain this perfect unison or synchronism, has involved unparalleled research and experiment upon his part—experiments that have varied from day to day. No one, in my opinion, who had not stood by his side, as his shadow, watching every experiment, could have kept fully abreast of him. To pursue my simile, I may say that his harp (engine) is not yet perfectly attuned ("graduated"); when it is so, it will produce nothing but harmony (regularity of motion), and his work will be finished.

"At such time, I doubt not that he will be able to give to Mr. Boekel, myself or another, the scale with which to reconstruct and attune another apparatus so as to produce like results with it; but to go over the ground that he has gone over, to explore the wilderness in which he has been the pioneer, in other words, the study, to a full understanding of them, of his experiments and researches, as recorded in his writings and illustrated in the beautiful charts which he has produced, will be a work rather for scientists than for mechanicians or engineers."

Keely's "Theoretical Exposé" is in preparation for the press; and, when these volumes are issued, we may look for a change of attitude towards him in all men who hold themselves "ready to abandon preconceived notions, however cherished, if they be found to contradict truths;" which, Herbert Spencer says, is the first condition of success in scientific research. The Rev. J. J. Smith, M.A., D.D., tells us that the only way the great problem of the universe can ever be scientifically solved is by studying, and arriving at just conclusions with regard to *the true nature and character of force*. This has been Mr. Keely's life study; and he is able to demonstrate all that he asserts.

Laurence Oliphant writes: " Recent scientific research has proved conclusively that all force is atomic—that electricity consists of files of particles, and that the interstellar spaces contain substances, whether it be called ether or astral fluid (or by any other name), which is composed of atoms, because it is not possible to dissever force from its transmitting medium. The whole universe, therefore, and all that it contains, consists of matter in motion, and is animated by a vital principle which we call God.

" Science has further discovered that these atoms are severally encompassed by an ethereal substance which prevents their touching each other, and to this circumambient, inter-atomic element they have given the name of dynasphere; but, inasmuch as has further been found, that in these dynaspheres there resides a tremendous potency, it is evident that they also must contain atoms, and that these atoms must in their turn be surrounded by dynaspheres, which again contain atoms, and so on *ad infinitum*. Matter thus becomes infinite and indestructible, and the force which pervades it persistent and everlasting.

"This dynaspheric force, which is also called etheric, is conditioned as to its nature on the quality of the atoms which form its transmitting media; and which are infinite both in variety and in their combinations. They may, however, be broadly divided into two categories; viz. the sentient and the non-sentient atoms. Dynaspheric force, composed of non-sentient atoms, is the force that has been already mechanically applied by Mr. Keely to his motor; and which will probably ere long supersede the agencies now used for locomotive, projectile, and other purposes. When the laws which govern it come to be understood, it will produce materially a great commercial and industrial revolution. . . .

" The most remarkable illustration of the stupendous energy of atomic vibratory force is to be found in that singular apparatus in Philadelphia—which for the last fifteen years has excited in turn the amazement, the scepticism, the admiration, and the ridicule of those who have examined it—called ' Keely's Motor.' " . . . " In the practical land of its origin, it has popularly been esteemed a fraud. I have not examined it personally, but I believe it to be based upon a sound principle of dynamics, and to be probably the first of a series of discoveries destined to revolutionize all existing mechanical theories, and many of the principles upon which they are founded." . . . " Those who are sufficiently unprejudiced to connect the bearings of this discovery, of what must be dynaspheric force, with phenomena which have hitherto been regarded as supernatural by the ignorant, will perceive how rapidly we are bridging over the chasm which has divided the seen from the unseen." . . .

In 1882 a lady, conversing with Mr. Keely, said, "You have opened the door into the spirit-world." He answered, "Do you think so? I have sometimes thought I might be able to discover the origin of life." At this time Mr. Keely had given no attention whatever to the occult bearing of his discovery; and it was only after he had pursued his researches, under the advantages which his small Liberator afforded him for such experiments, that he realized the truth of this woman's assertion. It was then, in 1887, that a "bridge of mist" formed itself before him, connecting the laws which govern physical science with the laws which govern spiritual science, and year by year this bridge of mist has solidified, until now he is in a position to stand upon it, and proclaim that its abutments have a solid foundation—one resting in the material and visible world, and the other in the spiritual and unseen world; or, rather, that no bridge is needed to connect the two worlds, one law governing both in its needed modifications.

"The physical thing," writes a modern scientist, "which energizes and does work in and upon ordinary matter, is a separate form of matter, infinitely refined, and infinitely rapid in its vibrations, and is thus able to penetrate through all ordinary matter, and to make everywhere a fountain of motion, no less real because unseen. It is among the atoms of the crystal and the molecules of living matter; and, whether producing locked effects or free, it is the same cosmic thing, matter in motion, which we conceive as material energy, and with difficulty think of as only a peculiar form of matter in motion."

The President of the British Association, Sir Henry Roscoe, in his address before that body, said: "In nature there is no such thing as great or small; the structure of the smallest particle, invisible even to our most searching vision, may be as complicated as that of any of the heavenly bodies which circle round our sun." As to the indivisibility of the atom, he asks this question: "Notwithstanding the properties of these elements have been studied, and are now known with a degree of precision formerly undreamt of, have the atoms of our present elements been made to yield?" He continues: "A negative answer must undoubtedly be given, for even the highest of terrestrial temperatures, that of the electric spark, has failed to shake any one of these atoms in two."

This is an error, for it is well known by those who are fully acquainted with the principle involved in Keely's inventions that the intense vibratory action which is induced in his "Liberator" has accomplished what the retort of the chemist has failed to do, what the electric spark has left intact, and what the inconceivably fierce temperature of the sun and of volcanic fires has turned over to us unscathed. The mighty Geni imprisoned within the molecule, thus released from the chains and fetters which Nature forged, has been for years the tyrant of the one who rashly intruded, without first paving the way with the gold which he has since been accused of using in experiments with reckless and wanton waste! For more than a score of years has Keely been fighting a hand-to-hand fight with this Geni; often beaten back by it, paralyzed at times, even, by its monstrous blows; and only now so approaching its subjugation as to make it safe to harness it for the work that is calling for a power mightier than steam, safer and more uniform in operation than electricity; a power which, by its might and beneficence, will ameliorate the condition of the masses, and reconcile and solve all that now menaces our race: as it was never menaced before, as has been said.

The structure of the air molecule, as believed in by Keely, is as follows:—Broken up, by vibratory action, he finds it to contain what he calls an atomic triplet. The position of a molecule, on the point of a fine cambric needle sustains the same relation to the point of the needle that a grain of sand sustains to a field of ten acres.

Although, as Sir H. Roscoe has said, "In nature there is no such thing as great or small," the human mind cannot conceive such infinitesimal minuteness. We will, then, imagine a molecule magnified to the size of a billiard ball, and the atomic triplet magnified to the size of three marbles, in the triangular position, within that molecule, at its centre; unless acted upon by electricity, when the molecule, the billiard ball, becomes oblate, and the three atoms are ranged in a line within, unless broken up by the mighty force of vibratory action. Nature never gives us a vacuum; consequently, the space within the molecule not occupied by the atomic triplet must be filled with something. This is where the Geni—"the all-pervading ether"—has made its secret abode through untold æons, during which our world has been in course of preparation for its release, to fulfil its appointed task in advancing the progress of the human race.

Step by step, with a patient perseverance which some day the world will honour, this man of genius has made his researches, overcoming the colossal difficulties which have raised up in his path what seemed to be insurmountable barriers to further progress: but never before has the world's index finger so pointed to an hour when all is making ready for the advent of the new form of force that mankind is waiting for. Nature, always reluctant to yield her secrets, is listening to the demands made upon her by her master, necessity. The coal mines of the world cannot long afford the increasing drain made upon them. Steam has reached its utmost limits of power, and does not fulfil the requirements of the age. Electricity holds back, with bated breath, dependent upon the approach of her sister colleague. Air ships are riding at anchor, as it were, waiting for the force which is to make aerial navigation something more than a dream. As easily as men communicate with their offices from their homes by means of the telephone, so will the inhabitants of separate continents talk across the ocean. Imagination is palsied when seeking to foresee the grand results of this marvellous discovery when once it is applied to art and mechanics. In taking the throne which it will force steam to abdicate, dynaspheric force will rule the world with a power so mighty in the interests of civilization, that no finite mind can conjecture the results.

In 1746, when Franklin's attention was drawn to the phenomena of electricity, little more was known on the subject than Thales had announced two thousand years before. Von Kleist in Leyden, Collinson in London, and others in as widely-separated cities in Europe, were experimenting in the same field of research. What our last century has done toward subduing this tyrant which Franklin succeeded in bringing down to earth, from the clouds, the next century will see surpassed beyond man's wildest conjectures, should Keely's utilization of this unknown force of nature bestow upon humanity the *costless motive power*, which he anticipates it will. Reynolds predicted that those who "studied the mysteries of molecular vibration would win the victorious wreaths of successful discovery." After such discoveries as Mr. Keely has made in this field of research, it matters not to him whether he succeeds commercially or not. His work of discovery commenced when, as a boy of twelve, he held the sea-shells to his ear as he walked the shore and noted that no two gave forth the same tone. From the construction of his first crude instrument, his work of evolution progressed slowly for years; but within the last five years he has made giant strides towards the "Dark Tower" which is his last fortress to take. When he is ready, "Dauntless the slug-horn to his lips" he will set; and the world will hear the blast, and awaken from its slumber into new life.

Molecular vibration is thus seen to be Keely's legitimate field of research; but more than once has he had to tear down portions of the vibratory scaffolding which aided him in the building up of his edifice of philosophy; therefore, he is ever ready to admit that some of the present scaffolding may have to be removed. The charge of "abandoning his base," recently brought against him by one of the editors of *The New York Times*, could only have been made by one who is utterly ignorant of the subject upon which he writes. Under the heading "A Cool Confession," this editor asserts that Keely has "given up the Keely Motor as a bad job," and that he admits that he is a "bogus inventor" and a "fraud." This is not true.

What Keely does admit is that, baffled in applying vibratory force to mechanics, upon his first and second lines of experimental research, he was obliged either to confess a commercial failure, or to try a third departure from his base or principle; seeking success through another channel of experiment. While experimenting upon this third line, until his efforts were crowned with success, he kept his secret from all men; with the approbation of the one who furnished the money for these experiments. There is a time when silence is golden; and the charge made by the same editor that Keely had been "receiving money from the Keely Motor Company on false pretences from the time that he abandoned his original plans," could only have been made by one who knows nothing of the facts of the case: for years have passed away since the Keely Motor Company broke its contract with him, and since it has furnished him with any money for his experiments.

But let Keely speak for himself in reference to his work :—

"In considering the operation of my engine, the visitor, in order to have even an approximate conception of its *modus operandi*, must discard all thought of engines that are operated upon the principle of pressure and exhaustion, by the expansion of steam or other analogous gas which impinges upon an abutment, such as the piston of a steam-engine. My engine has neither piston nor eccentrics, nor is there one grain of pressure exerted in the engine, whatever may be the size or capacity of it.

"My system, in every part and detail, both in the developing of this power and in every branch of its utilization, is based and founded on sympathetic vibration. In no other way would it be possible to awaken or develop this force, and equally impossible would it be to operate my engine upon any other principle.

"All that remains to be done is to secure a uniform speed under different velocities and control reversions. That I shall accomplish this is absolutely certain. Some few years ago, I contemplated using a wire as a connective link between two sympathetic mediums, to evolve this power as also to operate my machinery—instead of tubular connections as heretofore employed—I have only recently succeeded in accomplishing successfully such change. This, however, is the true system; and henceforth all my operations will be conducted in this manner—that is to say, the power will be generated, my engines run, my cannon operated, through a wire.

"It has been only after years of incessant labour, and the making of almost innumerable experiments, involving not only the construction of a great many most peculiar mechanical structures, and the closest investigation and study of the phenomenal properties of the substance "ether," *per se*, produced, that I have been able to dispense with complicated mechanism, and to obtain, as I claim, mastery over the subtle and strange force with which I am dealing.

"When my present process of adjustment is completed, the force, the mechanism, and all that pertains to it, will be fully explained in a theoretical exposition of the subject, with appropriate diagrams, which I shall publish to the world; through which medium, and my patents, when taken out, a knowledge of all that is required for its commercial employment will be more easily acquired than is the necessary skill required to enable one to safely operate a steam-engine.

"The power will be adapted to engines of all sizes and capacities, as well to an engine capable of propelling the largest ship as to one that will operate a sewing machine. Equally well and certain is it that it will be adapted as a projectile force for guns and cannons of all sizes, from the ordinary shoulder-piece to the heaviest artillery." . . . .

When Keely obtained continuity of motion (for a time) in his engine he thought that his last difficulty had been overcome : but, up to the present time, he has not succeeded in governing its speed nor in controlling reversions. He has, however, again reduced in size the instrument with which he produces the force. From 1882 to 1884 the "Generator" was a structure six feet long and correspondingly wide and high; but, failing in his attempt to make an automatic arrangement upon which its usefulness in mechanics depended, Keely found a new standard for research in an experiment often made by himself, but never before successful, which resulted in the production of a machine in 1885 which he named a "Liberator"—not so large as a lady's small round work-table. Continuing his labour of evolution Keely within one year made such astonishing progress, from experiments with this beautiful piece of vibratory mechanism, as to combine the production of the power, and the operation of his cannon, his engine and his disintegrator in a machine no larger than a dinner plate, and only three or four inches in thickness. This instrument was completed in 1886, up to which time his experiments had been conducted upon a principle of sympathetic vibration, for the purpose of liberating a vapoury or etheric product. His later experiments have been confined to another modification of vibratory sympathy; and the size of the instrument used now, '88, for the same purposes is no larger than an old-fashioned silver watch, such as we see in Museum collections. The raising of a lever with an apparent uplifting expansive force of between 20,000 and 30,000 pounds to the square inch, the running of the engine, the firing of the cannon, are conducted without one ounce of pressure in any part of the apparatus, and without the production or presence of what has been known as Keely's ether. The force is now transmitted along a wire (of platinum and silver), and when the lever is lowered there is no exhaustion, into the atmosphere of the room, of any up-lifting vapour, as was always the case when the ether was used in this experiment; nor is there any vapour impinging upon the piston under the lever to raise it.

Keely has named this new modification of the one force in nature "Negative Attraction," which to the uninitiated does not suggest as much as it would had he called it "Negative Humbug."

The two forms of force which he has been experimenting with, and the phenomena attending them, are the very antithesis of each other. Keely does not feel the shadow of a doubt as to his eventual success in producing engines of varying capacities; small enough, on the one hand, to operate sewing machines with, and large enough, on the other hand, to propel the largest ships that plough the seas. Every fact and feature surrounding the case warrants the belief, notwithstanding the incredulity of all who have not witnessed the progress of Mr. Keely, step by step, that his success will be complete, and his work stand as the most colossal example of the survival of the fittest, in the process of inventive evolution. Cox says: "Not one of the great facts which science now accepts as incontrovertible truths but was vehemently denied by the scientists of its time:—declared to be *a priori* impossible, its discoverers and supporters denounced as fools or charlatans, and even investigation of it refused as being a waste of time and thought." "History repeats itself," and Amiel's definition of science gives the key to the incredulity of scientists in reference to Mr. Keely's discovery; for if, as Amiel has said, "science is a lucid madness occupied with tabulating its own hallucinations," it is not strange that men of science should refuse to investigate what they consider the hallucinations of others.

It is an undisputed fact that "too much has been conceded to science, too little to those sublime laws which make science possible." But the one law which regulates creation, and to which all other laws are made subservient, keeping in harmony the systems upon systems of worlds throughout space, developing sound and colour, animal and vegetable

The Key to the Problems.

growth, the crystallization of minerals, is the hidden law, which develops every natural science throughout the universe ; and which both Kepler and Newton anticipated would be revealed in our age. " You can even trace the poles in sound," writes Mrs. F. J. Hughes, in her work upon the " Evolution of Tones and Colours." The experiments made by Mrs. Watts Hughes, at the annual Reception of the Royal Society, and the [1]Pendulograph writings by Andrew of Belfast, have a bearing upon Keely's discovery; illustrating the workings of this hidden law of nature.

Of the law of periodicity, Hartmann writes : "Its actions have long ago been known to exist in the vibrations producing light and sound, and it has been recognized in chemistry by experiments tending to prove that all so-called simple elements are only various states of vibration of one primordial element, manifesting itself in seven principal modes of action, each of which may be subdivided into seven again. The difference which exists between so-called single substances appears, therefore, to be no difference of substance or matter, but only a difference of the function of matter in the ratio of its atomic vibration." It is by changing the vibrations of cosmic ether that Mr. Keely releases this energy, and Dr. Kellner in Austria produces electricity in the same way; while it is said that a chemist in Prague produces magnetism; also Dr. Dupuy, of New York, who has been for years experimenting in this field without meeting with Keely's progressive successes.

Horace Wemyss Smith, in commenting upon the fact that, at the time of Franklin's discovery, men in France, in Belgium, in Holland, and in Germany were pursuing the same line of experiment, says that there is something worthy of observa-

---

[1] A system of Pendulums tuned to swing the various ratios of the musical scale, form a " Silent Harp " of extraordinary interest. This " Silent Harp," D. C. Ramsay, of Glasgow, has shown to his students of harmony for many a year. A pen, placed by means of a universal-jointed arrangement between any two pendulums of this " Silent Harp," so as to be moved by a blend of their various motions, writes, with all the precision of gravitation, a portrait of the chord which two corresponding strings of a sounding harp would utter to the ear. This spiral writing is a Pendulograph; exquisite forms such as no human hand could trace.

tion in the progress of science and human genius, inasmuch as in countries far distant from each other men have fallen into the same tracks, and have made similar and corresponding discoveries, at the same period of time, without the least communication with each other.

Laurence Oliphant's recent works give us the clue to an explanation of this fact; and Lowe, in his "Fragments of Physiology," condenses the answer in these words: "Man is not the governor and commander of the created world; and were it not for superhuman influence constantly flowing into created forms, the world would perish in a moment."

There are men in various parts of the world, unknown even by name to each other, who tell us by "the signs of the times" that the season of harvesting is approaching; the season for gathering the fruit, which has been deferred, century after century, because mankind is not yet ready, in the opinion of many, to share the fruit with one another.

It has been said that when Keely's vibratory force shall have taken the place of steam-engines, the millions of working men who gain with difficulty their daily bread by the work of their hands, will find themselves without occupation. The same prediction was made in regard to steam, but instead we find the city of Boston giving work to thirty thousand men in one manufactory of boots and shoes by steam, in place of the three thousand shoemakers who were all that were occupied in this branch of labour in that city when the work was done by hand.

Dr. Kellner's colleague, Franz Hartmann, M.D., writing in reference to Keely's discovery, says: "I have taken great interest in him ever since I first heard of him in 1882. As gaslight has driven away, in part, the smoky petroleum lamp, and is about to be displaced by electricity, which in the course of time may be supplanted by magnetism, and as the power of steam has caused muscular labour to disappear to a certain extent, and will itself give way before the new vibratory force of Keely, likewise the orthodox medical quackery that now prevails will be dethroned by the employment of the finer forces of nature, such as light, electricity, magnetism, etc."

The Key to the Problems.

When the time is ripe, these are of the true scientists who will come to the front " to lead as progress leads," men who know how to wait upon God, viz., to work while waiting; and to such the end is, sooner or later, victory! "God never hurries." He counts the centuries as we count the seconds, and the nearer we approach to the least comprehension of His "underlying purpose" the more we become like Tolstoi's labourer, who knew that the fruit was ripening for him and his fellow-men, trusting implicitly in the superior wisdom of his master.

No man, whose spiritual eyes have been opened to "discern the signs of the times," can doubt that we are on the eve of revelations which are to usher in the dawn of a brighter day than our race has yet known; and no prophecy of this brighter day, foretold by prophets, apostles, and inspired poets, was ever made in truer strains than in these glorious lines of Elizabeth Barrett Browning:—

> Verily many thinkers of this age,
> Aye, many Christian teachers, half in heaven,
> Are wrong in just my sense who understood
> Our natural world too insularly, as if
> No spiritual counterpart completed it,
> Consummating its meaning, rounding all
> To justice and perfection, line by line,
> Form by form, nothing single nor alone;
> The Great Below clenched by the Great Above.

PART II.

ONE PHASE OF KEELY'S DISCOVERY IN ITS RELATIONS TO THE CURE OF DISEASE.

I know medicine is called a science. It is nothing like a science. It is a great humbug! Doctors are mere empirics when they are not charlatans. We are as ignorant as men can be. Who knows anything in the world about medicine? Gentlemen, you have done me the honour to come here to attend my lectures, and I must tell you now, frankly, in the beginning, that I know nothing about medicine, nor do I know anyone who does know anything about it. Nature does a great deal, imagination does a great deal, doctors do devilish little when they do not do harm. Sick people always feel they are neglected, unless they are well drugged, *les imbéciles!*

PROFESSOR MAGENDIE (before the students of his class in "The Allopathic College of Paris").

In the year 1871, the writer was sent from Paris to Schwalbach, by Dr. Beylard, and recommended to the care of Dr. Adolph Genth. She said to the physician, "I wish for your opinion and your advice, if you can give it to me without giving me any medicine." He replied, "With all my heart, madam; and I wish to God there were more women like you, but we should soon lose most of our patients if we did not dose them."

This is a terrible excuse for the use of those agencies which Dr. John Good says have sent more human beings to their graves than war, pestilence and famine combined. Keely holds the opinion that Nature works under the one law of Compensation and Equilibrium—the law of Harmony; and that when disease indicates the disturbance of this law Nature at once seeks to banish the disease by restoring equilibrium, He seeks to render assistance on the same plan; replacing grossly material agencies by the finer forces of nature; as has been so successfully done by Dr. Pancoast and Dr. Babbitt in America.

"Nature," says Dr. Pancoast, author of *The True Science of Light,* "works by antagonism in all her operations: when one of her forces overdoes its work, disease, or at least a local disorder, is the immediate consequence; now, if we attack this force, and overcome it, the opposite force has a clear field and may re-assert its rights—thus equilibrium is restored, and *Equilibrium is health*. The Sympathetic System, instead of attacking the stronger force, sends recruits to the weaker one, and enables it to recover its powers; or, if the disorder be the result of excessive tension of Nerves or Ganglia, a negative remedy may be employed to reduce the tension. Thus, too, equilibrium is restored."

Dr. Hartmann writes:—

Mr. Keely is perfectly right in saying that 'all disease is a disturbance of the equilibrium between positive and negative forces.' In my opinion, no doctor ever cured any disease. All he can possibly do is to establish conditions under which the patient (or nature) may cure himself.

If you enter the field of therapeutics and medicine, we find a decided ' fermentation of new ideas; not among

The Key to the Problems. 93

the fossil specimens of antediluvian quackery, but among those who are called "irregulars," because they have the courage to depart from the tracks trodden out by their predecessors. The more intelligent classes of physicians have long ago realized the fact that drugs and medicines are perfectly useless, excepting in cases where diseases can be traced to some mechanical obstruction, in some organ that may be reached by mechanical action. In all other cases our best physicians have become agnostics, leaving nature to have her own way, and observing the expectative method, which, in fact, is no method of cure at all, but merely consists in doing no harm to the patient. Recently, however, light, electricity, and magnetism have been employed; so that even in the medical guild the finer forces of nature are taking the place of grossly material, and therefore injurious substances. The time is probably near when these finer forces will be employed universally. Everybody knows that a note struck upon an instrument will produce sound in a correspondingly attuned instrument in its vicinity. If connected with a tuning fork, it will produce a corresponding sound in the latter; and if connected with a thousand such tuning forks, it will make all the thousand sound, and produce a noise far greater than the original sound, without the latter becoming any weaker for it. Here, then, is an augmentation or multiplication of power. If we had any means to transform sound again into mechanical motion, we would have a thousand-fold multiplication of mechanical motion. It would be presumptuous to say that it will not be as easy for the scientists of the future to transform sound into mechanical motion, as it is for the scientist of the present to transform heat into electricity. Perhaps Mr. Keely has already solved the problem. There is a fair prospect that in the very near future, we shall have, in his ethereal force, a power far surpassing that of steam or electricity. Nor does the idea seem to be Utopian if we remember that modern science heretofore only knew the law of the conservation of energy; while to the scientist of the future the law of the augmentation of energy will be unveiled.
. . . . As the age which has passed away has been the age of steam, the coming era will be the age of induction. There

will be a universal rising up of lower vibrations into higher ones, in the realm of motion. Mr. Keely will, perhaps, transform sound into mechanical motion by applying the law of augmentation and multiplication of force." . . .

Keely, writing on brain disturbance, says, In considering the mental forces as associated with the physical, I find, by my past researches, that the convolutions which exist in the cerebral field are entirely governed by the sympathetic conditions that surround them.

The question arises, what are these aggregations and what do they represent, as being linked with physical impulses? They are simply vibrometric resonators, thoroughly subservient to sympathetic acoustic impulses given to them by their atomic sympathetic surrounding media, all the sympathetic impulses that so entirely govern the physical in their many and perfect impulses (we are now discussing purity of conditions) are not emanations properly inherent in their own composition. They are only media—the acoustic media—for transferring from their vibratory surroundings the conditions necessary to the pure connective link for vitalizing and bringing into action the varied impulses of the physical.

All abnormal discordant aggregations in these resonating convolutions produce differentiation to concordant transmission; and, according as these differentiations exist in volume, so the transmissions are discordantly transferred, producing antagonism to pure physical action.

Thus, in Motor Ataxy a differentiation of the minor thirds of the posterior parietal lobule produces the same condition between the retractors and extensors of the leg and foot; and thus the control of the proper movements is lost through this differentiation. The same truth can be universally applied to any of the cerebral convolutions that are in a state of differential harmony to the mass of immediate cerebral surroundings. Taking the cerebral condition of the whole mass as one, it is subservient to one general head centre, although as many neutrals are represented as there are convolutions.

The introductory minors are controlled by the molecular; the next progressive third by the atomic; and the high third by the Etheric. All these progressive links have their positive, negative, and neutral position. When we take into consideration the structural condition of the human brain, we ought not to be bewildered by the infinite variety of its sympathetic impulses; inasmuch as it unerringly proves the true philosophy that the mass chords of such structures are governed by vibratory etheric flows—the very material which composes them. There is no structure whatever, animal, vegetable, mineral, that is not built up from the universal cosmic ether. Certain orders of attractive vibration produce certain orders of structure; thus, the infinite variety of effects—more especially in the cerebral organs. The bar of iron or the mass of steel, have, in each, all the qualifications necessary, under certain vibratory impulses, to evolve all the conditions that govern that animal organism—the brain: and it is as possible to differentiate the molecular conditions of a mass of metal of any shape so as to produce what you may express as a crazy piece of iron or a crazy piece of steel; or, *vice versâ*, an intelligent condition in the same.

I find in my researches, as to the condition of molecules under vibration, that discordance cannot exist in the molecule proper; and that it is the highest and most perfect structural condition that exists; providing that all the progressive orders are the same. Discordance in any mass is the result of differentiated groups, induced by antagonistic chords, and the flight or motions of such, when intensified by sound, are very tortuous and zig-zag; but when free of this differentiation are in straight lines. Tortuous lines denote discord, or pain; straight lines denote harmony, or pleasure. Any differentiated mass can be brought to a condition of harmony, or equation, by proper chord media, and an equated sympathy produced.

There is good reason for believing that insanity is simply a condition of differentiation in the mass chords of the cerebral convolutions, which creates an antagonistic molecular bombardment towards the neutral or attractive centres of such convolutions; which, in turn, produce a morbid irritation in the cortical sensory centres in the substance of ideation; accompanied, as a general thing, by sensory hallucinations, ushered in by subjective sensations; such as flashes of light and colour, or confused sounds and disagreeable odours, etc., etc.

There is no condition of the human brain that ought not to be sympathetically coincident to that order of atomic flow to which its position, in the cerebral field, is fitted. Any differentiation in that special organ, or, more plainly, any discordant grouping tends to produce a discordant bombardment —an antagonistic conflict; which means the same disturbance transferred to the physical, producing inharmonious disaster to that portion of the physical field which is controlled by that especial convolution. This unstable aggregation may be compared to a knot on a violin string. As long as this knot remains it is impossible to elicit, from its sympathetic surroundings, the condition which transfers pure concordance to its resonating body. Discordant conditions, *i.e.*, differentiation of mass, produce *negatization* to coincident action.

The question now arises, What condition is it necessary to bring about in order to bring back normality, or to produce stable equilibrium in the sympathetic centres?

The normal brain is like a harp of many strings strung to perfect harmony. The transmitting conditions being perfect, are ready, at any impulse, to induce pure sympathetic assimilation. The different strings represent the different ventricles and convolutions. The differentiations of any one from its true setting is fatal, to a certain degree, to the harmony of the whole combination.

If the sympathetic condition of any physical organism carries a positive flow of 80 per cent. on its whole combination, and a negative one of 20 per cent., it is the medium of perfect assimilation to one of the same ratio, if it is distributed under the same conditions to the mass of the other. If two masses of metal, of any shape whatever, are brought under perfect assimilation, to one another, their unition, when brought into contact, will be instant. If we live in a sympathetic field we become sympathetic, and a tendency from the abnormal to the normal presents itself by an evolution of a purely sympathetic flow towards its attractive centres. It is only under these conditions that differentiation can be broken up, and a pure equation established. The only condition under which equation can never be established is when a differential disaster has taken place, of $66\frac{2}{3}$ against the 100 pure, taking the full volume as one. If this 66⅔ or even 100 exists in one organ alone, and the surrounding ones are normal, then a condition can be easily brought about to establish the concordant harmony or equation to that organ. It is as rare to find a negative condition of 66⅔ against the volume of the whole cerebral mass, as it is to find a coincident between differentiation; or, more plainly, between two individuals under a state of negative influence. Under this new system, it is as possible to induce negations alike as it is to induce positives alike.

Pure sympathetic concordants are as antagonistic to negative discordants as the negative is to the positive; but the vast volume the sympathetic holds over the non-sympathetic, in ethereal space, makes it at once the ruling medium and re-adjuster of all opposing conditions if properly brought to bear upon them.

Until Keely's "Theoretical Exposé" is given to science, there are few who will fathom the full meaning of these views.

His discoveries embrace the manner or way of obtaining the keynote, or "chord of mass," of mineral, vegetable, and animal substances; therefore, the construction of instruments, or machines, by which this law can be utilized in mechanics, in arts, and in restoration of equilibrium in disease, is only a question of the full understanding of the operation of this law.

Keely estimates that, after the introductory impulse is given on the harmonic thirds, molecular vibration is increased from 20,000 per second to 100,000,000.

On the enharmonic sixths, that the vibration of the intermolecule is increased to 300,000,000.

On the diatonic ninths, that atomic vibration reaches 900,000,000; on the dominant etheric sixths, 8,100,000,000; and on the inter-etheric ninths, 24,300,000,000; all of which can be demonstrated by sound colours.

In such fields of research, Mr. Keely finds little leisure. Those who accuse him of "dilly-dallying," of idleness, of "always going to do and never doing," of "visionary plans," etc., etc., know nothing of the infinite patience, the persistent energy, which for a quarter of a century has upheld him in his struggle to attain this end. Still less, if possible, is he understood by those who think he is seeking self-aggrandizement, fame, fortune, or glory.

The time is approaching when all who have sought to defame this discoverer and inventor, all who have stabbed him with unmerited accusations, all who have denounced him as "a bogus inventor," "a fraud," "an impostor," "a charlatan," "a modern Cagliostro," will be forced to acknowledge that he has done a giant's work for true science, even though he should not live to attain commercial success. But history will not forget that, in the nineteenth century, the story of Prometheus has been repeated, and that the greatest mind of the age, seeking to scale the heavens to bring down the light of truth for mankind, met with Prometheus's reward.

NOTE.—Dr. Hartmann, in a report, or condensed statement, in reference to Keely's discovery, writes as follows: "He will never invent a machine by which the equilibrium of the living forces in a disordered brain can be restored."

As such a statement would lead the reader of the report to fancy that Keely expected to invent such an instrument, it is better to correct the error that Dr. Hartmann has fallen into. Keely has never dreamed of inventing such an instrument. He hopes, however, to perfect one that he is now at work upon, which will enable the operator to localize the seat of disturbance in the brain in mental disorders. If he succeeds, this will greatly simplify the work of "re-adjusting opposing conditions"; and will also enable the physician to decide whether the "differential disaster" has taken place which prevents the possibility of establishing the equation that is necessary to a cure.

According to Keely's theories it is that form of energy known as magnetism—*not* electricity—which is to be the curative agent of the future, thus reviving a mode of treatment handed down from the time of the earliest records, and made known to the Royal Society of London more than fifty years since by Professor Keil, of Jena, who demonstrated the susceptibility of the nervous system to the influence of the natural magnet, and its efficacy in the cure of certain infirmities.

The Key to the Problems.

As Cheston Morris, M.D., has well said in his paper on "Vital Molecular Vibrations," "We are entering upon a new field in biology, pathology, and of course, therapeutics, whose limits are at present far beyond our ken."

"The adaptability of drugs," says Dr. Henry Wood, "to heal disease is becoming a matter of doubt, even among many who have not yet studied deeper causation. Materia Medica lacks the exact elements of a science. The just preponderance, for good or ill, of any drug upon the human system is an unsolved problem, and will so remain. . . . After centuries of professional research, in order to perfect "the art of healing," diseases have steadily grown more subtle and more numerous. . . . Only when internal, divine forces come to be relied upon, rather than outside reinforcement, will deterioration cease. Said Plato, 'You ought not to attempt to cure the body without the soul.'"

CHAPTER VIII

1888.

HELPERS ON THE ROAD, AND HINDERERS.

> Blindfolded and alone we stand,
> With unknown thresholds on each hand:
> The darkness deepens as we grope,
> Afraid to fear, afraid to hope.
> Yet this one thing we learn to know
> Each day more surely as we go :
> That doors are opened, ways are made,
> Burdens are lifted, or are laid
> By some great law unseen and still
> Unfathomed purpose to fulfil.
>   " Not as I will."

THE next "helper on the road" was an Austrian nobleman, the Chevalier Griez de Ronse, who printed a series of papers on Keely's discoveries in a journal in Vienna, then owned by him—*The Vienna Weekly News*. One of these articles mentions that the attention of Englishmen of science had been drawn to Keely's claims, in regard to having imprisoned the ether, by Professor Henri Hertz's experiments in ether vibrations at the Bonn University. "Keely, like the late Dr. Schuster," says *The Vienna Weekly News*, " claims on behalf of science the right to prosecute its investigations until a mechanical explanation of all things is attained. The public are still but the children of those who murdered Socrates, tolerated the persecution of Galileo, and deserted Columbus. This remark is now illustrated by the imprisonment with felons last month of Inventor Keely in Moyamensing Prison, Philadelphia, where Judge Finletter committed him for contempt of court, without the shadow of an excuse in the opinions of men who had followed the proceedings against him.

Under the heading, "Keely's Sunday in Jail," says a Philadelphia journal, Inventor Keely spent a quiet Sunday in Moyamensing Prison. The outside iron doors of his cell were thrown open, when the religious services of the morning began. The imprisoned inventor listened with deep interest. The soft peals of the organ and the melody of the choir, singing "Nearer, my God, to Thee," floated into the narrow cell. Keely sat near the grated door while the minister read selections from the Scriptures and preached his sermon. While the inventor was resting in his cell, during the afternoon, a number of persons made inquiries at the "Untried Department." They were all told that no one could be admitted on Sunday, but a young man with a pallid face lingered. He told the gate-keeper that he was an inventor himself, and had been waiting for eight years for a patent from Washington; adding that, when he read of Keely's commitment, he was reminded of Galileo who was thrown in a dungeon because he said, "*The world moves.*"

The following day Keely was released by order of the Judges of the Supreme Court. His imprisonment exalted him, instead of degrading him as "the unjust judge" hoped to do; drawing the sympathies to him of all men who know what it is to be "persecuted for righteousness' sake;" of all men, in all parts of the world, who are truth-loving, justice-loving men.

The Keely Motor Company should learn a lesson in this experience. Tyndall said, long since, that the community that severs itself from great discoveries, that merely runs after the practical application without reference to the sources of a discovery, would by-and-by find itself at the end of its tether. This has been verified in the fate of the Keely Motor Company, which was organized for the purpose of reaping financial benefit from Keely's grand discovery of an unknown force before his "work of evolution," in obtaining mechanical results, had fairly commenced. This company has thrown upon the discoverer's shoulders the burden of its stock-jobbing operations, until Keely is looked upon by men of science, as well as by men ignorant of the A B C of science, as a man working for personal ends; instead of, as he should be regarded, a Prometheus seeking to give to his fellow-men a costless motive force; and who, whether he succeeds financially or not, is entitled to the admiration of all who believe, with Browning, that "effort, not success, makes man great." If the Keely Motor Company managers would profit by this lesson, they will in future seek to find, among scientific men of world-wide renown, some one man, broad enough in mind to care nothing for the ridicule of the ignorant, who will investigate the nature of Keely's discoveries, as demonstrated by his experiments, instead of inviting reporters to witness the demonstrations, in their efforts "to boom the stock" of their company, by a reporter's accounts of the marvels he has witnessed. For years Keely had nothing to show, beyond the generation of the force, the production of a 30 lb. vacuum and the discharge of a gun. When once his giant mind had grasped the knowledge, which again by seeming chance was imparted to him, he made colossal strides across that unknown tract, the boundaries of which others are now but beginning to explore. Colonel Le Mat was no false prophet, *Le Figaro* was no untrustworthy herald, when the announcement was made by this French inventor to Monsieur Chevreuil, and by this French journal to the public on the 1st day of September, 1888, that the chain which holds the aerial ship to the earth would be broken asunder by Keely's discovery. The nineteenth century holds in its strong arms the pledge, that sooner or later the aerial navy, so long waited for, will traverse the trackless high roads of space from Continent to Continent.

It has been supposed by many, Dr. Franz Hartmann among the number, that it requires Keely himself, or another person constituted like him, to set his machinery in motion. Therefore, it has been reasoned that the commercial success of an engine is only possible in case Keely is himself the engineer; or if another man possessing the same seemingly abnormal power could be the engineer. For this reason, says Dr. Hartmann, it is impossible for Keely to instruct any one in his method, so as to enable that one to do what he does. There has been ground in the past for such a statement, it is true, but not now. Keely asserts that when his system is completed, the knowledge of all that is needed for its commercial employment will be more easily acquired than is the necessary skill demanded to enable one to safely operate a steam-engine. When Dr. Hartmann's opinion was made known to Keely, he replied, "Dr. Hartmann's whole conception, in regard to other men being unable to control the operations of my inventions on the sympathetic attractive system, is as incorrect as would be the same conception in reference to operating an electric battery by anyone but its inventor."

Let anyone imagine the years on years of research that would have been necessary before Gilbert (who, after Thales, discovered electricity) could have perfected a system which would have enabled men to accomplish all that is accomplished in our age, with electricity as a motive power. Keely's labours would be better understood by those who accuse him of "always promising, and never performing," under such a conception. The inventor must be sanguine of success; he must day by day think that he is on the eve of perfecting his invention, in order to keep up his courage to persevere to the end; otherwise, how could he work, year after year, in the face of obstacle after obstacle that seems, each one, to be insurmountable? After Keely's imprisonment when, among the men who knew that he was incapable of fraud, there was one so incensed by Keely's repeated failures to perfect his engine that he had said he "hoped to live to see Keely rotting in a gutter," Mr. R. Harte wrote: "And now that it has been proved in a hundred ways and before thousands of persons competent to judge of the merits of Keely's claims, that he has really discovered previously unknown forces in nature, studied them, mastered some of their laws, invented and is perfecting researching apparatus that will make his discoveries of practical application in numerous ways—now that he has actually done this, how does the world treat him? Does Congress come forward with a grant to enable him to complete his marvellous work? Do men of science hail him as a great discoverer, or hold out the hand of fellowship? Do people do honour to the man whose sole entreaty to them will be to receive from his hands a gift a thousand times more precious to them than steam engine or dynamo? It is a literal fact that if Keely fell exhausted to-day, in the terrible struggle he has so long maintained, his failure to establish his claims would be received with a shout of malignant delight from nearly every lecture-hall, pulpit, counting-house and newspaper office in the so-called civilized world. The world has hardly ever recognized its benefactors until it has become time to raise a statue to their memory, ' in order to beautify the town.' Jealousy, stupidity, the malignity which is born of conscious inferiority, are at this moment putting in Keely's road every impediment which law and injustice can manufacture. Two hundred years ago he would have been burned, a century since he would have probably been mobbed to death; but thank God we are too civilized, too humane now to burn or mob to death those who make great discoveries, who wish to benefit their fellow-men, or whose ideas are in advance of their age—we only break their hearts with slander, ridicule, and neglect, and when that fails to drive them to suicide, we bring to bear upon them the ponderous pressure of the law, and heap upon them the '*peine forte et dure*' of injunctions, and orders, and suits, to crush them out of a world they have had the impertinence to try to improve, and the folly to imagine they could save from suffering, without paying in their own persons the inevitable penalty. Had it not been for the obligations incurred by Keely, in accepting the aid of the Keely Motor Company—in other words, had scientists, instead of speculators, furnished him with the means necessary to carry on his work of evolution, the secrets which he has so carefully guarded would now have been public property, so little does he care personally for financial results. As it is, those who have witnessed his beautiful experiments in acoustics and sympathetic vibration were often too ignorant to comprehend their meaning, and, consequently, even after expressing gratification to him, went away from his workshop to denounce him as a Cagliostro; while others, competent to judge, have refused to witness the production of the ether, as Sir William Thomson and Lord Raleigh refused, when they were in America a few years since. The company here mentioned has been a thorn in the inventor's side ever since it was organized. It has been 'bulled and beared' by greedy speculators, in whose varying interests the American newspapers for years have been worked, the results of which the inventor has had to bear. For many years the Company has contributed nothing towards Keely's expenses or support, and in the opinion of many lawyers it is virtually dead. How far it is entitled to his gratitude may be gathered from the fact, as stated, that 'when Mr. Keely abandoned his old generator of etheric force, baffled in his attempts to wrest from nature one of her most carefully guarded secrets, harassed by his connection with the Keely Motor Company, some of the officers and stockholders of which had instituted law proceedings against him, which threatened him with the indignity of imprisonment, he destroyed many of his marvellous models, and determined that, if taken to prison, it should be his dead body and not himself.

"Those who argue, if Keely had really obtained knowledge which contributes towards making man master of the material world, that science would hail the glad tidings with great joy, know but little of modern science and its votaries. An Anglican bishop never ignored a dissenting preacher with more dignified grace than the professor of orthodox science ignores the heterodox genius who has the audacity to wander beyond the limitations which 'received opinion' has placed upon the possibilities of nature. The fact is that men of science have persistently ignored, and know absolutely nothing about, the great department of nature into which Keely penetrated years ago, and in which he has now made himself at home. Not long ago a Fellow of the Royal Society of Edinburgh, Major Ricarde-Seaver, went to Philadelphia to convince himself as to the nature of Keely's discovery. He returned, saying that Keely was working with, and had the apparent command over forces, the nature, or even the very existence, of which was absolutely unknown to him, and, so far as he is aware, to modern science.

"Beyond disintegration lies dispersion, and Keely can just as easily disperse the atoms of matter as disintegrate its molecules. Disperse them into what? Well,—into ether, apparently; into the hypothetical substratum which modern scientists have postulated, and about whose nature they know absolutely nothing but what they invent themselves, but which to Keely is not hypothesis, but a fact as real as his own shoes; and which ether, indeed, seems to be 'the protoplasm of all things.' As to the 'law of gravity,' it appears in the light of Keely's experiments, but one manifestation of a law of very much wider application—a law which provides for the reversion of the process of attraction in the shape of a process of repulsion.

"While Major Ricarde-Seaver, F.R.S.,[1] was in Philadelphia, Keely, by means of a belt and certain appliances which he wore upon his person, moved single-handed, a 500 horse-power vibratory engine from one part of his shop to another. There was not a scratch on the floor, and astounded engineers declared that they could not have moved it without a derrick, the operation of which would have required the removal of the roof of the shop. Of course it is but a step in advance of this to construct a machine which, when polarized with a 'negative attraction,' will rise from the earth and move under the influence of an etheric current at the rate of 500 miles an hour, in any given direction. This is, in fact, Keely's 'air ship.'

"When the history of his discoveries and inventions come to be written there will be no more pathetic story in the annals of genius than that of John Worrell Keely. The world hereafter will find it hard to believe that in the last quarter of the 19th century a man with an insight into the secret workings of nature, and a knowledge of her subtler forces, which, whenever it is utilized, will relieve mankind from much of the grinding

---

[1] By his advocacy of Keely's claims, as a discoverer, Major Ricarde-Seaver had reason to fear that he would lose his election to membership of the Athenæum Club in London; as he was notified by Sir William Thomson (who had proposed him for membership in or about the year 1873) that such would probably be the case. The members however, rallied in force and, led by one of the Major's oldest friends Prince Lucien Buonaparte, he was elected by an overwhelming majority.

toil that now makes bitter the existence of the vast majority, that such a man should have been left unaided, because in all the ranks of science there was not found one man capable of understanding his colossal work—because in all the ranks of religion there was not found one man able to realize the enlarged conception of Deity immanent in Keely's great thoughts—because in all the ranks of commerce, of speculation, of literature, of art, there was not found one man large enough, generous enough, unselfish enough, to furnish money for a purpose that did not promise an immediate dividend."

Again in 1888, more than ever was Keely held up to ridicule by all those men who possess the instinct of the brute to hound down its prey, and his supporters came in for their share of abuse. Among this class, or of it, were men so ignorant of Keely's claims, and of the object of his researches, that they represented him as "a seeker of the impossible," a "perpetual motion crank," throwing upon his character other odium which the speculating managers of "The Keely Motor Company" were justly responsible for. One of these communications alone is enough to show the quality of the weapons used against him. It appeared in *The New York Daily Tribune*.

THE KEELY MOTOR CRAZE.

A Donkey-Cabbage Race.

HOW MUCH LONGER WILL THE CLEVER JUGGLER BE ABLE TO DELUDE HIS VICTIMS?

To the Editor of "The Tribune."

Sir,—The success with which Keely has deluded his victims by appealing to their credulity with a mystery, and to their cupidity with a promise of "all the kingdoms of the earth," which would not be of greater value than the monopoly of infinite power without cost, which he dangles before their astonished vision, makes him and his antics subjects of unusual interest. His last performance appears to be an issue of

5,000,000 dols. of new stock representing a new discovery veiled in mystery, which is to far outstrip his former one, on which 5,000,000 dols. of stock was issued and is now held by his dupes. Two of these new millions are to go to the old holders as a compensation to them for their disappointment in not realizing perpetual motion under the old discovery; two more to go to Keely to be sold to the public; and the remaining one million is in the treasury to be sold for the benefit of Keely and the others, half and half.

For fifteen years the donkey has been ridden by Keely with the cabbage on a pole held just in front of his hungry mouth, and now the donkey is told that the cabbage after all is only sham, but that the new cabbage is real, and if he will only consent to run fast enough and far enough he certainly will reach it and grow fat.

It would seem that the donkey ought to pause and consider before he begins another fifteen-year race after perpetual motion, and it is here proposed to assist him in his reflections by a few facts. More than fifteen years ago Keely made himself known to the public by exhibiting an apparatus in which a great pressure was manifested, which, he said, resulted from the discovery by him of a new force the nature of which was his secret. Several people, as usual, were astonished at the show, and bought and paid for shares in the patent which was promised. To give colour to the pretence, Keely applied for a patent before 1876, but did not assign to the purchasers their shares; whereupon some of them protested against the issue of the patent unless their shares were recognized in the grant. The Patent Office replied to these protests that it could not recognize the rights claimed unless there was a written assignment filed in the office, which the claimants did not have. The Commissioner, however, called upon Keely to furnish a "working model" of his invention, which, of course, he could not do, and his application was rejected. The specification and drawings of this apparatus show a very silly form of the common perpetual motion machine, of which there are thousands. It was open to the public for some years, when, under a new rule of the office, it, along with all other rejected applications, was withdrawn from inspection; but it is in the office, together with the protests of those who had paid Keely for a share in it. I examined it years ago, and informed Mr. Lamson, and others of Keely's stockholders, of it. Mr. Lamson told me that he had charged Keely with deception, because he had always said that he never had applied for a patent, and that Keely explained it by saying that he had purposely concealed his invention from the Patent Office in that application to which he had made oath.

Keely, however, finding the perpetual motion trick profitable, extended his operations and became well known to many influential people by his exhibitions. In the winter of 1875-76 he produced two metallic spheres, one about thirty inches in diameter, hung like an ordinary terrestrial globe, which, he said, would revolve with a force equal to two horse-power, and would continue to run when once started as long as the Centennial Exhibition should be open, and until the thing was worn out by friction. In starting it Keely used to have a blackboard in the room, on which he would write a few figures in chalk in the presence of his dupes, and would say that at a certain time the globe would start—and it did, and would revolve as long as the lookers-on remained to see it. Keely pretended to explain this phenomenon by a string of unintelligible jargon; but the point of it all was that he said the thing ran in consequence of its internal mechanical arrangement—or, in other words, that by combining pieces of metal in a certain way power was generated without any other expense than that required to construct the apparatus. Naturally he refused to show the interior construction which did the miracle; but if his statements were true, it existed inside of that globe, and could be produced indefinitely with the result of producing an indefinite amount of horse-power without current expense.

The stock about this time rose to a great price—about 600 per cent.—as it well might if this ball was an "honest ghost." Some of the stockholders had sense enough to see that if Keely's story were true, nothing more could be desired, for it must at once supersede coal and all other means of producing power, and its novelty could not be doubted. It was in effect, "all the kingdoms of the earth," which Satan once offered.

But, on the other hand, if Keely's story were not true, then he was simply an impostor who had been defrauding the stockholders out of their money; and they demanded of Keely that he should proceed at once to patent this miraculous machine, which could create power by a peculiar-shaped hole in a sphere of iron. Of course Keely refused to comply with this reasonable request, and many of his stockholders sold out and left him; since which time the stock has gradually declined down to the present time, when its value is admitted to be nothing.

In view of these facts the curious question is why the donkey goes on any further. The revolving ball is a fact known to hundreds of the stockholders. It is either a real cabbage capable of feeding the donkey with a perpetual feast, like the widow's cruse of oil, or it is only a sham such as any good mechanic could construct and operate as Keely did. Why doesn't the donkey balk and insist on biting into the cabbage? If it is real the Keely stock is worth untold millions. It would put an end to steam engines and electric batteries for ever. One of those balls in the corner of a room would make all the heat and light which could be used, and have power to sell; and all that would be needed would be to learn Keely's cabalistic signs on the blackboard in order to make it start, and to stop it when it had done enough. But if the ball is only a trick, then, of course, Keely could be sent to prison, and his victims could close their accounts and be sure that they would lose no more by him.

Without going any further into the history of this remarkable delusion, which is full of similar tricks too numerous to mention now, it seems clear that these facts ought to be used to bring to an end in one way or the other the Keely craze.

EDWARD N. DICKERSON.

New York, Nov. 30, 1888.

It is difficult to understand how anyone could concoct and put together such a tissue of fabrications as this, when the sole foundation for such a tissue lay in the fact that it was at this juncture that Keely made the announcement that he had

Helpers on the Road, and Hinderers.

proved the uselessness of building engines to employ the ether as a motive power; which could only be used as the medium for the power which he had discovered, namely, a condition of sympathetic vibration, associated both positively and negatively with the polar stream.

The statement made of the issue of new stock is absolutely untrue. The revolving globe was never created to be "the source of power," and the representation of the manner in which the globe was made to revolve, and that Keely affirmed he could produce with it "an indefinite amount of horse power without current expense," is denied. The suggestion that Keely could be sent to prison was welcomed by those who eventually acted upon it, with the result that Judge Finletter committed Keely to Moyamensing Prison, for contempt of court, but not for fraud. Mr. Keely, at that time, wrote of those who called him a perpetual motion seeker:—" I console myself by thinking that if they were not ignorant of the grand truths which I am devoting my life to develop into a system, they could never bring forward such an absurd charge. Perpetual motion is against nature, and it is only by following nature's laws that I can ever hope to reach the goal I am aiming to reach."

The Supreme Court reversed and set aside the order of the court committing Keely for contempt, and released him from custody, upon the writ of *habeas corpus* taken out on his behalf, within three days of his commitment.

The Chief Justice, in delivering his opinion, made some remarks which fully vindicated Mr. Keely's character. After alluding to the proper procedure which ought to have been taken in the court below, the Judge continued :—

"Instead of so proceeding, a commission of experts was appointed to examine the defendant's machine, and the order of April 7th was made, by which the defendant, in advance of any issue, was not only required to exhibit his machine, but also to operate it and explain the mode of its construction and operation, although it clearly appeared that it would require considerable expense to clean the machine, put it together and operate it. The defendant appears to have been willing to exhibit it, and in point of fact did so. That he might have been compelled to do so at a proper stage of the case is conceded. But to make an order not only to exhibit it, but to operate it, the practical effect of which was to wring from him his defence in advance of any issue joined, was an improvident and excessive exercise of Chancery powers. We are of opinion that the order was improvidently made. It follows that the learned court had no power to enforce it by attachment. The relator is discharged."

It was in this year, 1888, that a woman, interested in all branches of science, who had proved to her own satisfaction the value to humanity, as well as to science, of Keely's discoveries, was deprived of legal and maternal rights on account of the delusions that she was very generally believed to be under. A journalist, wishing to obtain information concerning Keely's work, called upon this woman, by appointment, and at the close of the interview said,—

"May I venture to ask you if it is true that you have furnished Mr. Keely with large sums of money as rumour declares; and that you have invested largely in the stock?"

"Were I not glad of the opportunity to answer this question in justice to Mr. Keely, I might have said that this is a subject which is of no interest to the public; but I have heard the amount estimated as nearly 100,000*l.* too often not to be willing to have the truth made known. What I have given to Mr. Keely has been saved by economies in my expenses; and, if not given to him, would have been given to others; as I believe in those who have the most doing all that lies in their power for those who have less. In regard to investments in Keely Motor stock, I have bought no stock excepting to give away."

"There is one other question I should like to ask you," said our representative, "Is Mr. Keely a spiritualist? I use the word in its ordinary sense. Does he claim that he has bridged the gulf between the finite and the infinite?"

"When Mr. Keely first commenced his wonderful investigations he would have scouted the idea of being in any way whatever associated with so-called spiritualism, but of recent years, and especially during the last few months, he has made such startling progress that he now admits—as I told him a long time ago he would come to admit—that if not in actual experiment, at least in theory he has passed into the world of spirit."

The interview being ended, our representative took his departure, after expressing his thanks for the information so willingly given. How far this lady's anticipations of the inventor's success will be realized, or how far her confidence in his integrity is justified, we must leave our readers to judge for themselves. The whole subject is enveloped in much mystery, but it is full of interest, and if half that is narrated of Mr. Keely be true, he is indeed a wonderful man!—*The Tatler.*

CHAPTER IX.

1889—1890.

KEELY SUPPORTED BY DISTINGUISHED MEN OF SCIENCE.
AERIAL NAVIGATION.

> Is not ether infinitely more rare and more subtle than air, and exceedingly more elastic and more active? Does it not easily penetrate all bodies? And is it not by its elastic force diffused through the universe?—SIR ISAAC NEWTON.

IN 1889 a series of short articles were written, which, for the first time, made known to the public that Keely had theories which he was able to sustain by mechanical demonstration : and once more an attempt was made to have men of science acquaint themselves with the theories, and witness the demonstrations. Capitalists also were appealed to, to convince themselves of the existence of an unknown force, and of Mr. Keely's honesty in his efforts to control it for commercial purposes ; money being required to enable him to complete his researches for science, and to protect him from those who were harassing him in such a way as to impede his progress at every step. The appeal to capitalists might as well have been made to stone walls ; but among the men of scientific and philosophical attainments who were invited, the late Professor Joseph Leidy, M.D., of the Pennsylvania University, and James M. Willcox, Ph.D., author of "Rational Philosophy," and other works, accepted the invitation and attended a series of Keely's researching experiments. For years Mr. Keely's experiments were confined to the production of the force; the raising of a lever ; the firing of a cannon ; and the showing of a vacuum greater than had ever been produced.

Since 1888 he has pursued his researches on a line which enabled him to show uninterrupted progress year after year: so that now he never repeats his experiments; but, discarding or improving his researching instruments, after he has gained the results which his theories lead him to expect, he continues his investigations, thereafter, from the solid basis which he has attained by those researches. The result of the attention given by Professor Leidy and Dr. Willcox is best set down in their own words:—

"April 8th, 1890.

"After having had the opportunity of witnessing a series of experiments made by Mr. John Keely, illustrative of a reputed new motor power, it has appeared to me that he has fairly demonstrated the discovery of a force previously unknown to science. I have no theory to account for the phenomena observed, but I believe Mr. Keely to be honest in his attempt to explain them. His demonstrations appear to indicate great mechanical power, which, when applied to appropriate machinery, must supersede all ordinary appliances.

"JOSEPH LEIDY."

"Philadelphia, April 8th, 1890.

"After having witnessed, on several occasions and under favourable circumstances, Mr. Keely's experiments in what he terms sympathetic vibration, I am satisfied that he has made new and important demonstrations in physical science. He has made manifest the existence of natural forces that cannot be explained by any known physical laws, and has shown that he possesses over them a very considerable control.

"JAMES M. WILLCOX."

Shortly after these announcements were made public, with the consent of the writers, *Anglo-Austria* contained two papers on the subject, from which, principally, the article on Etheric Philosophy is taken.

S. Zolver Preston, in his "Physics of the Ether," says: "A

quantity of matter representing a total mass of only one grain, and possessing the normal velocity of the ether particles, that of a wave of light, encloses a state of energy represented by upward of one thousand millions of foot tons. Or the mass of one single grain contains an energy not less than that possessed by a mass of 70,000 tons, moving at the speed of a cannon ball (1200 feet per second); or, otherwise, a quantity of matter, representing a mass of one grain, endued with the velocity of the ether particles, encloses an amount of energy which, if entirely utilized, would be competent to project a weight of 100 tons to a height of one mile and nine-tenths of a mile."

Etheric philosophy has a scientific basis in fact; and in the light of Keely's progressive demonstrations, his views are no longer abnormal to the scientific mind which is willing to admit the possibility of a discovery in which it has had no part. To discover an unknown power is one thing; to subjugate it is quite another thing. The one may be stumbled over; the other can only be attained after laborious investigation. No one who has followed Keely in his "dead work," during the last ten years, can doubt that he has been, and still is, dealing with the same force which, as Professor Hertz has disclosed to us, is already imprisoned, without our knowledge, in electro-magnetic engines. If thus, unknowingly, it has been made the servant of man, in machinery not especially constructed for its use, may it not also have been imprisoned by one who is adapting his inventions to its special requirements? Keely demonstrates, with what he calls vibratory machinery, that all corpuscles of matter may be subdivided by a certain order of vibration, thus showing up new elements; and having demonstrated what he asserts, by releasing the various orders of ether from the suspension in which it is always held in our atmosphere, he has answered the sceptical demand "Give us some bread." It has been said that as men penetrate deeper and deeper into a knowledge of the wonderful laws which govern the universe they may find mysterious forces which remain still undiscovered. Keely's discoveries promise to burst upon the world of science as the one mighty and complete revelation of the universe. There are more things in heaven and earth than are dreamt of in the materialistic science of our age, or in our philosophy. "All we have cognizance of around us are results, the causes of which are supersensuous. Of the nature which we behold around us, the cause is supernatural."

The Reverend Albert H. Plumb, of Roxbury, Mass., who has followed Mr. Keely's efforts, to obtain control of the unknown force which he discovered more than twenty years ago, up to his present successful demonstration before scientists, says : " Neither theological science nor any department of physical science, as it lies in the divine mind, is exactly expressed in any human system; yet no knowledge is to be decried nor despised, least of all in the highest realms of thought. The agnostic makes the mistake of confounding exhaustive knowledge with positive knowledge in declaring both unattainable. We can know positively that a thing is, if not how or why it is. As Gladstone says, ' Our hands can lay hold of truths which our arms cannot embrace. We can apprehend what we cannot comprehend.' If Keely should die, I fear no one could understand his writings. Every day we read of distinguished men dying. The other day a man carried with him into the grave his secret for the cheap production of aluminium. No one man entrusted by Providence with high interests has a right to allow a possibility of their sinking back, perhaps for ages, into the void of the unknown. Why not confine attention strictly to making the discovery practically intelligible to others, and thus securing to mankind the first steps by which the new force is evoked and controlled, and leave to later leisure the subtler relations of this power to the divine mind and to life ? "

For years Mr. Keely did "confine attention" to efforts to prove his discovery by practical methods, without making any advance; and it was not until he was led into the spiritual or philosophical bearings of his discovery that he himself gained "practically intelligible" ideas of its nature. To Dr. Macvicar's "Sketch of a Philosophy," from which Mrs. Moore compiled " Ether the True Protoplasm," and to Mrs. Hughes' book on the evolution of tones and colours, Mr. Keely is indebted for the pregnant germs which, falling from their writings upon his mind, took him from the line of experiment which he was pursuing, into the only line of research which can lead to scientific and commercial success. The hour in which he reaches one he reaches both; nor can one be gained without the other being gained. This should teach us that, though "the heart of man deviseth his way, the Lord directeth his steps." God never hurries, and He chooses His own instruments, employing them after a manner that is inscrutable to us, in our weak impatience for results. Admitting the truth of all that Dr. Plumb has said, but understanding fully the impossibility of directing Mr. Keely's steps, until he himself gains more control of the force that he has discovered, we must "wait upon the Lord," who is revealing to him "the deep mysteries of Creation." In the meantime, those in whom narrowness of mind has not caused stubbornness will hold themselves in readiness to prove all things and hold fast to the truth. We do not easily believe what is beyond our own knowledge, but faith in the claims of Keely as a discoverer, if not as an inventor, is steadily increasing. The following from a foreign publication about the Keely Motor will be of interest to all who have watched the progress of that enterprise. The correspondent writes:—" In the following brief article I purpose placing the latest aspect of Mr. Keely, perhaps the best abused man in America, and his investigations before the readers of *Anglo-Austria;*" continuing,—

" Under the heading of ' The Keely Motor Again,' *Invention,* of London, on October 19th, printed a communication, mentioning the leading scientist of America, Dr. Leidy, of the University of Pennsylvania, as supporting Mr. Keely's claims as a discoverer of an unknown force, as follows:—Dr. Leidy having expressed the wish that Professor Barker should again visit Mr. Keely and witness the experiments which had convinced himself that Keely had discovered a new force, has received the following letter:—

" 909, Walnut Street, Philadelphia, October 4, 1889.

" Dr. Leidy. Sir,—Referring to our conversation of a few days since, and the suggestion of another visit to the work-

shop of Mr. Keely, by Professor Barker, I would say that I
have presented the matter to Mr. Keely and he acquiesces in
what I stated to you. That is to say, if Dr. Barker desires to
visit Mr. Keely's workshops again, and will make this known
to him in writing or through yourself, for the purpose of
further observation and of having confirmed or removed from
his mind, as the case may be, the conclusions or impressions
arrived at by him, and published in the columns of the *Ledger*,
of this city, in 1878; and on condition that he will, if his
further observations satisfy him that he did injustice to Mr.
Keely, forthwith publish that fact through the same channel,
the *Ledger:* he being, of course, at full liberty to confirm by
further publication his previous condemnation, if satisfied
with the correctness of that conclusion; then Dr. Barker will
be cordially received by Mr. Keely, and a series of experiments will be conducted for him at an early day, say, Saturday,
12 inst. And in the event of the engagement being made, I
shall request the pleasure of your presence, and that of Dr.
McCook. I leave the matter in your hands for such action as
you in your wise discretion may think proper to take. Very
truly yours,

"CHARLES B. COLLIER."

Nothing could be fairer than Mr. Keely's proposal, and the
result of Professor Barker's visit will be watched for with
the keenest interest by all scientists on both sides of the
Atlantic.[1]

"Professor Barker, after due consideration, concluded not
to accept the invitation, and declined it on October 11th,
suggesting Professor Goodspeed, his associate in physics, as
one who would probably be disposed to witness the series of
experiments about to be given; showing the neutralizing or
overcoming of gravity and the separation of metallic plates by
vibration. After the date upon which these latter experiments were to have been made, and which I may mention, *en*

---

[1] The *Philadelphia Inquirer* of March 30, 1890, copied this article from *Anglo-Austria*, headed "The Keely Motor: some observations on the invention from a foreign publication."

passant, had been repeatedly made in the laboratory of Mr. Keely, this cablegram was sent from London to Philadelphia :—
' Ask Dr. Leidy's permission to announce here his conviction that Keely has discovered a new force.' "

The answer was returned as follows :—

" Having had the opportunity of seeing Mr. John Keely's experiments, it has appeared to me that he has command of some unknown force of most wonderful mechanical power.

"JOSEPH LEIDY."

Invention, in commenting upon the communication, says : " We wish to make it quite clear that we do not identify ourselves with any of the opinions which are expressed in this communication. It is certainly desirable that the motor should be thoroughly tested, and particularly that all the secrecy, which has hitherto been practised in connection with it, should be abandoned. There can be no reason why this invention, if invention it be, should not be published to the world as long as it is fully protected by patents. We agree, however, so far, that Professor Barker's report, if his visit be paid, will be of considerable interest."

These remarks of our English contemporary are based upon quite wrong premises. The motor cannot be tested nor patented until it is completed. Mr. Keely's work is one of experimental research. His machine for the production and liberation of the power is in daily operation. He has made many failures in constructing his commercial engine, but each failure has brought him nearer to perfection. When he has succeeded in building an engine in which he can regulate the speed, control reversions and govern its operations, as completely as the steam engine is now governed, then he will be ready to test its action publicly, take out patents for the same, and make known to the world the nature of his discovery. Up to the present time Mr. Keely's inventions have been principally devices, enabling him to experiment with the force which he has discovered and to obtain control over it. For years he was impeded by the frequency of the explosions which took place, breaking his ribs, paralyzing his left side for six weeks at one time, and frequently bursting iron tubes as if they were pipe stems.

Little by little he learned the laws which governed the unknown force, and now he never has an explosion. Mr. Keely has not preserved any secrecy with regard to his experiments, but on the contrary he has lost much time in exhibiting the production of this force to those who desire to see it. For instance, some years ago he stopped his work on the graduating of his engine to take his *liberator* to pieces, in order to show its interior construction to Sir William Thompson and Lord Raleigh: these gentlemen, misled by Professor Barker's assertion, that Keely was deceiving his dupes with compressed air, refused to witness his experiments. This was in 1884.

There is no "secrecy to be abandoned," therefore. The question to be settled was not one of *secrecy*, but whether Mr. Keely should continue his experimental research, unimpeded by exhibitions, until he should succeed in perfecting a commercial engine; or whether he should first convince scientists that he is not a modern Cagliostro as he has been called, and that he is a discoverer of an unknown force.

The ground taken by those who urged the latter course was that the interests of the Keely Motor Company would thus be better served; reasoning that, when scientists have been convinced that Mr. Keely's researches are in a field comparatively unknown to them, the cries of execration would be drowned in the applause which would resound throughout the world as the result of his stupendous labours became better known.

For this end several scientists were invited to witness the present stage of experiment, which Mr. Keely had reached in his efforts to provide his provisional engine with a governor, and Dr. Leidy was one of the number who, after witnessing the experiments on May 28th, 1889, confessed himself convinced that Keely was dealing with some unknown force.

When we call to mind Watt's persevering efforts during thirty years, before he succeeded in his attempt to invent a governor for the steam engine, we can afford to be more patient with Mr. Keely than we have been. Taking into consideration the marvellous advance which Mr. Keely has made in the past five years in perfecting his liberator, we should not be surprised to hear at any moment that he has also perfected his commercial engine, the so-called "Keely Motor," thus overcoming his sole remaining obstacle to financial success. Those who talk of "testing" the motor, or of patenting it in its present condition, are not aware of the exertions which have been made by Mr. Keely to bring the motor to its present stage of development; nor that, although the motor now seems to be approaching perfection, the work of evolution will not be completed until it is in a patentable form.

In 1759 James Watt made his first model of a steam carriage. In 1784 he took out a patent. In 1803 the first engine was built, but it was not until 1824 that the experiment of running a locomotive from Liverpool to Stockport was made. Until Mr. Keely's commercial engine is perfected and patented, now that scientists are beginning to support him as the discoverer of an unknown force, ridicule should give way to sympathy; for we know that nature never reveals one of her tyrant forces without at the same time showing how this force is to be transformed into the slave of man, and that complete success is only a question of time.—*Anglo-Austria*, March, 1890.

SOME RECENT EXPERIMENTS.[1]

Copy of a Letter addressed to PROFESSOR DEWAR *of the Royal Institution of Great Britain.*

DEAR PROFESSOR DEWAR,—As I have already informed you, I carried out your wishes in reference to Professor Rowland of the John Hopkins University, as far as extending to him an invitation to witness some of Mr. Keely's experiments in sympathetic vibration was concerned. Professor Rowland was not able to witness any demonstration whatever, on account of an accident which happened to the disintegrator, and he could not fail to have formed an unfavourable opinion

---

[1] From the *Evening Telegraph*, Philadelphia, April 13th, 1890: headed "Professor Leidy's Adherence to the New Force."

of Mr. Keely from all that transpired on that occasion. I next renewed the invitation to Professor Barker, which had already been extended to him by Professor Leidy, both of these gentlemen being Professors in the Pennsylvania University. Professor Barker was not able to be present. The series of experiments which have been given for scientists, mechanical engineers, and others since my return, closed on the 12th. The steady progress from week to week, since the accident to the disintegrator was repaired, has given beautiful evidence of the wisdom of the plan adopted by Mr. Keely in the winter of 1888-89, which led him to turn his attention to a class of experiments of quite a different nature from those which, up to that time, had been made for commercial ends; experiments which have not failed to convince all who attended the entire series that Mr. Keely is dealing with an unknown force, the laws governing which he is still in partial ignorance concerning. He admits now that he cannot construct a patentable engine to use this force till he has mastered the principle; and a fund, with the approval of scientists, has been appropriated for this end, upon the condition that he will waste no more time upon what is known as the Keely Motor Engine until he has demonstrated his ability to control reversions and in all points to govern the revolutions.

His last engine was built to exhibit the practical nature of his discovery to capitalists, the managers of "The Keely Motor Company"—which company died a natural death years since—hoping thereby to raise the price of its stock, and in this way to furnish Mr. Keely with the funds that he needed. But the exhibition of this engine was premature and did not succeed. There will be no further need for such exhibitions in future, for it is, as it always has been, in the interest of stock-holders that the stock should not rise until the system is completed, when it will rise to remain raised. From this time the interests of stock-holders will not be sacrificed to the interest of stock-jobbers. The experiments conducted on Saturday last surpassed preceding ones in the purity of the demonstrations, the instruments being in better condition.

In demonstrating what seems to be *the overcoming of gravity* for aerial navigation, Mr. Keely used a model of an air-ship, weighing about eight pounds, which, when the differentiated wire of silver and platinum was attached to it, communicating with the sympathetic transmitter, rose, descended, or remained stationary midway, the motion as gentle as that of thistledown floating in the air.

The experiment illustrating "chord of mass" sympathy was repeated, using a glass chamber, forty inches in height, filled with water, standing on a slab of glass. Three metal spheres, weighing about six ounces each, rested on the glass floor of the chamber. The chord of mass of these spheres was B flat first octave; E flat second octave, and B flat third octave. Upon sounding the note B flat on the sympathetic transmitter, the sphere having that chord of mass rose slowly to the top of the chamber; the positive end of the wire having been attached, which connected the covered jar with the transmitter. The same result followed the sound of the note in sympathy with the chord of mass of the other spheres, all of which descended as gently as they rose, upon changing the positive to the negative.

J. M. Willcox, Ph.D., who was present, remarked,—"This experiment proves the truth of a fundamental law in scholastic philosophy, viz., that when one body attracts or seeks another body, it is not that the effect is the sum of effects produced by parts of one body upon parts of another, one aggregate of effects, but the result of the operation of one whole upon another whole."

The experiments on the 12th closed with the disintegration of water, twelve drops of which we saw dropped, drop by drop, into the small sphere attached to the disintegrator after exhausting the air by suction. A pressure of over 20,000 pounds to the square inch was shown to the satisfaction of all present, and when Mr. Willcox accepted Mr. Keely's invitation to take a seat on the arm of the lever, adding his 260 pounds to the weight, applause broke forth. Mr. Keely showed control of the ether, inter-atomic subdivision, by graduating the escape of the residue, as he allowed it to discharge itself with a noise like the rushing of steam to an expulsion as gentle as the breathings of an infant. The three subdivisions acted simultaneously, showing instantaneous association and disassociation. The sympathetic globe was operated upon, 120 revolutions a second, ceasing the instant that the wire was detached.

I regret to say that Professor Ira Remsen was prevented, I fear by Professor Rowland, from witnessing any one of this series of experiments as he intended doing; nor have I been able to get the opinion of any physicist in whom I felt any confidence; but Mr. Keely is satisfied to have the support of such men as J. M. Willcox, Ph.D., and Professor Leidy, LL.D. Dr. Leidy was awarded the Lyell Medal in 1884, when in London, and the Cuvier Prize in 1888, from the Academy of Sciences in France. He is known in America not only as possessing the broadest of minds and the gentlest of natures, but as holding in his heart that love for, and reverence of, truth and justice which alone can confer the power of forming a correct and a just judgment.

I would like to have you make known in England that Mr. Keely is indebted to Macvicar's *Sketch of a Philosophy* for turning his attention, in 1884, to researches on the structure of ether, and to Mrs. F. J. Hughes (not Mrs. Watts Hughes), for the suggestions in her work on *Harmonies of Tones and Colours Developed by Evolution*, which led him into the line of experiment that will enable him to show on a disc the various colours of sound, each note having its colour, and to demonstrate in various ways Mrs. Hughes' own words " that the same laws which develop musical harmonies develop the universe," etc., etc.

On the 10th of June, 1890, the Rev. John Andrew, of Belfast, whose pendulographs illustrate the ratios which rule in the domain of atmospheric vibrations, in which audible music has been located by the great numberer, wrote: " I think that now, at last, Keely's labours are about to be honourably recognized by the world of science. May he live to rejoice in his triumphs." Mr. Andrew, who was the friend of the late Dr. Macvicar, was instrumental in bringing " A Sketch of a Philosophy " to Mrs. Moore's notice, and has maintained great interest in Keely's researches since he first heard of them. Miss Mary Green, a governess in the family of Lord Wimborne, was another instrument used to make known to Keely the important nature of the energy he had liberated from the suspension in which it is always held in our atmosphere. About this time Professor James Dewar, who had been following Keely's claims as a discoverer since 1884, wrote: " If Mr. Keely succeeds in making his discovery practically useful, as it is said that he is demonstrating to scientists his ability to do—if this information be true, it is strange to contrast the past history of science with the present. Fancy the discoverer of electricity having succeeded in inventing the modern dynamo machine! Such a fact would mean the concentration of *hundreds* of years of scientific discovery and invention into the single life of one man. Such a result would be simply marvellous."

At this time a number of the leading journals in various parts of the United States announced that, although Keely's methods and his failures had combined to engender distrust and arouse ridicule, it could no longer be denied that he had discovered what no other man has discovered. Still " penny-a-liners " continued to employ those " weapons of small souls and narrow minds," sneers and ridicule and calumny, which Lavater's allegorical vignette so well depicts: A hand holding a lighted torch is stung by a wasp, and the gnats that swarm around it are consumed in its flame. Underneath are these lines :—

> And although it singes the wings of the gnats,
> Destroys their heads and all their little brains,
>   Light is still light;
> And although I am stung by the angriest wasp,
>   I will not yield.

Every defender of the truth, at whom shafts of ridicule are levelled, should recall these words. Never, for one moment, has Keely turned aside from his work to answer his assailants.

It is not to be wondered at that the magical nature of his demonstrations, more inexplicable than any feats of legerdemain, should have brought upon him the suspicion of fradulent representation, concerning the production of the force and its manipulation; but his persistency alone in seeking to unravel the mysteries of nature, ought to have brought around him sooner men who, like the revered and great Leidy, were able to appreciate his researches in sympathetic vibration, the laws of which govern everything in creation, from the movements of the planets, down to the movements of atoms. From the time in which it was made known to Keely that the same principle underlies harmonies and the motion of heavenly bodies, as announced by Pythagoras, his grasping intellect conceived the idea that planetary bodies have a nerve-system, subject to conditions which govern it and keep it under control, just as our human mechanism is controlled by the law which governs its operation. In Keely's theories all is mechanical in nature. A molecule of steel, a molecule of gas, a molecule of brain matter are all of the one primeval substance—the Ether.

AERIAL NAVIGATION.

The instrument devised by Mr. Keely for bringing the airship under control in its ascent and descent, consists of a row of bars, like the keys of a piano, representing the enharmonic and the diatonic conditions. These bars range from 0 to 100. At 50 Mr. Keely thinks the progress of the vessel ought to be about 500 miles an hour. At 100 gravity resumes its control. If pushed to that speed it would descend like a rifle-ball to the earth. There is no force known so safe to use as the polar flow if, as Mr. Keely thinks, that, when the conditions are once set up, they remain for ever, with perpetual molecular action as the result, until the machinery wears out. In the event of meeting a cyclone, the course of the vessel, he teaches, can be guided so as to ascend above the cyclone by simply dampening a certain proportion of these vibratory bars.

The instrument for guiding the ship has nothing to do with the propelling of it, which is a distinct feature of itself, acting by molecular bombardment; moving the molecules in the same order as in the suspension process, but transversely. After the molecular mass of the vessel is sensitized, or made concordant with the celestial and terrestrial streams, the control of it in all particulars is easy and simple. In ascending the positive force is used, or the celestial, as Keely has named it, and in descending the negative or terrestrial. Passing through a cyclone the air-ship would not be affected by it.

The breaking up of cyclones will open a field for future research, if any way can be discovered for obtaining the chord of mass of the cyclone. To differentiate the chord of its thirds would destroy it; but to those who know nothing of the underlying principle, on which Keely has based his system, all such assertions are the merest " rubbish."

For a few months following the announcement of Professor Leidy's and Dr. Willcox's opinions, Mr. Keely continued his researches under favourable circumstances; but, in the autumn of 1890, he was again threatened with suits-at-law and harassed by demands to give exhibitions in order to raise the price of stock. A subscription was started to raise funds for the prosecution. These threats made it necessary to make public the history of Keely's connection with an organization which was supposed by many to have been formed for speculative purposes, before the stock of the company possessed any value other than prospective; but to which company, notwithstanding, the world is indebted for supplying Mr. Keely with the means to continue his work, at a time when it was impossible for him to gain the recognition of science or the aid of capitalists. The discovery would in all probability have been lost, but for the help which this organization gave, at a time when Keely needed help; he had made a discovery, and these shrewd business men, totally ignorant of physics, knew enough to comprehend its financial importance. Never doubting that Keely would be able to master the difficulties at once, in the way of its subjugation, and not realizing the width of the gulf that lies between discovery and invention, they expected him to leap it with one bound; and when he failed to do so they threw upon him all the odium which befell the enterprise. Keely, who had twice destroyed his researching instruments, when harassed and threatened by the managers of the company, first in 1882, and again in 1887, was now placed by their threatened proceedings in a position where he had to choose between continuing his researches with the end in view of completing his system; or diverting his course and resuming his efforts to perfect an engine, to continue exhibitions for the purpose of raising the stock of the company.

At this juncture an attempt was made to have circulated among the stock-holders a narrative setting forth facts to show that their interests would be better served by a continuance of the researches that had led to the results attained within the last two years; and which were of so important a character as to justify Keely in saying that he had learned more of the law, governing the operation of the force he was dealing with, in that time, than in the many preceding years during which he had been scarcely doing more than liberating the ether. The effort to have the narrative circulated failed; and, as a last resort, the history of the company was made public in a pamphlet, entitled *The Keely Motor Bubble;* which contained the *Minority Report* of Mr. John Lorimer, made, in 1881, when he was a member of the Board of Directors of " the now defunct Keely Motor Company;" giving a masterly analysis of the situation at that time. Mr. Lorimer's faith in, and loyalty to, Mr. Keely, has never been questioned. He is probably the best and most disinterested adviser that Mr. Keely has ever had; among those who are interested solely in the commercial aspect of the discovery.

CHAPTER X.

1881—1891.

THE KEELY MOTOR BUBBLE.   MACVICAR'S LOGICAL ANALYSIS.

For it is well known that bodies act upon one another by the attraction of gravity, magnetism, and electricity ; and these instances show the tenour and course of Nature and make it not improbable that there may be more attractive powers than these. For Nature is very consonant and comfortable to herself.—SIR ISAAC NEWTON.

THE Scotch author, Macvicar, from whose " Sketch of a Philosophy " has been compiled " Ether the True Protoplasm," published this year in the *New York Home Journal*, says in his "Enquiry into Human Nature," written in 1852, " Modern science is certainly on the way to the discovery that, so far as is cognizable by us, throughout the whole universe the same laws are at work and regulate all things. The *mécanique céleste* of mind is still waiting its Newton to disclose them to us."

Looking upon the discoverer of etheric force as the Newton, whose coming was forecast by Macvicar, it is satisfactory to see that Keely, in his field of research, eventually adopted the methods which his forerunner advocated nearly forty years ago ; but not until after many years of blind grappling with the mechanical difficulties which he encountered, in his efforts to control the unknown Genii, which he himself declares that he stumbled upon in quite another field of research. Keely was experimenting in 1875 on what he called a hydro-pneumatic-pulsating-vacuo engine, when, " accidentally," the first evolution of disintegration was made. The focalization of this quadruple force, acting on one general centre of concentration, produced partial molecular subdivision, resulting in a pressure of some three thousand pounds per square inch. Mr. Keely was himself amazed at this evidence of the energy which he had evoked, and at once turned his attention to researching its nature, with the result that he came to the conclusion that he had partially resolved the gaseous element of water by crude molecular dissociation. This was his first step, and the necessary introductory one, towards the elimination of ether; but at that time, to use his own words, he had not the remotest idea of the etheric element proper. Since then he has constructed innumerable machines to subdivide or dissociate the molecular; but it was not until he had instituted certain acoustic vibratory conditions that he began to realize the magnitude of the element that he is now controlling with his vibratory disintegrator. Yet, even this instrument was only the stepping-stone towards polar-sympathetic-negative-attraction.

In 1878 Mr. Keely conceived and constructed an instrument which he called a "vibratory lift," and, while experimenting on the improvised multiplication by this medium, he had occasion to put a piece of marble, weighing twenty-six pounds, on a steel bar to hold it in place, when then and there his first discovery of the disintegration of mineral substance took place. From that time progressive research of the most arduous nature has brought him to his present standard in vibratory physics. In the winter of 1881-82, when threatened with imprisonment by the managers of the Keely Motor Company for not disclosing his secret to them, which then would have been like pricking a bubble, he destroyed his vibratory lift and other instruments that he had been years in perfecting. At this time so hopeless was Keely, that his plans were made to destroy himself, after destroying his devices. At this critical juncture he received unexpected aid. Again, in 1888, before he was taken to a felon's cell in Moyamensing Prison by decree of Judge Finletter for alleged contempt of court, he broke up his vibratory microscope, his sympathetic transmitter, and some devices, which have taken much of his time since to reconstruct. It would seem to be incomprehensible that a man who believes he has been specially endowed by Providence to convey great truths to the world, should have destroyed instruments which were the result of the labour of many years of research; but Schopenhauer tells us that genius possesses an abnormally developed nervous and cerebral system that brings with it hyper-sensibility, which in union with intensity of will-energy, that is also characteristic of genius, occasions quick changes of mood and extravagant outbursts. Schopenhauer also explains why it is that men of genius are ignored by the age in which they appear :—" The genius comes into his age like a comet into the paths of the planets, to whose well-regulated and comprehensible order its entirely eccentric course is foreign. Accordingly he cannot go hand in hand with the existing regular progress to the culture of the age, but flings his works far out on the way in front (as the dying Emperor flung his spear among the enemy), which time has first to overtake. The achievement of the man of genius transcends not only the power of achievement of others, but also their power of apprehension; therefore they do not become directly conscious of him. The man of talent is like the marksman who hits a mark the others cannot hit; the man of genius is like the marksman who hits a mark that the sight of others cannot even reach." In one sense this truth applies to all men, for, says Cicero, no man is understood excepting by his equals or his superiors.

Admitting all that has been said of the difficulties attendant upon the comprehension of a genius by the age in which he lives, it does not require genius to understand the blunders which, perpetrated by the managers of the prematurely organized Keely Motor Company, have placed Mr. Keely, as well as themselves, in false positions with the public; leaving him since the winter of 1880-81 to bear the whole burden of the infamy brought about by their having offered stock for investment which could possess no tangible existence in the shape of property until the laws governing the unknown force that he was handling had been studied out and applied to mechanics in a patentable machine. To those informed that this company ceased to hold annual meetings as far back as 1881 it will be a matter of surprise to hear that, sitting up in its coffin, seven or eight years after its burial, it called another *annual* meeting, and that now its managers are again applying the thumb-screw, as in past years; pressing their claims and threatening a suit for obtaining money under false pretences, unless Mr. Keely renounces his plan of progressive research, and gives his time to the construction of engines for the Keely Motor Company. This requirement, as was said in 1881, of a similar effort, is as sensible, under existing conditions, as it would be to require Keely to devote his time to growing figs on thorn trees. It is from the "Minority Report to the Stockholders of the Keely Motor Company from the Board of Directors" (made by a member of that board in 1881, John H. Lorimer), that the material is gleaned for disclosing facts which it is due to Mr. Keely should now, since this last attempt to intimidate him, be given to the public. The stock of that company is not lessened in value by the mismanagement of its officers and directors; for Mr. Keely's moral obligations to its stockholders are as sacred to him as if the company had not long since forfeited its charter. When Mr. Keely became financially independent of the company last March, speculation in the stock of that company received its death blow, and the "Keely Motor Bubble" burst, leaving to the stockholders all that ever had any tangible existence in the shape of property in a more valuable position than it had ever been before. Mr. Lorimer is a gentleman of Scotch birth, who was elected a director of the Keely Motor Company in 1881, and who resigned in 1882, because he was "unable to carry the enterprise," and unwilling to fall in with the policy of the old directors. Before resigning, he set himself to studying the position of affairs with a view to forming for the Board a definite plan of action which ordinary business principles would justify.

This course resulted in a thoroughly business-like letter to Mr. Keely in which, under nine heads, Mr. Lorimer set down the conclusions he had reached as to the cause of the difficulties that had culminated in a threatened law suit, and Mr. Keely was ordered to ask that a special meeting of the Board should be called at once, to consider any proposition he should see fit to make towards settling the question whether he should proceed with the company's work or be permitted to defer it, as he so much desired, until he had fully developed the adaptations of his power already known to him or hereafter possible of discovery by him. Mr. Lorimer added:—" And now, in conclusion, I may say to you that the above deductions from the history of your motor are the result of patient and laborious inquiry on my part, and I am truly at a loss to understand how, or in what manner, other than that herein suggested, you can honourably vindicate your position; and as no one I have met connected with the enterprise, or personally acquainted with you, hesitates for an instant in crediting you with the most unswerving integrity, I have no hesitation in offering the above suggestions for your consideration; and I trust you will so far adopt them as to enable the active portion of your friends to bring the organization rapidly into harmonious accord with you in the development of what all seem to think is the greatest wonder of our civilization, the early completion of which will lift you to the highest pinnacle of fame as a scientist, and make them co-dispensers with you of the God-given wealth of which you hold the key." The date is 10th of February, 1881.

This letter was followed by another dated February 11th, in which Mr. Lorimer submitted certain conclusions, arrived at after meeting in New York with several members of the Board of Directors, one of which reads:—" It seems to be generally understood that without your hearty co-operation and good will, the company cannot realize value upon any existing contracts, or any they may hereafter make with you."

At this time Mr. Lorimer states that he had the opportunity presented of studying, semi-officially, the very peculiar man whose genius held his friends so spell-bound that they lost their power (if such they possessed) to adapt business methods to the enterprise. "To meet him socially in his shop," Mr. Lorimer writes, "after his day's work, was, I think, invariably to be impressed with his earnestness, honesty of purpose, and above all, with confidence in his knowledge of the plane of science he was working in (acoustics), and, at the same time to be impressed with the folly of basing calculations for the government of the business details of the organization upon the statements made by him while contemplating the possible result of his researches."

With the hopeful spirit of an inventor, Mr. Keely always

anticipated almost immediate mechanical success, up to the hour in which he abandoned the automatic arrangement that was necessary to make his generator patentable. From that time his line of perspective extended, and he began to realize that he had been too sanguine in the past. He had been like a man grappling in the dark with a foe, the form of which had not even presented itself to his imagination; but when, in 1884, Macvicar's work on the structure of ether came like a torch to reveal the face of his antagonist, what wonder that he, with the enthusiasm of Paracelsus, felt his

> . . . "fluttering pulse give evidence that God
> Means good to me, will make my cause His own;"

and, as in 1881, again rashly bound himself anew, by fresh promises, made to those who had the power to give or to withhold the sinews needed in the warfare he was waging?

To return to the report. During the negotiations which followed, facts in the history of the company were developed which convinced Mr. Lorimer that Mr. Keely was totally unable to measure time, or define his plans, because of the ever-changing results attained by him, in researching the laws governing the force he was trying to harness. At this time the treasurer of the company was proposing to bring over from New York to Philadelphia a number of capitalists to witness an exhibition of the production of the force, in order to dispose of 500 shares at 25.00 dollars a share. To this plan Mr. Lorimer objected, writing to the treasurer, "I fear that you would be putting yourself in a false position with the friends you might induce to take stock at the figures named," and Mr. Keely himself at first refused to give the exhibition, but upon the application of the thumb-screw, kept in readiness, it took place. At this time Mr. Lorimer wrote to the president of the company, "If Keely gives us the benefit of his discoveries, it will require all our energies to guide our enterprise; and, on the other hand, if he dies or is forestalled, it will need all our care and attention to take care of our reputations. . . . The fact that the Board has some delicate and important work to perform, brings us to the question, Are we properly organized to perform our part? If we are, let us show it by our acts, and, if not, let us act like men, worthy the important trust before us. If I am overestimating the character and importance of this work, you can show it to me; and *per contra*, if I am correct, you can and will accept the responsibilities of the position you hold, no matter how unpleasant, no matter how irksome, if understood by you and honourably supported by us."

Mr. Lorimer then prepared this summary, or analysis of the situation.

SUMMARY.

26th July, 1881.

"*First.*—The existence of a discovery or invention which from evidences of its adaptability (when complete) to the industrial arts and sciences, may be esteemed the most valuable discovery of civilization in modern or in ancient times, inasmuch as it revolutionizes all known methods of generating power.

"*Second.*—The retention by the discoverer and inventor of all the secrets whereby these discoveries can be utilized by the public, thus making their future existence, so far as the Keely Motor Company is concerned, depend entirely upon his life and goodwill.

"*Third.*—The existence of a corporated company, organized for the purpose of furnishing funds for the development and completion of the discovery, and for the final control of certain specified inventions, in certain specified localities.

"*Fourth.*—The contracts under which the above-mentioned control of certain inventions is vested in the Keely Motor Company, being mere evidences of intention, have no real value until the inventor has received his patents and verified the contracts by transfer of the same to the company.

"*Fifth.*—If any conflict should arise between the company and the inventor, in which the latter *felt justified* in withholding the transfer, the existing contracts might be a good foundation to build litigation upon but not good for investment in.

"*Sixth.*—The uncertainty of the future of the enterprise, as thus indicated, must of necessity invite speculative management; and while speculation under some circumstances is legitimate and laudable, under other conditions it may become illegitimate and reprehensible.

"*Seventh.*—The existence of a speculative management in Keely Motor affairs has, of necessity, developed two interests—one which holds that the completion of the discovery in all its possible grandeur should ever be the sole object of its management, and the other, believing that on account of the human uncertainty of the completion of the invention, they are in duty bound to make quick recoveries on their investments, so that they may be safe financially, in the event of a failure by Keely to perfect his inventions."

It is not necessary to pursue this summary farther, as the manner in which Mr. Lorimer has set down the facts already given, makes clear the nature of the conflicting interests that brought about the antagonism which he attempted to subdue, bringing such a spirit of fairness and justice into his efforts as must have crowned them with success, supported as he was by Mr. Keely, had it not been that those who advocated following a policy which, at best, aimed no farther than at the recouping of losses to themselves, were in the majority. It was at this time that Mr. Keely manifested his willingness to assume, on the one hand, all the responsibility of the proper development of his discovery; or, on the other hand, all the disgrace accompanying failure by his offer to purchase a controlling interest in the stock, fifty-one thousand shares of which, in order to prevent speculation, he agreed to lock up for five years, and to give the company a bond restraining him from negotiating or parting with a single share of it in that time, the stock to be paid for as soon as certain deferred payments had been made to him. This proposition of Mr. Keely to the Board of Directors, October 25th, 1881 (and laid upon the table by a large majority as unworthy of consideration), was made from his earnest desire to control the presentation of his life's work to the world in a just and honourable way; having recognized, with Mr. Lorimer, the utter impossibility of reconciling the numerous interests created by mistakes of himself and the mismanagement of the Board, unless he could thus obtain the power to deliver an unencumbered enterprise to the world. In the opinion of Mr. Lorimer, during the negotiations which he conducted between the management and Mr. Keely, the latter was the only one who had manifested any consistency or strength of purpose, so far as the facts gave evidence, which were brought before him, of the history of the company. When the validity of the contracts made with Mr. Keely while he was president, or director of the company, were disputed, he was called upon to resign, which he did ; and yet no steps were taken to ascertain the value of the existing contracts, which had all been made with him while he was both president and director, and which were therefore illegal. Proceedings in equity were commenced against Mr. Keely, by the Committee of the Board of Directors having the matter in charge, late in the year 1881, while Mr. Lorimer's report was still in the hands of the printer. " The spectacle of a Board of thirteen Directors, composed of business men," writes Mr. Lorimer, " claiming that they have been foiled in their business calculations by a man whose mind has been so thoroughly absorbed in researching the problems presented by his wonderful discoveries that he could not possibly compare with any of them in *business* tact, is truly a phenomenon which is not easy of explanation on any hypothesis, but the one that their visions of prospective wealth have been so overpowering as to undo their prudence ; and then having in due process of time discovered their error, it certainly is an edifying spectacle to see them now trying to throw all the blame on one poor mortal wholly absorbed in his inventions, and by these efforts disturbing that mental equilibrium of both the inventor and themselves, which is absolutely necessary to ultimate success. When boys, in early summer, pick unripe fruit and eat it, because of their unwillingness to await the ripening thereof, they sometimes suffer acutely for their haste. Yet no one ever thinks of punishing the tree because of their sufferings ; nor is it deemed necessary to justice to preserve the fruit of the tree, when ripe, for the sole use of the impatient ones as a recompense for their early sufferings ! So it has been with the Keely Motor Company ; undue haste to gather the golden fruit that was to come from it, has led to a great deal of suffering financially among a few impatient believers. Still it does not seem to me to be wise to curse the inventor, or his inventions because he has not given us the fruit when we expected it would be ripe." ...

The effort to force Keely to divulge his secrets failed, for at that time he had nothing of a practical nature to divulge, and though possessing no business qualifications, he was too shrewd to cut off any of his resources for supplies, necessary to enable him to persevere in his efforts to attain some practical result, as he surely would have done, had he said, "I know very little more than you know of the laws governing the force I have discovered. I can only control their operation by experimental research, and the more time that is wasted in building engines, until I have made myself acquainted with these laws, the longer will you have to wait for your golden fruit." Mr. Keely was no more able at that time to give the faintest idea of the present stage of his researches than Professor Leidy or Dr. Wilcox could now, after witnessing the experiments in sympathetic attraction, write out a clear formulation of its governing law, and an inductive substantiation of it. Even were it possible, no reader could understand it because the discovery made by Mr. Keely is not in accordance with any of the facts known to science. Mr. Keely's experiments in disintegrating water prove that incalculable amounts of latent force exist in the molecular spaces; but in the opinion of scientists, molecular aggregation is attended with dissipation of energy, not with absorption of energy. If the men of science are right, then there must be an absolute creation of energy, for only by admitting its absorption in aggregation, could molecular dissociation supply the force witnessed. Keely, of course, denies any creation of energy, claiming only that he can produce an indefinite supply by the expenditure of an infinitesimally small amount of energy. Every new discovery necessitates a new nomenclature. The vocabulary coined by Mr. Keely, to meet his requirements in formulating his hypotheses into theories as he progresses, conveys as little meaning to those who read his writings, as the word "electricity" conveyed 200 years ago. Professor Crookes remarked that reading Mr. Keely's writings was like reading Persian without a dictionary. Another learned professor said that they seemed to him to be composed in an unknown tongue, so profoundly unintelligible had he found the extracts sent to him. One must be familiar with Mr Keely's instruments and their operation, in order to comprehend even the nature of his researches.

An author of philosophical works, who was present at some experiments illustrative of varying chords of mass, and whose theories had not been in unison with those of Mr. Keely on that subject, sat for some time after the demonstration with his eyes fixed upon the floor, wearing as serious an expression of countenance as if he were looking on the grave of his most cherished views. The first remark that he made was, " What would Jules Verne say if he were here ? " The rotation of the needle of a compass, the compass placed on a glass slab and connected with the transmitter by a wire, 120 revolutions in a second, had the same effect upon the scientists present, one of awe; so completely were they transfixed and unable to form a conjecture as to the mysterious influence from any known law of science. There was only one professor present, *a very young man*, who ventured the whispered suggestion of concealed mechanism under the pedestal; and as Mr. Keely soon after had occasion to wheel the pedestal across the room, showing that it was not stationary, and could have no concealed connection within or without, the young professor took up another line of conjecture. As Macvicar says, it has grown to be the fashion, to a marvellous extent, to give predominance in education to physical and mathematical studies over moral and mental. Hence a very general and growing prepossession in favour of material nature. Astronomy, natural philosophy, chemistry, natural history, geology, these and the like are in our day held to be everything. He continues :—

Now, all these branches of study, however various in detail, agree in this, that they exclude the conception of a true self-directive power from the field of thought. They offer for consideration nothing but figures, movements, and laws. And thus they tend to form the popular mind to the habit of looking for figures, movements, and laws everywhere, and for rejecting all other conceptions as intruders. But of all such other conceptions, there is nothing so difficult and so intractable, under physical modes of investigation, as self-directive power. It therefore runs a great risk of being rejected, and thus the mind, from its first training, having been in physics, carrying out here, as it usually does everywhere, its first love into all its after thoughts, shuts up the student surreptitiously with materialism as his philosophy. Thus it is easy to see how materialism should come to be a current opinion, when the popular education runs all in favour of physical pursuits. But if philosophy must yield to the demands of the logical faculty for an extreme simplicity, unity, identity, at the fountain-head of nature, it were more logical to regard those phenomena and laws named physical, such as the laws of motion, elasticity, gravitation, etc., as manifestations, when existing under certain limiting conditions, of substances or beings which have also in them, when not so limited, and when existing under certain conditions, ability to manifest self-directive power. That every body is compounded, constituted, or made up of molecules, is universally agreed. Every body is therefore a fit subject for analysis. But when any body is submitted to analysis in reference to its mere corporeity or bodily nature, that is, its extension and impenetrability, what do we ultimately arrive at? Do we not, in reference to the attribute of extension, arrive at particles, of which the physical limit is that they have at least ceased to be extended, and are but mere points in space? And as to the attribute of impenetrability, what do we in the last analysis arrive at, but the idea of a substance that can resist the intrusion into its place of other similar substances, and, therefore, ultimately, a centre of force. And thus, under a logical analysis, which must be admitted to be legitimate, it may be maintained that a body or chemical element resolves itself into a system of centres of force balancing each other at certain distances, and thus rendering the whole molecule or mass extended, as body is known to be. The elements of body, therefore, are things of which these attributes are to be affirmed in the first instance, that they possess unextended substance and extensive power. But, if so, do they not touch upon the confines of the spiritual world to say the least? asks Macvicar; and the Newton whom he anticipated would give a *mécanique celeste* to mankind, solves the problem, answers the question by his discovery of the cerebelic stream or will-flow.

Body and spirit, one at the fountain-head, when rising into existence, form, as it were, the first breath of creation; for, as Sir Wm. Thompson says : " Life proceeds from life and from nothing else." They are the opposite poles of being and constitute the two principles by the harmonious interweaving of which the beautiful system of creation is constituted, and its economy worked out. Such a view, far from being contrary to the canons of science, is even the necessary complement of science. That unity, which is the last word of science, must always include two objects, existing in contrast after all. The law of couples, of opposites, of reciprocal action between two contrasted yet homogeneous and harmonizing elements, each of which opens a field for the other, and brings it into action, is of universal extent. In the organic world, also, no less than in the purely physical and chemical, all is framed according to the same law of couples. In the sphere of sensibility, in like manner, everything turns on the antagonism of pleasure and pain, and in the moral sphere of good and evil. Nor is the world of pure intellect exempt from this law, but on the contrary displays its influence everywhere. Hence faith and sight, identity and difference, finite and infinite, objective and subjective, space and time, cause and effect, the world of realities and the world of ideas. In a word, every system of thought and of things, when complete, present as its basis two co-ordinate elements, the reciprocals of each other; or one parted into two reciprocally, and by the harmonious antagonism of both the beautiful web of nature is woven. If we are to be consistent, mind and matter ought always to be viewed as distinct, and the opposite poles of being ; *inertia*, or unvarying submissiveness to the laws of motion being the characteristic of the one; self-directive power the characteristic of the other.

The universal analogy of science sanctioned Macvicar in the characteristic he thus arrived at as that of animated nature, for if inertia, or the obedience to pressures and impulses from without, be the characteristic of matter, then that which is needed as the other term to complete the couple is just what has been insisted on, viz., self-directive power, the power to cause pressures and impulses. Here is shown the symmetrical relation in which this power, when viewed as the characteristic of the whole animal kingdom (which plainly points to man, and culminates in human nature), places the animal in relation with the vegetable and the mineral kingdoms. Of minerals or crystals, the characteristic is simply self-imposing or *self-concreting* power. They are, so to speak, merely insoluble seeds without an embryo. To this, *self-developing* power is added in plants, and forms their acknowledged characteristic. While of animals the characteristic, according to the view here advanced (the same seed-producing, self-developing, powers continuing) is *self-directive* power superadded. This relationship between these three kingdoms of nature is as homogeneous and symmetrical as is necessary to appear to be legitimate, and is a true expression of the order of nature.

Granting these two principles, the inert and the self-directive, the necessary and the free, we obtain the materials for a universe, without disputing the fact of human liberty and bringing into suspicion even the possibility either of morality or immorality. If man be really free as well as under law, in this union of body and spirit, then in human nature heaven and earth truly embrace each other; and no reason appears why, as the ages roll on, our own free thought may not have the run of the universe. . . . What study then can be more replete with interest, what researches can possess more of fascination, than those which Mr. Keely's discoveries are preparing the way for?

The discoveries of Mr. Keely (demonstrated—as he is now prepared to demonstrate them) cannot be disputed, though his system may be called in question. With the humility of genius, he calls his theories hypotheses, and his hypotheses conjectures. The solidity of the principles, as laid down by himself, cannot be decided upon by others until he has brought to light the whole system that grows out of them. But it is time the public should know that the odium thrown upon him by the Keely Motor Company, he does not deserve. It is time that the Press should cease its sneers, its cry of "Crucify him, crucify him!" morally speaking, and extend to him that discriminating appreciation of his work and encouragement which the *New York Home Journal*, *Truth*, *Detroit Tribune*, *Chicago Herald*, *Toledo Blade*, *Atlanta Constitution*, *The Statesman*, and *Vienna News* have been the first to do. Let the Press contrast the past history of science with the present position of Keely, as Professor Dewar has done. Only such a man who knows from experience the labour, the difficulties, the uncertainties, attendant upon researching unknown laws of nature is able to appreciate all that is now being concentrated in the single life of one man. It is time that capitalists should step from their ranks to protect Keely from the selfish policy of the managers of a speculative company, which has long since forfeited all claims upon him, to continue mechanical work for it, even admitting that it ever possessed that right; and, more than all else, it is time that science should send her delegates to confer with the broad-minded men who have had the courage to give testimony, without which Keely could not have stood where, this year, he stands for the first time, fearless of threats, pursuing his researches on his own line, to acquire that knowledge of the laws governing his discoveries by which alone he can gain sufficient control of machinery to insure financial success. Meanwhile, are there no men who are able to feel an interest (without reference to commercial results) in a discovery which sweeps away the *débris* of materialism as chaff is swept before a whirlwind?—giving indisputable proof that, as St. Paul teaches, "we are the offspring of God;" or, as Aratus wrote, from whom he quoted:—

> "From God we must originate,
> Not any time we break the spell
> That binds us to the ineffable.
> Indeed, we all are evermore
> Having to do with God: for *we*
> *His very kind and offspring be:*
> And to His offspring the benign
> Fails not to give benignant sign."

From *New York Truth*, 3rd July, 1890.

"I think it is safe, for even the most conservative and pigheaded of scientists, to admit that Keely, the contemned, the scoffed at, the derided, the man whom every picayune peddler called charlatan because he could not harness the hitherto undiscovered forces of ether in less time than one might hitch up a mule, is the most original and the most straightforward of inventors, and that in his own good time he will give to the world a power that will throw steam and electricity into disuse, open the realms of air as a public highway for man, and send great ships careering over ocean with a power developed by sound. His theory of etheric vibration is now conclusively established, and it is only a question of time and material that delays its use as a servant to man. The fact is patent, so that he who runs may read, but the ox must have the yoke, the horse the collar, the engine the cylinder, and the dynamo the coil, ere they can work their wonders. While Keely was hampered by mere tradesmen, who only looked to the immediate recoupment of their outlay, men more anxious for dividends than discoveries, he could do little save turn showman, and exhibit his partial control of the harmonies of nature as springs catch woodcocks, and was forced to open his crude contrivances to divert the eternal will of the cosmos to work-a-day uses, that he might coax from the greed and credulity of mere mammon-worshippers the sorely grudged means to continue his exploration of the infinite. His genius was prisoned in a test tube, and only let out to play monkey tricks before muddle-headed merchants, who could see the effect, but not the means, and so the greatest discovery of the age was turned into a raree show, and the eternal music of the spheres was set, figuratively speaking, to play tunes to attract custom like a barrel organ before a dime museum."

CHAPTER XI.

VIBRATORY SYMPATHETIC POLAR FLOWS.—KEELY'S CONTRIBUTIONS TO SCIENCE.

> " Evermore brave feet in all the ages
>   Climb the heights that hide the coming day,—
> Evermore they cry, these seers and sages,
>   From their cloud, 'Our doctrines make no way.'
> All too high they stand above the nations,
>   Shouting forth their trumpet-calls sublime,
> Shouting downwards their interpretations
>   Of the wondrous secrets born of Time."

... Who can say what secrets the now unread 'fairy tales of science' may have to tell to those who live in this later age?—*The Globe.*

THE question has often been asked, "How much energy does Keely expend in the production of the force he is handling ?" or again, "Can Keely show that a foot-pound of vibratory sympathy can be more easily developed from the resources of nature, than a foot-pound of good honest work ?"

In the economy of nature profit and loss must balance in mechanical conditions; but Keely is not dealing with mechanical physics. There is an immense difference between vibratory physics, in which field Keely is researching, and mechanical physics. The consumption of coal to expand water for the production of steam power, in the operation of engines, cannot be compared to a force which is yielded in sympathetic vibration or by sympathetic flows. In mechanical physics, no matter what the nature of the force may be, its production must necessarily be accompanied by a corresponding expenditure of force in some form or other. The amount of force covered by a human volition cannot be measured, yet it produces the wonderful effects that are exhibited on the human frame in its overt actions. Something like this is the difference between sympathetical and mechanical force. The force of will cannot be multiplied by mechanical means, making it give pound for pound. This would annihilate both the mental and the physical, were it possible.

In his researches, Mr. Keely, who is dealing entirely with VIBRATORY SYMPATHETIC and POLAR flows, is hopeless in regard to convincing the scientific world of the value of his discoveries until he has compelled its attention by commercial success. To the question, "What does the supply cost in dollars and cents, per horse-power developed?" he answers, "It costs nothing more after the machinery is made, than the vibratory concordant impulse which associates it with the polar stream." The twanging of a taut string, the agitation of a tuning-fork, as associated with the resonating condition of the sympathetic transmitter, is all that is necessary to induce the connective link, and to produce this "costless motive power." As long as the transmitter is in sympathy with the sympathetic current of the triune polar stream, the action of the sympathetic instrument or engine continues.

Again, mechanical conservation of energy is one thing; sympathetic conservation is another, and we cannot expect Keely will reveal what he has discovered concerning the forces that he is dealing with until he has himself acquired that full knowledge of their action which will protect the rights of those who are interested in the "dollars and cents" part of "the enterprise."

Macvicar said that "if extreme vicissitudes of belief on the part of men of science are evidences of uncertainty, it may be affirmed that of all kinds of knowledge none is more uncertain than science;" but slow as mankind is in the progress of discoveries bearing upon unknown laws of nature, men of science are still slower in recognizing truths after they have been discovered and demonstrated. Two centuries elapsed between the discoveries of Pythagoras and their revival by Copernicus. Tycho Brahe opposed the Pythagorean system until his death; Galileo, adopting it and demonstrating it in all its purity, suffered for his support of it at the hands of bigots. And so history now repeats itself. Were it possible to convince scientists *en masse* of the grandeur of Keely's work, they would protect him from the interruptions and lawsuits which have so retarded his progress that now it looks very much as though he would never be permitted to complete his system. The world is full of inventors, but there is but one man able to unfold, to this age and generation, the wonderful mysteries attendant upon vibratory physics, while there are thousands who, when a mastery of the principle has been gained, can invent machinery to apply it to commercial uses. Macvicar asks, " Who that goes so far as to make a question of all, or almost all, the data of common sense can legitimately refrain from making it a question whether the laws of phenomena which men of science discover may not be laws of thinking, merely imposed upon nature as her laws? Nay, who can refrain from admitting with Kant that they can be nothing more?"

As a suggestion to those interested in psychological researches I will mention that Keely has copied nature in all his instruments from the Vibrophone, which is fashioned after the human ear, up to the Disintegrator, in which the neutral centre represents the human heart. With the system which Keely is unfolding to us we may well say, with Buckle, " A vast and splendid career lies before us, which it will take many ages to complete. As we surpass our fathers, so will our children surpass us. Waging against the forces of nature what has too often been a precarious, unsteady, and unskilled warfare, we have never yet put forth the whole of our strength, and have never united all our faculties against our common foe. We have, therefore, been often worsted, and have sustained many and grievous reverses. But, even so, such is the elasticity of the human mind, such is the energy of that immortal and godlike principle which lives within us, that we are baffled without being discouraged, our very defeats quickening our resources, and we may hope that our descendants, benefiting by our failures, will profit by our example, and that for them is reserved that last and decisive stage of the great conflict between man and nature, in which advancing from success to success, fresh trophies will be constantly won;

every struggle issuing in a conquest, and every battle ending in a victory."

The force discovered by Keely—no, the force revealed to him—will rule the earth with an influence mighty in the interests of humanity. The completion of his system for science and commerce will usher in the dawning of a new era.

While our leading men of science are everywhere occupying themselves with the mysteries of electro-magnetic radiation, with the action of the ether, with the structure of the molecule, the instruments with which they are researching are, in comparison with those which Keely has invented, for his researches, like the rudest implements of the savage, compared to those developed by modern civilization. A discussion has recently been carried on in one of our Reviews, as to whether the energy which feeds the magnet comes from the atmosphere, from gravity, from solar rays, or from earth currents. Nothing is more simple than Keely's explanation, as proved by his demonstrations. The energy of the magnet comes from the polar stream; and, though the introductory impulse is so slight that it cannot be weighed any more than can the flow of the mind, yet, if kept up for years, it could not be computed by billions of tons in its effect. The magnet that lifts pounds to-day, if the load of the armature is gradually increased day by day, will lift double the amount in time. Whence comes this energy? Keely teaches that it comes from sympathetic association with one of the triune currents of the polar stream, and that its energy will increase as long as sympathetic flows last, which is through eternity.

The physicist tells you that "you cannot make something out of nothing;" that "in the *economy* of nature profit and loss must balance;" that "no matter what the nature of the force may be, its production must necessarily be accompanied by a corresponding expenditure of force in some form or other," etc., etc. But, in the *prodigality* of nature, this energy flows, without measure and without price, from the great storehouse of the Infinite Will. From the sympathetic portion of the etheric field, all visible aggregations of matter emanate, and on the same order that molecular masses of all living organisms are vitalized by the sympathetic flow from the brain.

"Our most learned men," said Buckle, "know not what magnetism is, nor electricity, nor gravity, nor cohesion, nor force." Keely shows us, by mechanical means, what magnetism is. By neutralizing or overcoming gravity, he proves to us that he understands its nature; electricity he declares to be a certain form of atomic vibration; and, in the disintegration of quartz, he demonstrates that cohesive force, like gravity, is an ever-existing force, holding together all molecular masses by the infinite velocity of its vibrations; which, were these vibrations to cease for one instant, would fall apart, molecules and atoms, and return to the ether in which they originated.

KEELY'S CONTRIBUTIONS TO SCIENCE.[1]

An infinitely subtle substance, out of which all other substances are constituted, in varying forms, passes back again into simplicity. The same principle underlies the harmonies of music and the motion of heavenly bodies.—PYTHAGORAS.

One of the most arduous problems is that of energies acting at distances. Are they real? Of all those that appear incontrollable, one only remains, gravitation. Will it escape us also? The laws of its action incline us to think so. The nature of electricity is another problem which recalls us to the condition of electric and magnetic forces through space. Behind this question arises the most important problem of all, that of the nature and properties of the substance which fills space,—the ether,—its structure, its motion, its limits, if it possesses any. We find this subject of research, day by day, predominating over all others. It seems as though a knowledge of ether should not only reveal to us the nature of that imponderable substance, but will unveil to us the essence of matter itself and of its inherent properties, weight and inertia. Soon the question set by modern physics will be, "Are not all things due to conditions of ether?" That is the ultimate end of our science; these are the most exalted summits to which we can hope to attain. Shall we ever reach them? Will it be soon? We cannot answer.—PROF. HENRI HERTZ, in *La Revue Scientifique*, October 26, 1888.

In the long delay attendant upon the application to mechanics of the unknown force which John Ernest Worrell Keely has discovered in the field of vibration, the question is often heard, "What has Keely done?" with the remark, "He has never done anything; he is always promising to do something, but he never keeps his promises."

[1] From *Lippincott's Magazine*, July, 1890. Edited by J. M. Stoddart.

Let us see what Keely, in his researches, has done for science; although, as yet, he has done nothing for commerce.

We are quick to forget the experiences of history, which show what a length of time has invariably elapsed between the discovery of a new force and its use in mechanics. Watt commenced his experiments on the elastic force of steam in 1764, obtaining about forty pounds total pressure per square inch. (It has been stated that it was thirty years before he succeeded in perfecting his safety-valve, or governor, which made it possible to use steam without running great risks.) Fifty years later, in 1814, the first steam locomotive was built; but it was not until 1825 that the locomotive was used for traffic—travelling at a speed of from six to eight miles in an hour. Keely commenced his experiments with ether in the winter of 1872-73, showing a pressure of two thousand pounds per square inch. It does not look now as though half a century would elapse before Keely's discovery will supersede steam in travel and traffic. In experimenting with ether, he has shown, from time to time, since 1873, a pressure of from twenty thousand to thirty-two thousand pounds per square inch; but he was occupied many years in his researches before he obtained sufficient control over the ether to prevent the explosions which made wrecks of his machines, bursting iron and steel pipes, twelve inches in circumference, as if they were straws. He has now arrived at a stage in his experimental research in which he can, without danger of explosions, exhibit to scientists such manifestations of an unknown force as to place him before the world where he would have stood many years ago, had it not been for the calumnious attacks of those men of science who found it easier to denounce him than to account for the phenomena which they witnessed in his workshop.

Professor Ira Remsen, in his "Theoretical Chemistry," writes, "As regards the cause of the phenomena of the motion of the heavenly bodies, we have no conception at the present day. It is true we say that these phenomena are caused by the attraction of gravitation; but, after all, we do not know what pulls these bodies together."

Let us see what Keely knows on this subject?

1st. After a lifetime of research into the laws governing vibrations, which develop this force, Keely is able to demonstrate partial control of the power that he has discovered,—a power which he believes to be the governing medium of the universe, throughout animate and inanimate nature, controlling the advance and recession of the solar and planetary masses, and reigning in the mineral, the vegetable, and the animal kingdom, according to the laws that rule its action in each, as undeviatingly as it governs the motions of the earth itself, and of all the heavenly bodies in space.

Keely calls this power, which he is endeavouring to apply in mechanics for the benefit of mankind, " sympathetic negative attraction,"—it being necessary to use the word " attraction," as no other word has yet been coined to take its place.

2nd. He has determined and written out a system of the vibratory conditions governing the aggregation of all molecular masses, as to their relation sympathetically one to the other, stating the conditions to be brought about in order to induce antagonism or repellent action, disintegration, etc.; but he has not yet been able to control the operation of his Disintegrator so as to use it with safety to the operator, for mining purposes, etc.

3rd. He has proved by demonstration that the subdivision of matter under different orders of progressive vibration evolves by such subdivision entirely new and distinct elements, too multiple to enumerate. He has systematized the proper vibratory chords, progressively, from the introductory molecular to the inter-etheric, embracing seven distinct orders of triple subdivision. He has elaborated a system of inducing sympathetic negative attraction on metallic masses, with great range of motion, and instant depolarization of the same, by vibratory change of their neutral centres. Keely controls the transmission of these sympathetic streams by a medium of high molecular density, viz., drawn wires of differentiated metals, gold, silver, platinum, German silver, etc. In some recent experiments he took apart, for inspection of its interior construction, the instrument which he has invented for the production of the force, cutting the wires with which he had operated in sympathetic attraction and propulsion, and distributing the fragments to those who were present, among whom was Professor Leidy, to whom the Geological Society of London has awarded the Lyell Medal, and the Academy of Sciences of France the Cuvier Prize.

4th. Keely has discovered that all sympathetic streams, cerebellic, gravital, magnetic, and electric, are composed of triple flows; this fact governing all the terrestrial and celestial orders of positive and negative radiation. In gravity it would be more correct to speak of triple connective links, as there is no flow of gravity.

5th. Keely has discovered and was the first to demonstrate that electricity has never been handled; that it is in principle as material as is water; that it is not merely a force or a form of energy,—that it is matter; and that what we call electricity, and have diverted for commercial use in electric lighting, is but one of the triune currents, harmonic, enharmonic, and diatonic, which are united in pure electricity; that the enharmonic current seems to be sympathetically and mysteriously associated with the dominant current; and that the dominant current can no more be brought under control than can the lightning itself. The diversion of the dominant current would mean destruction to any mechanical medium used for that purpose, and death to the operator. The intense heat evolved by the electric stream Keely attributes to the velocity of the triple subdivision at the point of dispersion, as each triple seeks its medium of affinity. Sudden unition induces the same effect; but demonstration shows that the concentration of this triple force is as free of percussion as is the breath of an infant against the atmosphere; for the three currents flow together as in one stream, in the mildest sympathetic way, while their discharge after concentration is, in comparison to their accumulation, as the tornado's force to the waft of the butterfly's wing. The enharmonic current of this triple stream, Keely thinks, carries with it the power of propulsion that induces disturbance of negative equilibrium; which disturbance is essential to the co-ordination of its flow, in completing the triune stream of electricity. When this fluid is discharged from the clouds, each triplet or third seeks its terrestrial concordant, there to remain until that supreme law which governs disturbance of equilibrium again induces sympathetic concordant concentration, continuing to pass through its evolutions, positively and negatively, until the solar forces are expended.

"My researches have proved to me," writes Keely, "the subtle and pure conditions of the power of negative attraction and positive propulsion."

6th. These same researches have enabled Keely to pronounce definitely as to the nature of what is recognized as gravity, an ever-existing, eternal force, coexistent with the compound etheric, or high luminous, entering into all forms of aggregated matter at their birth. Keely thinks that gravity is the source from which all visible matter springs, and that the sympathetic or neutral centre of such aggregation becomes at birth a connective concordant link to all neutral centres that have preceded it and to all that may succeed it, and that disturbance of equilibrium, like gravity, is an ever-existing force. His researches in the vibratory subdivision of matter have revealed to him some of the mysteries of the hidden sympathetic world, teaching that "the visible world," as Coleridge wrote, "is but the clothing of the invisible world;" that "true philosophy," as Professor George Bush said, "when reached will conduct us into the realm of the spiritual as the true region of causes, disclosing new and unthought-of relations between the world of matter and of mind."

Professor Thurston writes, in the January number of the *North American Review*, "We are continually expecting to see a limit reached by the discoverer, and by the inventor, and are as constantly finding that we are simply on a frontier which is being steadily pushed further and further out into the infinite unknown. The border-land is still ahead of us, constantly enlarging as we move on. The more we gain, the more is seen to be achievable."

All planetary masses Keely calls terrestrial, showing in his writings that the beauty of the celestial concordant chords of sympathy forming the harmonious connective link, in what may be denominated "the music of the spheres," is seen in the alternate oscillating range of motion between the planetary systems; for at a certain range of the greater distance, harmony is established, and the attractive forces are brought into action, under the command, "Thus far shalt thou go, and no further." Then in the return towards the neutral centres, when at the nearest point to each other, the opposite or propulsive force is brought into play; and "thus near shalt thou come, and no nearer;" advancing and receding under the celestial law of etheric compensation and restoration, as originally established by the Great Creator.

7th. Keely has constructed instruments by which he is endeavouring to determine the nature of the triune action of the polar terrestrial stream, or envelope, as regards its vibratory philosophy. He is seeking to demonstrate its sympathetic association with the celestial stream, or luminiferous track,—the compound etheric field, from which all planetary masses spring. He considers the electric stream to be one of the triune sympathetic streams which help to build up, in their order of triple concentration, the high vitality of the polar stream, or, more correctly, the magnetic-electric terrestrial envelope, without which all living organisms would cease to exist. He classes the cohesive force of molecular masses as the dominant order of the electric stream, the molecule owing its negative attractive quality to the magnetic element.

In Keely's beautiful experiments in antagonizing the polar stream, recently given before men of science, he has copied in his instruments the conditions which Nature has established in all her terrestrial ranges,—conditions necessary in order to equate a state of sympathetic disturbance for the revitalization of what is continually being displaced by negative dispersion. These mechanical conditions are principally differential vibratory settings on molecular aggregations of the metallic masses of gold, silver, and platinum.

8th. He has discovered that the range of molecular motion in all quiescent masses is equal to one-third of their diameters, and that all extended range is induced by sound-force, set at chords of the thirds which are antagonistic to the combined chords of the mass of the neutral centres that they represent, no two masses being alike, and that at a certain increased range of molecular motion, induced by the proper acoustic force, the molecules become repellent, and that when the sympathetic centres are influenced by a vibration concordant to the one that exists in themselves, the molecules become attractive; that the repellent condition seems to take place at a distance of about ten of the diameters of the molecules, this distance representing the neutral line of their attractive force, or the dividing line between the attractive and the repellent. Beyond this line, perfect triple separation takes place; inside of it, perfect attractive association is the result.

The force which Mr. Keely uses in running machinery is the sympathetic attractive,—the force which, according to his theories, draws the planets together; while in his system of aërial navigation, should he live to perfect it, he will use a negation of this force,—the same that regulates the motion of the planets in their recession from each other. It is the sympathetic attractive force which keeps the planets subservient to a certain range of motion, between their oscillations. If this condition were broken up, the rotation of planets would cease; if destroyed at a given point of recession, all planets would become wanderers, like the comets; if destroyed at another given point, assimilation would take place, as two bullets fired through the air, meeting, would fuse into one mass. Nature has established her sympathetic concordants from the birth of the neutral centres of the planets, in a manner known only to the Infinite One. This is gravity.

"The music of the spheres" is a reality. "The finer the power the greater the force." Thus, the inaudible atomic, etheric, and inter-etheric sounds, which control and direct the harmony of the movements of the celestial universe, are the most powerful of all sounds. If our faculty of hearing were a hundred billions of times intensified, we might be able to hear the streams of light as plainly as we now hear the sighings of the wind.

Again, to answer the often-asked question, "What has Keely done?"

9th. He has broken joints of his fingers and thumbs, he has broken his ribs, he has had his left side paralyzed for weeks, he has lost the sight of one eye for months, in his hand-to-hand fight with the genii that he has encountered, and cannot completely subdue until he has effected the condition of polarization and depolarization which is necessary for the control of rotation and reversions in his commercial engine. An illness of nine weeks followed his abandonment of water in disintegrating; and he was obliged to return to its use, to avoid the percussion that was induced by the rapid vibration of the atmospheric air. To illustrate: if a bullet is fired at a man through a vessel of water a foot thick, the bullet is flattened out without injuring the man; while if nothing intervenes the man is killed.

The question naturally arises, "Are not the forces with which Keely is dealing of too subtle a nature to be harnessed to do the daily work of the world?" Even were it so, the fascination attendant upon his researches would prevent him from abandoning them; but his faith in his ability to accomplish all that he has undertaken to do for the Keely Motor Company and for others is equalled only by the persistent energy which, in the face of gigantic obstacles, of cruel obloquy, of baffled endeavours, leads him to persevere to the end. He believes that the successful result is as positive as are the continued revolutions of our globe, under the great law which governs all Nature's highest, grandest, and most sensitive operations. And when has Nature ever revealed a force save to permit man to subjugate it for the progress of our race?

Another question often heard is, "Why does not Keely make known his discoveries?"

10th. He has written three treatises to explain his system, the titles of which are as follows:—

I. Theoretical Exposé or Philosophical Analysis of Vibro-Molecular, Vibro-Atomic, and Sympathetic Vibro-Etheric Forces, as applied to induce Mechanical Rotation by Negative Sympathetic Attraction.

II. Explanatory Analysis of Vibro-Acoustic Mechanism in all its Different Groupings or Combinations to induce Propulsion and Attraction (sympathetically) by the Power of Sound-Force; as also the Different Conditions of Intensity, both Positive and Negative, on the Progressive Octaves to Ozonic Liberation and Luminosity.

III. The Determining Principle of Matter, or the Connective Link between the Finite and the Infinite, progressively considered from the Crude Molecular to the Compound Inter-Etheric; showing the Control of Spirit over Matter in all the Variations of Mass-Chords and Molecular Groupings, both Physical and Mechanical.

If these treatises were read from the first page to the last, by men of science, they would not at present be any better understood than were Gilbert's writings in his age, author of " De Magnete."

Newton was indebted to Gilbert for his discovery of the so-called law of gravitation. Keely defines gravity as transmittive inter-etheric force under immense etheric vibration, and electricity as a certain form of atomic vibration. When Gilbert, court-physician to Queen Elizabeth, announced his discovery of electricity, he was asked by his compeers of what use it was. No one dreamed then of it as a motive power. He replied, " Of what use is a baby? It may develop into a man or a woman, and, although we cannot make any use of electricity now, the world may in time find out uses for it." Just as little understood would Keely's writings be now on sympathetic negative attraction as were Gilbert's writings then on electricity and magnetism. Men found no sense in the words " electric " and " electricity," although derived from the Greek root for amber. The same fault is found with Keely for coining new words which no one understands.

" Every branch of science, every doctrine of extensive application, has had its alphabet, its rudiments, its grammar: at each fresh step in the path of discovery the researcher has had to work out by experiment the unknown laws which govern his discovery." To attempt to introduce " the world " —even scientists—to any new system without previous preparation would be like giving a Persian book to a man to read who knew nothing of the language. As has been said, we do not expect a complicated problem in the higher mathematical analysis to be solved by one who is ignorant of the elementary rules of arithmetic. Just as useless would it be to expect every scientist to comprehend the laws of etheric physics and etheric philosophy after having witnessed Keely's experiments. The requirement of every demonstration is that it shall give sufficient proof of the truth that it asserts. A demonstration which does less than this cannot be relied upon, and no demonstration ever made has done more. The success of a demonstration is in proportion as the means applied are adequate or inadequate. As different principles exist in various forms of matter, it is quite impossible to demonstrate every truth by the same means or the same principles. It is only the prejudice of ignorance which exacts that every demonstration shall be given by a prescribed canon of science; as if the science of the present were thoroughly conversant with every principle that exists in nature. Yet physicists exact this, though they must know its inadequacy.

Mr. Keely does not expect more from scientists than that they should withhold their defamatory opinions of him until they have witnessed his demonstrations and acquainted themselves with his theories. Yet, notwithstanding Professor Crooke's psychical researches and Professor Rücker's experiments in molecular vibration, demonstrating that molecules seem to have a "mental attribute, a sort of expression of free will," physicists still look upon the human organism as little more than a machine, taking small interest in experiments which evince the dominion of spirit over matter. Keely's researches in this province have shown him that it is neither the electric nor the magnetic flow, but the etheric, which sends its current along our nerves; that the electric and magnetic flows bear but an infinitely small ratio to the etheric flow, both as to velocity and tenuity; that true coincidents can exist between any mediums,—cartilage to steel, steel to wood, wood to stone, and stone to cartilage; that the same influence, sympathetic association, which governs all the solids holds the same control over all liquids, and again from liquid to solid, embracing the three kingdoms, animal, vegetable, and mineral; that the action of mind over matter thoroughly substantiates the incontrovertible laws of sympathetic etheric influence; that the only true medium which exists in nature is the sympathetic flow emanating from the normal human brain, governing correctly the graduating and setting-up of the true sympathetic vibratory positions in machinery, necessary to commercial success; that these flows come in on the order of the fifth and seventh positions of atomic subdivision, compound inter-etheric sympathy a resultant of this subdivision; that if metallic mediums are brought under the influence of this sympathetic flow they become organisms which carry the same influence with them that the human brain does over living physical positions, and that the composition of metallic and that of physical organisms are one and the same thing, although the molecular arrangement of the physical may be entirely opposite to the metallic on their aggregations; that the harmonious chords induced by sympathetic positive vibration permeate the molecules in each, notwithstanding, and bring about the perfect equation of any differentiation that may exist—in one the same as in the other—and thus they become one and the same medium for sympathetic transmission; that the etheric, or willflow, is of a tenuity coincident to the condition governing the seventh subdivision of matter, a condition of subtlety that readily and instantaneously permeates all forms of aggregated matter, from air to solid hammered steel, the velocity of the permeation being the same with the one as with the other; that the tenuity of the etheric flow is so infinitely fine that a magnifying glass, the power of which would enlarge the smallest grain of sand to the size of the sun, brought to bear upon it would not make its structure visible to us; and that, light traversing space at the speed of two hundred thousand miles per second, a distance requiring light a thousand centuries to reach would be traversed by the etheric flow in an indefinite fragment of a second.

11th. Keely has given such proof of genius as should bring all scientists who approach him into that attitude of mind which would lead them to receive without prejudice the evidence of the truth of the claims he offers.

Genius has been defined as an extraordinary power of synthetic creation. Another definition of the man of genius is, the man who unceasingly cultivates and perfects such great natural aptitudes and facilities as he has been endowed with at his birth.

No man has ever lived on this earth who, according to these qualifications, so deserved to be known and acknowledged as a man of genius as John Worrell Keely. History will determine whether he is a man of genius or "a charlatan," as some scientists still persist in calling him. It is easier, as has been said, to accuse a man of fraud than to account for unknown phenomena. A system of doctrine can be legitimately refuted only upon its own principles, viz., by disproving its facts and invalidating the principles deduced from them. Abercrombie said that the necessary caution which preserves us from credulity should not be allowed to engender scepticism,—that both of these extremes are equally unworthy of a mind which devotes itself with candour to the discovery of truth.

"We must not decide that a thing is impossible," says Lebrun, "because of the common belief that it cannot exist; for the opinion of man cannot set limits to the operations of Nature, nor to the power of the Almighty. He who attempts to hold up to contempt a scientific subject of which he is profoundly ignorant has but small pretensions to the character of a philosopher." Galileo said, after pronouncing his abjuration, "*E pur si muove*" ("But it does move"). What signified to him the opinion of men, when Nature confirmed his discovery? Of what value were their prejudices or their wisdom in opposition to her immutable laws? Kedzie, speculating upon the nature of force, writes, "Molecules and masses act precisely as they are acted on; they are governed by the iron instead of the golden rule. They do unto others as others have done unto them. Whence comes this energy? Not from atoms, but from the Creator, in the beginning."

The Duke of Argyll says, "We know nothing of the ultimate seat of force. Science, in the modern doctrine of the conservation of energy and the convertibility of forces, is already getting something like a firm hold of the idea that all kinds of forces are but forms or manifestations of some one central force, arising from one fountain-head of power."

12th. Keely's researches have taught him that this one fountain-head is none other than the omnipotent and all-pervading Will-Force of the Almighty, which creates, upholds, guides, and governs the universe. "The whole world-

Keely's Contributions to Science. 161

process," says Von Hartmann, " in its context is only a logical process ; but in its existence it is a continued act of will."

Lilly says, "This is what physical law means. Reason and will are inseparably united in the universe as they are in idea. If we will anything, it is for some reason. In contemplating the structure of the universe, we cannot resist the conclusion that the whole is founded upon a distinct idea." Keely holds to the harmony of this " distinct idea " throughout creation, and he demonstrates by vibratory machinery that all forces are indestructible, immaterial, homogeneous entities, having their origin and unity in one great intelligent personal will-force.

Were it not for this will-force eternally flowing into all created forms, the entire universe would disappear. As the workman employs his instrument to accomplish his designs, so Omnipotence may be said, in all reverence, to regulate His systems of worlds through and by the vibratory ether which He has created to serve His purpose. Well did Hertz reason when he wrote, "Soon the question set by modern physics will be, 'Are not all things due to conditions of ether?'" He had never heard of the toiler on this side of the Atlantic, when, after his own discovery, in 1888, that ether was imprisoned and used in every electro-magnetic engine, without this fact having been even so much as suspected by a single scientist, he wrote, in the *Revue Scientifique*, "We have gained a greater height than ever, and we possess a solid basis which will facilitate the ascent, in the research of new truths. The road which is open to us is not too steep, and the next resting-point does not appear inaccessible. Moreover, the crowds of researchers are full of ardour. We must therefore welcome with confidence all the efforts that are being made in this direction."

Keely has found no " resting-point " in his researches of a lifetime ; and, instead of being "welcomed with confidence" by his fellow-researchers in science, he has suffered at their hands more than will ever be known by his detractors. Keely's discoveries would have died with him, through the calumnies of these same scientists, as far as demonstration was concerned, had not a company been formed, in the early days of his inventions, which for many years furnished him with the necessary funds, expecting almost immediate financial success. The sneers of men of science crying "Charlatan," the ridicule of the public press, and the denunciations of the ignorant have been mighty factors in debasing the value of the shares of the company. The courage, faith, and contributing capacity of nearly all the stockholders have given out; and it is fortunate that now Mr. Keely's work of evolution has at last reached the point where he is able to convince those scientists of his integrity whose minds are broad enough to conform to what Herbert Spencer has said is the first condition of success in scientific research,—viz. "an honest receptivity, and willingness to abandon all preconceived notions, however cherished, if they be found to contradict the truth."

Keely may be said to have spent years of his valuable time in giving exhibitions whereby to raise the funds needed for his scientific researches. Again and again has he taken apart his various machines, to show their interior construction to the sceptical; and what this means, in the attendant delay, will be better understood when he has made known how slight a thing, by the laws of sympathetic association, may retard his progress for days, even for weeks.

Take, for example, his last experience with his preliminary commercial engine, to which, before he had completed his graduation, he was induced, in November 1889, to apply a brake, to show what resistance the vibratory current could bear under powerful friction. A force sufficient to stop a train of cars, it was estimated, did not interfere with its running; but under additional strain a "thud" was heard, and the shaft of the engine was twisted.

The engine should not have been submitted to such a test until after the differentiation had been equated, and perfect control in reversions established. And yet, so often has Keely made what seemed to be disasters an advantage in the end, it is possible that the interruption and delay may enable him to produce a perfect engine sooner than he would have done on this model. The world will never know how many mechanical difficulties Keely has conquered before attaining his present degree of success, in which he thinks he has mastered all that pertains to the principle of the force that he is dealing with, so far as necessary for commercial purposes, the difficulties that he still has to contend with being merely the minor ones of mechanical detail. The fact that so much of Mr. Keely's success, in conducting his experiments when giving exhibitions, depends upon the complete perfection of his instruments, is one of the strongest arguments that could be advanced in proof of the genuineness of his claims. Has any one ever heard of a performer in legerdemain who, after assembling an audience to witness his tricks, announced that something was wrong with his conjuring apparatus and that he was unable to exhibit his dexterity? Feats of legerdemain can be performed, night after night, year in and year out, without any hitch on the part of the operator; but all who are conversant with the failures attendant upon a certain order of experiments, as for instance in the liquefying of oxygen gas, will be able to appreciate the uncertainty which characterizes the action of Mr. Keely's instruments at times.

It is only by progressive experimental research that knowledge of the laws governing Nature's operations can be gained, and a system evolved to perpetuate such knowledge. The hypothesis of to-day must be discarded to-morrow, if further research proves its fallacy. Is it not, then, another strong argument in favour of Keely's integrity that, confessing ignorance of the laws that govern the force he has discovered, he has plodded on through all these years, experimenting upon its nature, with instruments of his own invention, which from their delicate and imperfect construction are uncertain in their operations, until he has so improved the defective machine as to make it a stepping-stone, by which he ascends to perfection? Take the imperfect comparison of a ladder: no workman can attain the summit in one effort; he must mount step by step.

To quote from Keely's writings, "The mathematics of vibratory etheric science, both pure and applied, require long and arduous research. It seems to me that no man's life is long enough to cover more than the introductory branch.

The theory of elliptic functions, the calculus of probabilities, are but pygmies in comparison to a science which requires the utmost tension of the human mind to grasp. But let us wait patiently for the light that will come, that is even now dawning." [1]

On the 28th of May, 1889, Mr. Keely's workshop was visited by several men interested to see and judge for themselves of the nature of his researches. Among them were Professor Leidy, of the University of Pennsylvania, and James M. Willcox, author of "Elemental Philosophy." After seeing the experiments in acoustics, and the production, storage, and discharge of the ether, Mr. Willcox remarked that no one who had witnessed all that they had seen in the line of associative vibration, under the same advantages, could assert any fraud on the part of Keely without convicting himself of the rankest folly. These gentlemen met Mr. Keely with their minds open to conviction, though with strong prejudices against the discovery of any unknown force. They treated him as if he were all that he is, keeping out of sight whatever doubts they may have had of the genuineness of his claims as a discoverer; and, in the end, all who were present expressed their appreciation of his courtesy in answering the questions asked, and their admiration of what he has accomplished on his unknown path. In doing this, they were simply doing justice to him and to themselves,—to that self-respect which leads men to respect the rights of others, and to do unto others as they would be done by. Had they questioned Keely's integrity, or betrayed doubts of his honesty of purpose, he would at once have assumed the defensive, and would have informed them that he has no wish to conduct experiments for scientists who are ready to give their opinions of his theories before having heard them propounded, or of his experiments before witnessing them. When Keely's system of "sympathetic vibration" is made known ("sympathetic seeking" Mr. Willcox would call it), it will be seen how sensitive Mr. Keely's instruments are to the vibrations caused by street-noises, to vibrations of

---

[1] Quotation from one of Keely's letters in 1885.

air from talking in the operating room, to touch even, as well as why it is that, although he is willing to take apart and explain the construction of his instruments in the presence of investigators, he objects to having them handled by others than himself, after they have been "harmonized," or "sensitized," or "graduated."

Mr. Keely is his own worst enemy. When suspected of fraud he acts as if he were a fraud; and in breaking up his vibratory microscope and other instruments which he had been years in perfecting, at the time he was committed to prison in 1888, he laid himself open to the suspicion that his instruments are but devices with which he cunningly deceives his patrons. Yet these same instruments he has, since their reconstruction, dissected and explained to those who approached him in the proper spirit. It is only when he has been subjected to insulting suspicions by arrogant scientists that he refuses to explain his theories, and to demonstrate their truth, as far as it is in his power to do so. "Keely may be on the right track, after all," remarked an English scientist, after Prof. Hertz had made known his researches on the structure of ether; "for if we have imprisoned the ether without knowing it, why may not Keely know what he has got a hold of?"

Norman Lockyer, in his "Chemistry of the Sun," confirms Keely's theories when he writes, "The law which connects radiation with absorption and at once enables us to read the riddle set by the sun and stars is, then, simply the law of 'sympathetic vibration.'"

"It is remarkable," says Horace W. Smith, "that in countries far distant from each other, different men have fallen into the same tracks of science, and have made similar and correspondent discoveries, at the same period of time, without the least communication with each other." So has it been in all periods of progress and in all branches of science, from the discoveries of Euclid and Archimedes down to those of Galileo and Descartes and Bacon, and, in later days, of Gilbert and Newton and Leibnitz, then Franklin and Collison and Von Kliest and Muschenbröck; and now Keely and Hertz and Depuy and Rücker and

Lockyer are examples. Never has a discovery leading to a new system been begun and perfected by the same individual so far as Keely is doing; but, as Morley has said, "the representative of a larger age must excel in genius all predecessors."

The application of his discovery to the service of humanity is the aim and end of Keely's efforts; his success means "vastly more than the most sanguine to-day venture to predict," promising "a true millennial introduction into the unseen universe, and the glorious life that every man, Christian or sceptic, optimist or pessimist, would gladly hope for and believe possible." (Thurston.)

Not the least among the ultimate blessings to our race which Keely's discovery foreshadows is the deeper insight that it will bestow into the healing power of the finer forces of nature, embracing cures of brain and nerve disorders that are now classed with incurable diseases.

Only a partial answer has been given to the question, "What has Keely done for science?" But enough has been said to convey some idea of the subtle nature of the force he is dealing with, and of the cause of the delays which have again and again disappointed the inventor, as well as the too sanguine hopes of immediate commercial success which have animated the officers and stockholders of "The Keely Motor Company." Keely has no secret to wrest from him. Instead of "Keely's Secret," it should be called "Nature's Secret;" for the problem has still to be worked out, the solution of which will make it "Keely's Secret;" and until this problem is fully solved to the inventor's satisfaction for commercial application, Keely has no secret that he is not willing to disclose, as far as it is in his power to do so.

CHAPTER XII.

1891.

VIBRATORY PHYSICS.—TRUE SCIENCE.

We seem to be approaching a theory as to the construction of ether. Hertz has produced vibrations, vibrating more than one hundred million times per second. He made use of the principle of resonance. You all understand how, by a succession of well-timed small impulses, a large vibration may be set up.—PROF. FITZGERALD.

DR. SCHIMMEL, in his lecture on "The Unity of Nature's Forces," says:—"The Greek philosophers, Leucippus, Anaxagoras, Democritus, and Aristotle, base their philosophies on the existence of an ether and atoms." According to Spiller's system, "both ether and atoms are material. The atoms are indivisible. Chemistry, being based on the correctness of this statement, forces us to accept it." But we are not forced to accept it if it is proved to be false.

Keely has now reached a stage in his researches at which he is able to demonstrate the truth of the hypotheses which he is formulating into a system; and consequently the stage where he can demonstrate whether theories, that have prevailed concerning the cause of physical phenomena, are sound or without basis in fact. Until this stage was reached it would have been as useless to make Mr. Keely's theories known, as it would be to publish a treatise to prove that two and two make five. Scientific men reject all theories in physics in which there is not an equal proportion of science and mathematics, excluding all questions of pure metaphysics.

They are right; for, until the world had undergone a state of preparation for another revelation of truth, the man who demonstrated all that Keely is now prepared to demonstrate would have been burned alive as a wizard. To use the words of Babcock, one of Keely's staunchest adherents, in 1880:— " This discoverer has entered a new world, and although an unexplored region of untold wealth lies beyond, he is treading firmly its border, which daily widens as with ever-increasing interest he pursues his explorations. He has passed the dreary realm where scientists are groping. His researches are made in the open field of elemental force, where gravity, inertia, cohesion, momentum, are disturbed in their haunts and diverted to use; where, from unity of origin, emanates infinite energy in diversified forms," and, to this statement I would add—where he is able to look from nature up to nature's God, understanding and explaining, as no man before ever understood and explained, how simple is " the mysterious way in which God works His wonders to perform."

Mr. Babcock continues:—"Human comprehension is inadequate to grasp the possibilities of this discovery for power, for increased prosperity, and for peace. It includes all that relates mechanically to travel, manufacture, mining, engineering, and warfare." Up to within two years, Keely, this discoverer of unknown laws of nature, has been left partially to the mercy of men who were interested only in mechanical "possibilities." In the autumn of 1888, he was led into a line of research which made the mechanical question one of secondary interest; and yet the present results are such as to prove that on this line alone can he ever hope to attain commercial success. The course then adopted has also been the means of placing his discoveries before the world, endorsed in such a manner as to command attention to his views and theories. It has been said that if extreme vicissitudes of belief on the part of men of science are evidences of uncertainty, it may be affirmed that of all kinds of knowledge none is more uncertain than science. The only hope for science is more science, says Drummond. Keely now bestows the only hope for science—" more science." He accounts for the non-recognition by scientists of his claims, in these words:

"The system of arranging introductory etheric impulses by compound chords set by differential harmonies, is one that the world of science has never recognized, simply because the struggles of physicists, combating with the solution of the conditions governing the fourth order of matter, have been in a direction thoroughly antagonistic, and opposite to a right one. It is true that luminosity has been induced by chemical antagonism, and, in my mind, this ought to have been a stepping-stone towards a more perfect condition than was accepted by them; but independent of what might be necessary to its analysis, the bare truth remains that the conditions were isolated—robbed of their most vital essentials—by not having the medium of etheric vibration associated with them."

In order to subdivide the atoms in the atomic triplet, the molecular ether, liberated from the molecule, is absolutely necessary to effect the rupture of the atoms; and so on, progressively, in each order of ether, molecular, intermolecular, atomic, inter-atomic, etheric, inter-etheric, the ether liberated in each successive division is essential to the next subdivision.

The keynote of Mr. Keely's researches is that the movements of elastic elements are rhythmical, and before he had reached his present stage in producing vibrations, on the principle of resonance, he has had problems to solve which needed the full measure of inspiration or apperception that he has received.

Hertz has produced vibrations about one metre long, vibrating more than one hundred million times a second. Keely has produced, using an atmospheric medium alone, 519,655,633 vibrations per second; but, interposing pure hydrogen gas between soap films and using it as a medium of acceleration, he asserts that on the enharmonic third a rate of vibration may be induced which could not be set down in figures, and could only be represented in sound colours. *He has invented instruments which demonstrate in many variations the colours of sound, registering the number of necessary vibrations to produce each variation.* The transmissive sympathetic chord of B flat, third octave, when passing into inaudibility, would induce billions of billions of vibrations, represented by sound colour on a screen illuminated from a solar ray. But this experiment is one of infinite difficulty, from the almost utter impossibility of holding the hydrogen between the two films long enough to conduct the experiment. Keely made over 1200 trials before succeeding once in inducing the intense blue field necessary, covering a space of six weeks, four hours at a time daily; and should he ever succeed in his present efforts to produce a film that will stand, he anticipates being able to register the range of motion in all metallic mediums. On this subject Keely writes:—The highest range of vibration I ever induced was in the one experiment that I made in liberating ozone by molecular percussion, which induced luminosity, and registered a percussive molecular force of 110,000 lbs. per square inch, as registered on a lever constructed for the purpose. The vibrations induced by this experiment reached over 700,000,000 per second, unshipping the apparatus, thus making it insecure for a repetition of the experiments. The decarbonized steel compressors of said apparatus moved as if composed of putty. Volume of sphere, 15 cubic inches; weight of surrounding metal, 316 lbs.

Recently some questions, propounded to Mr. Keely by a scientist, elicited answers which the man of science admitted were clear and definite, but no physicist could accept Keely's assertion that incalculable amounts of latent force exist in the molecular spaces, for the simple reason that science asserts that molecular aggregation is attended with dissipation of energy instead of its absorption. The questions asked were:—

I. "In disintegrating water, how many foot-pounds of energy have you to expend in order to produce or induce the vibratory energy in your acoustical apparatus?"

Answer.—"No foot-pounds at all. The force necessary to excite disintegration when the instrument is sensitized, both in sensitization and developments, would not be sufficient to wind up a watch."

II. "What is the amount of energy that you get out of that initial amount of water, say twelve drops, when decomposed into ether?"

Answer.—" From twelve drops of water a force can be developed that will fill a chamber of seven pint volume no less than six times with a pressure of ten tons to the square inch."

III. " In other words, if you put so many pounds of energy into vibratory motion, how many foot-pounds do you get out of this ? "

Answer.—" All molecular masses of metal represent in their interstitial molecular spaces incalculable amounts of latent force, which, if awakened and brought into intense vibratory action by the medium of sympathetic liberation, would result in thousands of billions more power in foot-pounds than that necessary to awaken it. The resultant development of any and all forces is only accomplished by conditions that awaken the latent energy they have carried with them during molecular aggregation. If the latent force that exists in a pound of water could be sympathetically evolved or liberated up to the seventh subdivision or compound inter-etheric, and could be stored free of rotation, it would be in my estimation sufficient to run the power of the world for a century."

This statement gives another of Keely's discoveries to the world, viz., that molecular dissociation does not create energy, as men have asserted Keely has claimed, but supplies it in unlimited quantities, as the product of the latent energy accumulated in molecular aggregation. This is to the physicist as if Keely had asserted that two and two make a billion, but as a man of science, who is held to be "the scientific equal of any man in the world," has come forward to make known that, in his opinion, " Keely has fairly demonstrated the discovery of a force previously unknown to science," the discoverer at lasts feels at liberty to make public the nature of his discoveries. Until Dr. Joseph Leidy had taken this stand, Mr. Keely could not, without jeopardizing his interests, and the interests of the Keely Motor Company, have made known in what particulars his system conflicts with the systems upheld by the age in which we live.

After the warning given in the history of Huxley's " Bathybius," we may feel quite sure that if Keely had failed to demonstrate the genuineness of his claims by actual experiment, no scientist would have risked the world-wide reputation of a lifetime by endorsement of the discovery of an unknown force, as Professor Leidy has done, while Keely himself was under such a cloud that, to advocate his integrity and uphold the importance of his discovery, has hitherto been enough to awaken doubts as to the sanity of his upholders. Among many others who have written of it from the standpoint of Keely's accountability for the mistakes of the managers of the Keely Motor Company—men who made no pretence of caring for anything but dividends—was one who asserted, in the *New York Tribune*, that it was a "remarkable delusion, full of tricks too numerous to mention, the exposure of which ought to be made to bring the Keely craze to an end." In the same journal an editorial states that "Mr. Keely appears to have no mechanical ingenuity, his strong point being his ability as a collector. He has one of the largest and best arranged collections of other people's money to be found in the United States. Having, a number of years ago, during a fit of temporary insanity, constructed a machine which, if any power on earth could start it, would explode and pierce the startled dome of heaven with flying fragments of cog-wheels and cranks, he now sits down calmly, and allows this same mechanical nightmare to make his living for him. This is genius; this is John W. Keely; he toils not, neither does he spin, but he has got an hysterical collection of crooked pipes and lob-sided wheels tied up in his back room that extract the reluctant dollar from the pocket of avarice without fail."

This is a specimen of the nature of the ridicule which was encountered by Keely's "upholders," as well as by himself. Until Professor Leidy and Dr. Willcox came to the front, in March, 1890, Mr. Keely had no influential supporters, and not one scientist could be found who was ready to encounter the wasps.

Such is the position of all defenders of the truth in all ages; but the torch being held aloft, in such hands as have now seized it, the opportunity is given to see what Keely proclaims as truth.

We know that science denies the divisibility of atoms, but Keely affirms and demonstrates that all corpuscules of matter may be divided and subdivided by a certain order of vibration. During all these years in which he has given exhibitions of the operation of his generators, liberators, and disintegrators, in turn, each being an improvement, successively, on the preceding one, no one has attempted to give to the public any theory, or even so much as a sensible conjecture, of the origin of the force.

When Mr. Keely was asked, by a woman in 1884, if it were not possible that he had dissociated hydrogen gas, and that his unknown force came from that dissociation, he replied that he thought it might be; but he made no assertion that he had. This conjecture was repeated to an English scientist, who replied that he was willing to make a bet of 10,000*l*. that hydrogen is a simple element. The same scientist says now that he should answer such a question with more caution, and say that he had never known hydrogen to be dissociated.

THEORY AND FORMULA OF AQUEOUS DISINTEGRATION.

The peculiar conditions as associated with the gaseous elements of which water is composed, as regards the differential volume and gravity of its gases, make it a ready and fit subject of vibratory research. In submitting water to the influence of vibratory transmission, even on simple thirds, the high action induced on the hydrogen as contrasted with the one on the oxygen (under the same vibratory stream), causes the antagonism between these elements that induces dissociation. The differential antagonistic range of motion, so favouring the antagonistic thirds as to become thoroughly repellent. The gaseous element thus induced and registered, shows thousands of times much greater force as regards tenuity and volume than that induced by the chemical disintegration of heat, on the same medium. In all molecular dissociation or disintegration of both simple or compound elements, whether gaseous or solid, a stream of vibratory antagonistic thirds, sixths, or ninths, on their chord mass will compel progressive subdivisions. In the disintegration of water the instrument is set on thirds, sixths, and ninths, to get the best effects.

These triple conditions are focalized on the neutral centre of said instrument so as to induce perfect harmony or concordance to the chord-note of the mass-chord of the instrument's full combination; after which the diatonic and the enharmonic scale located at the top of the instrument, or ring, is thoroughly harmonized with the scale of ninths which is placed at the base of the vibratory transmitter with the telephone head. The next step is to disturb the harmony on the concentrative thirds, between the transmitter and disintegrator. This is done by rotating the syren so as to induce a sympathetic communication along the nodal transmitter, or wire, that associates the two instruments. When the note of the syren becomes concordant to the neutral centre of the disintegrator, the highest order of sympathetic communication is established. It is now necessary to operate the transferable vibratory negatizer, or negative accelerator, which is seated in the centre of the diatonic and enharmonic ring, at the top of disintegrator, and complete disintegration will follow (from the antagonisms induced on the concordants by said adjunct), in triple progression, thus :—First, thirds : Molecular dissociation resolving the water into a gaseous compound of hydrogen and oxygen. Second, sixths : resolving the hydrogen and oxygen into a new element by second order of dissociation, producing what I call, low atomic ether. Third, ninths : The low atomic ether resolved into a new element, which I denominate high or second atomic harmonic. All these transmissions being simultaneous on the disturbance of sympathetic equilibrium by said negative accelerator.

Example :—Taking the chord mass of the disintegrator B flat, or any chord mass that may be represented by the combined association of all the mechanical parts of its structure (no two structures being alike in their chord masses), taking B flat, the resonators of said structure are set at B flat first octave, B flat third octave, and B flat ninth octave, by drawing out the caps of resonators until the harmony of thirds, sixths, and ninths are reached; which a simple movement of the fingers on the diatonic scale, at the head, will determine by the tremulous action which is highly sensible to the touch, on said caps. The caps are then rigidly fixed in their different positions by set screws. The focalization to the neutral centre is then established by dampening the steel rods, on the scale at the back, representing the thirds, sixths, and ninths, drawing a piece of small gum tube over them, which establishes harmony to the chord mass of the instrument. Concordance is thus effected between the disintegrator and the ninths of the scale at base of transmitters with telephonic head.

This scale has a permanent sympathetic one, set on the ninth of any mass chord that may be represented, on any and all the multiple variations of mechanical combinations. In fact, permanently set for universal accommodation.

The next step is to establish pure harmony between the transmitter and the disintegrator, which is done by spinning the syren disk, then waiting until the sympathetic note is reached, as the syren chord, decreasing in velocity, descends the scale. At this juncture, the negative accelerator must be immediately and rapidly rotated, inducing high disturbance of equilibrium between the transmitter and the disintegrator by triple negative evolution, with the result that a force of from five to ten, fifteen, twenty, and thirty thousand pounds to the square inch is evolved by the focalization of this triple negative stream on the disintegrating cell, or chamber, whether there be one, two, three, five, or ten drops of water enclosed within it.

Graduation of Machines.

Mr. Keely gives a few introductory words concerning the necessary graduating of his instruments, for effecting conditions necessary to ensure perfect sympathetic transmission, which will serve to show how great are the difficulties that have been attendant upon getting his machines into a condition to control and equate the differentiation in molecular masses, requiring greater skill than in researching the force of a sunbeam. He writes:—The differentiation in molecular metallic masses, or grouping, is brought about in their manipulations in manufacturing them for commercial uses; in the forging of a piece of metal, in the drawing of a length of wire, and in the casting of a molten mass to any requisite form.

The nearest approach to molecular uniformity in metallic masses is in the wire drawn for commercial uses, gold and platina being the nearest to freedom from differentiation. But even these wires, when tested by a certain condition of the first order of intensified molecular vibration for a transferring medium between centres of neutrality, I find to be entirely inadequate for the transfer of concordant unition, as between one and the other, on account of nodal interferences. We can appreciate the difficulty of converting such a medium to a uniform molecular link, by knowing that it can be accomplished only after removing all nodal interference, by inducing between the nodal waves a condition in which they become subservient to the inter-sympathetic vibratory molecular link of such structure or wire.

Therefore, it is necessary to submit the wire to a system of graduation in order to find what the combined chords of these nodal interferences represent when focalized to one general centre. Then the differentiation between these nodal waves and the inter-molecular link must be equated, by what I call a process of vibratory induction, so as to induce pure concordance between one and the other. To elaborate on this system of graduation, for effecting conditions necessary to ensure perfect and unadulterated transmission, would make up a book that would take days to read and months to study.

The graduating of a perfectly constructed instrument, to a condition to transmit sympathetically, is no standard whatever for any other one that may be built, nor ever will be, because no concordant conditions of compound molecular aggregation can ever exist in visible groupings. If it were even possible to make their parts perfectly accurate one to the other, in regard to atmospheric displacement and weight, their resonating qualities would still have a high rate of sympathetic variation in their molecular groupings alone. If one thousand million of coins, each one representing a certain standard value, and all struck from the same die, were sympathetically graduated under a vibratory subdivision of 150,000, the most amazing variation would present itself, as between each individual coin throughout the number, in regard to their molecular grouping and resonance. . . .

It will be realized in the future what immense difficulties have been encountered by Mr. Keely in perfecting his system of graduation, and in constructing devices for the guidance of artificers and mechanicians, whereby those who are not as abnormally endowed as he is for his work, can bring a proper vibratory action into play to induce positive sympathetic transmission; as will also be realized the stupidity of the men who still seek to confine his researches to perfecting the so-called Keely motor, before his system is sufficiently developed to enable others to follow it up, should his physical strength give out. His system of graduating research, when completed, will enable men to take up the work, *not* from the standard of an already completed structure that is true in its operation, though a perfect duplicate as to size and gravity be made, for each successively constructed machine requires a knowledge of its own conditions of sensity, as regards its mass chords. Keely writes:—

"That tuning forks can be so constructed as to show coincident or concordant association with each other, is but a very weak illustration of the fact which governs pure acoustic assimilation. The best only approach a condition of about a fortieth, as regards pure attractive and propulsive receptiveness. By differentiating them to concordant thirds, they induce a condition of molecular bombardment between themselves, by alternate changes of long and short waves of sympathy. Bells rung in vacuo liberate the same number of corpuscules, at the same velocity as those surrounded by a normal atmosphere; and hence the same acoustic force attending them, but they are inaudible from the fact that, in vacuo, the molecular volume is reduced. Every gaseous molecule is a resonator of itself, and is sensitive to any and all sounds induced, whether accordant or discordant.

Answers to Questions.

The positive vibrations are the radiating or propulsive; the negative vibrations are the ones that are attracted towards the neutral centre. The action of the magnetic flow is dual in its evolutions, both attractive and propulsive. The sound vibrations of themselves have no power whatever to induce dissociation, even in its lowest form. Certain differential, dual, triple and quadruple, chords give introductory impulses which excite an action on molecular masses, liquid and gaseous, that increase their range of molecular motion and put them in that receptive state for sympathetic vibratory interchange which favours molecular disintegration; then, as I have shown, the diatonic enharmonic is brought into play, which further increases the molecular range of motion beyond fifty per cent. of their diameters, when molecular separation takes place, giving the tenuous substance that is necessary to induce progressive subdivision. This molecular gaseous substance, during its evolution, assumes a condition of high rotation in the sphere or tube in which it has been generated, and becomes itself the medium, with the proper exciters, for further progressive dissociation. The exciters include an illuminated revolving prism, condenser, and coloured lenses, with a capped glass tube strong enough to carry a pressure of at least one thousand pounds per square inch. To one of these caps a sectional wire of platinum and silver is attached; the other cap is attached to the tube, so screwed to the chamber as to allow it to lead to the neutral centre of said chamber.

MINERAL DISINTEGRATION.

I have been repeatedly urged to repeat my disintegrations of quartz rock; but it has been utterly out of my power to do so. The mechanical device with which I conducted those experiments was destroyed at the time of the proceedings against me. Its graduation occupied over four years, after which it was operated successfully. It had been originally constructed as an instrument for overcoming gravity; a perfect, graduated scale of that device was accurately registered, a copy of which I kept; I have since built three successive disintegrators set up from that scale, but they did not operate. This peculiar feature remained a paradox to me until I had solved the conditions governing the chords of multiple masses;

when this problem ceased to be paradoxical in its character. As I have said, there are no two compound aggregated forms of visible matter that are, or ever can be, so duplicated as to show pure sympathetic concordance one to the other. Hence the necessity of my system of graduation, and of a compound device that will enable anyone to correct the variations that exist in compound molecular structures ; or in other words to graduate such, so as to bring them to a successful operation. . . .

KEELY.

DISTURBANCE OF MAGNETIC NEEDLE.

If Keely's theories are correct, science will in time classify all the important modifications of the one force in nature as sympathetic streams, each stream composed of triple flows. Mr. Keely maintains that the static condition which the magnetic needle assumes, when undisturbed by any extraneous force outside of its own sympathetic one, proves conclusively that the power of the dominant third, of the triple combination of the magnetic terrestrial envelope, is the controlling one of this sympathetic triplet, and the one towards which all the others co-ordinate. All the dominant conditions of nature represent the focal centres towards which like surrounding ones become sympathetically subservient. The rapid rotation of the magnetic needle of a compass which Mr. Keely shows in his experiments, rests entirely on the alternating of the dominant alone, which is effected by a triple condition of vibration that is antagonistic to its harmonious flow as associated with its other attendants. A rapid change of polarity is induced, and rapid rotation necessarily follows.

Quoting from Keely's writings,—"The human ear cannot detect the triple chord of any vibration, or sounding note, but every sound that is induced of any range, high or low, is governed by the same laws, as regards triple action of such, that govern every sympathetic flow in Nature. Were it not for these triple vibratory conditions, change of polarity could never be effected, and consequently there could be no rotation. Thus the compounding of the triple triple, to produce the effect, would give a vibration in multiplication reaching the ninth, in order to induce subservience, the enumeration of which it would be folly to undertake, as the result would be a string of figures nearly a mile in length to denote it.

When the proper impulse is given to induce the rotation with pure alternating corpuscular action, the conditions of action become perpetual in their character, lasting long enough from that one impulse to wear out any machine denoting such action, and on the sympathetic stream eternally perpetual. The action of the neutral or focalizing centres represents molecular focalization and redistribution, not having any magnetism associated with them; but when the radiating arms of their centres are submitted to the triple compound vibratory force, representing their mass thirds, they become magnetic and consequently cease their rotation. Their rotation is induced by submitting them to three different orders of vibration, simultaneously giving the majority to the harmonic third.

Theory of the Induction of Sympathetic Chords to excite rotation, by vibrophonic trajection to and from centres of neutrality, as induced and shown to Professor Leidy, Dr. Willcox, and others, on revolving globe.

All hollow spheres, of certain diameters, represent, as per diameters and their volume of molecular mass, pure, unadulterated, sympathetic resonation towards the enharmonic and diatonic thirds of any, and in fact all, concordant sounds. In tubes it is adversely different, requiring a definite number of them so graduated as to represent a confliction by thirds, sixths, and ninths, as towards the harmonic scale. When the conditions are established, the acoustic result of this combination, when focalized, represents concordant harmony, as between the chord mass of the instrument to be operated and chord mass of the tubes of resonation. Therefore the shortest way towards establishing pure concordance, between any number of resonating mediums, is by the position that Nature herself assumes in her multitudinous arrangements of the varied forms and volumes of matter—the spherical. The great difficulty to overcome, in order to get a revolution of the said sphere, exists in equating the interior adjuncts of same. In other words, the differentiation induced must be so

Vibratory Physics. 181

equated as to harmonize and make their conditions purely concordant to the molecular mass of the sphere. Example: Suppose the chord of the sphere mass represents B flat, or any other chord, and the internal adjuncts by displacement of atmospheric volume differentiates the volume one-twentieth; this displacement in the shell's atmospheric volume would represent an antagonistic twentieth against the shell's mass concordance, to equate which it would be necessary to so graduate the shell's internal adjuncts as to get at the same chord;—an octave or any number of octaves that comes nearest to the concordance of the shell's atmospheric volume. No intermediates between the octaves would ever reach sympathetic union.

We will now take up the mechanical routine as associated with adjuncts of interference, and follow the system for chording the mechanical aggregation in its different parts, in order to induce the transmissive sympathy necessary to perfect evolution, and to produce revolution of the sphere or shell.

Example.—Suppose that we had just received from the machine shop a spun shell of twelve inches internal diameter, 1·32 of an inch thick, which represents an atmospheric volume of 904·77 cubic inches. On determination by research we find the shell to be on its resonating volume B flat, and the molecular volume of the metal that the sphere is composed of, B natural. This or any other antagonistic chord, as between the chord mass of the shell and its atmospheric volume, would not interfere but would come under subservience. We now pass a steel shaft through its centre, ½ inch in diameter, which represents its axial rest. This shaft subjects the atmospheric volume of the shell to a certain displacement or reduction, to correct which we first register the chord note of its mass, and find it to be antagonistic to the chord mass of the shell, a certain portion of an octave. This must be corrected. The molecular volume of the shaft must be reduced in volume, either by filing or turning, so as to represent the first B flat chord that is reached by such reduction. When this is done the first line of interference is neutralized, and the condition of sympathy is as pure between the parts as it was when the globe was minus its axis. There is now introduced on its axis a ring which has seven tubes or graduating resonators, the ring being two-thirds the diameter of the globe, the resonators three inches long and ¾ inch diameter, each one to be set on the chord of B flat, which is done by sliding the small diaphragm in the tube to a point that will indicate B flat. This setting then controls the metallic displacement of the metallic combination, as also of the arms necessary to hold the ring and resonators on shaft or axis. Thus the second equation is established, both on resonation and displacement. We are now ready to introduce the diatonic scale ring of three octaves which is set at two-thirds of the scale antagonistic to the chord mass of the globe itself. This is done by graduating every third pin of its scale to B flat, thirds, which represent antagonistic thirds to the shell's molecular mass. This antagonism must be thoroughly sensitive to the chord mass of one of the hemispheres of which the globe is composed. The axis of the scale ring must rotate loosely on the globe's shaft without revolving with the globe itself; which it is prevented from doing by being weighted on one side of the ring by a small hollow brass ball, holding about two ounces of lead. The remaining work on the device is finished by painting the interior of the globe, one hemisphere black and one white, and attaching a rubber bulb such as is used to spray perfume, to the hollow end of the shaft. This bulb equates vibratory undulations, thus preventing an equation of molecular bombardment on its dark side when sympathetically influenced. It is now in condition to denote the sympathetic concordance between living physical organisms, or the receptive transmittive concordance necessary to induce rotation.

PHILOSOPHY OF TRANSMISSION AND ROTATION OF MUSICAL SPHERE.

The only two vibratory conditions that can be so associated as to excite high sympathetic affinity, as between two physical organisms, are:—Etheric chord of B flat, 3rd octave, and on etheric sympathetic chords transmission E flat on the scale 3rd, 6ths, and 9ths; octaves harmonic; having the 3rd dominant; the 6th enharmonic, and the 9th diatonic.

Vibratory Physics. 183

The chord mass representing the musical sphere, being the sympathetic etheric chord of B flat third octave, indicated by the focalization of its interior mechanical combination, as against the neutral sevenths of its atmospheric volume, makes the shell highly sensitive to the reception of pure sympathetic concordance, whether it be physical, mechanical, or a combination of both. Taking the chord mass of the different mechanical parts of the sphere and its adjuncts, as previously explained, when associated and focalized to represent pure concordance, as between its atmospheric volume and sphere mass, which means the pure unit of concordance, we have the highest position that can be established in relation to its sympathetic susceptiveness to negative antagonism. The beauty of the perfection of the laws that govern the action of Nature's sympathetic flows is here demonstrated in all the purity of its workings, actually requiring antagonistic chords to move and accelerate. The dark side of the shell, which represents fifty per cent. of its full area of pure concordant harmony, is the receptive area for the influence of the negative transmissive chords of the thirds, sixths and ninths to bombard upon; which bombardment disturbs the equilibrium of said sphere, and induces rotation. The rotation can be accelerated or retarded, according as the antagonistic chords of the acoustic forces are transmitted in greater or lesser volume. The action induced by the mouth organ, transmitted at a distance from the sphere without any connection of wire, demonstrates the purity of the principle of sympathetic transmission, as negatized or disturbed by discordants; which, focalizing on the resonating sevenths of resonators, or tubes attached to ring, the sympathetic flow is by this means transmitted to the focalizing centre, or centre of neutrality, to be re-distributed at each revolution of sphere, keeping intact the sympathetic volume during sensitization, thus preventing the equation or stoppage of its rotation.

Again, the sphere resting on its journals in the ring, as graduated to the condition of its interior combinations, represents a pure sympathetic concordant under perfect equation ready to receive the sympathetic, or to reject the non-sympathetic. If a pure sympathetic chord is transmitted coincident to its full combination, the sphere will remain quiescent; but if a transmission of discordance is brought to bear upon it, its sympathetic conditions become repellent to this discordance. . . .

KEELY.

Hertz in his conjectures that a knowledge of the structure of ether should unveil the essence of matter itself, and of its inherent properties, weight and inertia, is treading the path that leads to this knowledge. Professor Fitzgerald says:—"Ether must be the means by which electric and magnetic forces exist, it should explain chemical actions, and if possible gravity." The law of sympathetic vibration explains chemical affinities as a sympathetic attractive, but inherent, force; in short, as gravity. This opens up too wide a territory even but to peer into in the dawning light of Keely's system of vibratory physics. The boundary line is crossed, and the crowds of researchers in electro-magnetism are full of ardour. Hertz constructed a circuit, whose period of vibration for electric currents was such that he was able to see sparks, due to the increased vibration, leaping across a small air-space in this resonant circuit; his experiments have proved and demonstrated the ethereal theory of electro-magnetism:—that electro-magnetic actions are due to a medium pervading all known space; while Keely's experiments have proved that *all things are due to conditions of ether.*

Professor Fitzgerald closes one of his lectures on ether in these words:—" There are metaphysical grounds for reducing matter to motion, and potential to kinetic energy. Let us for a moment contemplate what is betokened by this theory that in electro-magnetic engines we are using as our mechanism the ether, the medium that fills all known space. It was a great step in human progress when man learnt to make material machines, when he used the elasticity of his bow, and the rigidity of his arrow to provide food and defeat his enemies. It was a great advance when he learnt to use the chemical action of fire; when he learnt to use water to float his boats, and air to drive them; when, by artificial selection, he provided himself with food and domestic animals. For two hundred years he has made heat his slave to drive his machinery. Fire, water, earth, and air have long been his slaves, but it is only within the last few years that man has won the battle lost by the giants of old, has snatched the thunderbolt from Jove himself, and enslaved the all-pervading ether."

Of the experiments of Hertz, in inducing vibrations "in ether waves," Professor Fitzgerald says : " If we consider the possible radiating power of an atom, we find that it may be millions of millions of times as great as Professor Wiedermann has found to be the radiating power of a sodium atom in a Bunsen burner; so if there is reason to think that any greater oscillation might disintegrate the atom, we are still a long way from it."

Here we have an admission that the atom *may be* divisible ; but the professor's conjecture is made upon an incorrect hypothesis. The "*possible theory of ether and matter*" which Professor Fitzgerald puts forward, in his lecture on Electro-Magnetic Radiation, is in harmony with Keely's theories. This hypothesis explains the differences in nature as differences in motion, ending : " Can we resist the conclusion that all motion is thought ? Not that contradiction in terms, 'unconscious thought,' but *living thought;* that all nature is the language of One in whom we live, and move, and have our being ? " This great truth the Buddhists have taught for ages. *There is no such thing as blind or dead matter, as there is no blind nor unconscious thought.*

CHAPTER XIII.

1891.

"MORE SCIENCE."

The only hope for science is more science.—DRUMMOND.

Philosophy must finally endeavour to be itself constructive." Here Professor Seth laid stress on the necessity of a teleological view of the universe, not in the paltry, mechanical sense sometimes associated with the word teleology, but as vindicating the existence of an end or organic unity in the process of the world, constituting it an evolution and not a series of aimless changes. . . . As Goethe taught, in one of his finest poems, we do well to recognize in the highest attributes of human-kind our nearest glimpse into the nature of the divine. The part was not greater than the whole, and we might rest assured that whatever of wisdom and goodness there was in us had not been born out of nothing, but had its fount, somewhere and somehow, in a more perfect Goodness and Truth.—Review of PROFESSOR SETH's address.

Believe nothing which is unreasonable, and reject nothing as unreasonable without proper examination.—GAUTAMA BUDDHA.

I do not believe that matter is inert, acted upon by an outside force. To me it seems that every atom is possessed by a certain amount of primitive intelligence.—EDISON.

HISTORY tells us that Pythagoras would not allow himself to be called a sage, as his predecessors had done, but designated himself as a lover of wisdom; ardent in the pursuit of wisdom, he could not arrogate to himself the possession of wisdom. Yet, in our time, so unwilling are the searchers after wisdom to admit that there can be anything "new under the sun," anything that they do not already know, that we find the number of men of science to be marvellously small who possess the first condition of success in scientific research, as set down by Herbert Spencer, very few who do not arrogate to themselves too much learning to permit them to admit the possibility of any new revelation of truth. In every age of our world, to meet the requirements of the age, in its step-by-step progress from barbarism to civilization and enlightenment, there have appeared extraordinary men, having knowledge far in advance of the era in which they lived. Of such, among many, were Moses, Zoroaster, Confucius, Plato, and above these, Gautama the Buddha. But Moses, with all his knowledge of bacilli and bacteria, could not have met the requirements of any later age. The " eye for an eye " and " tooth for a tooth " period passed, and King David, who was so superior to other Kings of marauding tribes, that he was called " a man after God's own heart," satisfied his desire for punishment, to be meted out to his personal enemies, by prayer to God to "put out their eyes," and to "let them fall from one wickedness to another." This was a step in advance, for it gave those who had offended him a chance to escape all such summary proceedings as Moses had authorized. Still, the time was a long way off before a greater than Moses appeared to teach the world that such prayers are unavailing, that we can hate sin without hating the sinner, and that the Alpha and Omega of religion is to live in love and in the performance of duty. The Jewish prophets foretold the coming of Jesus of Nazareth; and the interpreters of Scripture are not alone now in having predicted that we are approaching a new dispensation, an age of harmony, which the twentieth century is to usher in, according to Biblical prophets. Renan has said that he envies those who shall live to see the wonders which the light of the new dawn that is breaking upon the world of science will unfold ; that those who live in this coming age will know things of which we have no conception. Morley, in the spirit of prophecy, has said that in the near future a great intellectual giant will arise to bless our globe, who will surpass all other men of genius, reasoning that the representative of a larger age must be greater in genius than any predecessor. When the system is made known by which Keely dissociates the molecule and atoms by successive orders of vibration, proving two laws in physics as fallacious, we shall not hesitate to say that " the light of the new dawn " has now broken upon the world of science, and that the discoverer of the divisibility of the atom and of the absorption of energy in all molecular aggregation is the genius foretold by Morley. One quality of true genius is humility. "What a brain you must have!" said a man of science to Keely, not long since, "to have thought this all out." This man of genius replied, "I was but the instrument of a Higher Power." We are all instruments of a Higher Power, but the instruments chosen and set apart for any special work are always choice instruments which have been fitted or adapted to that work—the furnace perhaps seven times heated before the annealing was perfected.

It has been said that man enters upon life as a born idiot; and there are many who think that, in comparison with the possibilities which the future promises in the way of the physical evolution of the race, we are but as idiots still. Having reached our present stage of physical and mental development, the history of the civilization of our race cannot but lead reflecting men and women into the opinion that the work of evolution will become more purely psychical in future. After which, as a consequence, there can be no doubt that physical development will again take its turn; for, as Tennyson has said,—

"When reign the world's great bridals, chaste and calm,
Then springs the coming race that rules mankind."

Not the least among the many applications of Keely's discoveries will be that which will prove, by demonstration, whether the chord of mass in a man and woman is near enough in the octaves to be beneficial, or so far apart as to be deteriorating.

"There is no truer truth obtainable
By man than comes of music."

The earlier processes of civilization belonged to an age of spontaneity, of unreflective productivity; an age that expressed itself in myths, created religions and organized social forms and habits of life in harmony with these spontaneous creations.

> " O, ye delicious fables! where the wave
> And woods were peopled and the air with things
> So lovely! Why, ah why, has Science grave
> Scattered afar your sweet imaginings?"

asks Barry Cornwall. But now that we have entered upon a more advanced age in thought, as in all things pertaining to discovery and practical application, or invention, a critical defining intellectual age, we must henceforth depend upon true science for our progress toward a higher enlightenment. Science, as will be seen, embraces religion, and must become, as Keely asserts, the religion of the world, when it is made known in all its glory and grandeur, sweeping away all footholds for scepticism, and spreading the knowledge of God, as a God of love, until this knowledge covers the earth as the waters cover the sea. As has been said, the word science, in its largest signification, includes intellectual achievement in every direction open to the mind, and the co-ordination of the results in a progressive philosophy of life. Philosophy has been defined as the science of causes or of first principles, and should be limited, almost exclusively, to the mental sciences. This is the field which Keely is exploring; the knowledge of the "hidden things" which he is bringing to the light is pure philosophical knowledge, in the widest acceptation of the term: the knowledge of effects as dependent on their causes.

> " Behold an infinite of floating worlds
> Dividing crystal waves of ether pure
> In endless voyage without port."

Is it not a marvel of inspiration to have been able to cast line and plummet in such a sea of knowledge, to be able to demonstrate the power of that "sympathetic outreach" which, acting from our satellite upon the waters of our oceans and seas, through the vast space that separates it from our earth, lifts these waters, once in every twenty-four hours, from their beds; and, as gently as a mother would lay her infant on its couch, places them again where they rest?

God hath chosen, as Paul said, the foolish things of the

world to confound the wise; and God hath chosen the weak things of the world to confound the things which are mighty, and base things of the world and things which are despised hath God chosen, yea, and things which are not to bring to naught things which are; that no flesh should glory in His presence. Christ said, "I thank Thee, O Father, Lord of heaven and earth, because Thou hast hid these things from the wise and prudent, and hast revealed them unto babes."

Truth never changes; but as new truths are revealed to us, to meet the necessities of progress (in our development from ignorance into the wisdom of angels), our point of view is ever changing, like the landscape which we look out upon from the swiftly gliding railway-carriage that bears us to our destination. As yet, "Earth has shown us only the title-page of a book" that we may, if we will, read its first pages here, and continue reading throughout eternity.

When Bulwer wrote of "a power that can replenish or invigorate life, heal and preserve, cure disease: enabling the physical organism to re-establish the due equilibrium of its natural powers, thereby curing itself," he foreshadowed one of Keely's discoveries. "Once admit the possibility that the secrets of nature conceal forces yet undeveloped," says the author of "Masollam," "which may contain a cure for the evils by which it is now afflicted, and it is culpable timidity to shrink from risking all to discover that cure." This author teaches that humanity at large has a claim higher than the claims of the blood-tie; that a love based upon no higher sentiment, makes us blind to the claims of duty; and this is why, when men or women are chosen to do a great work, for the human family, the ligaments which have bound them too exclusively to their own families, are cut and torn apart.

No greater work has ever been committed to a man to do than that which Keely's discoveries are preparing the way for. Science was rocking the world into the sleep of death—for materialism is death—its votaries declaring atoms to be eternally active, and the intellect which had discovered the existence of these atoms to end with the life of the molecular body. On this subject Simmons has written :—

"Shall impalpable light speed so swiftly and safely through

infinite space—and the mind that measures its speed, and makes it tell its secrets in the spectroscope, be buried with the body? Shall mere breath send its pulsations through the wire and, after fifty miles of silence, sound again in speech or music in a far-off city, or stamp itself in the phonograph to sound again in far-off centuries—and the soul that has wrought these wonders pass to eternal silence? Shall physical force persist for ever—and this love, which is the strongest force in nature, perish? It would seem wiser to trust that the infinite law, which is everywhere else so true, will take care of this human longing which it has made, and fufil it in eternal safety. We make no argument, but we cannot ignore all the intimations of immortality. Cyrus Field tells us of the night when, after his weary search for that long-lost cable two miles deep in mid-ocean, the grapnel caught it and, trembling with suspense, they drew it to the deck, hardly trusting their eyes, but creeping to feel it and make sure it was there. And when, as they watched, a spark soon came from a finger in England, showing that the line was sound, strong men wept and rockets rent the midnight darkness. We and our world float like a ship on the mysterious sea of being, in whose abysses the grapnel of science touches no solid line of logic connecting us to another land. But now and then there come from convictions, stronger than cables, flashes of light bidding us trust that our dead share in divine immortality, and are safe in the arms of Infinite Law and Eternal Love."

Keely's demonstrations suggest "the missing link" between matter and mind, the solid line of logic which may yet be laid in "the widening dominion of the human mind over the forces of nature." In " Keely's Secrets," No. 9, Vol. I. of the T.P.S., some of the elements of the possibilities resulting to the world from Keely's discoveries were set down. War will become an impossibility; and, as Browning's poem of "Childe Roland" forecasts, "The Dark Tower" of unbelief will crumble at the bugle-blast which levels its walls to their foundation, revealing such a boundless region of research as the mind of man could never conceive were he not the offspring of the Creator. Not long since, Mr. Keely was congratulated upon having secured the attention of men of science, connected with the

University of Pennsylvania, to his work of research. "Now, you will be known as a great discoverer, not as Keely the motor-man," said one of them present; whom he answered, "I have discovered so little, in comparison with what remains to be discovered, that I cannot call myself a discoverer." One of the professors present took Keely by the hand and said, "You *are* a great discoverer."

All thoughtful men who have witnessed the latest developments of the force displayed by Keely, in his researching experiments for aerial navigation, are made to realize that more through his discoveries, than by the progressive development of the altruistic element in humanity (dreamed of by speculative optimists), our race will be brought into that dispensation of peace and harmony, anticipated by "seers" and foretold by prophets as the millennial age. It requires no great measure of foresight to discern, as a natural consequence of the control and application of this force in art and commerce, that ameliorated condition of the masses which will end the mighty conflict now so blindly being waged between capital and labour.[1] And to the eye of faith, it is not difficult to look beyond the intervening æons of centuries, to the literal fulfilment of the promise of that millennial period when men shall live in brotherly love together; making heaven of earth as even now it is in our power to do if we live up to Christ's command: "Whatsoever ye would that others should do unto you, that do ye also unto them." Had some of the dogmatic scientists of this age followed this command, Keely's discovery might have been sooner known in all its importance, protecting him, as their acknowledgment would have done, from the persecutions that have operated so detrimentally against the completion of researches which should have been finished before any attempt was made to apply the discovery to commercial ends.

[1] The steam engines of the world now represent the work of 1,000,000,000 men, or more than double the working population of the earth, whose total population is about 1,500,000,000 inhabitants. Steam has accordingly trebled man's working power, enabling him to economize his physical strength while attending to his intellectual development. Our race, which seems to have reached its limit of physical development, is ready to enter upon the foretold stage of psychical evolution.

No scientist who witnessed the production of the force, displayed by Keely, in a proper spirit, but would have been welcomed by him to further experiments in its operations, as were Professor Leidy and Dr. Wilcox in 1889. So, in truth, those who printed their edicts against Keely about ten years since are, in part, responsible for the loss to the world which this long delay has occasioned. Still, in view of the acknowledged fact that not one of the great laws which science now accepts as incontrovertible truths, but was vehemently denied by the scientists of its time, declared to be *à priori* impossible; its discoverers and *supporters* denounced as fools or charlatans, and even investigation refused as being a waste of time and thought; it would be too much to expect from the thinkers of this age any greater degree of readiness to investigate claims, that threatened to demolish their cherished notions, than characterized their predecessors.

But the time was not ripe for the disclosure: "God never hurries." He counts the centuries as we count the seconds, and the nearer that we approach to the least comprehension of His "underlying purpose," the better fitted are we to do the work He assigns us, while waiting patiently for our path of duty to be made clear to us; like the labourer, in Tolstoi's Confession, who completed the work that had been laid out for him, without understanding what the result would be, and unable to judge whether his master had planned well. If the prophecies of Scripture are fulfilled, the twentieth century will usher in the commencement of that age in which men and women will become aware of the great powers which they inherit, and of which Oliphant has said that we are so ignorant that we wholly fail to see them, though they sweep like mighty seas throughout all human nature.

What is the character of these powers which Oliphant has written so eloquently concerning? Can we not form an inference from St. Paul's most precious and deeply scientific context, in which he introduced the quotation from the Greek poet Aratus, who was well known in Athens, having studied there?

If we are the offspring of God, how rich must be our inheritance! If we are the children of God, why do we not trust our Father? But this is not science! A philosopher has said that if ever a human being needed divine pity, it is the man of science who believes in nothing but what he can prove by scientific methods. Scientists will have to admit, in the light of Keely's discoveries, that the sensibility and intelligence, which confer upon us our self-directive power, do not have their origin in our molecular structures. That they take their first beginning in matter is one of the most inadequate conceptions that was ever proposed for scientific belief. If it were so, we could not claim to be the offspring of God, who is the Fountain of all life, the ever living, from whom, as " His very kind," we inherit this self-directive power; not the molecular bodies which are our clothing. God is our Father. The material structure is the mother and nurse. The hypothesis that there are no beings in the universe but those which possess molecular bodies, is the conjecture of a mind that has no conception of the illimitable power of the Almighty. The link, which connects mind with matter, gives us a higher conception of the Deity. Keely places it in the mind flow, the result of the sixth subdivision. When we are done with "the things of Time," and not before, we are ready to rise out of our molecular bondage into the freedom we inherit as heirs of God and co-heirs with Christ of sonship with the Father.

The problem of the origin of life would become a matter of easy analysis, writes Keely, if the properties governing the different orders of matter could be understood in their different evolutions. Disturbance of equilibrium is the prime mover, aggregator and disperser of all forces that exist in nature. The force of the mind on matter is a grand illustration of the power of the finer over the crude, of the etheric over the molecular. If the differential forces of the brain could become equated, eternal perpetuity would be the result. Under such a condition the physical would remain free of disintegration or decomposition. But the law, laid out by the Great Master, which governs the disturbance of equilibrium, making the crude forms of matter subservient to the finer or higher forms, forbidding anything molecular or terrestrial to assimilate with the high etheric, the law that has fixed the planets in their places, is an unknown law to the finite mind, comprehended only by the Infinite One. . . .

Some of our men of science once settled the problem of the origin of life to their own satisfaction, only to learn that "speculation is not science;" for a substance which, when dissolved, crystallizes as gypsum, cannot produce vital force ; and it is like groping among the bones of a graveyard to look for spontaneous generation in a shining heap of jelly on the floor of the sea.

When our learned men are forced to admit that "all motion is thought," that "all nature is the language of One in whom we live, and are moved, and have our being," the attempts to evolve life out of chemical elements will cease ; the Mosaic records will no longer be denied, which tell us that the Creator's law for living organisms is that each plant seeds, and each animal bears, after its kind; not that each seeds and bears after *another* kind. The doctrine of evolution, as made known to us in Geology, is a fundamental truth ; proving that "there has been a plan, glorious in its scheme, perfect in system, progressing through unmeasured ages, and looking ever toward man and a spiritual end."

The Rev. John Andrew, in his "Thoughts on the Evolution Theory of Creation," mentions that Haeckel gives the pedigree of man from primeval moneron in twenty-two stages. Stage twenty is the man-like ape ; stage twenty-one is the ape-like man ; stage twenty-two is the man ; but he confesses that the twenty-first stage—the ape-like man—is entirely wanting in all the records.

There is no missing link in the evolution theory, as laid down in Keely's pure philosophy. Inasmuch as the Father of all is Himself a Spiritual Being, cosmical law leads us to expect that the type of created being, His offspring, shall be spirit also. Nor can Being in any object be so attenuated, or so far removed from Him who filleth all in all, but it must surely retain an aura of His spiritual nature. The corner-stone of this philosophy is one power, one law; order and method reigning throughout creation; spirit controlling matter, as the Divine order and law of creation that the spiritual should govern the material—that the whole realm of matter should be under the dominion of the world of spirit. Nor is this a new truth. According to Diogenes Laërtius, Thales taught that souls are the motive forces of the universe. Empedocles affirms that spiritual forces move the visible world. Virgil asserted that mind animates and moves the world; that the spiritual realm is the soul of the universe. The universe is not a mass of dead matter, says Gilbert (in his work, "De Magnate"), but is pervaded with this soul, this living principle, this unseen cause of all visible phenomena, underlying all movements in the earth beneath and in the heavens above. Joseph Cook affirms that as science progresses it draws nearer in all its forms to the proof of the spiritual origin of force—that is of the Divine immanence in natural law: and that God was not transiently present in nature—that is in a mere creative moment; nor has He left the world in a state of orphanage, bereft of a deific influence and care, but He is immanent in nature, as the Apostle Paul and Aratus and Spinoza declared. As certainly as the unborn infant's life is that of the mother, so is it divinely true that somehow God's life includes ours; and we shall understand the nature of that relationship when, in due time, we have been "born again" into the life of the spirit. "The economy of creation is not regarded in this philosophy as a theory of development all in one direction; but as a cycle in which, after development, and as its fruit, the last term gives again the first. Herein is found the link by which the law of continuity is maintained throughout—the link which is missing in the popular science of the day; with this very serious consequence that, to keep the break out of sight, the entire doctrine of spirit and the spiritual world is ignored or altogether denied." Science admits that nature works with dual force, though at rest she is a unit. "Nature is one eternal circle." Keely's discoveries prove that the doctrine of the Trinity should be set down as an established canon of science—the Trinity of force. All nature's sympathetic streams—cerebellic, gravital, electric and magnetic—are made up of triple currents. The ancients understood this dogma in a far deeper sense than modern theology has construed it. The great and universal Trinity of cause, motion and matter—or of will, thought and manifestation—was known to the Rosicrucians as *prima materia*. Paracelsus states that each of these three is also the other two; for, as nothing can possibly exist without cause, matter and energy—that is, spirit, matter and soul (the ultimate cause of existence being that it exists), we may therefore look upon all forms of activity as being the action of the universal or Divine will operating upon and through the ether, as the skilled artificer uses his tools to accomplish his designs; making the comparison in all reverence.

"The existence of an intelligent Creator, a personal God, can to my mind, almost be proved from chemistry," writes Edison; and George Parsons Lathrop, in commenting upon Edison's belief, says :—" Surely it is a circumstance calculated to excite reflection, and to cause a good deal of satisfaction, that this keen and penetrating mind, so vigorously representing the practical side of American intelligence—the mind of a remarkable exponent of applied science, and of a brilliant and prolific inventor who has spent his life in dealing with the material part of the world—should so confidently arrive at belief in God through a study of those media that often obscure the perception of spiritual things." Edison, it seems, like Keely, has never been discouraged by the obstacles which he meets with, in his researches, nor even inclined to be hopeless of ultimate success.

Unlike Keely, Edison through all his years of experimental research has never once made a discovery. All the work of this great and succesful inventor has been deductive, and the results achieved by him have been simply those of pure invention. Like Keely he constructs a theory, and works on its lines until he finds it untenable; then, he at once discards it and forms another theory. In connection with the electric light, he evolved or constructed *three thousand successive theories;* each one reasonable and apparently likely to be true; yet, only in two cases was he able to prove by experiment that his theories were correct. Of such a nature is the "dead-work" which all researchers on scientific principles must toil through to attain success.

They must keep their minds open to every suggestion or idea, no matter how fanciful it may seem to others, and they must never let go their hold of it until it has been tested in all its possibilities. The same words which Lathrop uses, in describing Edison's characteristics, are equally applicable to Keely, who, in addition to his native endowment of a genius for science and mechanics, brings to bear vast patience in logical deduction, careful calculation, unlimited experiment, a ceaseless industry, and a persistence which refuses to be discouraged.

Edison has said that he does not philosophize. Like General Grant, he is a man of action. When asked what theory he held upon a subject under discussion, General Grant replied, "I never theorize: when there is anything to be done, I do it."[1] Edison is always doing something which the public can see and appreciate, but, unlike Keely, he has no system to work out and transmute into the pure philosophy which is now revealing to the world " the further link in the chain of causation," " the cause of the cause," which hitherto has rather been assumed than demonstrated.

"If we believe," says Professor Sir G. G. Stokes, "that what are called the natural sciences spring from the same supreme source as those which are concerned with morals and Natural Theology in general, we may expect to find broad lines of analogy between the two; and thus it may conceivably happen that the investigations, which belong to natural science, may here and there afford us hints with respect even to the moral sciences, with which at first sight they might appear to have no connection. And if such are to be found, perhaps they are more likely to be indicated by one whose studies have lain mainly in the direction of those natural sciences than by one whose primary attention has been devoted to moral subjects."

Mr. Keely's first discovery of an unknown force and the releasing of an unknown energy seemed to be by accident; and most certainly no one could then have foreseen that his researches in physical science would lead him on step by step, and very slow steps they have been, to such important findings. In the pursuit of physical science he encountered

---

[1] Carried out in the taking of the forts one after another during our civil war, which other generals had been unable to do.

paradoxes and anomalies, the study of which led him on to fresh discoveries whereby he has been able to extend the boundary of ascertained truth and separate the wheat of science from the chaff.

The late Dr. Macvicar said when he considered how difficult he had found it to believe that such insight into nature as his views imply is possible to be attained, he was not so unreasonable as to expect that others would, in his time, regard them even as probable, much less as proved. He expressed himself as content with the private enjoyment which these views imparted to himself, "especially as that enjoyment is not merely the gratification of a chemical curiosity, but attaches to a much larger field of thought." One of the points to which he refers, as possessing great value to his own mind, is the place which his investigation assigns to material nature in the universe of being. He says that it is much the fashion in the present day to regard matter and force, more shortly matter, as all in all. But, according to the view of things which has presented itself to both of these men, "matter comes out rather as a precipitate in the universal ether, determined by a mathematical necessity; a grand and beautiful cloud-work in the realm of light, bounded on both sides by a world of spirits; on the upper and anterior side, by the great Creator Himself, and the hierarchy of spirits to which He awarded immediate existence; and on the lower and posterior side, by that world of spirits of which the material body is the mother and nurse." Macvicar says the hypothesis that there are no beings in the universe but those which possess a molecular structure, and that sensibility and intelligence take their first beginnings in such structures, is one of the most inadequate conceptions that was ever proposed for scientific belief. Science is not only very blind, but glories in her blindness. She gropes among the dead seeking the origin of life, instead of going to the Fountain of all life, the Ever Living, as Dr. Macvicar and Keely have done.

In theorizing on the philosophy of planetary suspension Mr. Keely writes :—As regards planetary volume, we would ask in a scientific point of view—How can the immense difference of volume in the planets exist without disorganizing the harmonious action that has always characterized them? I can only answer this question properly by entering into a progressive synthesis, starting on the rotating etheric centres that were fixed by the Creator with their attractive or accumulative power. If you ask what power it is that gives to each etheric atom its inconceivable velocity of rotation, or introductory impulse, I must answer that no finite mind will ever be able to conceive what it is. The philosophy of accumulation," assimilation, Macvicar calls it, "is the only proof that such a power has been given. The area, if we can so speak of such an atom, presents to the attractive or magnetic, the elective or propulsive, all the receptive force and all the antagonistic force that characterizes a planet of the largest magnitude; consequently, as the accumulation goes on, the perfect equation remains the same. When this minute centre has once been fixed, the power to rend it from its position would necessarily have to be as great as to displace the most immense planet that exists. When this atomic neutral centre is displaced, the planet must go with it. The neutral centre carries the full load of any accumulation from the start, and remains the same, for ever balanced in the eternal space.

Mr. Keely illustrates his idea of "*a neutral centre*" in this way:—We will imagine that, after an accumulation of a planet of any diameter—say, 20,000 miles more or less, for the size has nothing to do with the problem—there should be a displacement of all the material, with the exception of a crust 5000 miles thick, leaving an intervening void between this crust and a centre of the size of an ordinary billiard ball, it would then require a force as great to move this small central mass as it would to move the shell of 5000 miles thickness. Moreover, this small central mass would carry the load of this crust for ever, keeping it equi-distant; and there could be no opposing power, however great, that could bring them together. The imagination staggers in contemplating the immense load which bears upon this point of centre, where weight ceases. This is what we understand by a neutral centre.

Again, Mr. Keely, in explanation of the working of his engine, writes:—In the conception of any machine heretofore constructed, the medium for inducing a neutral centre has never been found. If it had, the difficulties of perpetual-motion seekers would have ended, and this problem would have become an established and operating fact. It would only require an introductory impulse of a few pounds, on such a device, to cause it to run for centuries. In the conception of my vibratory engine, I did not seek to attain perpetual motion; but a circuit is formed that actually has a neutral centre, which is in a condition to be vivified by my vibratory ether, and while under operation, by said substance, is really a machine that is virtually independent of the mass (or globe), and it is the wonderful velocity of the vibratory circuit which makes it so. Still, with all its perfection, it requires to be fed with the vibratory ether to make it an independent motor. . . .

Alluding to his illustration of a neutral centre, Mr. Keely says:—The man who can, even in a simple way, appreciate this vast problem has been endowed by the Creator with one of the greatest gifts which He can bestow upon a mortal. It is well known that all structures require a foundation in strength according to the weight of the mass they have to carry, but the foundations of the universe rest on a vacuous point far more minute than a molecule; in fact, to express this truth properly, on an inter-etheric point, which requires an infinite mind to understand. To look down into the depths of an etheric centre is precisely the same as it would be to search into the broad space of heaven's ether to find the end; with this difference, that one is the positive field, while the other is the negative field. . . .

Again, Mr. Keely gives some suggestive thoughts as follows:—In seeking to solve the great problems which have baffled me, from time to time, in my progressive researches, I have often been struck by the fact that I have, to all seeming, accidentally tripped over their solution. The mind of man is not infinite, and it requires an infinite brain to evolve infinite positions. My highest power of concentration failed to attain the results which, at last, seeming accident revealed. God moves in a mysterious way His wonders to perform; and if He has chosen me as the tool to carve out certain positions, what credit have I? None; and, though it is an exalting thought that He has singled me out for a specific work, I know that the finest tool is of no value without a manipulator. It is the artist who handles it that makes it what it is. Indifference to the marvels which surround us is a deep reproach. If we have neither leisure nor inclination to strive to unravel some of the mysteries of nature, which task to the utmost the highest order of human intelligence, we can at least exercise and improve our intellectual faculties by making ourselves acquainted with the operation of agencies already revealed to man; learning, by the experience of the past, to be tolerant of all truth; remembering that one of Nature's agencies, known once as of use only in awakening men's minds to an awful sense of the Creator's power, has now become a patient slave of man's will, rushing upon his errands with the speed of light around the inhabited globe. . . .

In comparing the tenuity of the atmosphere with that of the etheric flows, obtained by Mr. Keely from his invention for dissociating the molecules of air by vibration, he says, It is as platina to hydrogen gas. Molecular separation of air brings us to the first subdivision only; inter-molecular, to the second; atomic, to the third; inter-atomic, to the fourth; etheric, to the fifth; and inter-etheric, to the sixth subdivision, or positive association with luminiferous ether. In my introductory argument I have contended that this is the vibratory envelope of all atoms. In my definition of atom I do not confine myself to the sixth subdivision, where this luminiferous ether is developed in its crude form, as far as my researches prove. I think this idea will be pronounced, by the physicists of the present day, a wild freak of the imagination. Possibly, in time, a light may fall upon this theory that will bring its simplicity forward for scientific research. At present I can only compare it to some planet in a dark space, where the light of the sun of science has not yet reached it. . . .

I assume that sound, like odour, is a real substance of unknown and wonderful tenuity, emanating from a body where it has been induced by percussion, and throwing out absolute corpuscles of matter—inter-atomic particles—with a velocity of 1120 feet per second, in vacuo 20,000. The substance which is thus disseminated is a part and parcel of the mass agitated, and if kept under this agitation continuously would, in the course of a certain cycle of time, become thoroughly absorbed by the atmosphere; or, more truly, would pass through the atmosphere to an elevated point of tenuity corresponding to the condition of subdivision that governs its liberation from its parent body. The sounds from vibratory forks, set so as to produce etheric chords, while disseminating their compound tones permeate most thoroughly all substances that come under the range of their atomic bombardment. The clapping of a bell in vacuo liberates these atoms with the same velocity and volume as one in the open air; and were the agitation of the bell kept up continuously for a few millions of centuries, it would thoroughly return to its primitive element. If the chamber were hermetically sealed, and strong enough, the vacuous volume surrounding the bell would be brought to a pressure of many thousands of pounds to the square inch, by the tenuous substance evolved. In my estimation, *sound truly defined is the disturbance of atomic equilibrium, rupturing actual atomic corpuscles; and the substance thus liberated must certainly be a certain order of etheric flow.* Under these conditions is it unreasonable to suppose that, if this flow were kept up, and the body thus robbed of its element, it would in time disappear entirely? All bodies are formed primitively from this high tenuous ether, animal, vegetable and mineral, and they only return to their high gaseous condition when brought under a state of differential equilibrium.

As regards odour, continues Mr. Keely, we can only get some definite idea of its extreme and wondrous tenuity by taking into consideration that a large area of atmosphere can be impregnated for a long series of years from a single grain of musk; which, if weighed after that long interval, will be found to be not appreciably diminished. The great paradox attending the flow of odorous particles is that they can be held under confinement in a glass vessel! Here is a substance of much higher tenuity than the glass that holds it, and yet it cannot escape. It is as a sieve with its meshes large enough to pass marbles, and yet holding fine sand which cannot pass through; in fact, a molecular vessel holding an atomic substance. This is a problem that would confound those who stop to recognize it. But infinitely tenuous as odour is, it holds a very crude relation to the substance of subdivision that governs a magnetic flow (a flow of sympathy, if you please to call it so). This subdivision comes next to sound, but is above sound. The action of the flow of a magnet coincides somewhat to the receiving and distributing portion of the human brain, giving off at all times a depreciating ratio of the amount received. It is a grand illustration of the control of mind over matter, which gradually depreciates the physical till dissolution takes place. The magnet on the same ratio gradually loses its power and becomes inert. If the relations that exist between mind and matter could be equated, and so held, we would live on in our physical state eternally, as there would be no physical depreciation. But this physical depreciation leads, at its terminus, to the source of a much higher development—viz., the liberation of the pure ether from the crude molecular; which in my estimation is to be much desired. Thus God moves in a simple way His wonders to perform. . . ."

When my theoretical *exposé* is finished and brought out, I shall be ready for the attacks that will be made upon it, and able to demonstrate what I assert. One would think that modern physicists, knowing the lesson taught by the disastrous overthrow of the primitive system of astronomy, would be somewhat cautious in reference to jeering at any announcement of scientific research, however preposterous, without first carefully weighing its claims. It is my belief that there are many to-day who occupy positions as professors in our colleges and in universities abroad, who for bigotry and ignorance can discount the opinion of the religionists of the dark ages; but those to whom has been given mental force to boldly investigate new truths in science may congratulate themselves upon the fact that there are investigators of truth who are not afraid to acknowledge its claims, in whatever garb it may appear, welcoming whatever new message it may have to deliver. . . .

Professor Rücker, in closing his address read at the meeting of the British Association in 1891, said :—

"In studies such as these we are passing from the investigation of the properties of ordinary matter to those of the ether, which may perhaps be the material of which matter is composed. We may some day be able to control and use it, as we now control and use steam."

For nearly fifteen years, Keely constructed engines of various models, with this end in view, before he discovered that it is impossible to use the ether in any other way than as a medium for the energy that he is now experimenting with; and which he defines, in its present operation, as a condition of sympathetic vibration associated with the polar stream positively and negatively.

Should Keely succeed in controlling and directing this subtle energy, we shall then be able to "hook our machinery on to the machinery of nature." A writer in the *Nineteenth Century* says,—" Whether the molecules or particles of what we know as matter are independent matter, or whether they are ether-whirlpools; we know that they keep up an incessant hammering one on another, and thus on everything in space. Professor Crookes has shown that the forces contained in this bombardment are immensely greater than any forces we have yet handled. . . . It has also been found that the vibrations keep time in some unknown way with the vibrations of solid matter."

Thus it is seen that Keely is not the only man of science who is trying to effect a passage over the untrodden wild lying between acoustics and music : " that Siberian bog where whole armies of scientific musicians and musical men of science have sunk, without filling it up." Helmholtz, it is said, has, by a series of daring strides, made a passage for himself; while Keely stands alone in seeking to build a solid causeway ; over which all the nations of the earth may pass in safety, to the " new order of things," that lies in this " land of promise."

CHAPTER XIV.

VIBRATORY PHYSICS.—THE CONNECTING LINK BETWEEN MIND AND MATTER.

The elements of Nature are made of the will of God.—*Hermes Trismegistus.*

Newton and Faraday have indicated how force instead of leaping over nothing, acting at a distance, is transmitted consecutively through the ethereal substance.

We must become as little children, not presuming to think of causes efficient, or causes final; for these are things we cannot grasp; but reverently and patiently waiting until, like a revelation, the hidden link between the familiar and the unfamiliar flashes into our mind, and thus an additional step is gained in the endless series of successive generalizations.—The REV. H. W. WATSON, F.R.S., President of the Birmingham Philosophical Society.

All truth comes by inspiration.—*Scripture.*

There is but one Deity, the Supreme Spirit: he is of the same nature as the soul of man.—*Vedic Theology.*

As for truth it endureth and is always strong, it liveth and conquereth for evermore.—*Esdras.*

Everything happens according to the will of God and has its appointed time, which can neither be hastened nor avoided.—*Mohammed.*

IN the paper of the Rev. H. W. Watson, on "The Progress of Science, its Conditions and Limitations," he tells us that every thinking man recognizes the subjective Self and the objective non-Self, and that this non-Self, so far as it manifests its existence through the senses, is the object of investigation of natural philosophers; but he admits that their investigations have not bestowed upon modern science any results to justify the language of causation. Universal gravitation is declared to be a vast generalization, telling us that there is no more, but yet just as much, of mystery in the whole sequence of astronomical phenomena, as in the most humdrum processes of every-day experiences. The unfamiliar has been explained by the familiar, and both remain in their original mystery. The mystery, attendant upon gravitation, Kepler prophesied would be revealed to man in this age: and the cautious and inductive investigations which Keely has been pursuing, since 1888, have enabled him to demonstrate that the unknown force, which for fifteen years had baffled all his skill, is the same condition of sympathetic vibration which controls nature's highest and most general operations:—the identical force which Faraday divined when he wrote, in 1836: "*Thus, either present elements are the true elements, or else there is the probability before us of obtaining some more high and general power of nature even than electricity, and which at the same time might reveal to us an entirely new grade of the elements of matter, now hidden from our view and almost from our suspicion.*"

It was good advice given by the late Professor Clifford,—"Before teaching any doctrine wait until the nature of the evidence can be understood." But without attempting to teach Keely's system of vibratory physics, we may look into some of his views, notwithstanding the fact that, whatever truths there may be in them, they are approached from such a different standpoint, than that of the platform of mechanical physics, that it is utterly impossible to bring them into any definite relations with each other.[1] Dr. Gérard, of Paris, in

---

[1] The paper which Mr. J. F. Nisbet was commissioned to write, in behalf of this discoverer's claims on the world for patience, while pursuing his researches (and paid in advance for writing), illustrates the truth of this assertion. Mr. Nisbet's essay, entitled "The Present Aspect of the Molecular Theory, or Mr. Keely's Relations to Modern Science," closes with these lines:—"If science looks askance at Mr. Keely's professions, therefore, it has its reasons for doing so. These reasons, as I have shown, are not mere prejudices. In more than one line of inquiry they have, what seems to be, a substantial basis of fact, which must be explained away before Mr. Keely's theory of 'etheric force' can commend itself to the mind of the impartial observer."

Fortunately, for the interests of science and of humanity, the threatened prosecution of Mr. Keely (for obtaining money under false

his work on "Nervous Force," writes of this founder of a new system of philosophy: "The force discovered by Keely appears to me to be so entirely the counterpart of what passes primarily in the brain cells that we see in him but a plagiarist of cerebral dynamics—that is, he has had but to copy the delicate human mechanism to make a wonderful discovery; probably, the greatest the world has ever known. The word plagiarist has no deprecatory meaning as applied to the great American inventor, for he must possess an extraordinary power of assimilation to read so fluently the open book of nature, and to be able wisely to interpret her admirable laws: it is, therefore, with profound admiration that I here render homage to this man of science."

Dr. Gérard's work treats of the production of electricity in the nerve centres, and its accumulation in storage. He says that fifty years ago it would have been difficult to explain this fact intelligently; but thanks to the scientific progress of the period, everyone now knows how electricity is produced, and how applied, to use in lighting our houses. He continues: "Let us say, then, in few words, how matters stand, for it will serve to illustrate how it is with our brain, the mechanism of which is precisely the same—only that our apparatus is much more perfect and much less costly.

"A dynamo-electric machine is placed at any given spot; its object, being put in action, is to withdraw from the earth its neutral electricity, to decompose it into its two conditions and to collect, upon accumulators, the electricity thus separated. As soon as the accumulators are charged, the electricity is disposable; that is, our lamps can be lighted. But what is marvellous in all this is that the forces of nature can be transformed at will. Should we not wish for light, we

pretences) was checkmated by Provost Pepper's action, early in January, before Mr. Nisbet wrote to America that he could not commence his paper until he had received more information; sending a series of questions to be answered by Mr. Keely. The superficial character of the essay will be seen, when printed, as well as that Mr. Nisbet promised more than he was able to perform when he accepted the cheque in order to enable him to devote time to the writing of a paper, for an influential quarter, which it was hoped would enlist public sympathy in Keely's behalf. But that power which is mightier than the sword, in putting down error and injustice, has hitherto turned its weapons against Keely (with some rare exceptions) as Mr. Nisbet did in his essay.—C.J.M.

turn a knob and we have sound, heat, motion, chemical action, magnetism. Little seems wanting to create intelligence, so entirely do these accumulated forces lend themselves to all the transformations which their engineer may imagine and desire. But let us consider how greatly superior is our cerebral mechanism to all invented mechanism. In order to light a theatre we require a wide space, a dynamo-electric machine of many horse-power, accumulators filling many receptacles, a considerable expense in fuel, and clever mechanicians. In the human organism these engines are in miniature, one décimètre cube is all the space occupied by our brain; no wheels, no pistons, nothing to drive the apparatus, we suffice ourselves. In this sense, each of us can say, like the philosopher Biaz:—*Omnia mecum porto*. Our cerebral organ not only originates motion, heat, sound, light, chemical actions, magnetism; but it produces psychic forces, such as will, reasoning, judgment, hatred, love, and the whole series of intellectual faculties. They are all derived from the same source, and are always identical to each other, so long as the cerebral apparatus remains intact. The variations of our health alone are capable of causing a variation in the intensity and quality of our productions.

"With a maximum of physical and moral health, we produce a maximum of physical and moral results. Our manual labour and our intellectual productions are always exactly proportionate to the integrity of our mechanism."

Dr. Gérard has, it will be seen, grasped the same truth that Buckle enunciated in his lecture, The Influence of Women on the Progress of Knowledge, when he affirmed that not one single discovery that had ever been made has been connected with the laws of the mind that made it: declaring that until this connection is ascertained our knowledge has no sure basis, as "the laws of nature have their sole seat, origin, and function in the human mind." This is the foundation stone of vibratory physics, that all force is mind force.

All the forces of nature, writes Keely, proceed from the one governing force; the source of all life, of all energy. These sympathetic flows, or streams of force, each consists of three currents, harmonic, enharmonic, and dominant; this classification governing all orders of positive and negative radiation. The sympathetic flow called "Animal Magnetism" is the transmissive link of sympathy in the fourth, or inter-atomic, subdivision of matter. It is the most intricate of problems to treat philosophically; isolated as it is from all approach by any of the prescribed rules in "the orthodox scheme of physics." It turns upon the interchangeable sub-division of inter-atomic acting agency, or the force of the mind. The action of this etheric flow, in substances of all kinds, is according to the character of the molecular interferences which exist in the volume of their atomic groupings. These interferences proceed from some description of atomic chemical nature, which tend to vary the uniformity of structure in the atomic triplets of each molecule. If these groupings were absolutely uniform there would be but one substance in nature, and all beings inhabiting this globe would be simul-taneously impressed with the same feelings and actuated by the same desires; but nature has produced unlimited variety. Science, as yet, has not made so much as an introductory attempt to solve this problem of "the mind flow," but has left it with the hosts of impostors, who always beset any field that trenches on the land of marvel.

Professor Olive Lodge, in his address before the British Association, at Cardiff, said: "Let me try to state what this field is, the exploration of which is regarded as so dangerous. I might call it the borderland of physics and psychology. I might call it the connection between life and energy; or the connection between mind and matter. It is an intermediate region, bounded on the north by psychology, on the south by physics, on the east by physiology, and on the west by pathology and medicine. An occasional psychologist has groped down into it and become a metaphysician. An occasional physicist has wandered up into it and lost his base, to the horror of his quondam brethren. Biologists mostly look at it askance, or deny its existence. A few medical practitioners, after long maintenance of a similar attitude, have begun to annex a portion of its western frontier. . . . Why not leave it to the metaphysicians? I say it has been left to them long enough. They have explored it with insufficient equipment. Their methods are not our methods; they are unsatisfactory to us, as physicists. We prefer to creep slowly from our base of physical knowledge; to engineer carefully as we go, establishing forts, constructing roads, and thoroughly exploring the country, making a progress very slow but very lasting. The psychologists from their side may meet us. I hope they will: but one or the other of us ought to begin. . . ."

In America, we have Buchanan and many others investigating in this field; and Dr. Bowne, the orthodox Dean of the Boston University, in his answer to Herbert Spencer, answering the question, "What is Force?" tells us: "Not gravitation, nor electricity, nor magnetism, nor chemical affinity, but will, is the typical idea of force. Self-determination, volition is the essence of the only causation we know. Will is the sum-total of the dynamic idea: it either stands for that or nothing. Now science professes itself unable to interpret nature without this metaphysical idea of power. The experiments made by Professor Barker and others, which are said to establish the identity of heat and mental force, really prove only a correlation between heat and the nervous action which attends thinking. Nervous action and heat correlate, but the real point is to prove that nervous action and mental force correlate. This has never been done."

"The concept of will," says Arthur Schopenhauer, "has hitherto commonly been subordinated to that of force; but I reverse the matter entirely, and desire that every force in nature be thought of as will. It must not be supposed that this is mere verbal quibbling and of no consequence: rather it is of the greatest significance and importance."

Thus it will be seen that the field which Professor Lodge, with rare courage, invited his fellow-physicists to enter and bring with them their appropriate methods of investigation (unless these philosophers are astray) may prove to be "the immense and untrodden field" which Buckle said must be conquered before Science can arrogate to herself any knowledge of nature's laws that is not purely empirical. A little reflection will enable the average mind to see in the signs of the times a tendency to movements on a grander scale, such as are involved in the higher view which Keely is himself now taking since his researches have extended beyond the order he was pursuing when he was thinking only of mechanical success.

Man's progress has been so enormous that nothing too extravagant can be imagined for the future, when once psychical investigation is conducted as proposed by Professor Lodge; who is trying to unravel the mystery as to what force is, and by what means exerted. There is something here not definitely provided for in the orthodox scheme of physics; but Keely's themes explain this mystery. "Luminiferous ether," he writes, "or celestial mind force, a compound inter-etheric element, is the substance of which everything visible is composed. It is the great sympathetic protoplastic element; life itself. Consequently, our physical organisms are composed of this element. This focalizing, or controlling media, of the physical, has its seat in the cerebral convolutions; from which sympathetic radiation emanates. This sympathetic outreach is mind flow proper, or will force; sympathetic polarization to produce action; sympathetic depolarization to neutralize it. Polar and depolar differentiation, resulting in motion. The true protoplastic element sympathetically permeates all forms and conditions of matter; having, for its attendants, gravity, electricity, and magnetism; the triple conditions born in itself. In fact, it is the soul of matter; the element from which all forms of motion receive their introductory impulse."

Not long since, Mr. Keely was congratulated upon having secured the attention of men of science, connected with the University of Pennsylvania, to his work of research. Now, you will be known as a great discoverer, not as Keely the motor-man, said one of the professors present. Keely answered, I have discovered so little, in comparison with what remains to be discovered, that I cannot call myself a discoverer. Another of the professors present took Keely by the hand and said, *You are a great discoverer.*

Had the discoverer of this unknown force not been dependent upon a company, "a ring," for funds to pursue his investigations, scientists would have better understood the nature of this work at an earlier stage of his experimental research ; but following close upon Keely's production of the latent force carried in all forms of aggregated matter, he became entangled in the meshes of an organization that cared nothing for science, and a great deal for the wealth which, it was seen by practical business men, must sooner or later accrue as the result of a costless motive power. In other words, those who interested themselves in Keely's discoveries were interested solely in their marketable value ; or if there chanced to be one who was not so interested, that one was not of sufficient influence in the scientific world to be able to induce capitalists to come forward and contribute towards saving the discovery to this age, by protecting the discoverer from the persecution that he was subjected to from those who had the management of the commercial affairs of the company.

Aratus, the poet of Cilicia, the author of " Phenomena," wrote, " We are the offspring of God ; " and St. Paul, quoting Aratus, continued, " In Him we live and move and have our being." From that hour, down the blood-stained path of the age to the present, there have been men, spiritually endowed, who have taught that He who created, commands and governs, the universe, sustains it by the power of His will ; and that were it not for the celestial streams of radiation, this superhuman influence, constantly flowing into all created forms, the universe would pass out of existence, would perish in a moment. So well did Macvicar, the great Scotch divine, understand this conception of Deity, that he wrote, " The nearer we ascend to the fountain-head of being and of action the more magical must everything inevitably become ; for that fountain-head is pure volition. And pure volition as a cause is precisely what is meant by magic ; for by magic is merely meant a mode of producing a phenomenon without mechanical appliances—that is, *without that seeming continuity of resisting parts and that leverage which satisfy our muscular sense* and our imagination, and bring the phenomenon into the category of what we call 'the natural ;' that is, the sphere of the elastic, the gravitating ; the sphere into which the ' *vis inertiæ* ' is alone admitted."

We call this the sphere of the natural; but, when we come to higher workings of natural laws, with which we are not familiar, we designate them as "supernatural;" and scientists witnessing some of Keely's experiments, like those of overcoming gravity, of rotation of the needle of a compass,[1] of the disintegration of water, etc., and not believing in any workings of laws unknown to them, followed in the footsteps, still unobliterated, of the narrow-minded, bigoted persecutors of Galileo; and have denounced Keely as "a modern Cagliostro." When men of more extended research have been on the eve of investigating for themselves they have, until 1889, been deterred from doing so by the representations made to them that Keely was "using compressed air to humbug his audiences." Until Professor Leidy and Dr. Willcox gave their attention to Mr. Keely's claims as the discoverer of a new form of energy, the way was not open for Mr. Keely to disclose his conjectures, his hypotheses and his theories. Regrettable as this fact has seemed to be, it is now seen that any previous revelation of his discovery, other than to scientists, might have been premature; so little did Keely himself know, until within two years, of the developments he has at last reached in his work of evolution. The time was not ripe for the disclosure.

It is a canon of science that molecular aggregation generally *involves dissipation of energy*. On the contrary, for more than fifteen years Keely has demonstrated that *all molecular aggregation is attended with an absorption of energy*; relieving by vibratory power the latent force held in a few drops of water and showing thereby a pressure of from ten to fifteen tons per square inch; claiming that resultant development of any force and of all forces is only accomplished by conditions that awaken the latent energy carried during molecular aggregation. It is conceded by those most conversant with the nature of Keely's discoveries that he must either create force, or *liberate latent energy*. As Omnipotence alone creates, it follows that science must be wrong in two of her most

---

[1] This is effected by polarization and depolarization, and the rotation of a non-magnetic needle by molecular differentiation: both needles revolving about 120 times in a second.

fundamental laws; one relating to the indivisibility of the atom; the other to the dissipation of energy in molecular aggregation. This, Keely establishes in the one experiment of disintegration of water, releasing from three drops the latent energy carried, during and from the time of molecular aggregation, and showing a pressure of fifteen tons to the square inch. Therefore, it is not "a waste of time and thought" to give attention to Keely's theories, and to investigate from the standpoint of vibratory physics, instead of setting limits to the operations of Nature and the power of the Almighty from the narrow platform of mechanical physics?

KEELY'S THEORIES.

The action of Nature's sympathetic flows, writes Keely, regulates the differential oscillatory range of motion of the planetary masses as regards their approach toward and recession from each other. These flows may also be compared to the flow of the magnet which permeates the field, existing between the molecules themselves, sensitizing the combined neutral centres of the molecules without disturbing, in the least, the visible molecular mass itself. In the planetary masses—balanced as it were in the scales of universal space, like soap-bubbles floating in a field of atmospheric air—the concentration of these sympathetic streams evolves the universal power which moves them in their oscillating range of motion to and from each other. This sympathetic triple stream focalizes and defocalizes on the neutrals of all such masses; polarizing and depolarizing, positive and negative action, planetary rotation, etc., etc. It is thus that all the conditions governing light, heat, life, vegetation, motion, are all derived from the velocity of the positive and negative interchange of celestial sympathy with the terrestrial.

Every harmonious condition of Nature's evolutions is governed by one incontrovertible law; that of concordant assimilative harmony. This concordant key is the ruling one over all the antagonistic, negative, discordant ones; the one that diverts the disturbance of sympathetic equilibrium to one general concentrative centre for redistribution. Harmony concentrates, harmony distributes. The focalizing point of concordant sympathetic concentration is the percussive electric field, where the velocity of its sympathetic streams rebounds with a power that throws them far out into universal space; and so far beyond their equative centre of equilibrium as to bring them in sympathy with the universal attraction of the combined neutral centres of all planetary masses.

Sympathetic Streams which Control the Action and Reaction of all Visible Forms of Matter.

What is light and heat, and how are they evolved? and why are they so intensely perceptible as emanating from the solar world?

Light and heat, considered theoretically, belong to the highest orders of the phenomenal. They can only be accounted for by the velocity of sympathetic streams, as interchangeable to and from centres of negative and attractive focalization. In considering the velocity of vibration, as associated with the projection of a ray of light, to be at least one hundred thousand billions per second, it is easy to account for the origin and demonstration of these two elements by the action of celestial sympathetic streams.

1st. *Light and heat are not evolved until the force of the vibratory sympathetic stream, from the neutral centre of the sun, comes into atomic percussive action against the molecular atmosphere or envelope of our planet.* The visibility of the planets can only be accounted for in this way, some in a great degree, some in less. Innumerable thousands, it may be, remain invisible to us by not having the conditions surrounding them, and associated with them, which favour the atomic and molecular antagonistic friction necessary to make them visible. The velocity of a steel ball passing through the atmospheric envelope, at a speed of thousands of billions times less than an etheric sympathetic stream, would be dissipated into vapour in an indefinite period of a second of time. Light and heat, in a certain sense, are one and the same; light giving heat, and heat giving light. The whole mystery, as associated with their evolution, is explained by the bombardment of the sympathetic etheric stream on the dense portion of the molecular, in seeking the sympathetic, concordant, neutral centre of the planetary mass that surrounds the point of focalization.

The positive and negative interchange of this true sympathetic stream keeps intact the magnetic force of the polar envelope of the earth; making it, as it were, a great magnet of itself. The fact of this magnetic force being universally present, on and in our planet, proves the immeasurable speed and power of etheric sympathetic interchange. Thus it is that, from the velocity of these sympathetic rays, the earth's standard of heat and light is evolved and kept in balance. This interchange of sympathetic radiation, between the solar world and its system of planets, equates the sympathetic volume by the reception of the full amount expended on sympathetic distribution; thus showing the never-ending restoration of equilibrium by the same medium that disturbs it during intermittent sympathetic action. There are very many facts in vibratory physics which prove that the volume of heat, supposed by many to emanate from the sun, if concentrated upon a centre of the volume represented by the sun, would give enough focal force, if projected upon the system of planets that is under its control, to vaporize them in one month's time. A ray of heat one billion times greater than the whole volume of the sun represents could not pass through the dark vacuous boundaries which lie between us and the sun without being neutralized and absorbed.

What is Electricity?

Electricity is the result of three differentiated sympathetic flows, combining the celestial and terrestrial flows by an order of assimilation negatively attractive in its character. It is one of Nature's efforts to restore attractive differentiation. In analyzing this triple union in its vibratory philosophy, I find the highest order of perfection in this assimilative action of Nature. The whole condition is atomic, and is the introductory one which has an affinity for terrestrial centres, uniting magnetically with the Polar stream; in other words, uniting with the Polar stream by neutral affinity. The magnetic or electric forces of the earth are thus kept in stable equilibrium by this triune force, and the chords of this force may be expressed as 1st, the dominant, 2nd, the harmonic, and 3rd, the enharmonic. The value of each is, one to the other, in the rates of figures, true thirds. E flat—transmissive chord or dominant; A flat—harmonic; A double flat—enharmonic. The unition of the two prime thirds is so rapid, when the negative and the positive conditions reach a certain range of vibratory motion, as to be compared to an explosion. During this action the positive electric stream is liberated and immediately seeks its neutral terrestrial centre, or centre of highest attraction.

The power of attractive vibration of the solar forces is the great coincident towards which the terrestrial-magnetic-sympathetic flow is diverted. This force is the celestial current that makes up the prime third of the triple association. It also induces aqueous disintegration and thermal concentration, the two prime conductors towards this coincident chord of sympathy with itself. Without this aqueous disintegration there would be no connective link between the celestial and terrestrial. There would exist nothing but a condition of luminous radiation on the order of the aurora—a reaching out for the concordant without any sympathetic diversion to create unstable equilibrium of terrestrial magnetism. In fact, under such a condition, the absence of the sun on one side, or the absence of water on the other, the magnetic or electric force would remain in a stable state of equilibrium, or the highest order of the chaotic. Disturbance of equilibrium and sympathetic equation constitute the dual power that governs all the varied forms of life and motion which exist terrestrially, of which the electric or magnetic is the prime mover and regulator. All electrical action, no matter of what character, has its sympathetic birth by the intervention of that current of the triune flow, which I call the dominant, with the Polar harmonic current; all sympathetic flows being composed of three currents. They become associative one with the other only near the junction of terrestrial interference. The great vacuous field which exists between the planetary ranges holds this portion of the etheric flow free of all antagonism, molecularly or otherwise, till the associative point is reached; so wonderfully planned by the Great Creator, for instant electric evolution and assimilation with terrestrial centres of attraction. I call this intervention, atomic-inter-molecular and molecular density. The combination of the action of the triune sympathetic-celestial stream with the same intervening medium induces heat and light, as the resultant of these corpuscular conflictions with sympathetic celestial and terrestrial focalized centres of neutral radiation. I do not recognize electricity, nor light, nor heat as coming from the sun. These conditions, according to my theories, emanate from atomic and interatomic interference on induced molecular vibration, by sympathetic etheric vibration, the celestial-attractive being the prime mover. In my estimation this is not at all phenomenal; it is only phenomenal as far as the knowledge of its action in mechanical physics is concerned. Physicists have been working in the wrong direction to lead them to associate themselves with Nature's sympathetic evolutions.[1] The expression " Electricity attracts at a distance " is as bad as, if not worse than, the " microbe of the magnet." Clerk Maxwell seems, when theorizing on sound transmission by an atmospheric medium, not to have taken into consideration the philosophy attending the phenomena of the origination of electric streams in celestial space. Light is one of the prominent evolved mediums in electric action, and is evolved by corpuscular bombardment induced by sympathetic streams acting between the neutral centres of planetary masses, all of which are under a condition of unstable equilibrium. These unstable conditions were born in them, and were thus designed

---

[1] Electricians are now admitting that, in electric currents the energy does not flow through, or along the wire, itself; but is actually transmitted by the ether vibrations outside of the wire, just as in Keely's experiments, running his musical sphere with a fine "thread" of silk, the energy is not transmitted through the sewing-silk, which acts only as the medium that makes the transfer of energy in this way possible; though not itself transferring it.

by the Architect of Creation in order to perpetuate the connective link between the dispersing positive and the attractive negative. The action that induces this link I call sympathetic planetary oscillation.

Attraction, Propulsion, &c.

The action of the magnetic flow is dual in its evolution, both attractive and propulsive. The inclination of the plane on which the subtle stream moves, either to the right or to the left, has nothing to do with positive or negative conditions. The difference in conditions of what is called, by electricians, positive and negative electricity, is the difference between receptive and propulsive vibrations. They can be right or left receptive, or right or left propulsive. The positive vibrations are the radiating; the negative vibrations are the ones that are attracted toward the neutral centre.

The negative-sympathetic polar stream is the magnetic flow proper, and it is in sympathetic coincidence with the second atomic flow; the electric current is the first and second order of atomic vibration, a dual force, the flow of which is too tenuous to displace the molecules. It can no more do so than the flow from a magnet can displace the molecules of a glass plate when it is passed under it. The flow from a magnet is too fine to disturb the plate molecules, but passes as freely between them as a current of air would through a coarse sieve.

Like poles do not repel each other, simply because there is a perfect sympathetic equation between them; the same in unlike poles. If a differentiation of $33\frac{1}{3}$ against 100 is established between them, whether like or unlike, they become attractive to each other. They become repellent after differentiating them, $66\frac{2}{3}$ of the one against 100 of the other, by sympathetic vibration.

Taking into consideration even the introductory conditions of the etheric stage, etheric vibration has proved to me that the higher the velocity of its rotating stream the greater is its tendency towards the neutral centre or centre of sympathetic

Vibratory Physics. 221

coincidence. Were it otherwise, how could there ever be any planetary formations or the building up of visible structures? If a billiard ball were rotated to a certain velocity, it would separate in pieces, and the pieces would fly off in a tangent; but if it were a ball of ether, the higher the velocity of rotation the stronger would be the tendency ·of its corpuscules to seek its centre of neutrality, and to hold together.

It is not a magnetic force that is borne on the etheric atom which gives it its power to draw to it streams of coincidence. The magnet is only susceptive to certain aggregated forms of matter; iron, for instance, and its preparations.

All moving bodies of visible matter produce heat as according to their velocity. The flow of gases only induces thermal reduction from molecular friction. By this term it must not be understood that the molecules actually come in contact, and rub against each other. There is no pressure, however great, that can cause molecular contact. The area of the volume of the molecule can be reduced by enormous pressure, and the tension thus brought to bear on their rotating envelopes induces heat. The heat thus induced is a positive proof of the wonderful velocity of the etheric envelope. If the molecules were dead—which is an infinite impossibility—to sympathetic vibration, and without a rotatory envelope if all the pressure possible to conceive were brought to bear upon them, it would not induce the slightest thermal change.

Energy.

Energy is a sympathetic condition inherent in all forms of aggregated matter, visible and invisible. It is ever present, in its latent condition, and is aroused by the sympathetic disturbers of its equilibrium. By this conservation it becomes transferable. The sympathetic correlation of will-force in the cerebral convolutionary centres transfers its energy to the physical organism.

Bring a steel rod in contact with a magnet, and the latent energy in the rod is brought into action without its becoming impregnated by its magnetic exciter. Energy is an infinite latent force. If it did not exist it could not be generated. Consequently, there would be no energy to lose nor to conserve. The volume of latent energy in the etheric domain never increases nor ever grows less. It will remain the same, as yesterday to-day and for ever.

INAUDIBLE VIBRATIONS.

Nature has established her sympathetic concordants from the birth of the neutral centres of the planets. This is gravity; therefore gravity is fixed, inherent. There is no flight of gravity. The difference in the condition of the sympathetic nerve centres, and the variations in the chord aggregation of the masses, as established in the man or woman at birth, constitutes the molecular condition of the individual. The molecular state of animals, vegetables, and minerals, depends upon the aggregation of their chord centres. It is impossible to make two coins from one die the same in its molecular aggregation. The mere picking up of a coin and replacing it causes billions of molecules to be lost. This produces a change in the chord of mass of the coin. As this fact has only been developed by persistent progressive research, it is quite easy to comprehend the nature of the difficulties that lie in the way of perfecting devices for the guidance of artificers and mechanics, whereby they can bring a proper vibratory action into play to induce positive sympathetic transmission. In order to transmit my knowledge by demonstration it will be necessary to have much more perfect instruments than those crude devices which I first constructed for my researches. One of my perfected instruments shows to the eye, in the molecular effects produced by a certain order of vibration, when the chord of harmony is established between two neutral centres. Another, when connected with the sympathizer, denotes accurately, by the colour of a certain sound or combination of sounds the number of vibrations that are necessary to induce certain effects of mechanical combinations.

Inaudible vibrations are tested by the magnetic needle

and sound colours. Every gaseous molecule is a resonator of itself and is sensitive to any and all sounds induced, whether accordant or discordant. At the normal density of the atmosphere we hear a volume of sound, focalized by the combined association of every molecule brought under sound influence. When we reduce the atmospheric volume of a chamber to 50/100, then the ear is sensitive to the reduction of the acoustic force evolved on the same ratio, and so on, until sound becomes inaudible. This inaudibility to our organ of hearing is no proof whatever of any reduction of the acoustic force evolved on the introductory impulse given to the bell. It is only a proof that the number of the molecules left for the acoustic force to act upon has been so reduced by increasing the vacuum, that the concentration of sound from the diminished number cannot be heard. The ear is not susceptible to the acoustic force emanating from one molecule, nor even from the concentration of one hundred millions of billions of molecules. The highest vacuum that can be induced, taking but a cubic inch in volume to act upon, will leave a residual number of molecules one hundred billion times as great as the above given number, and yet be perfectly inaudible when all their acoustic forces are focalized.

The audible has been conquered in my instruments to that extent which brings me into sympathetic contact with the inaudible, the vitalized conditions of which as regards sympathetic union with the terrestrial are the pure and only essentials necessary towards establishing the sensitive link, between the instrument and terrestrial chord-masses, in order to run sympathetic machinery. But there is still before me a vast region to be explored before the keystone of this sympathetic arch is set in position to carry the high order of sympathetic transfer that I aim at. I have every reason to hope that when I have mastered these mechanical difficulties I shall be able to control this most subtle of Nature's forces. When this is done, the commercial engine will soon follow. There is no truer nor quicker way to reach that end than the one I am now pursuing. My obligations on this line once fulfilled, I shall be at liberty to turn my attention to the consideration of the mental forces associated with the physical, and in fact the solution of the mechanical problem is one and the same in principle, as is the physical and mental. When one is solved all is solved. The convolutions which exist in the cerebral field are entirely governed by the sympathetic conditions that surround them.

"The force which binds the atoms, which controls secreting glands,
Is the same that guides the planets, acting by divine commands."

All abnormal discordant aggregations in these resonating convolutions produce differentiation to concordant transmission; and according as these differentiations exist in volume, so the transmissions are discordantly transferred, producing antagonism to pure physical action. Thus, in motor ataxy, a differentiation of the minor thirds of the posterior parietal lobule produces the same condition between the retractors and exteriors of the leg and foot, and thus the control of the proper movements is lost through this differentiation. The same truth can be universally applied to any of the cerebral convolutions that are in a state of differential harmony to the mass of immediate cerebral surroundings. Taking the cerebral condition of the whole mass as one, it is subservient to one general head centre; although as many neutrals are represented as there are convolutions. The introductory minors are controlled by the molecular; the next progressive third by the atomic; and the high third by the etheric. All these progressive links have their positive, negative, and neutral position. When we take into consideration the structural condition of the human brain, we ought not to be bewildered by the infinite variety of its sympathetic impulses, inasmuch as it unerringly proves the true philosophy that the mass-chords of such structures are governed by vibratory etheric flows. There is no structure whatever—animal, vegetable, or mineral—that is not built up from the cosmic ether. Certain orders of attractive vibration produce certain orders of structure; thus the infinite variety of effects; more especially in the cerebral organs. Discordance cannot exist in the molecule proper. Discordance in any mass is the result of differentiated groups induced by antagonistic chords, and any differentiated mass can be

Vibratory Physics. 225

brought to a condition of harmony or equation by proper chord media, and an equated sympathy produced whether the mass be metal or brain.

There is good reason for believing that insanity is simply a condition of differentiation in the mass-chords of the convolutions, which creates an antagonistic molecular bombardment towards the neutral or attractive centres of such convolutions. This may be compared to a knot on a violin string. As long as this knot remains, it is impossible to elicit, from its sympathetic surroundings, the condition which transfers pure concordance to its resonating body. Discordant conditions (*i.e.*, differentiation of mass) produce negatization to coincident action. Pure sympathetic concordants are as antagonistic to negative discordants as the negative is to the positive; but the vast volume the sympathetic holds over the non-sympathetic, in ethereal space, makes it at once the ruling medium and re-adjuster of all opposing conditions, when properly brought to bear upon them. . . .

Josiah Royce is right as regards correspondent sympathetic association between two conditions. If concordance can be established, even of unlike states, no matter whether it be of the high tenuous forces of nature, gases with liquids, liquids with solids, solids with gases, the structural conditions can be perfectly adverse. Their neutral centres are the focalized seat of sympathetic concordance for controlling any differentiation that may exist outside, or in the mass that surrounds them. Certain orders of vibration can reach these centres and establish a concordant flow of sympathy, independent of any and all mass antagonism; in other words, certain orders of sympathetic vibratory transmission can correct and equate all differentiation that may exist between physical organisms and their cerebellic flows. Discord is disease. Harmony is health.—KEELY.

The *Standard* calls attention to the fact that Lord Rosebery has pointed out how fast mental disease of one form or another is growing among the population of London—so fast that a new asylum, containing 5000 patients, must be built every five years. "This," said his lordship, "is a penalty of civilization."

When we take into consideration the effect upon the nerves, in sensitive organizations, of living in the vicinity of railways, more especially of the elevated railways in cities, the incessant jarring vibrations which are communicated to houses, even from underground railways, to say nothing of the piercing shrieks of the steam whistle, is it to be wondered at that mental disorders and nervous diseases are on the increase? With this increase of the most terible form of affliction, the remedy will follow; for our necessities are known to One who "with a Father's care and affectionate attention supplies the wants, as they arise, of the worlds which lie like children in His bosom." Sympathetic Vibratory Physics will, in due time, make known the curableness of many disorders now considered incurable.

On this subject Mr. Keely writes:—Every disease that the physical organism is subject to has its connective link in the cerebral domain; where it unerringly telegraphs, as it were, its molecular differentiations, through the spinal dura mater or physical sympathetic transmitter, and *vice versâ* back again. The sympathetic communication, as between the physical and mental forces, shows up truthfully the pure conditions that govern the celestial and terrestrial link of sympathy, as between the finite and the Infinite in planetary suspension. The whole system governing the suspension of the innumerable planetary masses,—the infinite certainty and harmony of their eccentric and concentric evolutions and revolutions, in their orbital and oscillating ranges of motion, —the triune sympathetic streams of Infinity that permeate their molecular masses—focalizing and defocalizing on their neutral centres of attraction—are all subservient to that Great Ruling Power: Mind-Flow. There is not a grain of sand, nor an invisible corpuscule of floating matter, that does not come under the same rule that governs the most mighty of planets. . . .

"All's love, yet all's law."

As the offspring of God, only by living in love and

harmony can we fulfil the law and maintain health and happiness, either individually in family life, or collectively in our intercourse with the world. As Goethe taught :—

> Let the God within thee speak,
> Love all things that lovely be,
> And God will show His best to thee.

CHAPTER XV.

THE PHILOSOPHY OF HISTORY.—KEELY THE FOUNDER OF A SYSTEM.

"Were half the power that fills the world with terror,
Were half the wealth bestowed on camps and courts,
Given to redeem the human mind from error,
There were no need of arsenals and forts."

As long as men remain "demons of selfishness and ignorance," so long will they fight for their turn to tyrannize over their brother men. Instruction and education can alone prepare the way for a peaceful solution of the greatest problem that mankind has ever had to deal with; for, before we can hope to enter into a 'brotherhood of humanity,' the earth must be 'filled with the knowledge of the Lord.'—H. O. WARD, in the *Nationalization News*.

As for myself I hold the firm conviction that unflagging research will be rewarded by an insight into natural mysteries such as now can rarely be conceived.—PROF. WM. CROOKES.

Though "it is the spirit that quickeneth, and the flesh profiteth nothing," the grand reign of the Spirit will not commence until the material world shall be completely under man's control.—RENAN, *Future of Science*.

If truth is to obtain a complete victory, if Christianity is ever really to triumph on the earth, then must the State become Christian and science become Christian. Such then is the two-fold problem which our age is called upon to solve.—FREDERICH VON SCHLEGEL.

I come soon and will renew all things.—*Scripture*.

FREDERICH VON SCHLEGEL, in his Lecture "On the General Spirit of the Age," (1846) says, There are in the history of the eighteenth century, many phenomena which occurred so suddenly, so instantaneously, that although on deeper consideration we may discover their efficient causes in the past, in the natural state of things, and in the general situation of the world, yet are there many circumstances which prove that there was a deliberate, though secret, preparation of events, as, indeed, in many instances has been actually demonstrated. In tracing the origin of this "secret and mysterious branch of illuminism," and its influence in regard to the true restoration of society founded on the basis of Christian justice, Schlegel gives it as his opinion that the order of Templars was the channel by which this esoteric influence was introduced into the West, handing down the Solomonian traditions connected with the very foundation of this order, and the religious masonic symbols which admit of a Christian interpretation : but, as he says, the idea of an esoteric society for the propagation of any secret doctrine is not compatible with the very principle of Christianity itself; for Christianity is a divine mystery which lies open to all.

Continuing from Schlegel's writings, the Christian faith has the living God and His revelation for its object, and is itself that revelation ; hence every doctrine taken from this source is something real and positive, while, in science, the absolute is the idol of vain and empty systems, of dead and abstract reason. In the absolute spirit of our age, and in the absolute character of its factions, there is a deep-rooted intellectual pride, which is not so much personal or individual as social, for it refers to the historical destiny of mankind and of this age in particular. Actuated by this pride, a spirit exalted by moral energy, or invested with external power, fancies it can give a real existence to that which can only be the work of God ; as from Him alone proceed all those mighty and real regenerations of the world, among which Christianity—a revolution in the high and divine sense of the word—occupies the first place. For the last three hundred years this human pride has been at work; a pride that wishes to originate events, instead of humbly awaiting them and of resting contented with the place assigned to it among those events. . . . It was indeed but a very small portion of this illuminism of the eighteenth century that was really derived from the truths of Christianity and the pure light of Revelation. The rest was the mere work of man, consequently vain and empty ; or at least defective, corrupt in parts, and on the whole destitute of a solid foundation ;—therefore devoid of all permanent strength and duration. But when once, after the complete victory of truth, the divine Reformation shall appear, that human Reformation which till now has existed will sink to the ground and disappear from the world. Then, by the universal triumph of Christianity, and the thorough religious regeneration of the age, of the world, and of governments themselves, will dawn the era of a true Christian *Illuminism*. This period is not perhaps so remote from our own as the natural indolence of the human mind would be disposed to believe, says Schlegel.

Never was there a period that pointed so strongly, so clearly, so generally towards the future, as our own. In order to comprehend in all its magnitude the problem of our age, the birth of Christianity must be the great point of survey to which we must recur; in order to examine clearly what has remained incomplete, what has not yet been attained. For, unquestionably, all that has been neglected, in the earlier periods and stages of Christian civilization, must be made good in this true, consummate regeneration of society. If truth is to obtain a complete victory—if Christianity is really to triumph on the earth, then must the state become Christian and science become Christian. Such then is the two-fold problem which our age is called upon to solve. Whatever man may contribute towards the religious regeneration of government and science, Schlegel reasons that we must look for the consummation, in silent awe, to a higher Providence, to the creative fiat of a last period of dispensation, to "the dawn of an approaching era of love and harmony," which will emancipate the human race from the bondage in which it has been held by false teachings; leading men and nations to consider and estimate time, and all things temporal, not by the law and feeling of eternity :—but for temporal interests, or from temporal motives; forgetting the thoughts and faith of eternity. All progress in the great work of the religious regeneration of science Schlegel hails as the noblest triumph of genius; for it is, he says, precisely in the department of physics that the problem is the most difficult; and all that rich and boundless treasure of new discoveries in nature, which are ever better understood when viewed in connection with the high truths of religion, must be looked upon as the property of Christian science. Our various systems of philosophic Rationalism, he foretells, will fall to the ground: and vulgar Rationalism, which is but an emanation of the higher, will finally disappear. Then science will become thoroughly Christian. In the progress of mankind now, as in the past, a divine hand and conducting Providence are clearly discernible. Earthly and visible power has not alone co-operated in this progress;—that the struggle has been, in part, carried on under divine, and against invisible might, has been substantiated by Schlegel on firm and solid grounds, if not proved to mathematical evidence; which evidence, as he remarks, is neither appropriate nor applicable to the subject. Schlegel concludes his work on The Philosophy of History, by a retrospective view of society, considered in reference to that invisible world and higher region, from which a pure philosophy teaches us the operations of this visible world proceed; in which its great destinies have their root, and which is the ultimate and highest term of all its movements.

Both Schlegel and Keely teach that we shall prize with deeper, more earnest and more solid affection the great and divine era of man's redemption and emancipation, by Christianity, the more accurately we discriminate between what is essentially divine and unchangeably eternal in this revelation of love, and those elements of destruction which false teachings have opposed thereto or intermingled therewith; tracing in the special dispensations of Providence, for the advancement of Christianity and the progress of civilization and regeneration, the wonderful concurrence of events towards the single object of divine love, or the unexpected exercise of divine justice long delayed. (See *Vera Vita*, by David Sinclair.)

Sir G. G. Stokes Bart., M.P., reasoning on the difficulties as to good arising out of evil, says, In our study of nature we are most forcibly impressed with the uniformity of her laws. Those uniform laws are, so far as we can judge, the method by which the ordinary course of nature is carried on. That is to say, if we recognize the ordinary course of nature as designed by a Supreme Being, that it is according to His will that the course of Nature should, as a rule, be carried on in this regular methodical manner, we should expect, therefore, to find the operation of regular laws in the moral, no less than in the physical world, although their existence is less obvious on account of the freedom of the will. . . .

There is a conflict of opinion and a restlessness of men's minds at the present day ; but we may confidently hope that if men will in a straightforward manner seek after what is true, and that in a humble spirit, without arrogating to themselves the monopoly of truth and contemning others whose opinions may be different, the present conflict of opinion will in time settle down. . . .

It is in this frame of mind that searchers after truth are now examining the claims of Keely as a discoverer, and as the founder of a new and pure philosophy. If the most important subject and the first problem of philosophy is, as Schlegel declares, the restoration in man of the lost image of God, so far as this relates to science, all revolution, as well as all revelation, must tend toward the full understanding of this restoration in the internal consciousness, and not until it is really brought about will the object of pure philosophy be fully attained.

The philosophy of history shows clearly how, in the first ages of the world, the original word of Divine revelation formed the firm central point of faith for the future reunion of the dispersed race of man; how later, amidst the various powers intellectual as well as political which (in the middle period of the world) all ruling nations exerted on their times, according to the measure allotted to them, it was alone the power of eternal love in the Christian religion which truly emancipated and redeemed mankind ; and how the pure light of this Divine truth, universally diffused through the world and *through all science,* will crown in conclusion the progress of this restoration in the future.

The fulfilment of the term of all Christian hope and Divine promise is reserved for the last period of consummation—for the new dispensation which the closing century is ushering in. The esoteric meaning of the second coming of our Lord is thus intimated to those who are watching for the triumph of justice and truth. " Behold I come quickly ; and my reward is with me, to give every man according to his work."

Theosophy interprets the often-quoted Scripture passage of " the seven Spirits which are before His throne " as the cosmical, creative, sustaining, and world-governing potencies, the principles of which God avails Himself as His instruments, organs, and media. This is what the Kabbala implies with its seven " Sephiroth," what Schelling means by the " potencies," or principles in the inner life of God ; and it is by their emergence, separation, and tension that they become cosmical potencies. If we stop short at these general considerations, this is precisely the idea of Theosophy. When it is asked what special activities are to be ascribed to each of the seven Spirits, striving to apprehend more closely the uncreated potencies through which the Deity works in its manifestation, and to which Scripture itself makes unmistakable allusion, revelation is silent, intimating only by veiled suggestions. It is here that Theosophy leads the way to the open book of Nature : the title-page of which we have only begun to turn.

Theosophy, says Bishop Martensen, signifies wisdom in God : " Church Theology is not wise in assuming a hostile attitude towards Theosophy, because it hereby deprives itself of a most valuable leavening influence, a source of renewal and rejuvenescence, which Theology so greatly needs, exposed as it is to the danger of stagnating in barren and dreary scholasticism and cold and trivial criticism. In such a course no real progress can be made in the Christian apprehension of truth." Jacob Böhme, who was the greatest and most famous of all Theosophists in the world,[1] said of philosophers and other disputants who attack not only Theosophy but also theology, and even Christianity itself, in the name of modern science :—" Every spirit sees no further than its mother, out of which it has its original, and wherein it stands ; for it is impossible for any spirit, in its own natural power to look into another principle, and behold it, except it be regenerated therein." This is what Christ taught : " Ye must

---

[1] See "Jacob Bohme, his Life and Teaching; or, Studies in Theosophy," by Dr. Hans Lassen Martensen.

be born again." Only those who are regenerated, by the principle of which Christ spoke to Nicodemus, can understand the quickening of the Spirit which comes alone from Him who gives this new birth to all who seek it, and in whom all the treasures of wisdom and knowledge are hidden :—"hidden, not in order that they may remain secret, but in order that they may ever increasingly be made manifest and appropriated by us."

Jacob Böhme, who was born in 1575, "brought to the birth" an idea which, three centuries later, is developing into a system of pure philosophy, that promises to "cover the earth with wisdom and understanding in the deep mysteries of God."

Böhme gave birth to an idea. Keely is giving birth to a system. Both are exceedingly imperfect in the expression of their views; yet in points of detail each possesses a firm dialectical grip. In their writings both seem overwhelmed by the vast extent of the realm they are exploring. Both find in harmony the object and the ending of the world's development. Conflicting with modern science at very many points, visionary as both appear to be, powerful expression is given to an idea of life both in the macrocosm and the microcosm, the validity of which can be questioned only by materialism. The idea of the one and the system of the other teach that when Nature is affirmed in God it is in a figurative and symbolical sense :—that it is, in comparison with what we call nature, something infinitely more subtle and super-material than matter; that it is the source of matter; a plenitude of living forces and energies. This system teaches, as "Waterdale" has expressed it, "the existence of a Great Almighty, as being in virtue of the perfect organization of the universe, even as the existence of man is incidental to the organic structure of his body;" and that the attribute of omniscience is represented by "the perfect conveyance of signs of atomic movement in vibratory action through the length and breadth of our universe." We are led by it to look from nature up to nature's God and to comprehend the attributes of deity as never before in any other system. It lays hold, with a giant's grasp, of the heart of the problems which science is wrestling with. It answers the question asked by Professor Oliver Lodge in his paper, read at Cardiff, last August, "By what means is force exerted, and what definitely is force?" It was a bold speculation of Professor Lodge, who is known as "a very careful and sober physicist," when, after admitting that there is herein something not provided for in the orthodox scheme of physics, he suggested that good physicists should carry their appropriate methods of investigation into the field of psychology, admitting that a line of possible advance lies in this direction. Without speculation science could never advance in any direction; discussion precedes reform, there can be no progress without it. It required rare courage for a physicist to step from the serried ranks that have always been ready to point their javelins at psychologists, and to show, with the torch of science, the hand on the signpost at the cross roads pointing in the right direction. It is the great high road of knowledge; but those who would explore it must do so with cautious tread, until the system of sympathetic association is completed which Keely is bringing to birth, for the road is bordered with pitfalls and quicksands and the mists of ignorance envelop it.

Ernest Renan, in "The Future of Science," illustrates the thesis that, henceforth, the advancement of civilization is to be the work of science; the word science being used in its largest signification as covering intellectual achievement in every direction open to the mind, and the co-ordination of the results in a progressive philosophy of life. The fundamental distinction which is expressed or implied, on every page, is that the earlier processes of civilization belong to an age of spontaneity, of unreflective productivity; an age that expressed itself in myths, created religions, organized social forms and habits, in harmony with the spontaneous creations; and that we have now entered upon the critical, defining, intellectual age; in short, as Mr. Nisbet has said, that the evolution of the human race has passed from the physiological into the psychical field; and that it is in the latter alone, henceforward, that progress may be looked for toward a higher civilization.[1] Philosophy, that is to say, rational research, is alone capable of solving the question of the future of humanity, says Renan. "The really efficacious revolution, that which will give its shape to the future, will not be a political, it will be a religious and moral revolution. Politics has exhausted its resources for solving this problem. The politician is the offscouring of humanity, not its inspired teacher. The great revolution can only come from men of thought and sentiment. It does not do to expect too much from governments. It is not for them to reveal to humanity the law for which it is in search. What humanity needs is a moral law and creed; and it is from the depths of human nature that they will emerge, and not from the well-trodden and sterile pathways of the official world." In order to know whence will come a better understanding of the religion which Christ taught, "the religion of the future, we must always look in the direction of liberty, equality, and fraternity." Not the French Commune liberty to cut one another's throats (an equality of misery, and a fraternity of crime), but that liberty to know and to love the truth of things which constitutes true religion, and which when it is bestowed without money and without price, as it will be, "humanity will accomplish the remainder, without asking anyone for permission." No one can say from what part of the sky will appear the star of this new redemption. The one thing certain is that the shepherds and the Magi will be once more the first to perceive it, that the germ of it is already formed, and that if we were able to see the present with the eyes of the future, we should be able to distinguish, in the complication of the hour, the imperceptible fibre which will bear life for the future. It is amid putrefaction that the germ of future life is developed, and no one has the right to say, "This is a rejected stone," for that stone may be the corner-stone of the future edifice. Human nature is with-

---

[1] The apparent comprehension of Keely's discovery by Mr. Nisbet, was what led the compiler of this work to apply to him for help, in making known the nature of the researches which Keely is pursuing, at the time that Keely was threatened with imprisonment, in 1890, for obtaining money under false pretences.

out reproach, continues Renan (*L'Avenir de la Science*), and proceeds toward the perfect by means of forms successively and diversely imperfect. All the ideas which primitive science had formed of the world appear narrow, trivial, and ridiculous to us after that which progressive research has proven to be true. The fact is that science has only destroyed her dreams of the past, to put in their stead a reality a thousand times superior; but were science to remain what it is, we should have to submit to it while cursing it, for it has destroyed and not builded up again; it has awakened man from a sweet sleep without smoothing the reality to him. What science gives us is not enough, we are still hungry. True science is that which belongs neither to the school nor the drawing-room, but which corresponds exactly to the wants of man. Hence true science is a religion which will solve for men the eternal problems, the solution of which his nature imperatively demands. Herein lies the hope of humanity; for, like a wild beast, the uneducated masses stand at bay; ready to turn and rend those who are willing to keep them in their present condition, in order to be able to make them answer their own purposes. . . . I am firmly convinced, continues Renan, for my own part, that unless we make haste and elevate the people, we are upon the eve of a terrible outbreak of barbarism. For if the people triumph in their present state, it will be worse than it was with the Franks and Vandals. They will destroy of their own accord the instrument which might have served to elevate them; we shall then have to wait until civilization once more emerges spontaneously from the profound depths of nature. Morality, like politics, is summed up, then, in this grand saying: To elevate the people. If I were to see humanity collapse on its own foundations, mankind again slaughter one another in some fateful hour, I should still go on proclaiming that perfection is human nature's final aim, and that the day must come when reason and perfection shall reign supreme.

> Sailing, sailing in the same staunch ship—
> We are sailing on together;
> We see the rocks and we mark the shoals,
> And we watch for cyclone weather.

The perils we run for one alone
  Are perils for all together,—
The harbour we make for one alone,
  Makes haven for all, through the weather.

Stand by your ship: be brave, brothers mine!
  Be brave, for we'll stand together!
We'll yet reach the port for which we sail
  In this black and stormy weather.

Sailing, sailing the same stormy sea,
  We are sailing all together!
There are rocks ahead and shoals beneath,
  And 'round us hurricane weather.

I see in the West a star arise,
  That will guide us all together:—
Stand firm by your helm and trust in God
  Who pilots us through this weather.

The dawn of morning breaks in the skies
  Which will bring mankind together;—
To havens of peace, to havens of bliss,
  We'll ride through this cyclone weather.

CLARA JESSUP MOORE

CHAPTER XVI.

1891.

AN APPEAL IN BEHALF OF THE CONTINUANCE OF KEELY'S RESEARCHES.

There is a distinct advantage in having one section of scientific men beginning their work untrammelled by preconceived notions.—*Engineering*.

A knowledge of scientific theories seems to kill all knowledge of scientific facts.—PROFESSOR SCHUSTER.

Tizeau found that the speed of light is increased in water which moves in the same direction as the light. This result must be due either to the motion of matter through the medium, or to the fact that moving matter carries the ether with it. The whole question of matter and motion as a medium is a vital one, and we shall hardly make any serious advance *before experiment has found a new opening.*—PROFESSOR SCHUSTER.

How MR. KEELY, IN 1891, WAS ABLE TO SECURE THE ATTENTION OF MEN OF SCIENCE TO HIS RESEARCHING EXPERIMENTS.

DURING the summer of 1890, Mr. Keely was harassed by threats, said to proceed from disappointed stockholders in the Keely Motor Company, of suits at law for "obtaining money under false pretences." After making many unsuccessful attempts with the editors of leading magazines in London, Boston, and New York, to bring before the public the claims of Mr. Keely for sympathy in his colossal work, the proposals of an editor, on the staff of the *London Times* (who had the year before introduced himself to Mrs. Bloomfield Moore to obtain information of Keely) to make known the researches of the persecuted discoverer and his need of assistance, at that time, were accepted. The programme, as laid out by this editor, was to use his extended influence with the leading journals throughout Great Britain, and to have brief notices of Keely inserted; to be followed up with a magazine article, for which the material was furnished. Later this arrangement was modified by the editor, who then proposed to write an essay for some influential journal, handling the various molecular and atomic theories; pointing out wherein Keely's views were original, and showing their revolutionizing tendencies. This work, which was to have been commenced in November, was delayed until all need was over. When the editor wrote to Philadelphia in January, 1891, that he had been unable to commence his work for want of sufficient material (enclosing questions to be answered by Mr. Keely before he could set about it), the answer returned was that the threatened troubles were over, that Mr. Keely had gained the protection of men of science, and the order for the essay was countermanded. At this very time a subscription was in circulation to raise money from disaffected stockholders for the purpose of bringing the threatened action at law, in case Mr. Keely did not resume work on his engine, instead of pursuing researches in order to gain more knowledge of the operation of this unknown polar force in nature.

It was at this juncture that the late Professor Joseph Leidy, that eminent man of science who had been the first to recognize the importance of Keely's discovery to the scientific world, arranged with the Provost of the University of Pennsylvania that an appeal should be made to the trustees, the faculty and the professors of that institution, to permit Keely to continue his researches for science under their protection.

Accordingly, on the 14th of January, 1891, a paper entitled "Keely's Discoveries" was read at the house of Provost Pepper. The answer sent by one of the professors, in reply to Dr. Pepper's invitation, probably expressed the views held by all the distinguished men who assembled to listen to the appeal, which was to the effect that the professor would be present to hear the paper read, if the Provost wished it; but, if he came, he should make it very unpleasant for the reader, as he had no faith in Keely nor in his discoveries. All those who were present listened with attention, and among the few who

An Appeal in Behalf of Science.

became interested in the claims of Keely as a discoverer, was the professor who had made this remark. The preamble to the appeal was read by the Provost, Dr. Pepper.

Preamble.

Before commencing to read my paper I wish to lay before you the object of this effort to interest men of science in the researches of a man who, in the cause of justice alone, is entitled to have his life's work fairly represented to you. Some of our men of science have, unwittingly, been the medium by which great injustice has been done to Mr. Keely; and to others also, by placing me before the world as a woman whom the Keely Motor Company management has robbed of large sums of money; whereas, in truth, I have never been in any way involved by the Keely Motor Company.

In the winter of 1881-82, Mr. Keely, who was dependent upon "The Keely Motor Company" for the means to continue his researches, as to the nature of the unknown force he had discovered, was virtually abandoned by the Company. Himself as ignorant as were its managers of the source of the mysterious energy he had stumbled over, he was driven to despair by their action; and, when I was led to his assistance, I found his wife's roof mortgaged over her head, and that, his honour assailed, he had resolved to take his life rather than submit to the indignities threatening him. At this time I had taken from my private estate ten thousand dollars, to found a small public library to my father's memory, in the town of Westfield, Hampden Co., Massachusetts. After convincing myself that Mr. Keely had made a great discovery, I felt that if this money could save his discovery, jeopardized as it was, it was my duty to so appropriate it. At that time, Mr. Keely thought half of the amount so appropriated would be all that he should require; but, unfortunately, his efforts were for years confined to the construction of an engine for the Company that had abandoned him. Later, he commenced researches which resulted in the discovery that he had unknowingly imprisoned the ether; greatly increasing my interest in his work.

The plan to which I shall allude in my paper, as framed by Professor Leidy for Mr. Keely to follow, and approved by Professor Hertz, of Bonn, and Professor Fitzgerald, of Trinity College, Dublin, may be summed up as one that permits Mr. Keely to pursue his researches on his own line, without further investigation, up to the completion of his system in a form which will enable him to give to commerce with one hand his model for aerial navigation, and to science, with the other, the knowledge that is necessary for extending its researches in the field of radiant energy—which Mr. Keely has been exploring for so many years. I ask the prestige of your sympathy, as well as for your interest in Mr. Keely's work, on this basis; and if in one year you are not convinced that satisfactory results have been attained for science, I will promise to leave Mr. Keely in the hands of the "usurers and Shylocks of commerce," who have already forced him into renouncing seven-eighths of his interest in what the Keely Motor Company claims as its property.

At present I do not desire from anyone endorsement of Keely's discoveries. Until his system is completed he wishes to avoid all discussion and all public mention of the anticipated value of his inventions. Mr. Keely's programme of experimental research, as laid down by himself last March, when I first proposed to furnish him with all the funds needed to carry it out, comprises its continuance until he has gained sufficient knowledge of the energy he is controlling—which is derived from the disintegration of water—to enable him to impart to others a system that will permit men of science to produce and to handle the energy, and enable him to instruct artisans in the work which lies in their province; viz., the construction of machines to apply this costless motive power in mechanics.

The prestige of your interest in Mr. Keely's labours can alone secure to him freedom to pursue researches on his own road; a course pronounced by Professor Leidy, Professor Hertz, and Professor Fitzgerald, to be "the only proper line for him to pursue."

The building of an engine is not in Mr. Keely's province. His researches completed to that point which is necessary, for perfect control of the force, practical application will follow. The result of his experimental work for nine months on this line has been such as to revive the interest of the speculative management of the Keely Motor Company, to that extent that Mr. Keely is now offered the support of its stockholders if he will resume construction of an engine ; and this after more than seven years of failure on the part of the company to furnish him with one dollar to carry on "the enterprise."

The official Report put forth in January by the Keely Motor Company managers annulled my contract with Mr. Keely ; but he is willing to abide by it, if I am able to continue to furnish him with the necessary funds. This position of affairs has forced me to the front, to ask whether you will place it in my power to renew the contract with Mr. Keely ; or leave him under the control of men who seem to be oblivious of the interests of the stockholders of the company in their "clamour" for an engine. When this system is completed, in its application to mechanics, the present mode of running engines with shafts and beltings will disappear, creating a revolution in all branches of industry.

Looking at my request from another point of view, do you not think it due to extend to Mr. Keely an opportunity to prove all that one of your number is ready to announce as his conviction in regard to the claims of Mr. Keely ? You all know to whom I refer—Professor Joseph Leidy. "Oh, Leidy is a biologist," said an English physicist not long since ; "get the opinion of a physicist for us." If I did not wish for the opinion of physicists, I should not have appealed to you for help at this most critical juncture. But I also ask that no opinion be given by any physicist until Mr. Keely's theories are understood and demonstrated, by experiment. Yes, Dr. Leidy is a biologist, and what better preparation could a man have than a study of the science of life to enable him to discern between laws of nature as invented by physicists, and nature's operations as demonstrated by Keely ?

The science of life has not been the only branch to which Dr. Leidy has given profound attention; it is his extensive and accurate knowledge of its methods, limits, and tendencies, which prepared the way for that quick comprehension of possibilities, lying hidden from the sight of those men of science whose minds have rested (rusted?) in the dead grooves of mechanical physics. In Dr. Leidy we find entire scientific and intellectual liberty of thought, with that love of justice and truth which keeps its possessor from arrogance and intolerance, leading him with humility to "prove all things and hold fast to truth." To such men the world owes all that we have of advance since the days when science taught that the earth is flat, arguing that were it round the seas and oceans would fall off into space. In Dr. Leidy's name and in justice to him, I ask your sanction to and approval of my efforts to preserve Keely's discoveries for science;—discoveries which explain, not only the causes of the planetary motions but the source of the one eternal and universal force.

An Appeal in Behalf of Science.

A paper read by Mrs. Bloomfield Moore at the house of Provost Pepper on the evening of January 14th, 1891, before members of the board of trustees and professors of the University of Pennsylvania.

> Each day he wrought, and better than he planned,
> Shape breeding shape beneath his restless hand;
> The soul without still helps the soul within,
> And its deft magic ends what we begin.
>   George Eliot.

I hope that I do not seem to be too presumptuous in my effort to awaken an interest, on your part, in the discoveries of Keely which have aroused a marked degree of attention among some of the most learned men in Europe.

I should hardly have ventured to ask the prestige of your support to be given to Mr. Keely, in his further scientific researches, were it not that one of your number fully realizes, I think, the important nature of these researches. You all know to whom I refer—Professor Joseph Leidy. In his book, "Fresh Water Rhizopods of North America," he says, in his concluding remarks: "I may perhaps continue in the same field of research and give to the reader further results, but I cannot promise to do so, for though the subject has proved to me an unceasing source of pleasure I see before me so many wonderful things in other fields, that a strong impulse disposes me to leap the hedges to examine them." I have reason to know that, had Dr. Leidy not followed this impulse, our age might have been robbed of its birthright.

It was not until I appealed to Professor Leidy and Dr. Willcox, to convince themselves whether I was right or wrong in extending aid to Mr. Keely, that their decision enabled me to continue to assist him until he has once more made such advances, in experimental research, as to cause the managers of the Keely Motor Company to believe that his engine is near completion, and that they can dispense with outside assistance hereafter.

But I know as it has been in the past so will it be again, and that, as the months glide away, if no engine is completed, the company will once more desert the discoverer; while, if he is allowed to pursue his researches, up to the completion of his system under your protection, his discoveries will be guarded for science, and the interests of the stockholders will not be sacrificed to the greed of speculators, as has so often been done in the past.

As I have had occasion to say, elsewhere, after the warning given in the history of Huxley's Bathybius, Professor Leidy would not have risked his world-wide reputation by the endorsement of Keely's claims, as the discoverer of hidden energy in inter-molecular and atomic spaces, had he not tested the demonstrations until fully convinced of the discovery of a force previously unknown to science, and of the honesty of Mr. Keely in his explanations. Therefore, following the advice of Professor G. Fr. Fitzgerald, of Dublin, I do not ask for further investigations. Until Professor Leidy and Dr. Willcox came to the front, in May, 1891, Mr. Keely had no influential supporters, and was under such a cloud, from his connection with speculators, that to advocate his integrity of purpose and to uphold the importance of his work, was enough to awaken doubts as to the sanity of his upholders.

We are told by Herodotus that science is to know things truly; yet past experience shows us that what has been called knowledge at one period of time is proved to be but folly in another age. Science *is* to know things truly, and the laws of nature are the same yesterday, to-day, and for ever. Throughout the universe the same laws are at work and regulate all things. Men interpret these laws to suit their own ideas. The system which Keely is unfolding shows us that there is not one grain of sand, nor one invisible corpuscule of floating matter, that does not come under the same law that governs the most mighty planet, and that all forms of matter are aggregated under one law. " The designs of the Creator as expounded by our latest teachers," writes Gilman, "have required millions of ages to carry out. They are so vast and complex that they can only be realized in the sweep of ages. One design is subordinated by another without ever being lost sight of, until the time has arrived for its complete fulfilment. These designs involve an infinitude of effort, ending often in what, to our view, looks like failure, to be crowned after a series of ages with complete success at last."

In this long chain of physical causes, says Dr. Willcox, seemingly endless, but really commencing with that one link that touches the hand of Him who made all matter, and all potencies that dwell within matter, this cosmical activity has been ceaseless, these cosmical effects numerous past conception, by which universal nature has slowly unfolded and become the universe of to-day.

In this way both Christianity and science unfold their truths progressively. Truth, like the laws of nature, never changes; yet truth as an absolute thing, existing in and by itself, is relatively capable of change; for as the atoms hold in their tenacious grasp undreamed-of potencies, so truths hold germs potential of all growth. Each new truth disclosed to the world, when its hour of need comes, unfolds and reveals undreamed-of means of growth. As the Rev. George Boardman has said of Christianity, so may it be said of science: Being a perennial vine, it is ever yielding new wine.

A philosopher has said that if ever a human being needed divine pity it is the pseudo-scientist who believes in nothing but what he can prove by his own methods. In the light of Keely's discoveries, science will have to admit that when she concentrates her attention upon matter, to the exclusion of mind, she is as the hunter who has no string in reserve for his bow. When she recognizes that a full and adequate science of matter is impossible to man, and that the science of mind is destined ultimately to attain to a much higher degree of perfection than the science of matter—that it will give the typical ideas and laws to which all the laws of physics must be referred—then science will be better supplied with strings than she now is, to bring her quarry down.

It is Professor Leidy's and Dr. Willcox's second strings, to their bows, which will enable you to secure to science the richest quarry that has ever been within its reach. I know that the experience of Professor Rowland, as related by him, must have had the effect to prejudice you against Mr. Keely. Professor Fitzgerald writes to me on this subject: "I am sorry that Mr. Keely did not cut the wire, wherever Professor Rowland asked to have it cut, because it will undoubtedly be said that he had some sinister reason for not doing so, whatever his real reasons were; but, of course, when one cuts a bit off a valuable string one prefers naturally to cut the bit off the end, as Keely did, rather than out of the middle." This very wire which Mr. Keely did cut at one end, twice, for Professor Rowland, one of the pieces falling into my hand, is now in Professor Fitzgerald's possession. It was the offensive manner of Professor Rowland when he seized the shears, telling Keely it was his guilty conscience which made him refuse to cut the wire, and that it must be cut in the middle, which put Keely on the defensive, causing him to refuse to allow Professor Rowland to cut it.

It would seem that the professor in the Johns Hopkins University, from his remarks on that occasion, thought, instead of an experiment in negative attraction, that Keely was imposing upon the ignorant by giving a simple experiment in pneumatics, familiar to all schoolboys. Professor Rowland did not realize how low he was rating the powers of discernment of a professor in the University of Pennsylvania who had witnessed Keely's experiments again and again, when his instruments or devices were in perfect working order. Mr. Keely, who was ambitious to show Professor Rowland that his disintegrator had no connection with any concealed apparatus, had suspended it from the ceiling by a staple. The hook had given way, and the jar to the instrument in falling to the floor disarranged its interior construction on that day. To those who have not witnessed any of Keely's experiments, under favourable conditions, his theories naturally seem vague speculations; but not one theory has Keely put forward, as a theory, which he has not demonstrated as having a solid foundation in fact. Some of our men of science once settled the problem of the origin of life to their own satisfaction, only to learn in the end that speculation is not science; but this very problem is one the solution of which Keely now seems to be approaching.

It would become a matter of easy analysis, writes Keely, if the properties governing the different orders of matter could be understood in their different evolutions. The force of the mind on matter is an illustration of the power of the finer over the crude, but the law making the crude forms of matter subservient to the finer or higher forms, is an unknown law to finite minds.

Buckle has asserted that the highest of our so called laws of nature are as yet purely empirical; and that, until some law is discovered which is connected with the laws of the mind that made it, our knowledge has no sure basis. So saturated has Mr. Keely's mind been with his discovery of this law that he has contented himself to remain ignorant in physics, as taught by the schools; and also with simpler matters it would seem; while testing and building up his hypotheses into a system which no one but himself can complete, and which without completion must be lost to the world. I should form a very poor opinion of the mind that would accept an hypothesis as anything more than the signpost at cross roads, which points to the direction that may be taken. In physics the very first fact to which the learner is introduced is already sophisticated by hypotheses. Every experiment in chemistry is but a member of a series, all based upon some one or other of many hypotheses; which are as necessary to the construction of a system as is the scaffolding which is used in building an edifice. If the scaffolding proves unsound it does not affect the edifice, as it can be at once replaced with material more solid. So an hypothesis, which is merely a conjecture or a suggestion, cannot affect the solidity of a philosophy or a system. It must be tested and found to support all the facts which bear upon it, and capable of accounting for them, before it can be accepted as a theory.

It is my wish to have the professors of the University of Pennsylvania meet at my house the founder of a system which, in my opinion, embraces a pure philosophy : to listen to his theories, and to elicit from him such information as to the nature of his researches, in what is called electro-magnetic radiation, as I trust will convince them that I have not been pursuing a will-o'-the-wisp during the years that my mind has been concentrated on the work in which Mr. Keely is engaged. The bearings of this work are so various that I shall not have time to touch upon more than the one which interests me beyond any or all of the others; namely, its connection with the medical art. Appreciating as I do the life of self-denial which physicians who are devoted to their profession must lead, and having in their ranks relatives and many warm friends on both sides of the ocean (one of them, my nephew, Dr. Jessup, is here to-night) I trust that what I say of the medical art will not be misconstrued.

The great sorrows of my life have come upon me through the ignorance of medical men, who, I know, followed their best judgment in the course of treatment that they pursued in the illnesses of those dear to me. When my children were in their infancy I had reason to embrace the opinions of Professor Magendie, as set forth in one of his lectures before the students of his class in the Allopathic College of Paris. These are his words : "I know medicine is called a science. It is nothing like a science. It is a great humbug. Doctors are mere empirics when they are not charlatans. We are as ignorant as men can be. Who knows anything about medicine ? I do not, nor do I know anyone who does know anything about it. Nature does a great deal ; imagination does a great deal, doctors do d——h little when they do no harm."

Later in life, in 1871, I was sent, while suffering with neurasthenia, from Paris to Schwalbach Baths by Dr. Beylard, who recommended me to the care of Dr. Adolph Genth ; to whom, in my first interview, I said: "I wish for your opinion, and for your advice, if you can give it to me without prescribing any medicine." He replied: "With all my heart, Madam, and I wish to God there were more women like you; but we should soon lose our patients, if we did not dose them." A terrible excuse for the use of those agencies which Dr. John Good has said have sent more human beings to their graves than war, pestilence and famine combined.

One of Mr. Keely's discoveries shapes his theory that all nervous and brain disorders may be cured by equating the differentiation that exists in the disordered structure. When his system is completed, medical men will have a new domain opened to them for *experiment*. Gross material agencies, such as drugs, will be replaced by the finer forces of nature: light, as taught by the late Dr. Pancoast of our city, and magnetism, as experimented with by the late Professor Keil of Jena, showing the efficacy of the ordinary magnet in the cure of certain infirmities,—these experiments were communicated by him more than fifty years since to the Royal Society of London.

Paracelsus taught that man is nourished and sustained by magnetic power, which he called the universal motor of nature. In Switzerland, in Italy and in France, the light-treatment is now being tested; red light used in cases of melancholia; blue light in cases of great nervous excitement, operating like magic in some instances. Dr. Oscar Jennings, the electrician at St. Anne's Hospital for the Insane in Paris, tells me that students, versed in Biblical lore, declare that the esoteric teachings of the Book of Job enunciate a system of light-cure. Ostensibly because of my faith in the importance of Keely's discoveries, as opening up new fields of research to medical men, an invalid daughter (suffering from puerperal mania after the birth of her third child) was taken from me, in conformance with orders of the Swedish guardian of her monied interests in Sweden, and I was summoned before the Police Direction, in Vienna, and required to bind myself not to experiment upon my child. It is well known to the London experts in mental disorders, the most distinguished of whom I have consulted, that my daughter's treatment, while she was under my care, had been confined to giving no medicine, forcing no food, and such changes from time to time in her surroundings as she needed, with a few electric baths.

The orthodox practice of medicine is nothing more and nothing less than " a system of blind experiment," as it has been called.

At the opening of a clinical society in London, Sir Thomas Watson said: " We try this and not succeeding we try that, and baffled again we try something else." Other eminent medical men have given utterance to these aphorisms: " The science of medicine is founded on conjecture and improved by murder;" "Mercury has made more cripples than war;" "Ninety-nine medical facts are medical lies;" "Every dose of medicine is a blind experiment;" " The older physicians grow the more sceptical they become of the virtues of their own medicines." Dr. Ridge said: " Everything in nature is acknowledged to be governed by law. It is singular, however, that while science endeavours to reduce this to actual fact in all other studies, those of health and disease have not hitherto been arranged under any law whatever."

Keely's system, should he live to complete it, will show that nature works under one law in everything; that discord is disease, that harmony is health. He believes that nervous and brain disorders are curable; but he will never have the leisure to enter this field of research himself, and it will be left for physicians to pursue their experiments to that point where they shall be able to decide whether he is right or wrong. This is why I seek to interest medical men in Keely's belief; his theories of latent energy he is able to handle without help, and to demonstrate a solid foundation for them on facts. " Nothing can lie like a fact," said Velpeau. But nature's laws are infallible facts, and the facts referred to by Velpeau are of the order of the fallible ones enunciated by science, such as " The atom is indivisible." " The atom is infinitely divisible," says Keely, repeating Schopenhauer's words, whose writings I dare say he has never read.

Professor George Fr. Fitzgerald, of Trinity College, Dublin, in closing a lecture delivered before the British Association last March, on " Electro-magnetic Radiation," enunciates a possible theory of ether and matter. This hypothesis, he says, explains the differences in nature as differences of motion. If it be true, ether and matter—gold, air, wood, brains—are but different motions. You will be able to judge of the marvellous mechanism invented by Keely, for his researches, when I tell you that by his demonstrations with these instruments, he is able to place this hypothesis in the rank of theories, boldly announcing that all motion is thought, and that all force is mind force. With a clearness that characterizes his great brain he has plunged through the deep and broad questions surrounding the mechanism of the universe, and he claims, on behalf of science, as did the late Provost Jellett of the British Association, "the right to prosecute its investigations until it attains to a mechanical explanation of all things."

In this lecture Professor Fitzgerald, commenting upon Professor Hertz's experiments in the vibration of ether waves, says: " If there is reason to think that any greater oscillation might disintegrate the atom, we are still a long way from it." Does not this statement border on an admission that the atom may be divisible? Those who are pursuing their researches in this field are farther off than they know from the great central truth which Faraday did not live long enough to reach, although conjectured by him.

We have not only Faraday's discoveries, but those of Scheele, the Swedish chemist, as an example of exact observations leading to erroneous conclusions. The investigations of Scheele led up to the rich harvest which has since been reaped from a knowledge of the nature of the compounds of organic chemistry. Scheele was one of the founders of quantitative analysis, but the phlogistic theory advanced by him was overthrown—the fate of all theories which are not based on solid foundations. Faraday admitted that his own ideas on gravitating force, and of the ether, were but vague impressions of his mind thrown out as matter for speculation. He left no theory on these lines, for he had nothing to offer as the result of demonstration, nor even of sufficient consideration to broach a theory: merely impressions, which are allowable for a time as guides to thought and farther research. Yet more than once did these speculations of his giant intellect touch upon one of nature's hidden laws, the greatest one yet made known to man. Had Faraday lived long enough to pursue his researches, from his starting point of conjecture, he would have been, without doubt, instead of Keely, the discoverer of the latent or hidden potencies existing in all forms of matter, visible and invisible. But the physicists of his time looked upon his speculations as contrary to the received dogmas of science, and preferred their own errors to his speculations. They saw the signpost, but took the road directly opposite to the one Faraday had pointed out.

It is admitted that even a false theory, when rightly constructed, has its uses, and that, instead of hindering, it hastens the advance of knowledge. Every one, possessing the slightest acquaintance with the history of astronomy, knows that the doctrines of cycles, epicycles and ellipses, were begotten naturally and necessarily out of each other; and that if Kepler had not propounded speculative errors Newton would not have hit upon speculative truth. It has been said that when men of science disclaim hypotheses, or speculation, they are either unfit for their vocation or, like Newton, they are better than their creed. Hypotheses are at once the effect and the cause of progress. One might as well attempt to preserve and employ an army without organization as to preserve and employ phenomena without a theory to weld them into one. But the theory must be provisionally, if not positively, true; it must be intelligible and consistent; it must explain a greater number of facts and reconcile a greater variety of apparent contradictions than any which has preceded it; and it must have become developed not by the addition merely, but by the addition and solution, of subsidiary explanations. I ask of you an examination of Keely's theories before giving an opinion of them.

Time only can decide whether Keely's hypotheses and theories will outlive these tests. If not, his system must be overthrown, as past systems have been, to make room for a better one. All that I ask is that he may have the opportunity to develop it under your encouragement. There are scientists in Europe ready to assist him with pecuniary assistance. They know enough—those who are interested in his discoveries—to know that they can help him in no other way.

Professor Hertz of Bonn, said to me: "Keely must work out his system himself to that point where he can instruct physicists to repeat his experiments." Picking up a photograph of Keely's instruments of research, grouped together, he added: "No man is likely to be a fraud who is working on these lines."

Science is alert, on tiptoe as it were, waiting for the one mighty explanation of the force, "behind the framework of nature," which has hitherto "eluded its skill;" and which the system of Keely makes clear to the understanding, demonstrating that one power, one law, reigns throughout creation; the immaterial controlling the material, after the divine order and law of creation that the immaterial should govern the material—that the whole realm of matter is under the dominion of the immaterial. But "the known always excludes the unknown" when in opposition to it. As in past generations, so now in ours, physicists have said: "We will not waste our time in looking at facts and phenomena which cannot be accepted in opposition to established principles of science and to known laws of nature; and which, even if we beheld we should not believe."

The recognition and practical application of new truths are, as has been said, notoriously slow processes. Harvey's beneficent discovery excited vehement opposition from his contemporaries. Professor Riolan combated this discovery with as much obstinacy as violence; even denying the existence and the functions of lymphatic vessels. Harvey himself united with Riolan in opposing the discoveries of Aselli and Pacquet respecting the lymphatic system. Jenner's discovery met with the same opposition, and more than forty years elapsed before the suggestion of Sir Humphrey Davy became of practical use. Mr. Wills was so affected by the ridicule which he encountered in his experiments with nitrous oxide in destroying physical pain, that he abandoned them. Nearly half a century later Dr. Morton was assailed by several of our journals in America for the use of ether in producing anæsthesia; as also was Sir James Simpson for his use of ether and chloroform.

The scientists excommunicated Dr. Wigan, who had proved by anatomical examination that each brain-hemisphere is a perfect brain ; that we have, in fact, two brains, as we have two eyes and two ears. His experiences as a physician were declared to be impostures or delusions ; his deductions fallacious. They could not be true, because they were inconsistent with the established principles of physiology and mental science. And with such experiences in the past, we should keep in mind that the powers of nature are so mysterious and inscrutable that men must be cautious in limiting them to the ordinary laws of experience. Proclus wrote of the power of mind or will to set up certain vibrations—not in the grosser atmospheric particles whose undulations beget light, sound, heat, electricity—but in the latent immaterial principle of force, of which modern science knows scarcely anything.

What is beyond their own power, men cannot comprehend to be in the power of others. Said Sextus : "If by magic you mean a perpetual research among all that is most latent and obscure in nature, I profess that magic, and he who does so comes nearer to the fountain of all knowledge."

Sir Isaac Newton said : " It is well known that bodies act upon one another by the attractions of gravity, magnetism and electricity ; and these instances show the tenour and course of nature, and make it not improbable that there may be more powers of attraction than these. For nature is very consonant and conformable to herself."

With such intimations of the hidden force that is ever in operation, "behind the framework of nature," shall we, because it is hidden from science, refuse to listen to the explanations which Mr. Keely is now prepared to give? All nature is a compound of conflicting, and therefore of counterbalancing and equilibrating, forces. Without this there could be no such thing as stability. In nature nothing is great and nothing is little, writes Figuier. Sir Henry Roscoe says : "The structure of the smallest particle, invisible even to our most searching vision, may be as complicated as that of any of the heavenly bodies which circle around our sun." If you admit this, as stated by one of your own orthodox scientists, why refuse to admit the possibility of the subdivision of all corpuscles of matter, which Keely declares can be done by certain orders of vibration, thus showing up new elements? I do not ask endorsement of Keely's theories; but if physicists did not think it possible to rupture the atom, would they be calculating the chances of doing so, as Professor Fitzgerald has done?

Why not admit that certain tenets of science may prove to be nothing more than hypotheses, too hastily adopted as theories, and that Keely has succeeded, as he claims, to have discovered the order of vibration, which by increasing the oscillation of the atom, causes it to rupture itself? This introductory impulse is given at forty-two thousand eight hundred vibrations, instead of one hundred millions; which, having been reached by Professor Hertz, failed to tear apart the atom, and convinced Professor Fitzgerald of the "long way off" that they still are from rupturing it. But even this conclusion was arrived at under an erroneous hypothesis; for the atomic charge does not oscillate across the diameter of the atom, and its possible radiating power was calculated on this hypothesis.

Again, as to the canons of science, which are proved by Mr. Keely's researches to be erroneous: take the one which teaches that molecular aggregation is ever attended with dissipation of energy. From whence, then, comes the immense force which is liberated from the constituents of gunpowder by its exciter, fire?—which is a certain order of vibration. Concussion, another order of vibration, releases the hidden energy stored in the molecules of dynamite, which tears the rocks asunder as if they were egg-shells. Still another order of vibration, which Keely has discovered, dissociates the supposed elements of water, releasing from its corpuscular embrace almost immeasurable volumes of force.

The discoverer of this law of nature has long been harassed and made to feel like a galley-slave chained to a rock, while with Prometheus aspirations he is seeking to bring down fire and light from heaven for his fellow-men.

When Professor Leidy followed his impulse to leap the hedge which divided his special field of research from the domain that Keely was exploring, his was the first effort made by a man of science to save to the world "the hidden knowledge" bestowed upon one who, in my opinion, is alone capable of completing his system in a form to transmit this knowledge to others. I doubt not that this will seem to you as the language of fanaticism; but my convictions do not come from things hoped for. They are the result of the evidence of things seen, year after year, for nearly a decade of years.

As a school-girl, fifty years ago, I had the privilege of attending courses of lectures at Yale College, where experiments were given in natural philosophy and in chemistry; which kept up the interest that was awakened in earlier years; when, with my mineral hammer and basket, my father took me in his walks, laying the foundation of that love of true science which has made the discoveries of Keely of such intense interest to me.

Superficial as was and still is my knowledge of science, in its various branches, my interest has never abated; and thus, by my course of reading, I have kept myself abreast of the most advanced writers of modern thought, preparing the way for the help that I have been able to give Mr. Keely by putting books into his hands which, after more than twelve years of blind struggles to grapple with the force he had stumbled over, helped him to comprehend its nature, sooner than he would have done had he been left to work out his conjectures unaided, he tells me.

Marvellous as is the extent of Keely's knowledge of vibratory physics, I doubt very much whether he knows enough of mechanical physics to perform the trickery which Professor Rowland accused him of attempting. "Of course every one is looking for a trick where Keely is concerned," writes a Baltimore man; and, so long as speculations in the stock of the Keely Motor Company are authorized by the managers of that company, or efforts made to dispose of it before any practical result is attained, so long will Keely be unjustly suspected of being in league with them to obtain money under false pretences.

It was after six or seven years of failure on the part of the stockholders of the company to furnish Keely with one dollar, even, that I made a contract with him in April, 1890, to supply all that he needed for the completion of his system; having first received the assurance of Mr. Keely's lawyer that he would carry out the united wishes of Mr. Keely and myself. At that time this announcement was made in the public journals:—

"There has been placed in the hands of Professor Leidy a fund for the use of inventor John W. Keely. The stipulation attached is that no use shall be made of the financial assistance for speculative purposes. This provision, which is made in the interests of the Keely Motor Company as well as for science, will end with the first attempt to speculate on the stock by exhibitions given of the operations of unpatentable engines. Professor Leidy holds the fund at his disposition, and will pay all bills for instruments constructed for researching purposes."

The report issued last month by the directors of the Keely Motor Company annulled this contract; and it now remains for your board to decide whether I shall, in behalf of science, continue to supply Mr. Keely with the means of continuing his researches, under the protecting auspices of the University of Pennsylvania, or leave him in the hands of those who are so blind to their own interests, as holders of stock in the Keely Motor Company, they cannot be made to see that their only hope of commercial success lies in the completion of the system that Keely is developing; and that the course proposed by Professor Leidy, and commended by Professor Hertz and Professor Fitzgerald, for Keely to follow, is the only one that will ever enable him to complete it.

This system is as much a work of evolution as is any one of the slow operations of nature. "Truth can afford to wait:" she knows that the Creator of all things never hurries. In these twenty years of toil Keely's patient perseverance has been godlike. It is the sharpest rebuke that could be uttered to those whose impatient "hue and cry" has been, "Give us a commercial engine and we will immortalize you;"—grinding from him, meantime, seven-eighths of his interests in his inventions.

But in his labours Keely finds a recompense that, as yet,

"the world knows not of;" for day by day he sees the once, to him, obscure domain lit up with ever-increasing glory; a domain the boundaries of which are the boundaries of the universe: the entrance into which promises the fulfilment of the hopes of those who look forward to "a time when we shall no longer go to the blind to lead the blind in our search to make life worth living; but, instead, be able to promote, in accordance with scientific method and in harmony with law, the physical, intellectual and moral evolution of our race."

As of Newton, with the change of one word only, so one day will it be said of Keely:—

> All intellectual eye—our solar round
> First gazing through, he by the blended power
> Of laws etheric, universal, saw
> The whole in silent harmony revolve.
> What were his raptures then! How pure! How strong!
> And what the triumphs of old Greece and Rome
> With his compared? When Nature and her laws
> Stood all disclosed to him, and open laid
> Their every hidden glory to his view.

On the 23rd of March, following the reading of this address, Professor Koenig, who had become deeply interested in Mr. Keely's researches, wrote:—

"With regard to the experiments, which I saw at Mr. Keely's, I venture upon the following suggestion, as a test of the nature of the force Mr. Keely is dealing with. The revolution of the compass as a result of negative polar attraction. It is stated in Mr. Keely's paper that he finds gold, silver, platinum, to be excellent media for the transmission of these triple currents. Now it is well known that these same metals are most diamagnetic, that is, unaffected by magnetic influences. If, therefore, a needle be made of one of these metals and suspended in place of the steel needle, in the compass, and put under the influence of Mr. Keely's force, it ought to revolve the same as the steel needle will under magnetic and polar and anti-polar influence. If Mr. Keely could make such a needle revolve, it would convince me that he is dealing with a force unknown to physicists."

To this requirement Mr. Keely replied: "To run a needle, composed of non-magnetic material, by polar and depolar action is a matter of as infinite impossibility as would be the raising of a heavy weight from the bottom of a well by sucking a vacuum in it, or the inhalation of water into the lungs instead of air, to sustain life."

However, at Dr. Brinton's suggestion, Mr. Keely took up a line of research that was new to him, and succeeded in making a needle of the three metals, gold, silver and platinum, rotate by differential molecular action ; induced by negative attractive outreach, which is as free of magnetic force as a cork.

Professor Brinton had so mastered Keely's working hypotheses as to say, early in April, that he was sure he could make them understood by any intelligent person—writing of them : " All that is needed now is to show that Keely's experiments sustain the principles that underlie these hypotheses. As soon as Professor Koenig is prepared to report on the purely technical and physical character of the experiments, I shall be ready to go into full details as to their significance in reference to both matter and mind. It will be enough for me if Dr. Koenig is enabled simply to say that the force handled by Keely is not any one of the already well-known forces. Let him say that, and I will undertake to say *what it is*."

On the evening of the 20th of April, the Provost of the University of Pennsylvania, with others who were invited, met at Mrs. Moore's house to hear the report of the " observation " of Mr. Keely's researching experiments. The result was not made public; as it was desired, by all concerned, that nothing should be made known which could in any way influence the price of the stock of the company, to which Mr. Keely is under obligations; and which, as far as marketable value is concerned, is quite worthless until his system is completed to that point where some one device or machine can be patented. But, after Professor Koenig had made his report to those assembled, and Professor Brinton had read his abstract, all that had been asked for Mr. Keely, in behalf of the interests of science, was conceded to him. Mr. Keely has been able to continue his researches, up to the present time, without the delays which actions-at-law would have occasioned.

Professor Brinton, before making public his " Abstract of Keely's Philosophy," wishes to add two parts, one on the diffi-

An Appeal in Behalf of Science.

culties in the way of physicists in understanding Keely's theories; the other on the relations of the conditions of the inter-etheric order to the laws of mind.

The address of Mrs. Moore, type-copied, was sent to various editors and men of science in Philadelphia, as well as to leading capitalists; and, in this crisis of Keely's connection with the stockholders of The Keely Motor Company, some of these editors rendered substantial aid in making known his critical position; most notably the *Inquirer*, owned by Mr. Elverson, and the *Evening Telegraph*, owned by Mr. Warburton, with the result that a decided change in public opinion took place, after these journals announced, in April, that Professor Koenig had tested the energy, employed by Keely, with the most sensitive galvanometer of the university, in the presence of Professor Leidy, Professor Brinton, Doctor Tuttle (a Baltimore physicist) and others, finding no trace of electricity; and by other tests no magnetism. The two professors who thoroughly investigated Keely's theories, and observed his demonstrations, were chosen because they possessed the qualities of mind which Herbert Spencer said constitute the first condition of success in scientific research, viz. "an honest receptivity and a willingness to abandon all preconceived notions, however cherished, if they be found to contradict the truth."

Professor Leidy and Dr. Willcox, during their observations of Keely's progressive experimental researches, had expressed no opinion of Keely's theories, other than that they did not correspond with their own ideas; but Professor Koenig boldly said, "I not only think Mr. Keely's theories possible, but I consider them quite probable." Professor Brinton, who made a study of Keely's theories, so mastered them as to be able to suggest to Keely a new line of research, required by Dr. Koenig in the tests proposed; and the synopsis of Keely's philosophy, prepared by Doctor Brinton, has made Keely's hitherto unintelligible language intelligible to men of science.

Notwithstanding this favourable result, a New York journalist, under a fictitious name, pretended to have discovered that Keely is a fraud, using well-known forces;·which statements were published (with woodcuts of instruments discarded by

Keely two years before) in the *New York Herald* and *The Press*, in Philadelphia. It is amusing to see how "history repeats itself;" for, in the year 1724, in a letter to the Royal Society, Hatzfeldt attacked Sir Isaac Newton in much the same spirit. One would suppose in reading what Hatzfeldt has written of an invention of his time, that it had been written, word for word, of this ignorant investigator of Keely's experiments in researching. After commenting upon the corruption of human nature as shown, in his day, by want of veracity, and the tendency to vicious misrepresentation, he says: "If the said machine was contrived according to the weak sense and understanding of those who pretend it to be moved in other ways than that declared, it would have been discerned before this.

"And those who pretend it to be moved by water, or air, or magnetism, one of which (meaning water) even our most famous author did in the beginning affirm it to be moved by, is so very weak that I don't at all think it deserving to be considered.

"And what is still worse, to pretend it to be a cheat is a manner of proceeding which is neither consistent with equity nor common sense. As long as arts and sciences have the misfortune of depending on the direction of *such like persons*, no progress toward truth can be made, but I shall make it sufficiently appear that there is yet more truth behind the hill than ever has been brought to light. There be persons who, when disappointed of gain, turn their shafts against those who have circumvented them.

"All those who know anything of philosophy know that gravity is generally (and chiefly by Sir Isaac Newton and his followers) denied to be essential to matter, which I shall not only prove the contrary of, but I shall likewise show the properties in matter, on which the principle depends, to be the most glorious means to prove the existence of God, and to establish natural religion."

Is it not rather remarkable that, after a sleep of nearly two centuries, it is again claimed that gravity is inherent in all matter?

It has been very generally supposed that Keely is working at haphazard, as it were; in other words, that he has no theory to go upon. Professor Brinton writes of Keely's theories : " Mr. Keely has a coherent and intelligent theory of things, or philosophy, on which he lays out his work and proceeds in his experiments." March 6th, the same professor writes : " Keely's paper on Latent Force in intermolecular spaces is clear enough and instructive, but the average reader will find the perusal up-hill work, from lack of preliminary teaching. Naturally, Mr. Keely, whose mind has been busy with this topic for years, and who is more familiar with it than with any other, does not appreciate how blankly ignorant of it is the average reader. Also naturally he writes above the heads of his audience."

A correspondent in *Invention*, London, writes December 12, 1891 : We have at various times in these columns alluded to the investigations of the Philadelphia scientist, J. W. Keely, and this researcher—who is now stated to be engaged in finding a method whereby the power [1] which he professes to have discovered can be employed as a motor in the place of steam—is just now the object of considerable attention in the press of the United States. To summarize the present state of the criticism to which this man is subjected, we may mention that for some time past *The New York Herald*, among other papers, has been printing a series of articles that have been recently prepared by an American *inventor* named Browne, professing to show how Keely has, for nearly twenty years, been deceiving expert engineers, shrewd men of the world, some few university professors and others, by the use of compressed air, obtaining testimonials of his discovery of an unknown force in nature. In reading his articles any one who has seen the photographs—as the writer has done—of the researching instruments discarded by Keely, in past years, and those that he is now employing in their place, cannot fail to detect the misstatements and misrepresentations made.

Mr. Browne (?) even overrides the testimony of the late Professor Leidy, Dr. Willcox, Dr. Koenig, Dr. Brinton—the

---

[1] Mr. Keely explains the energy he is handling to be a condition of sympathetic vibration, associated with the Polar stream of our planet, positively and negatively.

Baltimore physicist—Dr. Tuttle, and the engineers Linville and Le Van, all of whom have tested the force used by Keely, and admitted that no electricity, no magnetism, no compressed air is used. Without endorsing in the slightest anything that Keely has discovered, or claims to have discovered, we think that, with the English love of fair play, both sides should always fairly be heard before either is condemned, and as Mr. Keely has consented to instruct a well-known English physicist in his method of producing the force handled, there is every chance of the truth being known, and the correct state of the matter divulged to the scientific world at large, when, mayhap, this rival inventor may have to retract his assertions or stand a suit for libel. We do not say it will be so—we only assert it may be. Professor Brinton, who has made a study of Keely's methods, writes this month to a friend in London :—" The *exposé* of Keely's alleged methods continues each week. Some of the proposed explanations are plausible, others are plainly absurd. They only serve to attract renewed attention to Keely. I have written to the editor to ask him to arrange a meeting for me with the writer, but I have not yet been able to discover the Mr. Browne,[1] of Brooklyn, who is the supposititious author."

Mr. Keely has chosen the successor [2] of Professor Tyndall, at the Royal Institution of Great Britain, as the physicist to whom he will communicate his method. This will be welcome news indeed to scientists on both sides of the Atlantic, and the result will be awaited with anxiety alike by both the friends and foes of Keely. We shall watch for the result, as will our American confrères.—*Wm. Norman Brown.*

---

[1] Mr. B. (not Browne) was afterwards discovered to be an inventing journalist, who had been " disappointed of gain," and whose statements concerning Dr. Leidy had to be corrected.

[2] Professor Dewar's visit to Keely's workshop has been delayed until he goes to America as Royal Commissioner this year.

CHAPTER XVII.

1891.

MORE OF KEELY'S THEORIES.—HIS TRADUCERS EXPOSED.

It was in India that man first recognized the fact that force is indestructible and eternal. This implies ideas more or less distinct of that which we now term its correlation and conservation. The changes which we witness are in its distribution.—PROFESSOR DRAPER.

"For all things that be not true, be lies."

There is a principle in music which has yet to be discovered.—SIR JOHN HERSCHEL.

From the *Chicago Tribune*.

THAT was a happy inspiration which led the Quintet Club, of Philadelphia, to pay a visit to the workshop of Keely a few weeks ago. Its members had been told that the illustrious inventor had employed the power of music to develop the wonderful forces of nature, and evolve by a law of sympathetic vibrations a mighty energy through the disintegration of a few drops of water. Naturally they were anxious to go. They were familiar with the claim made by Paganini that he could throw down a building if he knew the chord of the mass of masonry, and wanted to know if it were possible that the dream of the great violinist is realized at last.

So nearly as can be made out from the mysterious language of the man of many promises, there is a harmony of the universe that is controllable by the strains of music. Each of the molecules composing a mass of matter is in a state of incessant oscillation, and these movements can be so much changed by means of musical vibration that the matter will be disintegrated, its constituent molecules fly apart, and a propulsive force be generated similar to that which is evolved by the touching of a match to a single grain of powder stored in a magazine. He holds that matter is nothing but forces held in equilibrium, and that if the equilibrium be once destroyed the most tremendous consequences will ensue.

According to the report, he proved to the satisfaction of more than one member of the club that he has already discovered the means of calling out this force, and is able to partially control it. In their presence he caused a heavy sphere to rotate rapidly or slowly, according to the notes given by the instrument on which he played. The sphere was so isolated as to prove that it could not be acted on by electricity or in any other way than by the sound waves. He disintegrated water into what he calls "etheric vapour" by means of a tuning fork and a zither. The disintegration of only four drops of water produced a pressure of 27,000 pounds to the square inch, and three drops of the harmless liquid fired off a cannon "with a tremendous roar."

All this is wonderful—if true. And it is strangely parallel to the most advanced lines of modern thought in a scientific direction, if not coincident with them. There is the point. Is there a "thin partition" dividing the wisdom of the schools from the insanity of Keely, or will he yet prove his right to take rank among the greatest of earth's inventors? If he can do what is at present claimed for him, doing it honestly and without any hocus-pocus to beguile the fools, he has already earned a title higher than that worn by any man of the age. If he is simply cheating those to whom he exhibits his mechanism, he is one of the biggest charlatans that ever drew breath, and ought to be scouted accordingly. And here is the difficulty. The visit alluded to is claimed to have been made on May 9th, or fully six weeks ago. Surely if such results were achieved then, as reported by the *Philadelphia Inquirer*, many others would ere this have been asked and permitted to witness a repetition of the experiments, and the scientific world would now be in a blaze of excited admiration of the man and his methods. But nothing further is said about it. Keely is still plodding away in his workshop, and the world is still rolling round in happy

More of Keely's Theories.   267

ignorance of what he has done towards revolutionizing existing lines of thought and modes of action. Surely something is radically wrong. The scientists owe it to themselves as well as to the inventor to see to it that this condition is not allowed to continue. They should appoint a commission to investigate, and find out whether Keely is a genius worthy of the highest honours and rewards that can be bestowed, an arrant impostor, whose fittest place would be the penitentiary, or a crank that ought to be put in a lunatic asylum. It is hard to resist the conclusion that he is one or the other of these, and in either case he is not getting his deserts. Let Keely be scientifically investigated. He has been permitted to remain in obscurity too long already. He should be reported on, no matter whether the result be to raise a mortal to the skies or send an alleged angel down to the depths of infamy as a life-long deceiver of his species."

[The *Tribune* is informed that the report was correct in every particular, and that Professor D. G. Brinton, of the University of Pennsylvania, has prepared a paper on the subject, and will publish it when Mr. Keely is ready to have his system made known.—ED. *Inquirer*.]

The writer of this article in the *Chicago Tribune* has expressed the prevailing sentiment of our time, in regard to Keely, as far as those are concerned who are in ignorance of the fact that Keely has discovered an unknown energy, and is working out a system which he must himself first learn, by researches into the laws of nature governing it, before he can apply it to mechanics, or make it even so much as understood by others.

The unprincipled journalist before alluded to, after failing in an attempt to obtain admission to Mr. Keely's workshop, wrote a series of articles for the press, recounting Keely's researching experiments in 1889 and 1890, as then shown to Professor Joseph Leidy, Dr. James Willcox, and others. This journalist, who professed to give woodcuts of Keely's researching instruments, was entirely ignorant of the fact that the experiments which he described had never once been repeated, during the last eighteen months; Keely having taken up researches on another line, as soon as he had gained sufficient control of the force he was handling to cause the solid bronze weight weighing six and three quarters lbs., to rise in the jar, rest midway, or remain stationary at will. The "Generator," described by this journalist in the Philadelphia Press of November 1st, 1891, never had any existence beyond the journalist's brain and the woodcut. It was represented as a square structure, "big and thick walled enough to hold a donkey engine," whereas the true disintegrator (or improved generator) is round, and about the size of the wheel of a baby's perambulator. This form of generator Mr. Keely has been using for about three years; suspending it from a staple in the ceiling, or against the wall, when using it in the dissociation of the so-called elements of water. Consequently, it was impossible for the force to be "conducted from a reservoir eight or ten squares distance," as suggested by this inventing journalist, who says that he "spent sleepless nights" in devising the way in which the generator was operated by Keely : asserting that " this extraordinary force was loaded like electricity through a wire and discharged like steam through a pipe."

In a romance called "The Prince and the Pauper" these lines occur: "For, look you, an it were not true, it would be a lie. It surely would be. Think on't. *For all things that be not true, be lies,*—thou canst make nought else out of it." Never were truer words written, and equally true is it that, as another author has written, "If the boy who cannot speak the truth, lives to be a man, and becomes a journalist, he will invent lie after lie as long as he can get a Journal to print them and to pay him for them." There are very few men, who take up journalism in the spirit of a St. Beuve. Quite as few are there who are competent to write, in any way, of Keely's discoveries and all that they involve. Even among men of science, only one man has been found who is able to comprehend Keely's theories, and to handle them in a way to make them intelligible to others. S. Laing, in "Modern Thought," says, " Science traces everything back to primeval atoms and germs, and there it leaves us. How came these atoms and energies there, from which this wonderful universe of worlds has been evolved by inevitable laws? What are they in their essence, and what do they mean? The only answer is, "It is unknowable. It is behind the veil. Spirit may be matter, matter may be spirit." Keely's researches have been of a nature which, grappling with these mysteries, has brought them to the light. He tells us that spirit is the soul of matter, and that no matter exists without a soul.

More of Keely's Theories.

The sympathetic conditions that we call mind are no more immaterial in their character than light or electricity. The substance of the brain is molecular, while the substance of the mind that permeates the brain is inter-etheric, and is the element by which the brain is impregnated; exciting it into action and controlling all the conditions of physical motion, as long as the sympathetic equatative is in harmony, as between the first, second, and third orders of transmission; molecular, atomic and etheric. By this soul-substance is the physical controlled. In order to trace the successive triple impulses, taking the introductory one of sympathetic negative outreach, towards the cerebral neutrals, which awakens the latent element to action, we find that mind may be considered a specific order of inter-atomic motion sympathetically influenced by the celestial flow, and that it becomes when thus excited by this medium a part and parcel of the celestial itself. Only under these conditions of sympathetic assimilation can it assert its power over the physical organisms; the finite associated with the infinite.

The brain is not a laboratory. It is as static as the head of the positive negative attractor,[1] until influenced by certain orders of vibration, when it reveals the true character of the outreach so induced. The brain is the high resonating receptacle where the sympathetic celestial acts, and where molecular and atomic motion exhibits itself, as according to the intensification brought to bear upon it by the celestial mind flow.

The cerebral forces, in their control of the physical

[1] One of Keely's researching instruments.

organism, reveal to us the infinite power of the finer or spiritual fluid, though not immaterial, over the crude molecular. The luminous, etheric, protoplastic element, which is the highest tenuous condition of the ether, fills the regions of infinite space, and in its radiating outreach gives birth to the prime neutral centres that carry the planetary worlds through their ranges of motion.

If the minds of all the most learned sages, of all time, were concentrated into one mind, that one would be too feeble, in its mental outreach, to comprehend the conditions associated with the fourth order of sympathetic condensation. The controversies of the past in regard to the condensation of invisible matter prove this. The chemistry of the infinite and the chemistry of the finite are as wide apart, in their sympathetic ranges, as is the velocity of light from the movement of the hour-hand of a clock. Even the analysis of the visible conditions taxes our highest powers of concentration.

The question naturally arises, Why is this condition of ether always under a state of luminosity of an especial order? Its characteristics are such, from its infinite tenuity and the sympathetic activity with which it is impregnated, that it possesses an order of vibratory, oscillatory velocity, which causes it to evolve its own luminosity. This celestial, latent power, that induces luminosity in this medium, is the same that registers in all aggregated forms of matter, visible and invisible. It is held in corpuscular embrace until liberated by a compound vibratory negative medium.

What does this activity represent, by which luminosity is induced in the high etheric realm? Does not the force following permeation by the Divine Will show that even this order of ether, this luminiferous region, is bounded by a greater region still beyond?—that it is but the shore which borders the realm, from which the radiating forces of the Infinite emanate: the luminiferous being the intermediate which transfers the will force of the Almighty towards the neutral centres of all created things, animate and inanimate, visible and invisible; even down into the very depths of all molecular masses. The activity of the corpuscles, in all aggregations, represents the outflow of this celestial force, from the luminiferous track, towards all these molecular centres of neutrality, and reveals to us the connecting link between mind and matter. How plainly are we thus taught that God is everywhere, and at the same time in every place. It gives us a new sense of the omniscience and omnipresence of the Creator. In these researches I am brought so near to the celestial conditions that my pen is ready to fall from my hand while writing on this subject; so more and more sensibly do I feel my abject ignorance of its depths. . . .

These conditions of luminosity have no thermal forces associated with them; although, paradoxically, all thermal conditions emanate from that source. The tenuity of this element accounts for it. It is only when these sympathetic streams come in conflict with the cruder elementary conditions, either the molecular or atomic, that heat is evolved from its latent state, and a different order of light from the etheric luminous is originated, which has all the high conditions of thermal force associated with it: the sun being the intermediate transmitter. Thus is shown the wonderful velocity of these sympathetic streams emanating from celestial space.

The sympathetic forces transmitted by our solar planet, to which our earth is so susceptible, are continuously received from the luminiferous realm; the sympathetic volume of which, as expended, is constantly equated by the exhaustless willforce of the Creator. Had the solar energy been subservient to what physicists ascribe it, the sun would have been a dead planet thousands of centuries ago, as also all planets depending upon it as an intermediate.

In fact, all planetary masses are sympathetic-transferringmediums, or intermediates, of this prime, luminous, dominant element. In the vibratory subdivision of matter, as progressive evolution has been analyzed, it is evident that these transfers of sympathetic force extend beyond the limits of our orbital range, from system to system, throughout the realms of space : these progressive systems becoming themselves, after a certain range of sympathetic motion, sympathetic intermediates, as included in the whole of one system, exemplified so beautifully in the cerebral convolutions, with their connective sympathy for each other; transferring as a whole on the focalizing centre, from which it radiates to all parts of the physical organism, controlling in all its intricate variety the sympathetic action, of our movements.

"What is there that we really know?" asks Buckle. "We talk of the law of gravitation, and yet we know not what gravitation is; we talk of the conservation of force and distribution of forces, and we know not what forces are." "The vibratory principles now discovered in physics," says Hemstreet, "are so fine and attenuated that they become an analogy to mental or cerebral vibrations." Let us see what Keely's system of vibratory physics says of gravity, cohesion, etc.

What is Gravity?—Gravity is an eternal existing condition in etheric space, from which all visible forms are condensed. Consequently, it is inherent in all forms of matter, visible and invisible. It is not subject to time nor space. It is an established connective link between all forms of matter from their birth, or aggregation. Time is annihilated by it, as it has already traversed space when the neutral centres of the molecules were established.

Gravity, then, is nothing more than an attractive, sympathetic stream, flowing towards the neutral centre of the earth, emanating from molecular centres of neutrality; concordant with the earth's centre of neutrality, and seeking its medium of affinity with a power corresponding to the character of the molecular mass.

What is Cohesion?—*Cohesion* is sympathetic negative attraction. It is the negative, vibratory assimilation, or aggregation, of the molecules, acting according to the density or compactness of the molecular groupings on their structures. The differing character of molecular densities, or molecular range of motion, represents differing powers of attraction. The lower the range of motions on the molecular vibrations of these structures, the greater is the attractive force that holds them together; and *vice versâ*.

What is Heat? *Heat* may be classed as a vibro-atomic element, not exceeding 14,000 vibrations per second at its greatest intensity, latent in all conditions of matter both visible and invisible. The velocity of the sympathetic flows which emanate from our solar world, the sun, coming into contact with our atmospheric medium, liberates this element in all the different degrees of intensity that give warmth to our earth. Light is another resultant; the different intensities of which are produced according to the different angles of this sympathetic projectment.

The light that emanates from a glow-worm is the resultant of the action of the sympathetic medium of the insect itself on a centre of phosphorescent matter, which is included in its structure. The resultant of the two conditions are quite different, but they are governed by the same laws of sympathetic percussion.

Radiation is the term used to express the reaching out of the thermal element, after its liberation from its corpuscular imprisonment, to be re-absorbed or returned again to its sympathetic environment; teaching us a lesson in the equation of disturbance of sympathetic equilibrium.

Force.

"By what means is force exerted, and what definitely is force? Given that force can be exerted by an act of will, do we understand the mechanism by which this is done? And if there is a gap in our knowledge between the conscious idea of a motion and the liberation of muscular energy needed to accomplish it, how do we know that a body may not be moved without ordinary material contact by an act of will?" These questions were asked by Professor Lodge in his paper on "Time;" and as Keely contends that all metallic substances after having been subjected to a certain order of vibration may be so moved, let us see how he would answer these questions. When Faraday endeavoured to elaborate some of his "unscientific notions in regard to force and matter," men of science then said that Faraday's writings were not translatable into scientific language. The same has been said of Keely's writings. Pierson says, "The very fact that there is about the product of another's genius what you and I cannot understand is a proof of genius, i.e., of a superior order of faculties." Keely, who claims to have discovered the existence of hidden energy in all aggregations of matter, imprisoned there by the infinite velocity of molecular rotation, asserts that "physicists in their mental rambles in the realm of analytical chemistry, analytical as understood by them, have failed to discover the key-note which is associated with the flow of the mental element;" that "they have antagonized or subverted all the conditions," in this unexplored territory of negative research, which he has demonstrated as existing in reference to latent energy locked in corpuscular space. These antagonisms might have been sooner removed had those physicists who witnessed some of Keely's experiments, while he was still working blindfold as it were, in past years, not belonged to that class of scientists "who only see what they want to see, and who array facts and figures adroitly on the side of preconceived opinion." Since the last meeting of the British Association, Keely, in writing of some of the addresses delivered, says : " It delights me to find that physicists are verging rapidly toward a region which, when they reach, will enable them to declare to the scientific world what they now deny; *viz., that immense volumes of energy exist in all conditions of corpuscular spaces.* My demonstrations of this truth have been ignored by them and now they must find it out for themselves. I do not doubt that they will reach it in their own way. I accept Professor Stoney's idea that an apsidal motion might be caused by an interaction between high and low tenuous matter; but such conditions, even of the highest accelerated motion, are too far down below the etheric realm to influence it sympathetically, even in the most remote way. I mean by this that no corpuscular action, nor interaction can disturb or change the character of etheric vibrations. The conception of the molecule disturbing the ether, by electrical discharges from its parts, is not correct; as the highest conditions associated with electricty come under the fourth descending order of sympathetic condensation, and consequently its corpuscular realm is too remote to take any part towards etheric disturbance. Hypothesis is one thing and actual experimental demonstration is another; one being as remote from the other as the electrical discharges from the recesses of the molecule are from the tenuous condition of the universal ether. The conjecture as regards the motion being a series of harmonic elliptic ones, accompanied by a slow apsidal one, I believe to be correct. . . . The combination of these motions would necessarily produce two circular motions of different amplitudes whose differing periods might correspond to two lines of the spectrum, as conjectured, and lead the experimenter, perhaps. into a position corresponding to an ocular illusion. Every line of the spectrum, I think, consists not of two close lines, but of compound triple lines : though not until an instrument has been constructed, which is as perfect in its parts as is the sympathethic field that environs matter, can any truthful conclusion be arrived at from demonstration.

It must be remembered that Keely claims to have demonstrated the *subdivision of matter in seven distinct orders : molecular, intermolecular, atomic, inter-atomic, etheric, interetheric, reaching the compound inter-etheric in the seventh order.* In commenting further upon the experimental researches of men of science to show whether ether in contact with moving matter is affected by the motion of such matter, Keely writes : " The motion of any matter of less tenuity than the ether cannot affect it any more than atmospheric air could be held under pressure in a perforated chamber. The tenuous flow of a magnet cannot be waived aside by a plate of heavy glass, and yet the magnetic flow is only of an inter-atomic character and far more crude than the introductory etheric. The etheric element would remain perfectly static under the travel of the most furious cyclone ; it would pass through the molecular interstices of any moving projectile with the same facility that atmospheric air would pass though a coarse sieve. Ether could not be affected by the motion of less tenuous matter, but if the matter were of the same tenuous condition it would sympathetically associate itself with it ; consequently there would be no motion any more than motion accompanies gravity.

In the same way that the mind flow induces motion on the physical organism, sympathetic flows on molecular masses induce motion on the molecular. The motion of the molecules in all vegetable and mineral forms in nature are the results of the sympathetic force of the celestial mind flow, or the etheric luminous. over terrestrial matter. This celestial flow is the controlling medium of the universe, and one of its closest associates is gravity. . . . . The molecule is a world in itself, carrying with it all the ruling sympathetic conditions which govern the greatest of the planetary masses. It oscillates within its etheric rotating envelope with an inconceivable velocity, without percussing its nearest attendant, and is always held within its sphere of action by the fixed gravital power of its neutral centre, in the same sympathetic order that exists between the planetary worlds. The dissociation of aggregated molecules by intermolecular vibration does not disturb even to an atomic degree these fixed neutral points. Each molecule contributes its quota to the latent electrical force, which shows up by explosion after its gathering in the storm clouds, and then it returns to the molecular embrace it originally occupied. You may call this return, absorption; but it gets there first during corpuscular aggregation, and comes from there, or shows itself, during sympathetic disturbance of equilibrium.

There are three kinds of electricity, the harmonic and enharmonic, which, with their leader, the dominant, form the first triple. Their sympathetic associations evolve the energy of matter. The dominant is electricity luminous, or propulsive positive. The harmonic, or the magnetic, which is the attractive, with its wonderful sympathetic outreach, is the negative current of the triune stream. The enharmonic, or high neutral, acts as the assimilative towards the reinstatement of sympathetic disturbance. In electric lighting, the velocity of the dynamos accumulates only the harmonic current—by atomic and inter-atomic conflict—transferring one two hundred thousandth of the light that the dominant current would give, if it were possible to construct a device whereby it could be concentrated and dispersed. But this supreme portion can never be handled by any finite mode. Each of these currents has its triple flow, representing the true lines of the sympathetic forces that are constantly assimilating with the polar terrestrial envelope. The rotation of the earth is one of the exciters that disturbs the equilibrium of these sensitive streams. The alternate light and darkness induced by this motion helps to keep up the activity of these streams, and the consequent assimilation and dissimilation. The light zone being ever followed by the dark zone, holds the sympathetic polar wave constant in its fluctuations. This fact may be looked upon as the foundation of the fable that the world rests upon a tortoise. The rotation of the earth is controlled and continued by the action of the positive and negative sympathetic celestial streams. Its pure and steady motion, so free from intermitting impulses, is governed to the most minute mathematical nicety by the mobility of the aqueous portion of its structure, *i.e.*, its oceans and ocean's anastomosis. There is said to be a grain of truth in the wildest fable, and herein we have the elephant that the tortoise stands on. The fixed gravital centres of neutrality, the sympathetic concordants to the celestial outreach, that exist in the inter-atomic position, are the connective sympathetic links whereby the terrestrial is held in independent suspension. We cannot say that this corresponds to what the elephant stands upon, but we can say, " This is the power whereby the elephant is sympathetically suspended."

The Atom.

Question asked in Clerk Maxwell's memoirs : "Under what form, right, or light, can an atom be imagined?" Keely replies, It eludes the grasp of the imagination, for it is the introductory step to a conception of the eternity of the duration of matter. The magnitude of the molecule, as compared to the inter-atom, is about on the same ratio as a billiard ball to a grain of sand ; the billiard ball being the domain wherein the triple inter-molecules rotate, the inter-molecules again being the field wherein the atomic triplets sympathetically act, and again progressively, in the inter-atomic field, the first order of the etheric triplets begins to show its sympathetic inreach for the centres of neutral focalization. It is impossible for the imagination to grasp such a position. Inter-atomic subdivision comes under the order of the fifth dimensional space in etheric condensation. Atoms and corpuscules can be represented by degrees of progressive tenuity, as according to progressive subdivision, but to imagine the ultimate position of the atomic alone would be like trying to take a measurement of immeasurable space. We often speak of the borders of the infinite. No matter what the outreach may be, nor how minute the corpuscular subdivision, we still remain on the borders, looking over the far beyond, as one on the shore of a boundless ocean who seeks to cross it with his gaze. Therefore, philosophically speaking, as the atom belongs to the infinite and the imagination to the finite, it can never be comprehended in any form or light, nor by any right; for in the range of the imagination it is as a bridge of mist which can never be crossed by any condition that is associated with a visible molecular mass, that is, by mind as associated with crude matter.

Sympathetic Outreach

is not induction. They are quite foreign to each other in principle. Sympathetic outreach is the seeking for concordance to establish an equation on the sympathetic disturbance of equilibrium. When a magnet is brought into contact with a keeper, there is no induction of magnetism from the magnet into the keeper. The static force of the magnet remains unchanged, and the action between the two may be compared to a sympathetic outreach of a very limited range of motion. The sympathetic outreach of the moon towards the earth, has a power strong enough to extend nearly a quarter of a million of miles to lift the oceans out of their beds. This is not the power of induction. . . .

The sympathetic envelope of our earth owes its volume and its activity entirely to celestial radiating forces. Reception and dispersion are kept up by atomic and inter-atomic conflict, as between the dominant and enharmonic.

Silver represents the 3rd, gold the 6th, and platina the 9th, in their links of association, one to the other, in the molecular range of their motions, when submitted to vibratory impulses.

If an introductory impulse, representing the sympathetic chord of transmission, say B flat, or any other chord, be given to a sectional transmitting wire, the molecular triple, that is carried sympathetically along the path of such transmitter by the differentiation' induced, excites high sympathy with the polar terrestrial stream. The polar terrestrial, being triune in its character, requires a triune sympathizer to meet its differential requirements: silver the harmonic, gold the enharmonic, and platina the dominant. When this triple metallic condition is properly sensitized, by any chord on the dominant, combined molecular, differentiated action is induced; showing a condition approaching magnetism in its development of related sympathy, without having the conditions that are truly magnetic, as this term (magnetic) is understood by all physicists.

Magnetism is not polar negative attraction, any more than polar negative attraction is magnetism; for polar negative attraction shows positive sympathetic outreach, of a high order; which is a condition entirely foreign to magnetism.

Sympathetic negative attraction is not the resultant of electrical sympathization, but it includes the full triune flow; the dominant being the leader and associate of the celestial. The sympathetic outreach, of negative attraction, is the power that holds the planetary masses in their orbital ranges of oscillatory action. Magnetism has no outreach, but it pervades all terrestrial masses—all planetary masses. It is highly electrical in its character, in fact magnetism is born of electricity; whereas negative attraction is not, but it has a sympathetic outreach for magnetism. Magnetism is static. Sympathetic negative attraction reaches from planet to planet; but electricity does not, nor does magnetism. Sympathetic negative attraction is born of the celestial, and impregnates every mass that floats in space: seeking out all magnetic or electric conditions; and all these masses are subservient to celestial outreach. All the magnets in the world could not induce rotation, no matter how differentiated, but polar negative attraction induces rotation.

HYDROGEN.

The horizon of matter, which has been thought to rest over attenuated hydrogen, may extend to infinite reaches beyond, including stuffs or substances which have never been revealed to the senses. Beings fashioned of this attenuated substance might walk by our side unseen, nor cast a shadow in the noon-day sun.—*Hudson Tuttle.*

This supposition of itself admits that hydrogen is a compound. If it were indivisible it would assimilate with the high luminous, from which all substances are formed or aggregated. If hydrogen were a simple it could not be confined. No molecular structure known to man can hold the inter-luminous; not even the low order of it that is chemically liberated. The word "attenuated" admits that hydrogen is a compound. I contend that hydrogen is composed of three elements, with a metallic base, and comes under the order of the second atomic, both in vibration and sympathetic outreach.

Hydrogen exists only where planetary conditions exist: there it is always present, but never in uninterfered space. There is much celestial material that has never been revealed to the senses. My researches lead me to think that hydrogen carries heat in a latent condition, but I do not believe it will ever be possible to originate a device that will vibrate hydrogen with a velocity to induce heat.

The word imponderable as applied to a molecule is incorrect. All gases as well as atmospheric air are molecular in their structures. If atmospheric air is subdivided, by atomic vibration, it merely dissociates the hydrogen from the oxygen; neither of which, though disunited, passes from the intermolecular state; and not until hydrogen is sympathetically subdivided in its inter-molecular structure by inter-atomic vibrations can it assimilate with the introductory etheric element. There is a wonderful variation of gravital sympathy between the gaseous elements of compounds, all of which comes under the head of molecular. . . .

Under date of October 1st, 1891, Mr. Keely writes: I see no possibility of failure, as I have demonstrated that my theories are correct in every particular, as far as I have gone; and if I am not handicapped in any way during the next eight months, and my depolarizer is perfect, I will then be prepared to demonstrate the truth of all that I assert in reference to disintegration, cerebral diagnosis, aerial supension and dissociation, and to prove the celestial gravital link of sympathy as existing between the polar terrestrial and equation of mental disturbance of equilibrium. It is a broad assertion for one man, and 'an ignorant man' at that, to make; but the proof will then be so overwhelming in its truthful simplicity that the most simple-minded can understand it. Then I will be prepared to give to science and to commerce a system that will elevate both to a position far above that which they now occupy.

Again, November 4th, Mr. Keely says: The proper system for the treatment of cerebral differentiation is not yet known to the physician of to-day. The dissimilarities of opinion existing, with regard to any case, are confounding. When the true system is recognized, the vast number of physical experimentalists, now torturing humanity, will die a natural death. Until this climax is reached, physical suffering must go on multiplying at the same ratio that experimentalists increase. Molecular differentiation is the fiend that wrecks the physical world, using the seat of the cerebral forces as its intermediate transmitter. It is the devastating dragon of the universe, and will continue to devastate until a St. George arises to destroy it. The system of equating molecular differentiation is the St. George that will conquer.

When my system is completed for commerce, it will be ready for science and art. I have become an extensive night worker, giving not less than eighteen hours a day, in times of intensification. I have timed my race for life and I am bound to make it. . . .

New York Truth, 15th May, 1890, in commenting upon Keely's claims to have "annihilated gravity and turned the mysterious polar current to a mill-race," continues: "I sincerely hope that Mr. Keely may prove, AS FROM LATE DEVELOPMENTS HE IS LIKE TO DO, that the hidden spirit of the Cosmos, which men call Deity, First Cause, Nature, and other sonorous but indefinite names, has manifested itself to him; that the music of the spheres is a truth, not an imagination, and that vibration, which is sight, hearing, taste and smell, is in serious verity, all else. The fable of Orpheus and Arion may have a foundation in actual physics, the harmonies that move our souls to grief or joy as music, may be the same as those that govern and impel the stars in their courses, cause molecules to crystallize into symmetry, and from symmetry into life. Who shall say? IF THE ACCOUNTS OF KEELY'S LATE ACHIEVEMENTS BE TRUE, AND THEY ARE HONESTLY VOUCHED FOR BY MEN OF WORTH AND NOTE, THEN THE SECRET IS LAID BARE, THE CORE OF BEING IS OPENED OUT. In this age of dawning reason the candle cannot always be hidden under a bushel; some enterprising hand will lift the obstruction and let the light shine before men."

Two years have nearly passed away since this was written, during which time Mr. Keely has been engaged in perfecting his system for aerial navigation. He has, one by one, overcome all obstacles, and so far gained control, of the mysterious polar current, that he has been able to exhibit on the thirds, or molecular graduation of the propeller of his air-ship, 120 revolutions in a minute; and on the sixths, or atomic graduation, 360 revolutions in a minute. He still has the etheric field to conquer; but those who know how many years he has been making his mistakes stepping-stones in his upward progress, surmounting obstacle after obstacle which would have dismayed a less courageous soul, feel little doubt that he will "make the race," which he has timed for life, and reach the goal a conqueror, notwithstanding he is still so often "handicapped."

All those who had the privilege of witnessing Keely's researching experiments, in the spring of 1890, when he first succeeded in raising the metal weight, and who were sufficiently acquainted with the laws of physics to understand the conditions under which the weight was raised, pronounced the force by which it was affected to be an unknown force. Had the weight been but a nail or a feather, lifted under such conditions, physicists know that, after he has gained as perfect control of it as we now have of steam, air-ships weighing thousands of tons can be raised to any height in our atmosphere, and the seemingly untraversable highways of the air opened to commerce.

This force is not, like steam or electricity, fraught with danger in certain states to those who use it; for, after the molecular mass of the vessel has been fitted to the conditions required, its control becomes of such a nature that seemingly a star might as soon go astray, and be lost to the universe, as for the aerial ship to meet with an accident, unless its speed was pushed to that point where gravity resumes its control. In fact, Keely asserts that there is no known force so safe to use as the polar terrestrial force, for when the celestial and terrestrial conditions are once set up, they remain for ever; perpetual molecular action the result.

In using the word *celestial*, Keely refers to the *air*, in the same sense that *terrestrial* refers to the *earth*.

> Wide through the waste of ether, sun and star
> All linked by harmony, which is the chain
> That binds to earth the orbs that wheel afar
> Through the blue fields of Nature's wide domain.
> PERCIVAL.

From the New York Home Journal.

THE SONG OF THE CARBONS.[1]

> A weird, sweet melody, faint and far,
>   A humming murmur, a rhythmic ring,
> Floats down from the tower where the lenses are:—
>   Can you hear the song which the carbons sing?
>
> Millions of æons have rolled away
>   In the grand chorale which the stars rehearse,
> Since the note, so sweet in our song to-day,
>   Was struck in the chord of the universe.
>
> The vast vibration went floating on
>   Through the diapason of space and time,
> Till the impulse swelled to a deeper tone,
>   And mellowed and thrilled with a finer rhyme.
>
> Backward and forward the atoms go
>   In the surging tide of that soundless sea,
> Whose billows from nowhere to nowhere flow,
>   As they break on the sands of eternity.
>
> Yet, through all the coasts of the endless All,
>   In the ages to come, as in ages gone,
> We feel but the throb of that mystic thrall
>   Which binds responsive the whole in one.

---

[1] The universal physical law of molecular vibration is finely illustrated in the carbon pencils of the electric arc light used in some of the largest lighthouses. The molecular stir set up in the armatures of the dynamo machines by rapid magnetization and demagnetization is transmitted to the carbon points of the lantern, and reappears as a distinct musical tone.

We feel but the pulse of that viewless hand
   Which ever has been and still shall be,
In the stellar orb and the grain of sand,
   Through nature's endless paternity.

The smile which plays in the maiden's glance,
   Or stirs in the beat of an insect's wing,
Is of kin with the north light's spectral dance,
   Or the dazzling zone of the planet's ring.

From our lonely tower aloft in air,
   With the breezes around us, tranquil and free,
When the storm rack pales in the lightning's glare
   Or the starlight sleeps in the sleeping sea,

We send our greeting through breathless space,
   To our distant cousins, the nebulæ,
And catch in the comet's misty trace,
   But a drifting leaf from the tribal tree.

The song we hum is but one faint sound
   In the hymn which echoes from pole to pole,
Which fills the domes of creation's round,
   And catches its key from the over-soul.

And when it ceases all life shall fail,
   Time's metronome shall arrested stand;
All voice be voiceless, the stars turn pale,
   And the great conductor shall drop his wand.

CHAPTER XVIII.

A PIONEER IN AN UNKNOWN REALM.

Thus, either present elements are the true elements, or there is a probability of eventually obtaining some more high and general power of Nature, even than electricity; and which, at the same time, might reveal to us an entirely new grade of the elements of matter, now hidden from our view and almost from our suspicion.—*The Nature of the Chemical Elements.* FARADAY, 1836.

A mysterious force exists in the vibrations of the ether, called sound, which science and invention have so far failed to utilize; but which, no doubt in the near future, will come under man's control, for driving the wheels of industry.—*Thought as Force.* E. S. HUNTINGTON.

Force and forces—
No end of forces! Have they mind like men?
BROWNING.

THE *Spectator*, commenting on the jubilee of the Chemical Society, last year, said it was notable for two remarkable speeches; one by Lord Salisbury, and the other by Sir Lyon Playfair. Lord Salisbury reminded his hearers that about one hundred years ago, a very celebrated tribunal had informed Lavoisier that the French Republic had no need of chemists; "but," said his Lordship, "Lavoisier, though a man of very advanced opinions, was behind this age." Lord Salisbury proceeded to exalt chemistry as an instrument of the higher educational discipline. Astronomy, he said, was hardly more than a science of things that probably are; for, at such distance in space, it was impossible to verify your inferences. Geology he regarded as a science of things as they probably were; verification being impossible after such a lapse of time. But chemistry he treated as a science of things as they actually are at the present time. The *Spectator* remarks:—

Surely that is questionable. All hypothesis is more or

less a matter of probability. No one has ever verified the existence of atoms.

Sir Lyon Playfair, following Lord Salisbury, said, Boyle has been called the father of chemistry and the brother of the Earl of Cork; ironically hinting, perhaps, that Lord Salisbury was reflecting as much immediate glory on chemistry, by his interest in it, as did the relationship of the first considerable chemist to the Irish earl. Sir Lyon, acknowledging the revolutionizing progress of chemistry, remarked that within the last fifty years it had seen great changes; then, oxygen was regarded as the universal lover of other elements; and nitrogen was looked upon as a quiet, confirmed bachelor; but oxygen had turned out to be a comparatively respectable bigamist, that only marries two wives at a time; and nitrogen had turned out to be a polygamist; generally requiring three conjugates, and sometimes five, at a time. The false teachings of physicists in the past were admitted, including Sir Lyon's own errors; his old conceptions concerning carbonic acid and carbonic oxide all having broken down, under the crushing feet of progress. After all, says the *Spectator*, it seems that the French revolutionists should have welcomed chemistry, instead of snubbing it, for it has been the most revolutionary of sciences.

At the present time, notwithstanding the experiences of the past, Science stands as calmly on the pedestal, to which she has exalted herself, as if not even an earthquake could rock its foundations. In her own opinion, she holds the key to nature's domains. Some few there are who are ready to admit that it is possible Nature still holds the key herself; and who are not unwilling to encounter another revolution, if they can extend their knowledge of Nature's laws; even though it may leave only ruins, where now all is supposed to be so solid as to defy earthquakes and other revolutionizing forces.

In reviewing the history of the onward march of chemistry in the past, we find that Robert Boyle, who lived from 1627 to 1691, was the first chemist who grasped the idea of the distinctions between an elementary and a compound body. He has been called the first scientific chemist, and he certainly did much to advance chemical science, particularly in the borderland of chemistry and physics, but he did this more by his overthrow of false theories, than in any other way. It was left for Scheele (born 1742), an obscure Swedish chemist whose discoveries extended over the whole range of chemical science, and his French contemporary, Lavoisier (born 1743), to bring about a complete revolution in chemistry. Thus, step by step, and period by period, experimental science has prepared the way to reach that elevation which humanity is destined eventually to attain, when all errors have been discarded and truth reigns triumphant. The question has been asked, in view of the past history of discovery, what may not the science of the future accomplish in the unseen pathways of the air? That still unconquered field lies before us, and we know that it is only a question of time when man will hold dominion there with as firm sway as he now holds it on land and sea.

Physics and chemistry walk hand in hand. Scientists cannot cut the tie that joins them together in experimental science. Physics treats of the changes of matter without regard to its internal constitution. The laws of gravitation and cohesion belong to physical science. They concern matter without reference to its composition. Chemistry makes us acquainted with the constituents of the different forms of matter, their proportions and the changes which they are capable of bringing about in each other. But notwithstanding the lessons of the past, both chemistry and physics are blind to what the future has in store for them. Scientists have erected barriers to progress, building them so as to appear of solid masonry on the ground of false hypotheses; but, when the hour is ripe, these will be swept away as if by a cyclone, leaving not one stone on another. It was Boyle who overthrew the so-called Aristotelian doctrine, and Paracelsus's teachings of the three constitutents of matter, disputed first by Van Helmont. Boyle taught that chemical combination consists of an approximation of the smallest particles of matter, and that a decomposition takes place when a third body is present, capable of exerting on the particles of the one element a greater attraction than is exercised by the particles of the element with which it is combined. In this conjecture there is just a hint of the grand potentialities in the unknown realm which is now being explored by Keely, the discoverer of the order of vibration that releases the latent force held in the interstitial spaces of the constituents of water; one order of vibration, being more in sympathy with one of the elements of water than with the other, possesses a greater attraction for that element and thereby ruptures its atoms, showing up new elements. Not all men of science are willing to admit the atomic theory; although it explains satisfactorily all the known laws of chemical combination. Dalton, accepting the teachings of the ancients as to the atomic constitution of matter, was the first to propound a truly chemical atomic theory; a quantitative theory, declaring that the atoms of the different elements are not of the same weight, and that the relative atomic weights of the elements are the proportions, by weight, in which the elements combine. All previous theories, or suggestions, had been simply qualitative. Berzelius, the renowned Swedish chemist, advancing Dalton's atomic theory, laid the foundation stones of chemical science, as it now exists. Since his day, by the new methods of spectrum analysis, elements unknown before have been discovered; and researchers in this field are now boldly questioning whether all the supposed elements are really undecomposable substances, and are conjecturing that they are not. On this subject Sir Henry Roscoe says :—

"So far as our chemical knowledge enables us to judge, we may assume, with a considerable degree of probability, that by the application of more powerful means than are known at present, chemists will succeed in obtaining still more simple bodies from the so-called elements. Indeed, if we examine the history of our science, we find frequent examples occurring of bodies, that only a short time ago were considered to be elementary, which have been shown to be compounds, upon more careful examination."

What the chemist's retort has failed to accomplish has been effected by the discoverer of latent force existing in all forms of matter, where it is held locked in the interstitial spaces, until released by a certain order of vibration. As yet, the order of vibration which releases this force, has not been discovered in any forms of matter, excepting in the constituents of gunpowder, dynamite, and water. The Chinese are supposed to have invented, centuries before the birth of Christ, the explosive compound gunpowder, which requires that order of vibration known as heat to bring about a rupture of the molecules of the nitre, sulphur, and charcoal, of which it is composed. Dynamite requires another order of vibration—concussion—to release the latent force held in the molecular embrace of its constituents. The order of vibration discovered by Keely, which causes the rupture of the molecular and atomic capsules of the constituents of water, must remain —though in one point only—a secret with the discoverer, until he has completed his system for science, and some one patentable invention. Let physicists be incredulous or cautious, it matters not to him. He has proved to his own satisfaction the actual existence of atoms and their divisibility—and, to the satisfaction of thousands capable of forming an opinion, the existence of an unknown force. Men of science have not been in any haste to aid him, either with money or with sympathy, in his researches; and he will take his own time to bestow upon them the fruit of those researches.

Those who have not clear ideas as to the nature of elementary bodies—molecules and atoms—may like to know that elements are defined as simple substances, out of which no other two or more essentially differing substances have been obtained. Compounds are bodies out of which two or more essentially differing substances have been obtained. A molecule is the smallest part of a compound or element that is capable of existence in a free state. Atoms are set down, by those who believe in the atomic theory, as the indivisible constituents of molecules. Thus, an element is a substance made up of atoms of the same kind; a compound is a substance made up of atoms of unlike kind.

Over seventy elements are now known, out of which, or compounds of these with each other, our globe is composed, and also the meteoric stones which have fallen on our earth. The science of chemistry aims at the experimental examination of the elements and their compounds, and the investigation of the laws which regulate their combination one with another.

For example, in the year 1805, Gay-Lussac and Von Humboldt found that one volume of oxygen combines with exactly two volumes of hydrogen to form water, and that these exact proportions hold good at whatever temperature the gases are brought into contact. Oxygen and hydrogen are now classified as elementary bodies.

The existence of atoms, if proved, as claimed by the pioneer of whom we write, confirms Priestly's idea that all discoveries are made by chance; for it certainly was by a mere chance, as we view things with our limited knowledge, that Keely stumbled over the dissociation of the supposed simple elements of water by vibratory force;[1] thus making good Roscoe's assumption that, by the application of more powerful means than were known to him, still more simple bodies would be shown up. Had Keely subdivided these corpuscles of matter, after a method known to physicists, he would have been hailed as a discoverer, when it was announced by Arthur Goddard, in the *British Mercantile Gazette*, in 1887, that Keely declared electricity to be a certain form of atomic vibration of what is called the luminiferous ether.

Had Keely been better understood, science might have been marching with giant strides across this unknown realm during the many years in which men of learning have refused to witness the operation of the dissociation of water, because one of their number decided, in 1876, that Keely was using compressed air. Fixing bounds to human knowledge, she still refuses to listen to the suggestion that what she has declared as truth may be as grossly erroneous as were her teachings in the days when the rotation of the earth was denied; this denial being based upon the assertions of all the great authorities of more than one thousand years, that the earth could not move because it was flat and stationary. Herodotus ridiculed those who did not believe this. For two thousand years after the daily rotation of the earth was first suggested,

---

[1] It will be a matter of interest to those who have given attention to the laws of heredity to know that John Ernst Worrell Keely is a grandson of a German composer, Ernst, who led the Baden-Baden orchestra in his day; and that Keely's experiments in vibration had their origin in his knowledge of music, and were commenced in his childhood.

the idea was disputed and derided. The history of the past, says General Drayson, who claims to have discovered a third movement of the earth, teaches us that erroneous theories were accepted as grand truths by all the scientific authorities of the whole world during more than five thousand years.[1] Although the daily rotation of the earth and its annual revolution around the sun had been received as facts by the few advanced minds, some five hundred years before Christ, yet the obstructions caused by ignorance and prejudice prevented these truths from being generally accepted until about three hundred years ago, when Copernicus first, and afterwards Galileo, revived the theory of the earth's two principal movements. Human nature is the same as in the days when Seneca said that men would rather cling to an error than admit they were in the wrong; so it is not strange that General Drayson, as the discoverer of a third movement, has not received the attention that he deserves, although his mathematical demonstrations seem to be beyond dispute.

With Keely's claim, that latent force exists in all forms of matter, it is different ; for it is susceptible of proof by experiment. In the days when the sphericity of the earth was denied, for the asserted reason that the waters of the oceans and seas on its surface would be thrown off in its revolutions were it so, because water could not stay on a round ball," the statement could not be disputed; the theory of the laws of gravitation being then unknown. Copernicus and Galileo had nothing but theories to offer; consequently it took long years to overcome the bigotry and the baneful influence of the great authorities of the time. It is otherwise with Keely, who, for fifteen years and more, has been demonstrating this discovery to thousands of men ; some of whom, but not all, were competent to form an opinion as to whether he was "humbugging with compressed air," or with a concealed dynamo, or, still more absurd, with tricks in suction, as asserted by a learned professor.

Now that some of our men of science have consented to form

[1] See "Untrodden Ground in Astronomy and Geology."

their opinions from observation, without interfering with the lines of progressive experimental research which the discoverer is pursuing, there seems to be no doubt as to the result; nor of the protection of the discovery by science. Truth is mighty, and must in the end prevail over mere authority.

It has been said that we need nothing more than the history of astronomy to teach us how obstinately the strongholds of error are clung to by incompetent reasoners; but when a stronghold is demolished, there is nothing left to cling to. Sir John Lubbock says :—The great lesson which science teaches is how little we yet know, and how much we have still to learn. To which it might be added, and how much we have to unlearn!

All mysteries are said to be either truths concealing deeper truths, or errors concealing deeper errors; and thus, as the mysteries unfold, truth or error will show itself in a gradually clearer light, enabling us to distinguish between the two. It is now left for men of science to decide as to the nature of the mysteries which Keely is slowly unfolding, and whether his demonstrations substantiate his theories. They have been invited to follow him in his experimental research, step by step; to bestow upon him sympathy and encouragement, so long withheld, until he reaches that stage where he will no longer need their protection. Then, if science is satisfied that he has gained a treasure for her, in his years of dead-work, she must step aside and wait patiently until he has fulfilled his obligations to those who organized themselves into a company to aid him, long before she came forward to interest herself in his behalf. Those men of science who have refused to countenance this great work, even by witnessing experiments made to prove the discovery of an unknown force, are men who attempt no explanation of the miracles of nature by which we are surrounded, assuming that no explanation can be given; but, as Bacon has said, he is a bad mariner, who concludes, when all is sea around him, that there is no land beyond.

If the multitude of so-called laws of nature could be resolved into one grand universal law, would it not be considered a great step in the progress of scientific knowledge? This is what our pioneer claims for his discoveries, one law working throughout nature, in all things; for, as Macvicar says, the productive and conservative agency in creation, as it exists and acts, does not consist of two things, "idea" and "power"; but of a unity embracing both, for which there is no special name. The relation between the Creator and the Creation, the First Cause and what he has effected, is altogether inscrutable; but intelligence acting analytically, as it cannot be kept from doing, insists on these two elements in the problem, viz. idea and power.

"The law of the universe is a distinct dualism while the creative energies are at work; and of a compound union when at rest."

The hypothesis that motion can only be effected mechanically, by pressure or traction or contact of some kind, is an utterly helpless one to explain even familiar movements. Gravitation itself, the grandest and most prevailing phenomenon of the material universe, has set all genius at defiance when attempting to conceive a mechanism which might account for it. The law of sympathetic association, or sympathetic assimilation, between two or more atoms, or masses of atoms, explains this grand phenomenon; but Roscoe, in theorizing on the atomic theory, says that from purely chemical considerations it appears unlikely the existence of atoms will ever be proved. It never could have been proved by mechanical physics nor by chemistry. The law which locks the atoms together would have remained an unknown law, had not Keely opened the door leading into one of nature's domains which was never entered before, unless by the fabled Orpheus, who, mythology tells us, was killed because he revealed to man what the gods wished to conceal. Certainly, whether Orpheus ever existed or not, the principle which Pythagoras promulgated as the teaching of Orpheus is disclosed in one of Keely's discoveries.

In the great fresco of the school of Athens, by Raphael, Pythagoras is represented as explaining to his pupils his theory that the same principle underlies the harmonies of music and the motion of heavenly bodies. One of these pupils holds in his hand a tablet, shaped like a zither, on which are inscribed the Greek words, Diapason, Diapente, Diatessaron. Of the diapason, or concord of all, Spenser writes, in The Faerie Queen :—

> Nine was the circle set in heaven's place,
> All which compacted made a goodly diapase.

Here we have a clue to the Thirds, Sixths and Ninths of Keely's theories, in the operation of his polar negative attractor. The conception of the Pythagoreans of music, as the principle of the creation's order, and the mainstay and supporter of the material world, is strictly in accordance with the marvellous truths which are now being unfolded to science. Rightly divined Browning when he wrote of

> . . . . music's mystery, which mind fails
> To fathom; its solution no mere clue;

and Cardinal Newman also, when he discoursed of musical sounds, "under which great wonders unknown to us seem to have been typified," as "the living law of divine government." Since the days of Leucippus, poets and philosophers have often touched upon the mysteries hidden in sound, which are now being revealed in the experimental researches of Keely. These truths make no impression on those who are not gifted with any comprehension of nature's harmonious workings, and are regarded as flights of fancy and of rhetoric. Among the utterances of inspiration—and all truth is inspired—one of the most remarkable, when taken in connection with these discoveries, is found in these eloquent words of the Dean of Boston University in his "Review of Herbert Spencer," printed in 1876 :—

"Think of the universal warring of tremendous forces which is for ever going on, and remember that out of this strife is born, not chaos void and formless, but a creation of law and harmony. Bear in mind, too, that this creation is filled with the most marvellous mechanisms, with the most exquisite contrivances, and with forms of the rarest beauty. Remember, also, that the existence of these forms for even a minute depends upon the nicest balance of destructive forces.

Abysses of chaos yawn on every side, and yet creation holds on its way. Nature's keys need but to be jarred to turn the tune into unutterable discord, and yet the harmony is preserved. Bring hither your glasses—and see that, from atomic recess to the farthest depth, there is naught but 'toil co-operant to an end.' All these atoms move to music; all march in tune. Listen until you catch the strain, and then say whether it is credible that a blind force should originate and maintain all this."

Sir John Herschel said :—There is some principle in the science of music that has yet to be discovered.

It is this principle which has been discovered by Keely. Let his theories be disputed as they have been, and as they still may be, the time has come in which his supporters claim that he is able to demonstrate what he teaches; is able to show how superficial are the foundations of the strongholds to which physicists are clinging ; and able to prove purity of conditions in physical science which not even the philosophers and poets of the past have so much as dreamed of in their hours of inspiration.

> . . . . . ways are made,
> Burdens are lifted, or are laid,
> By some great law unseen and still,
> Unfathomed purpose to fulfil.

Our materialistic physicists, our Comtist and agnostic philosophers, have done their best to destroy our faith.

Of him who will not believe in Soul because his scalpel cannot detect it, Browning wrote :

> To know of, think about—
> Is all man's sum of faculty effects,
> When exercised on earth's least atom.
> What was, what is, what may such atoms be ?—
> Unthinkable, unknowable to man.
> Yet, since to think and know fire through and through
> Exceeds man, is the warmth of fire unknown ?
> Its uses—are they so unthinkable ?
> Pass from such obvious power to powers unseen,
> Undreamed of save in their sure consequence :
> Take that we spoke of late, which draws to ground
> The staff my hand lets fall ; it draws at least—
> Thus much man thinks and knows, if nothing more.

These lines were written in reference to Keely's discovery

of the infinite subdivision of the atom; for not until a much later period was Browning influenced by a New York journalist to look upon Keely as "a modern Cagliostro." Keely's discovery was the key-note of "Ferishtah's Fancies," written by Browning before he met this journalist.

Professor Koenig writes:—I have long given up the idea of understanding the Universe; with a little insight into its microcosm, I would feel quite satisfied; as every day it becomes more puzzling.

But there are no boundaries set to knowledge in the life of the Soul, and these discoveries reach out so far towards the Infinite, that we are led by them to realize how much there is left for science to explore in the supposed unfathomable depths of the etheric domain, whence proceeds the influence that connects us with that infinite and eternal energy from which all things proceed.

The attitude of willingness to receive truths, of whatever nature, now manifested by men of science in regard to Keely's experimental research, is shared by all who are not "wise in their own conceit." They stand ready to welcome, while waiting for proof, the discovery of Darwin's grand-niece, Mrs. F. J. Hughes, as now demonstrated by Keely, viz., that the laws which develop and control harmonies, develop and control the universe; and they will rejoice to be convinced (as Keely teaches) that all corpuscular aggregation absorbs energy, holding it latent in its embrace until liberated by a certain order of vibration; that nature does not aggregate one form of matter under one law, and another form of matter under another law. When this has been demonstrated, to their entire satisfaction, they will acknowledge that Faraday's speculations on the nature of force and matter pointed the way to Keely's discoveries. Some broad-minded men have been pursuing lines of research which give evidence of their desire to solve the problem for themselves as to the mode of rupturing the atom, which science declares to be indivisible. Before any great scientific principle receives distinct enunciation, says Tyndall, it has dwelt more or less clearly in many minds. The intellectual plateau is already high, and our discoverers are those who, like peaks above the plateau, rise over the general level of thought at the time. If, as Browning has said,

> 'Tis not what man does which exalts him, but what man would do,

surely this discoverer merits the sympathy and the admiration of all men, whether he succeeds commercially or not, for his persistent efforts to make his discoveries of use to the world. Keely has always said that scientists would never be able to understand his discoveries until he had reached some practical or commercial result. Only now he sees an interest awakened among men of science, which is as gratifying to him as it is unexpected. For the first time in his life, he is working with the appreciation of men competent to comprehend what he has done in the past, and what remains to be done in the future, without one aspiration on their part for monetary results.

Foremost among these men was the late Joseph Leidy, Professor of Biology in the University of Pennsylvania; but physicists were not satisfied to take the opinion of this great man, because he was a biologist. What better preparation than the study of the science of life could a man have to qualify him for discriminating between laws of nature as conjectured by physicists, and Nature's operations as demonstrated by Keely?

To such men, possessing entire scientific and intellectual liberty of thought, with that love of justice and truth which keeps its possessor from self-conceit, arrogance and intolerance, the world owes all that we now possess of scientific advance, since the days when men believed the thunder and lightning to be the artillery of the gods.

LUCIFER, *September*, 1892.

CHAPTER XIX.

LATENT FORCE IN INTERSTITIAL SPACES—ELECTRO-MAGNETIC RADIATION—MOLECULAR DISSOCIATION.

(By John Ernst Worrell Keely.)

The atom is infinitely divisible.—*Arthur Schopenhauer.*

For thou well knowest that the imbecility of our understanding, in not comprehending the more abstruse and retired causes of things, is not to be ascribed to any defect in their nature, but in our own hoodwinkt intellect.—P. 6, *A Ternary of Paradoxes.*—VAN HELMONT.

The advance of science, which for a time overshadowed philosophy, has brought men face to face once more with ultimate questions, and has revealed the impotence of science to deal with its own conditions and pre-suppositions. The needs of science itself call for a critical doctrine of knowledge as the basis of an ultimate theory of things. Philosophy must criticize not only the categories of science but also the metaphysical systems of the past.—PROF. SETH.

LATENT FORCE.

SCIENCE, even in its highest progressive conditions, cannot assert anything definite. The many mistakes that men of science have made in the past prove the fallacy of *asserting.* By doing so they bastardize true philosophy and, as it were, place the wisdom of God at variance; as in the assertion that latent power does not exist in corpuscular aggregations of matter, in all its different forms, visible or invisible.

Take, for example, gunpowder, which is composed of three different mediums of aggregated matter, saltpetre, charcoal, and sulphur, each representing different orders of molecular density which, when associated under proper conditions, gives what is called an explosive compound. In fact it is a mass which is made susceptible at any moment by its exciter fire, which is an order of vibration, to evolve a most wonderful energy in volume many thousands of times greater than the volume it represents in its molecular mass. If it be not *latent force* that is thus liberated by its exciter, a mere spark, what is it? Are not the gases that are evolved in such great volume and power held latent in the molecular embrace of its aggregated matter, before being excited into action? If this force is not compressed there, nor placed there by absorption, how did it get there? And by what power was it held in its quiescent state? I contend that it was placed there at the birth of the molecule by the law of sympathetic etheric focalization towards the negative centres of neutrality with a velocity as inconceivable in its character as would be the subdivision of matter to an ultimate end. Again, what is the energy that is held in the molecular embrace of that small portion of dynamite which by slight concussion, another order of vibration, evolves volumes of terrific force, riving the solid rock and hurling massive projectiles for miles? If it is not latent power that is excited into action, what is it? Finally, what is held in the interstitial corpuscular embrace of water, which by its proper exciter another form of vibration, is liberated showing almost immeasurable volume and power? Is not this energy latent, quiet, until brought forth by its sympathetic negative exciter? Could the force thus evolved from these different substances be confined again, or pressed back and absorbed into the interstitial spaces occupied before liberation, where the sympathetic negative power of the Infinite One originally placed it?[1]

[1] There are some paradoxical conditions shown up in the disintegration of water which require further research to get at the solution. In disintegrating, say five drops of water in a steel bulb of two cubic inches volume of atmospheric air, the force generated by the triple order of vibration, when weighed on a lever, shows ten tons pressure per square inch. In using the same number of drops in the same bulb, and associating it with a tube of two hundred cubic inches, the result is the same in the force developed per square inch as is shown on the volume of the one of two cubic inches. The solution of this problem seems to rest in the fact that the gaseous element thereby induced even in minute quantities, must possess the property of exciting atmospheric air to that extent as to force it to give up, to quite an extended degree, the latent energy that is held in its corpuscular depths. This introductory medium seems to act on the air in the same manner that a spark of fire acts on a magazine of gunpowder.

If latent force is not accumulated and held in corpuscular aggregations how is it that progressive orders of disintegration of water induce progressive conditions of increased volume and of higher power? I hold that in the evolved gases of all explosive compounds, dynamite or any other, there exists deeper down in the corpuscular embrace of the gaseous element, induced by the first explosion, a still greater degree of latent energy that could be awakened by the proper condition of vibration; and still further on *ad infinitum*.[1]

Is it possible to imagine that mere molecular dissociation could show up such immense volumes of energy, unassociated with the medium of latent force?

The question arises, How is this sympathetic power held in the interstitial corpuscular condition?

Answer.—By the incalculable velocity of the molecular and atomic etheric capsules,[2] which velocity represents billions of revolutions per second in their rotations. We shall imagine a sphere of twelve inches in diameter, representing a magnified molecule surrounded by an atmospheric envelope of one sixteenth of an inch in depth; the envelope rotating at a velocity of the same increased ratio of the molecule's magnification. At the very lowest estimate it would give a velocity of six hundred thousand miles per second, or twenty-four thousand times the circumference of the earth in that time. Is it possible to compute what the velocity would be, on the same ratio, up to the earth's diameter?[2] It is only under such illustrations that we can be brought even to faintly imagine the wonderful sympathetic activity that exists in the molecular realm. An atmospheric film, rotating on a twelve inch sphere at the same ratio as the molecular one, would be impenetrable to a steel-pointed projectile at its greatest velocity; and would hermetically enclose a resisting pressure of many thousands of pounds per square inch. The latent

---

The ether is the capsule to the molecules and atoms all the way up to the perfect stream of structural ether.

[2] A volume of pure ether equivalent to the atmospheric displacement caused by our Earth, could be compressed and absorbed in a volume of one cubic inch, by the velocity and sympathetic power of the etheric triple flows, focalizing toward the neutral centre, at the birth of the molecule.

force evolved in the disintegration of water proves this fact; for under etheric evolution, in progressive orders of vibration, these pressures are evolved, and show their energy on a lever especially constructed for the purpose, strong enough for measuring a force over three times that of gunpowder. We shall continue this subject a little farther, and this little farther will reach out into infinity. The speculations of the physicists of the present age, in regard to latent energy, would neutralize the sympathetic conditions that are associated with the governing force of the cerebral and the muscular organism. The evolution of a volition, the infinite exciter, arouses the latent energy of the physical organism to do its work; differential orders of brain-force acting against each other under dual conditions. If there were no latent energy to arouse sympathetically, there would be no action in the physical frame; as all force is will-force.

All the evolutions of latent power in its varied multiplicity of action induced by its proper exciters, prove the connecting link between the celestial and the terrestrial, the finite and the infinite. (See Appendix I.)

There would be no life, and therefore no action in aggregated matter, had the latent negative force been left out of it.

If a bar of steel or iron is brought into contact with a magnet, the latent force that the steel or iron is impregnated with is aroused, and shows its interstitial latent action by still holding another bar. But this experiment does not give the most remote idea of the immensity of the force that would show itself on more progressive exciters. Enough alternate active energy could be evolved, by the proper sympathetic exciter, in one cubic inch of steel to do the work of a horse, by its sympathetic association with the polar force in alternate polarization and depolarization.

This is the power that I am now getting under control (using the proper exciters as associated with the mechanical media) to do commercial work. In other words, I am making a sympathetic harness for the polar terrestrial force: first, by exciting the sympathetic concordant force that exists in the corpuscular interstitial domain, which is concordant to it; and secondly, after the concordance is established, by negatizing the thirds, sixths, and ninths of this concordance, thereby inducing high velocities with great power by intermittent negation, as associated with the dominant thirds.

Again: Take away the sympathetic latent force that all matter is impregnated with, the connective link between the finite and the infinite would be dissociated, and gravity would be neutralized; bringing all visible and invisible aggregations back into the great etheric realm.

Here let me ask, What does the term cohesion mean? What is the power that holds molecules together, but electro-magnetic negative attraction? What is the state that is brought about by certain conditions of sympathetic vibration, causing molecules to repel each other, but electro-magnetic radiation?

It must not be understood that the character of the action of the latent force liberated from liquids and gases is the same, in its evolution, as that of the latent force existing in metals. The former shows up an elastic energy, which emanates from the breaking up of their rotating envelopes; increasing, at the same time, the range of their corpuscular action: thus giving, under confinement, elastic forces of an almost infinite character. By liberation from the tube it is confined in, it seeks its medium of concordant tenuity with a velocity greater than that of light.

In metals, the latent force, as excited by the same sympathizer, extends its range of neutral sympathetic attraction without corpuscular rupture, and reaches out as it were to link itself with its harmonic sympathizer, as long as its exciter is kept in action. When its exciter is dissociated, its outreach nestles back again into the corpuscular embrace of the molecular mass that has been acted upon.[1]

This is the polar sympathetic harness, as between metallic mediums and the polar dominant current,—the leader of the triune stream of the terrestrial flow. (See Appendix II.)

The velocity of the sympathetic bombarding streams, towards the centres of neutrality, in the corpuscular atoms, during sympathetic aggregation of visible molecular masses (in registering the latent force in their interstitial spaces), is

[1] This is what Keely terms "sympathetic outreach."

thousands of times greater than that of the most sensitive explosives. An atmospheric stream of that velocity would atomize the plate of an ironclad, if brought to bear on it.

If the evolution of the power of a volition be set down as one, what number would that represent in the power evolved by such volition on the physical organism? To answer this we must first be able, mentally, to get down to the neutral central depths of the corpuscular atoms, where gravity ceases, to get its unit; and in the second place we must be able to weigh it as against the force physically evolved.

How true, "the finer the force the greater the power!" and the greater is the velocity, also; and the more mathematically infinite the computation.

Yet all these conditions of evolution and concentration are accomplished by the celestial mind force, as associated with terrestrial brain matter.

The first seal is being broken, in the book of vibratory philosophy: the first stepping-stone is placed toward reaching the solution of that infinite problem,—the source of life.

Theory of Vibratory Lift for Air-Ships.

All molecular masses of terrestrial matter are composed of the ultimate ether,—from which all things originally emanated. They are sympathetically drawn towards the earth's centre, as according to the density of their molecular aggregation, minus their force or sympathetic outreach towards celestial association. In other words, the celestial flow as controlling terrestrial physical organisms.

The sympathetic outflow from the celestial streams reaches the infinite depths of all the diversified forms of matter. Thus it is seen that the celestial flow which permeates, to its atomic depths, the terrestrial convolutions of all matter, forms the exact sympathetic parallel to the human brain-flow and the physical organism,—a perfect connective link of controlling sympathy, or sympathetic control. Under certain orders of sympathetic vibration, polar and anti-polar, the attractive sympathies of either stream can be intensified, so as to give the predominance to the celestial or to the terrestrial.

If the predominance be given to the celestial, to a certain degree, on a mass of metal, it will ascend from the earth's surface, towards the etheric field, with a velocity as according to the dominant concentration that is brought to bear on the negative thirds of its mass chords, by inducing high radiation from their neutral centres, in combination with the power of the celestial attractive.

The power of the terrestrial propulsive and celestial attractive to lift; and these conditions reversed, or the celestial propulsive and the terrestrial attractive, to descend. Associating these conditions with the one of corpuscular bombardment, it is evident to me with what perfection an air-ship of any number of tons weight can, when my system is completed, be controlled in all the varied movements necessary for complete commercial use at any desired elevation, and at any desired speed. It can float off into atmospheric space as gentle in motion as thistle-down, or with a velocity outrivalling a cyclone.[1]

Electro-Magnetic Radiation.

If the persistency of our vision could be reversed, so as to have the power to follow the track of the molecule's oscillations under a high condition of vibratory acceleration, associated with the assisting power of the finest instruments known at present in scientific research, it would not help us to determine the period of time wherein the sympathetic actions in nature are propagated. Therefore, we cannot, with any degree of certainty, establish a foundation whereon observation, so associated, is reliable. (Theoretically explained in 'Soul of Matter.')

As far as my researches have gone, I find that there is but one condition approaching reliability; and that is in computing the intermittent periodic disturbances along a

---

[1] A facetious journalist commenting on this paper reprints its last paragraphs as "the only part that is perfectly lucid to the lay mind," continuing :—" We trust Keely will continue to bombard his corpuscles until he accomplishes it. And when he does, all other scientific men of this or any other age will sink by comparison into insignificance. Let no man say he cannot do it. Mr. Keely, the world is still waiting for you."

nodal vibratory transmitter—the nodes of gold, silver and platina—a fixed number placed at such different distances, along its line, as to take up and equalize (by a certain order of vibratory transmissions) the chord masses of the nodal interferences between the triple metals of which the nodes are composed, and also the acoustic introductory impulse of whatever chord is set. This will determine the rate of their accelerated molecular oscillation, so induced beyond their normal standard, and give us some definite figures in the computing of vibrations, thousands of billions of times more than those of light.

Light is induced by electro-magnetic percussion emanating from the ether, and in its action represents the plane of magnetism. In fact it is the plane of magnetism when under polarization.[1] Some scientific theories of the past have taught us that electricity and magnetism are one and the same thing. Sympathetic vibratory philosophy teaches that they are two distinct forces of one of the triune sympathetic family.

I will try to make comprehensible the computation of the number (even to infinity) of the corpuscular oscillations, induced on the introductory ninths, over their normal standard. The molecules of all visible masses, when not influenced by surrounding acoustic vibratory impulses, move at a rate of 20,000 oscillations per second, one third of their diameters. We have before us one of these masses; either a silver dollar, a pound weight, a horse-shoe, or any other metallic medium, which I associate to one of my nodal transmitters, the other end of which is attached to the clustered thirds (or third octave) of my focalizing neutral concentrator. Another transmitter, of gold, silver and platina sections, is attached to the sixth cluster of same disk, the other end of which is con-

---

[1] Platina wires the thickness of a fine hair associated with each of the nine nodal beads, and concentrated towards a general centre of focalization, attaching the other end of the wires to the focal centre, will determine, by the magnetic conduction, the number of corpuscular oscillations per second induced by a thought, either positive or negative, in the central centres. These are the only conditions—those of magnetic conduction—whereby the evolution of a thought can be computed in regard to its force under propagation, as against the amount of latent energy set free to act as induced by such thought on the physical organism.

nected to resonating sphere on my compound instrument: all of which must be brought to a state of complete rest. Then, a slight tap, with a vulcanite rubber hammer on the chladna resonating disk, will accelerate the 20,000 molecular oscillations to 180,000 per second,—an increase of nine times the normal number. The nine nodes each touching the extreme end, next the mass operated upon, in this arrangement; silver, gold, platina, make up the nine. When I associate the seventh, I start with gold and end with platina; always on the triplets. Silver represents the lowest introductory third, gold the next, and platina the highest. If we start with a gold node, the multiplication on oscillation will be nine times nine, or 81 times the 20,000; which is 1,620,000 per second. Each node represents one wave length of a certain number of vibrations when shifted along the transmitter, over the section representing its opposite metal. The shifting of the gold one over the silver extreme section will hold the corpuscular range of the mass velocity at 1,620,000 per second: the introductory chord being set at B, third octave. It requires an accelerated oscillation on the molecules of a soft steel mass, at that chord, of a transmissive multiplication of the full nine, in order to induce a rotary action on the neutral centre indicator of focalizing disk; which by computation, means, per second, 156,057,552,198,220,000 corpuscular intermittent oscillations to move the disk 110 revolutions per second. This only represents the multiplication on the first nodal dissociator of the ninth. The second transition, on same, would mean this number multiplied by itself, and the residue of each multiplication by itself 81 times progressively. This throws us infinitely far beyond computation, leaving us only on the second of the full ninth, towards reaching the sympathetic corpuscular velocity attending the high luminiferous. I have induced rotation up to 123 revolutions per second on a neutral indicator that required billions of vibrations per second to accomplish; but even this vibration represents only a minute fraction of the conditions governing the sympathetic vitality which exists in the far luminous centres.

The interposition of hydrogen gas between soap-film, of

the differential diameters of thirds, illuminated by a solar ray in whose focus a quiescent prism is set posteriorly—the prism to be adjusted at the proper distance and angle, to throw the seven colours through the film enclosing the hydrogen in a way that will give the bow an arch of three feet—will register deep down, inaudible tones or sounds, and indicate their different conditions by the dissolving and re-dissolving of certain of the colours of such arch. To conduct such experiments properly necessitates, first, a location as nearly isolated from all extraneous audible sounds as is possible to get; and second, a pedestal of the lowest vibrating material, the base of it set deep in the earth, to arrange the instruments upon; and third, a room of the highest resonating qualities to enclose them. Under such conditions the inaudible sounds emanating from the operator, would have to be neutralized by a negative device to get at the proper conditions while under his manipulation. Thus the hidden inaudible world of sounds could be shown up, as the microscope shows up to the eye the hidden invisible forms of nature.

The condition of the mechanical requirements necessary to conduct successfully the line of research that I am now pursuing, will never be properly appreciated until the beauty of this system is shown up under perfect control for commercial use.

I have spoken elsewhere of the almost infinite difficulties of getting into position, to hold hydrogen gas in suspension between soap-film a proper period of time, to conduct these experiments. The setting of the other parts of the apparatus is quite easy in comparison. All wave propagations, electromagnetic or otherwise, by being thus reflected can be measured in regard to the time of their propagation; all of which are introductorily subservient to the luminiferous ether. The theory put forward by "men of science," in regard to electro-magnetic forces shows that they are misled by the imperfection of their instruments. They are trying to measure the infinite by the finite; necessitating terms of avoidance, to the instantaneous propagation of nature's sympathetic evolutions, of the same nature as the one advanced in the assertion that force does not exist in the interstitial embrace of all matter.

Maxwell's theory is correct that the plane of polarized light is the plane of the magnetic force. The sympathetic vibrations associated with polarized light constitute the pure coincident of the plane of magnetism. Therefore, they both tend to the same path, for both are inter-atomic, assimilating sympathetically, in a given time, to continue the race together; although one precedes the other at the time of experimental evolution. The time is approaching when electromagnetic waves with an outreach of two feet will be produced, having an energy equal to that now shown up on the magnet when it is about to kiss its keeper; and showing a radiating force too stupendous for actual measurement.

I have already shown, to a certain point, the power of this radiation, by breaking a rope that had a resisting strain of over two tons, which was attached to the periphery of a steel disk, twelve inches in diameter, moving at the slow rate of one revolution in two minutes; its molecular structure vitalized with 42,800 vibrations per second. There was no retardation while breaking the rope, and no acceleration when it was broken. This experiment has been repeated scores of times, before scores of visitors who came to my laboratory for the purpose of seeing it.

A computation of the conditions, already shown up in part, proves conclusively that the power of an electro-magnetic wave at an outreach of ten inches would be, if properly developed, equal to a lifting force of 36,000 pounds on a disk but three inches in diameter. Ten of such on the periphery of a vibratory disk, 36 inches in diameter, would represent 360,000 pounds actual lift at one revolution per minute. Perfect depolarization at one hundred times per minute would represent 360,000,000 pounds, lifted twelve times per minute, or 1000 horse power in the same time. An excess of 100 extra revolutions, under the same conditions, would mean 2000 horse power per minute.

By this new system, to perfect which I am now devoting all my time and my energies, dynamos will become a thing of the past, eventually; and electric lighting will be conducted by a polar negative disk, independent of extraneous power to run it, other than that of sympathetic polar attraction, as simple in its construction, almost, as an ordinary type-writing machine.

ANSWERS MADE IN LETTERS FROM MR. KEELY, TO QUESTIONS ASKED OF HIM.

Light incident to any body that absorbs or reflects it does not press upon it. The radiometer of Professor Crookes's invention is not operated by the pressure of light, but by corpuscular bombardment on the reflecting side of its vanes.

You have called my attention to the receding movement in the metal silver, which it assumes when the flow of an alternating current from an electro-magnet, in front, is thrown upon it. This does not prove that light presses upon it to induce that movement. It moves by inter-atomic bombardment of some 800 millions of corpuscular percussions a second; or, more truly by inter-sympathetic vibrations. If a homogeneous disk of gold, silver and platina, in proper proportions, were made the medium of interference, the resultant action would be startling in showing up the movement of molecular antagonistic thirds. The movement would be very erratic and gyroscopic. If the same disk were used or an intermediate transmitter to a negative focalizer, or in other words a polar radiator only one of which is in existence, by a nodal wire of gold, silver and platina, the effect on the disk at the negative terminus would be to set into action the latent force held in its molecular embrace, and would cause it to sympathetically adhere to the focalizer, with a power that would make it practically inseparable.

Professor Fitzgerald's lecture on electro-magnetic radiation shows that scientific men are beginning to realize, and that fairly, the truths appertaining to the new philosophy. The professor admits that electricty and magnetism are of differential character, and he is right. The progressive subdivision, induced on molecules by different orders of sympathetic vibration, and the resultant conditions evolved on the inter-molecule and inter-atom, by introductory etheric dispersion, prove that the magnetic flow of itself is a triple one, as is also the electric. Again, the professor says that electricity and magnetism would be essentially interchangeable if such a thing existed as magnetic conduction, adding: 'It is in this difference that we must look for the difference between electricity and magnetism.' Thus you see how plain it is that progressive scientists are approaching true science. The rotation of the magnetic needle, as produced in my researching experiments, proves conclusively that the interchange spoken of, in Professor Fitzgerald's lecture, is a differentiated vibratory one, in which the dominant and enharmonic forces exchange compliments with each other, in a differential way; thus inducing rotation, in other words polarization and depolarization.

The transmission of sympathetic atomic vibration, through a triple nodal transmitter, induces an inter-atomic percussion, that results in triple atomic subdivision, *not oscillating across the diameter of the atom,* but accelerating to an infinite degree the atomic film that surrounds it and at the same time extending the vibratory range of the atom far enough to set free the gaseous atomic element.

Molecular Dissociation.

If our sight could reach into the remote depths of the interstitial spaces which exist between the molecular ranges, and observe their wonderful action, in their oscillating motion, to and from each other, as guided by the Infinite in their sphere of vibrating action—could we comprehend the astonishing velocity of their gaseous capsules, combined as it is with the accompanying acoustic force, we would be, as it were, paralyzed with amazement. But we would then only be bordering on the still more remote depths of the interstitial atomic realm, stretching far down towards the neutral depths of the interatomic; and again, still farther to the borders of its etheric neutral radiating centre.

If our earth were to be submitted to the force governing the rotative action of the molecule, in its gaseous envelope, and its oscillatory range of motion were in the same ratio to the differential magnitude of each, the force of the vibration induced by its atmospheric surrounding would, in a short

Latent Force in Interstitial Spaces. 311

time, disintegrate its full volume, precipitating it into a ring of impalpable inter-molecular dust, many thousands of miles in diameter. If brought face to face with such conditions we could better understand the mighty and sympathetic force which exists in the far remote domain of the molecular and atomic embrace.

The question arises, how and by what means are we able to measure the velocity of these capsules and the differential range of their vibratory action? Also, how can we prove beyond dispute the facts relating to their sympathetic government? By progressive disintegration; this is the only way; and it is accomplished by the proper exciters of vibratory focalization; the introductory acoustic impulses which negatize their molecular, inter-molecular, atomic and inter-atomic media of neutral attractions, towards their focalized centres of sympathetic aggregation.

I hold that the sympathetic neutral flow which exists in this remote region is the latent power that, under the disintegration of water, is liberated; showing immense volume and infinite pressure. The same condition of latent power exists in metallic masses and, paradoxical as it may seem, exerts its force, under the proper exciter, only in a negative attractive way, while in water in a positive one. In minerals under liberation this latent power seeks its medium of tenuous equilibrium, leaving behind an impalpable dust, that represents molecular dissociation.

In order to get at the conditions which govern and give introductory impulses to that peculiar force which acts on the sympathetic medium that associates matter with matter, inducing magnetic antagonisms, it will be necessary to explain the triune conditions that govern sympathetic streams; as also the triune conditions of corpuscular association.

All forces in nature are mind forces: magnetic, electric, galvanic, acoustic, solar, are all governed by the triune streams of celestial infinity; as also the molecular, inter-molecular, atomic, and inter-atomic. The remote depths of all their acoustic centres become subservient to the third, sixth, and ninth position of the diatonic, harmonic and enharmonic chords; which, when resonantly induced, concentrate concordant harmony, by reducing their range of corpuscular motion, drawing them as if towards each other's neutral centre of attractive infinity.

The sympathetic acoustic exciters, or impulses, are: 1st. the third diatonic; 2nd. the harmonic sixths neutralizing affinity; 3rd. the enharmonic ninths—positive acceleration, which induces infinite trajective velocity from neutral centres; in other words, neutral radiation.

Every molecule in nature represents, without variation, the same chord. Variations that show up in the mass chord of different visible aggregations, are accounted for by the non-uniformity of their molecular groupings. If all were molecularly homogeneous, the chord masses of all structures would be perfectly alike in their resonant impulses.

When the triple introductory impulse is transmitted towards the mass to be sensitized, it subserves the molecular concordant thirds and antagonizes the discordant sixths extending the range of their oscillating paths; and thus induces the highest order of repellent antagonism towards the centre of neutral equilibrium.

We will now follow out, in their progressive orders, the conditions necessary to give to these acoustic introductory impulses the power, as transmitted through the proper media, to induce molecular dissociation.

First: If I wish to disturb and bring into action the latent force held in the embrace of any molecular mass, I first find out what the harmonic chord or note of its mass represents; and as no two masses are alike, it would seem to necessitate an infinite number of variations to operate on different masses; but such is not the case. All masses can be subserved to one general condition by the compound mechanical devices which I use for that purpose. We will suppose that the mass to be experimented upon, when chorded, represents B flat. Then, first, the negative radiating focalizing bar on the disk is liberated from its dampening rod, and associated with the magnetic defocalizing one. There are seven ranges of bars in all.

Latent Force in Interstitial Spaces.

(See symbol representing sympathetic transmissive chord of B flat, third octave on third diatonic.)

The seven assemblings are in this order:

			Electro		Harmonic	
		Dominant 3rd.	Magnetic	Diatonic 6ths.	Enharmonic.	Negative 7ths.
I.	II.	III.	IIII.	IIIII.	IIIIII.	IIIIIII.

Twenty-eight in number.

The second step is to liberate, according to symbolic meaning, second harmonic bar on sixths, or neutralizing one, and third, enharmonic ninths, which is the one counting from negative sevenths. Now all is in readiness for the transmissive nodal wire, one end of which must be attached to the magnetic dispersing ring, over the negative-sevenths cluster, and the other end to the high polar negative attractor. Then, one end of a transmitting wire, of very fine proportions of gold, silver and platina, is connected to the resonating sphere, and the other end to the mass to be experimented upon. I then give to the syren a rotatory impulse of a velocity to indicate the concordant of the mass attached. If the introductory settings are all right, the neutral centre indicator will rotate with high velocity: and a single tap on the chladna wave-plate is all that is necessary to induce pure evolution.

Either attraction or dispersion can be induced on any mass by setting the instrument to the proper triple introductory positions, towards the mass chords it represents, either positive or negative.

This system of evolution might be expressed as disintegration induced by the intensified oscillations of inter-atomic-electro-magnetic waves.

How plainly this principle of harmonic sympathetic evolution indicates the structural condition of the atom as one of wonderfully complex form; as also is the progressive step toward it in the molecular and inter-molecular field.

During the effect induced by disintegration of molecular mineral masses, there is no molecular collision when forced asunder from their radiating centres of neutrality. Their atomic and inter-atomic centres seek their media of tenuous affinity in the far borders of the etheric field, leaving all metallic masses, that are associated with them, behind in their virgin form.

Keynote of electric-magnetic sympathy, transmissive combinations, 3rds, on the subdivision of first octave B flat, diatonic. 6ths, on same subdivision of 3rds, octave harmonic; and 9ths, on the same subdivision of 6ths, octave enharmonic.

I find that there is no medium in the range of vibratory philosophic research, that is as unerringly exact, towards the centre of sympathetic attraction, as the negative attractive influence of a certain triple association of the metallic masses of gold, silver and platina. In fact they are as accurate indicators of the earth's terrestrial sympathetic envelope, and its triple focalized action towards the earth's neutral centre, as the magnet is an indicator of the diversion of the attractive flow of the dominant current of the electric stream. Although much has been written on the subject, the conditions attending the continuous flow of the magnet remains a problem that has never been solved by any other theory. Yet the solution is very simple when harmonic vibratory influence is brought to bear upon it.

The harmonic attractive chord, thirds, induces a nodal interference on that third of the triune combination of the terrestrial envelope, that is immediately associated with this medium of interference, and moves towards the negative pole of the magnet, then flows through it to re-associate with the full triune combination, through the positive, thus :—

Dominant
Harmonic
Enharmonic

The triune stream; one current of which is diverted from the Dominant, flowing in at the Negative end of the magnet; and out to join the triune terrestrial stream at the Positive end.

The continuous flow of the magnet is merely a diversion of that portion of the terrestrial envelope that electricians have never controlled. This third current, of this triune stream, has never been subdivided and *only slightly diverted* towards the negative pole of the magnet, flowing unbrokenly back to associate sympathetically with the full triune combination of the earth's negative neutral force.[1] Thus the problem is solved of the continuous and never-ending force of the magnet, in carrying its load without any diminution of its energy. There is no influence, as yet known, that can break up its line of sympathetic flow as associated with the triune combination. Polarization and de-polarization, in its action, is nodal negative interference, intermittently excited, inducing differential disturbance of polar sympathetic equilibrium.

The attractive power, evolved by a magnet in sustaining its load, is no evidence that it is molecularly attractive: for, under the influence of the dominant current of the electric stream, the range of its molecular mass is not extended; but by the action induced in atomic vibration, the latent, or undisturbed power, that is locked up in its atomic embrace, is put into sympathetic action, and evolves the force that is recognized as magnetic. When its exciter is removed, it returns to atomic recesses to remain perfectly latent, until again brought into action by its proper exciter.

When a steel unmagnetized bar is associated with a magnetized one, the latent force in the unmagnetized one is sympathetically brought into action, associating itself to the magnetic one, without depreciating the power of it one iota. Dissociation and association between the two bars can go on indefinitely with the same result.

The suspension and propelling of an atmospheric navigator of any number of tons weight, can be successfully accomplished by thus exciting the molecular mass of the metal it is constructed of; and the vibratory neutral negative attraction evolved, will bring it into perfect control, commer-

---

[1] It is always interesting to trace the germ of a scientific idea, hypothesis, or established truth. A writer in *La Lumière Electrique*, vol. xlv., has drawn attention to the fact that Descartes gave a theory of magnetism, in 1656, which resembles the modern conception of lines of stress in the ether. He considers that all magnets are traversed by a subtle fluid which flows out at the North Pole, and curving round, in the ether, re-enters at the South Pole, thus completing the circuit. Some of the greatest doctrines of science have recurred again and again, like the *motif* of a piece of music, until they finally assume a definite shape and become a working part of human progress; as will be seen when Keely's system is recognized.

cially, by keeping it in sympathy with the earth's triune polar stream. There is enough of this latent power locked up in the embrace of the iron ore, that is contained in our planet, which, if liberated and applied to proper vibratory machinery, would furnish force enough to run the commercial power of the world: leaving millions of times more to draw upon, as the needs increase. The velocity of the vibration governing the flow of the magnetic stream, comes under the head of the first inter-atomic, and ranges from 300,000 to 780,000 vibrations per second; the first order above odour permeating the molecules, of the glass plate of the compass (with the same facility that atmospheric air would go through an ordinary sieve through which it passes), to arouse sympathetically in the needle the concordant condition that harmonizes with its own. The course of this sympathetic flow is governed by the full harmonic chord; and, consequently, moves in straight lines; thus transmitting its sympathy free of molecular interferences.

The order of vibration associated with the transmission of odour acts by sympathetic negative interference; and, consequently, moves in circles, with a velocity of 220,000 per second, at least.

If in any way the circle of its rotatory diameter could be reduced to that of its corpuscular structure, then a bottle containing an odorous substance, though sealed as hermetically as an Edison-light bulb, could no more confine its corpuscles than an open chimney the smoke ascending from the fire burning at its base.

The sympathetic influence of the terrestrial envelope gets its introductory impulse from the infinite depths of the earth's neutral centre. This impulse radiates in undulating lines far enough into etheric space to become sympathetically associated with the etheric (or Infinite) under the same conditions that associate the mental with the physical organism of man. We can define man's molecular condition in its physical organism as the earth, and its connective link with the convolutionary cerebral centres as the Infinite etheric domain. Thus, we have, represented in the planetary masses moving in etheric space, the same conditions of governing rule as exists between the mental and physical forces.

With this medium it is plain to see how simply God works, as well as mysteriously, His wonders to perform; the mental forces kept vitalized from the great store-house of the etheric realm; and, in controlling the physical, the deficit caused thereby renewed and kept balanced by the power of its sympathetic concordant receptiveness.

Any visible molecular mass of metal can be so impregnated by triple orders of sympathetic vibration as to give it the same sympathetic transmissive qualities that exist in the mental forces, which make such mass subservient to either the attractive or repulsive conditions of terrestrial sympathy.

Gravity is nothing more than a concordant attractive sympathetic stream flowing towards the neutral centre of the earth. This force is inherent in all visible and invisible aggregated forms of matter, from the very birth of a planet, around whose centre the molecules cluster by the sympathetic affinity which is thus induced. If these conditions had always maintained a neutral position in etheric space, no planet would ever have been evolved. These conditions have been fixed by the Infinite. These rotating neutral centres, set in celestial space, have been endowed with the power of rotation to become their own accumulators. It is through the action of these sympathetic forces of the Infinite etheric realm that planets are born, and their volume of matter augmented.

If we pick up an object, we feel a resisting power in it which physicists call gravity; but they do not explain what gravity is. It is simply a sympathetic flow, proceeding from the molecular centres of neutrality; which flow is concordant with the earth's neutral centre of same, seeking this medium of its affinity with a power corresponding to the character of its molecular mass. There is no actual weight in the molecules of the mass of which the earth is composed. If the sympathetic negative polar stream that flows towards the neutral centre of the earth were cut off from it, the earth's molecular mass would become independent, and would float away into space as would a soap-bubble filled with warm air.

The gravital flow comes, in this system, under the order of the sympathetic concordant of the 9ths, and belongs to that third of the triune combination called polar propulsive.

Magnetism is polar attraction.

Gravity is polar propulsion.

Both magnetism and gravity can be accelerated by the proper medium of sympathetic vibratory influences.

A Conjecture.

If we take into proper consideration the sympathetic affinity that exists between the centres of the cerebral convolutionary organism, and the polar terrestrial forces, as linked to the celestial, or Infinite, the harmonizing effects they have on the normal brain, and the antagonistic negative bombardment of these streams on the abnormal one, is it not possible, by the diversion of pure, sympathetic streams, to antagonize abnormal conditions, by concordant or magnetic polar sympathetic mechanical exciters, and thus to induce pure normal equilibrium of its corpuscular mass?—which means perfect mental restoration.

CHAPTER XX.

1892.

PROGRESSIVE SCIENCE—KEELY'S PRESENT POSITION.

(*A Review of the Situation.*)

This amount of repetition to some will probably appear to be tedious, but only by varied iteration can alien conceptions be forced on reluctant minds.—HERBERT SPENCER.

The researches of Lodge in England and of Hertz in Germany give us an almost infinite range of ethereal vibrations. . . . Here is unfolded to us a new and astonishing world,—one which it is hard to conceive should contain no possibilities of transmitting and receiving intelligence. . . . Here also is revealed to us the bewildering possibility of telegraphy without wires, posts, cables, or any of our present costly appliances. . . . As for myself, I hold the firm conviction that unflagging research will be rewarded by an insight into natural mysteries, such as now can rarely be conceived.—PROFESSOR WM. CROOKES, M.R.A., F.R.S., &c.

Vibratory Philosophy teaches that "in the great workshop of Nature there are no lines of demarcation to be drawn between the most exalted speculation and common-place practice, and that all knowledge must lead up to one great result; that of an intelligent recognition of the Creator through His works."

"Facts are the body of science; speculation is its soul."

IT has been said that there is nothing more sublime in the history of mind than the lonely struggles which generate and precede success. After the admission made by Professor Rücker, M.A., at the last meeting of the British Association, that the ether may be "the material of which all matter is composed," and that "we may, perhaps, be able to use and control the ether as we now use and control steam," there would seem to be grounds for hoping that Keely's "lonely and prolonged struggles" to utilize in mechanics the ether product which he obtains from his method of dissociating the elements of water, will be more universally recognized and appreciated than they have yet been. Discovery may be unsought and instantaneous, but the inventions for utilizing discoveries may be, and generally are, the work of years.

Keely first imprisoned the ether in 1872, when its existence was denied; or, if admitted by a few, it was called "the hypothetical ether." In 1888, Professor Henri Hertz discovered and announced, in the *Revue des Deux Mondes*, that the ether is held in a state of bondage in all electro-magnetic engines. Not until this fact had been made known, were there any scientific men, with one notable exception, who were willing to admit it was possible that Keely might also have "stumbled over" the manner of effecting its imprisonment.

The nature of Keely's researches, and the length of time in which he has been absorbed by the necessary dead-work, attendant upon research before a discovery can be utilized, may be gathered from a letter recently written by Mr. C. G. Till, of Brooklyn, New York:—

"In Keely's early struggles, somewhere about twenty years ago, I became acquainted with him, and helped him then to the best of my ability. Indeed I may say that I was godfather to his discovery; for I was with him when the idea first entered his head that he could combine steam and water to run an engine. At that time he made a crude machine, which he actually ran for some time; and this was the original model of the Pneumatic-Pulsating-Vacuo-Engine, in the operation of which he discovered his present force. From that day to this he has been in pursuit of some method as a medium to use what he calls his etheric force with. That he has actually discovered a new force there is not a shadow of doubt. In those days I have known him to sell and pawn everything of value in his house to obtain means to continue his investigations with the money thus acquired; and I am sure that he will eventually give to the world the greatest boon that has been received by it since the advent of Christianity," etc., etc.

It has been very generally thought that Keely is pursuing

Progressive Science. 321

the *ignis fatuus* of perpetual motion. No greater mistake could have been made. The genuineness of his claims as a discoverer rests upon a correct answer to the question, "*Is hydrogen gas an element or a compound?*"

Science, as Herodotus said, is to know things truly: but science tells us that hydrogen is a simple, that the atom is not divisible, and that latent energy is not locked in the interstitial spaces of all forms of matter from their birth or aggregation. Keely's system of Vibratory Physics refutes these canons of science. How absurd must seem the idea to many that the schools can be wrong, and that Keely, who has been branded by some of these schools as an impostor, should be right: but time will show whether Keely's discoveries have "come to stay." The history of the past shows us that science has never been infallible; that like Christianity she unfolds her truths progressively. Keely teaches that an unknown potency is held in the atom's tenacious grasp, until released by an introductory impulse given by a certain order of vibration, depending upon the mass-chord of the aggregation; which impulse so increases the oscillation of the atoms as to rupture their etheric capsules. All great truths hold germs potential of ever-increasing growth. It took half a century for the "Principia" of Newton to overcome the contempt that was showered upon it; and now progressive science is overshadowing Newton's vast attainments. In his giant mind was born the hypothesis that the ether is the cause of light and gravity. Keely has been teaching for years, that ether is the medium of all force. For every effect science requires an efficient cause. Hence, when Faraday found no definite knowledge in exact sciences to satisfy him on certain points he was led into speculative science, or the preliminary reaching after truths which we feel must exist by reason of certain effects that come under our observation, analogous to already known laws:—"reduced facts lie behind us; speculative ones lie before us;" and without these latter science could make no progress. Faraday was only speculating when he said: "Thus either present elements are the true elements; or else there is the probability before us of obtaining some more high and general power of nature even than electricity; and which, at the same time, might reveal to us an entirely new grade of elements of matter, now hidden from our view and almost from our suspicion."

Faraday's keen perception and acute practical judgment, were never better exemplified than in Keely's discovery of Negative Attraction; the laws governing which he is still researching; theorizing that it is the energy which controls the planetary masses in their advance toward each other, and in their recession from each other,—the energy which lifts the seas and the oceans out of their beds, and replaces them once in twenty-four hours; in other words, explaining the mystery of the action of gravity.

Had Faraday lived longer he might have anticipated Keely in one of his discoveries; for he certainly was on the road to it, in the views of force and matter which he held that were not in accordance with the accepted views of his time; and which were then set aside as "wild speculations," by the physicists who complained of his "want of mathematical accuracy," of his "entertaining notions altogether distinct from the views generally held by men of science," who continued their experimental researches on their own lines.

In 1885, before Keely's scientific explorations had taught him that no engine can ever be constructed by which the ether can be used and controlled, as we now use and control steam, he wrote, in a letter to a friend, "I shall not forestall an unproved conclusion, but fight step by step the dark paths I am exploring, knowing that, should I succeed in proving one single fact in science heretofore unknown, I shall in so doing be rewarded in the highest degree. In whatever direction the human mind travels it comes quickly to a boundary line which it cannot pass. There is a knowable field of research, bordered by an unknown tract. My experience teaches me how narrow is the strip of territory which belongs to the knowable, how very small the portion that has been traversed and taken possession of. The further we traverse this unknown territory, the stronger will become our faith in the immovable order of the world: for, at each advancing step, we find fresh fruits of the immutable laws that reign over all things,—from the falling apple, up to the thoughts, the words, the deeds, the will of man: and we find these laws irreversible and eternal, order and method reigning throughout the universe. Some details of this universal method have been worked up, and we know them by the names of 'gravitation,' 'chemical affinity,' 'nerve-power,' &c. These material certainties are as sacred as moral certainties. . . . The nearest approach to a certainty is made through harmony with nature's laws. The surest media are those which nature has laid out in her wonderful workings. The man who deviates from these paths will suffer the penalty of a defeat, as is seen in the record of 'perpetual motion' seekers. I have been classed with such dreamers; but I find consolation in the thought that it is only by those men who are utterly ignorant of the great and marvellous truths which I have devoted my life to demonstrate and to bring within reach of all. I believe the time is near at hand when the principles of etheric evolution will be established, and when the world will be eager to recognize and accept a system that will certainly create a revolution for the highest benefits of mankind, inaugurating an era undreamed of by those who are now ignorant of the existence of this etheric force." These views which have guided Keely in all his researches cannot be made known to any just, discerning mind without an accompanying perception of the gross way in which he has been misrepresented by his defamers; as well as some appreciation of the scientifically cautious manner in which he has pursued his investigations, since he abandoned his efforts to construct an engine that would hold the ether in rotation.

At the present time Keely is concentrating his efforts on the perfecting of his mechanical conditions to that point where, according to his theories, he will be able to establish, on the ninths, a sympathetic affinity with pure, polar, negative attraction, minus magnetism. In his own opinion he has so nearly gained the summit, or completion of his "graduation," as to feel that he holds the key to the control of the infinitely tenuous conditions which lie before him to be conquered, before he gains mastery of the group of depolar disks that he is now working upon. Twenty-six groups are completed, and when the twenty-seventh and last group is under equal control, Keely expects to establish a circuit of vibratory force, for running machinery: both for aerial navigation and for terrestrial use. If this result be obtained, Keely will then be in a position to give his system to science; and to demonstrate the ever-operative immanence of the Infinite builder of all things of whom our Lord said, "My Father worketh hitherto, and I work."

In commercial use Keely expects that when the motion has been once set up, in any of his machines, it will continue until the material is worn out. It is this claim which has caused Keely to be classed with perpetual-motion seekers.

For years Keely has been trying to utilize his discoveries for the material and moral advantage of humanity: and yet he feels, as Buckle has said of the present acquirements of science, that the ground only is broken, that the crust only is touched. The loftiest pinnacle which has been reached by the men who are foremost in their constructions of the method by which the one source of all energy works in the material world, is too insignificant a position to obtain even an outlook towards the vast realm that Keely figuratively describes as the infinite brain; or the source from which all "sympathetic-leads" emanate, that connect mind with matter. Realizing that all conditions of matter are but as vain illusions, he never falters in his determination to reach after the hidden things of God, if haply he may find them. Even the goal which he seeks to attain lies, in his own estimation, on the outermost border of this crust; and well he knows that it never can be reached in any other way than by principles of exact science and by pursuing a path that is at all times lighted by reason.

Believing that "the horizon of the world of matter, which has been thought to rest over hydrogen, extends to infinite reaches, including substances which have never been revealed to the senses," he knows how unfathomable is the ocean that lies beyond, and like Newton compares himself to one who is gathering pebbles on its shore.

Science, which has ever been interested both in the infinitely small and infinitely great, has in our age dropped the only clue that can guide through the obscure labyrinth which leads into depths of nature lying beyond the knowledge of our unaided senses.

The evolution of the human race, says Nesbit, has passed from the physiological into the psychological field; and it is in the latter alone that progress may be looked for.

This is the realm into which Keely's efforts, to give to the world a costless motive power, have slowly conducted him through the black darkness of the region in which he has been fighting his way, for a score of years, in behalf of true science and humanity.

Lord Derby has said that modern science, on its popular side, is really a great factory of popular fallacies; that its expounders in one decade are kept busy refuting the errors to which the preceding decade has given currency. There is hardly a branch of science, he says, susceptible of general and wide-reaching conclusions, which might not be revolutionized by some discovery to-morrow.

If Keely is able to establish his theories, physical science will have to abandon the positions to which she clings, and forced to admit that there exists a purity of conditions in Vibratory Physics unknown in mechanical physics, undreamed of even in philosophy; for he will then be in a position to demonstrate the outflow of the Infinite mind as sympathetically associated with matter visible and invisible.

Of this philosophy Professor Daniel G. Brinton has said, "It is so simple, beautiful and comprehensive in its vibratory theory that I hope it will be found experimentally to be true. To me all commercial and practical results, motors, air-ships, engines, are of no importance by the side of the theoretical truth of the demonstrations of this cosmic force. As soon as Dr. Koenig is prepared to report on the purely technical and physical character of the experiments, I shall be, in fact I am, ready to go into full details as to their significance in reference to both matter and mind. It will be enough for me if Dr. Koenig is able to say that the force handled by Keely is not gravity, electricity, magnetism, compressed air, nor other of the well-known forces. Let him say that, and I will undertake to say what the force is." Tests were made last year by Dr. Koenig and Dr. Tuttle, a Baltimore physicist, in the presence of other men of science with the most sensitive galvanometer belonging to the University of Pennsylvania, all of whom were satisfied that no known force had been detected.

The abstract of Keely's philosophy, written by Dr. Brinton, has made Keely's theories intelligible for the first time. Each new discovery necessitates a new vocabulary; and Keely's writings are obscure because of his new nomenclature. When Faraday's ideas differed from those held by the authorities of his time, they were pronounced to be "untranslatable into scientific language;" and as was then said of Faraday, so can it now be said of Keely, with equal truth, that, working at the very boundaries of our knowledge, his mind habitually dwells "in the boundless contiguity of shade" by which that knowledge is surrounded.

The brain of an Aristotle was needed to discern and grasp Keely's meaning, to interpret and define it. Dr. Brinton never touches a subject without throwing light upon it, and his penetrating mind perceived the ideas to be defined in all their relations. His keen logical acumen separated and classified them in their order, in a true, sound, and scientific manner. In the words of Sir James Crichton Browne, who heard Professor Brinton read this abstract in London, "Professor Brinton's synopsis is an able, lucid and logical paper."

Now that such distinguished men are interesting themselves in Keely's discoveries, there is no longer any danger of their being lost to science; nor to commerce, if his life is spared. The action of Dr. Pepper (Provost of the University of Pennsylvania) in January, 1891, gave Keely all the protection that he then needed in order to continue his researches up to the completion of his system.

Professor Dewar of the Royal Institution of Great Britain, whose Cambridge duties prevented him from keeping the engagement made for him to visit Mr. Keely's workshop in December, 1891, is now compelled to wait, until notified that Keely is in a position to demonstrate his theories, as it is desirable that he should not be interrupted in the critical work that is at present engrossing him, at times eighteen hours out of the twenty-four. But although Keely has not instructed anyone in his method of disintegrating water, to obtain the ether, which he uses as the medium of the polar force, he does not withhold the principle by which he obtains it. Sir John Herschell said, "There is a principle in the science of music that has yet to be discovered." Pythagoras taught that the principle which underlies the harmonies of music, underlies the motion of the heavenly bodies. It is this principle which Keely has discovered ; but until he has utilized it in mechanics, he has nothing more to sell than Sir Isaac Newton had when he discovered gravity, as Professor Fitzgerald has said.

Discovery and invention are walking side by side in our age, the glorious scientific age of the world. Never before have they so linked themselves together, working for humanity; and it is but natural that those *savants* who have seen no demonstrations of the force Keely is handling should regard with apathy claims, which, if established, would sweep away like chaff before a whirlwind, some of the canons of their schools. In fact, this apathy is a great improvement upon the active persecution of the learned men who hurried Copernicus and Galileo to prison, and established the Inquisition to deal with heretics in science as well as heretics in religion. Commerce rushed Keely into a dungeon; science looking on in approval; notwithstanding that conjectures of the most celebrated modern member of its school supported Keely's teachings. Galileo was brought before the Inquisition ; the tribunal pronounced him a deluded teacher and a lying heretic. They intended to subject him to the severest torture and death. Galileo was old, and felt that he could not endure such a terrible death. He knelt on the crucifix, with one hand on the Bible, and renounced all. When he arose, however, it is reported that he whispered to one of the attendants, "The earth does move for all that." Sir Isaac Newton has written of the possibility of discovering unknown forms of energy, in Nature, in these strong words: " For it is well known that bodies act upon one another by the attractions of gravity, magnetism and electricity, and these instances show the tenor and course of nature and make it not improbable that there may be more powers of attraction than these. For Nature is very consonant and conformable to herself."

All progress of whatever kind would be put back, if it were in the power of bigots to arrest its triumphal march, as they have done in the past, but the evolution of the human race remains in the hands of the Infinite One, who never fails to open up new paths when the farther development of humanity requires it. All systems may be said to have descended from previous ones. "The ideas of one generation are the mysterious progenitors of those in the next. Each age is the dawn of its successor; and in the eternal advance of truth,

'There always is a rising sun,
The day is ever but begun.'"

Religious and scientific reformation have always gone hand in hand, says Dr. Lowber. In fact, religious science is superior to any other science. As Christianity is the pure religion which contains the truth of all the rest, so it is the highest of the sciences, for it represents the development of the highest faculty of the human nature. Religion develops manhood as nothing else will, and Christianity represents the highest culture to which it is possible for man to attain. . . .

The system, now being evolved and worked out to demonstration by Keely, restores, by religious science, the faith of which materialistic science has been robbing the world, thus confirming Dr. Lowber's assertions that materialists will never be able to reduce all natural and spiritual forces to mere vibratory action of matter; and that the reformatory movement in philosophy, which characterizes our age, will continue until all the sciences point to God and immortality.

A writer in *Galignani's Messenger*, March 2, 1892, says: "When the nineteenth century closes, the most marvellous period ever known to man will be stored away in Time's granary. Can the twentieth century by any possibility be more productive, more fertile, more prolific of wonders than its predecessor? The face of the world has been changed; space has been annihilated; science puts 'a girdle round about the earth in forty minutes.' We may be almost excused if we are tempted to believe that the serpent's promise is fulfilled in our persons, and we are as gods. Alas for human complacency! Perhaps our descendants a thousand years hence will look upon us as pigmies. Be that as it may, the past and the present are ours, with their achievement, and we believe we shall hand down to posterity a goodly heritage."

The New York *Home Journal,* of the week before Christmas, 1892, points out, in its leader, the road on which this advance in the cause of humanity may be made. The writer, Mr. Howard Hinton, says: "The spirit of the salutation, ' A Merry Christmas,' lies in the desire that peace and goodwill shall reign among men, nor, if we may trust the intimations of the latest science, will this universality of good wishing be without avail in effecting its own accomplishment. For, as we are told by the wise men of science, every thought, every mental impulse of ours, sets in motion, in that realm of ether which it is said interfuses all coarser forms of matter, certain vibrations, corresponding in force to their cause, which have power to communicate themselves to other minds favourably conditioned to receive them, and so excite in them like thoughts and impulses.

"And are not common observation and individual experience in accord with this suggestion of science? Do we not say at times that a certain thought is in the air, revealing itself contemporaneously to many widely separated minds without any recognizable means of communication? And do we not sometimes find a noble, or it may be an ignoble, impulse breaking out in a community with a suddenness and universality that would seem to transcend all the ordinary forms of the contact of mind with mind? Perhaps, too, this theory of vibratory communication through an ethereal medium may explain, in part at least, that ' Welt-Geist,' that ' Spirit of the Age,' of which the philosophers discourse so bravely.

" Again, there are times—if the experiences and observations of sensitive minds have any worth—when a general spirit of expectancy seems to be awakened, as if the world were on the eve of some new and epoch-making revelation of science, or some new enthusiasm of regenerative impulse. Are we not now, at this hour, in this mood of silent expectancy, thrilled with an indefinable awe of what the brooding life of the world is maturing for the sons of men?—sensitive, perhaps, to ethereal vibrations that have not yet accumulated force for expression in conscious thought or for the definite determination of our hearts' desires?

"This may be fanciful. It may be simply that we are beginning to perceive that physical science has reached a stage of development when some new and more central truth, some profounder generalization, is needed to give further impulse to its essential progress. It may be that we are becoming aware that the conditions of society are such that some new unifying motive, some new enthusiasm of humanity is needed for its salvation; and that therefore we wait in expectancy for what—knowing that there can be no let nor hindrance in the onward movement of life—we feel in our hearts must come.

"And yet does not this sense of expectancy seem to communicate itself from mind to mind by some other means than that of oral or written expression, and to touch with more or less force even minds that are free from these intellectual anticipations? Are there not certain intellects at the fore-front of the world's progress, and certain hearts filled above the ordinary measure with the love of mankind, who are thus centres of power, from whom spread ever widening circles of vibratory emanations that gradually involve all minds in a common thought and all hearts in a common purpose? 'Many men of many minds.' Yes, truly; but there is the one mind of humanity that thinks and thinks, and alone has the power to externalize its thought as part of the world's history, while all purely individual thought is blown finally into the abyss of the Absolute Nothing.

"But it is not only the great souls that thus move and shape the world. We are all, in various degrees, centres and distributors of the ethereal force, so far as we are in touch with its waves of vibration. We can all make our thoughts, if they are one with the thought of humanity, and our desires, if they are one with the heart of humanity, felt by our fellows in extending circles of effluence till finally the very clods of human kind know the stirrings of a new life and wake to the higher reality as from a dream.

"And if individually we can thus set in movement this

ethereal medium, how must not this movement be quickened and extended when collectively we give utterance to some great thought and heart's desire, announcing it in song and prayer and merry-making. Hence the use and potency of the great festivals, the best and sweetest of which is the Christmas festival that we are now about to celebrate—the Evening Star of the year that is passing, the Morning Star of the new."

CHAPTER XXI.

FAITH BY SCIENCE: THE DAWN OF A NEW ORDER OF THINGS.

"All for each and each for all."

God will take account of the selfishness of wealth, and His quarrel has yet to be fought out.—REV. F. ROBERTSON.

All the great things of time have been done by single men, from Judas Maccabeus down to Cromwell. We hear the age spoken of as degenerative because of the vast accumulations of wealth. But wealth may be a power for beneficence, as great brains may be, and we have no more reason for regretting large fortunes than large heads. No doubt to secure a perfect equality of all people we need small heads, and small heads or empty heads go with empty purses. By no other means can you level us. So also by wealth the world has been moved, and will continue to be moved. Can we consecrate money power to humanity, as we do mind power? We do not see why not. And in our judgment anyone who does not feel the change that is going on must be blind. It is not legislation that will produce a moral revolution, but a new enthusiasm. The future holds for us a grand enthusiasm of this sort—a moralization of property and possession.—*Social Science in Science Siftings.*

A wave of unrest seems to be passing over the world. Uneasiness prevails on every side. We walk gingerly as though on the edge of a precipice. Discontent is spreading everywhere. The struggle between capital and labour threatens to reach unheard-of proportions. . . . . What is the meaning of the general restlessness? What are its causes? Is the world growing old and effete? Is the human race worn out? Is this generation incapable of the great achievements of the past? Does its materialism clog its powers and prevent its progress? Is the world going wrong for want of an ideal? A people which does not believe in its lofty mission will never accomplish it. Science has made gigantic strides in our days; but have its discoveries added much to the sum of human happiness? It has contributed to our material comfort in various ways, but it has not done much for the federation of the world. The great growth of luxury is not a good, but an evil, if it rob us of our belief in our great destiny and if it weaken our endeavour. If "the time is out of joint," is it not possible that worship of wealth is responsible for it? "He who makes haste to be rich shall not be innocent." Ours is emphatically the age in which men "make haste to be rich," without much regard to the means.

Capital has profited unduly at the expense of labour; employers have attained to fortune too quickly for the welfare of the employed. Commerce has forsaken the path of safety to indulge in rash and reckless speculation. Businesses have been converted into companies more for the benefit of vendors and financial houses than for the public. Company promotion has been carried to reckless lengths, and schemes for getting rich rapidly—schemes of the South Sea bubble order—have multiplied in every part of the civilized world. The Nemesis has come in the shape of restlessness, discontent, paralysis of trade, strikes, disorganization of finance, demoralization of Bourses, and general insecurity. It is a fact proved countless times in history that whenever a national need is felt, a man is raised up to supply the want.—*Galignani's Messenger.*

The first seal is being broken in the book of vibratory philosophy; the first stepping-stone is placed toward reaching the solution of that infinite problem, the origin of life.—JOHN ERNST WORRELL KEELY, 1890.

The seals are opened, as it were, under the sign Leo—as believing that such an age is coming on in which prophecy may be fulfilled that the earth be filled with the knowledge of the Lord, which shall cover it with wisdom and understanding in the deep mysteries of God.—JANE LEAD, 1699.

Evils bear in themselves the causes of their own extirpation. Providence is bringing the old order of things to a close in order to provide place for something better and higher.—JULIAN HAWTHORNE.

PROFESSOR ROWLAND, in his paper on the "Spectra of Metals," which he read at Leeds, says that the object of his research is primarily to find out what sort of things molecules are, and in what way they vibrate. The primary object of Mr. Keely's researches has been to find out all that he could about the laws that control vibrations, and on this line of research he made his discoveries, as to "what sort of things molecules and atoms are, and in what way they vibrate." One of the editors of the *Times*, in London, in January, 1891, wrote out this question for Keely to answer:—" What impulse led you primarily into the research of acoustic physics?" Keely replied, "An impulse associated sympathetically with my mental organism from birth, seemingly, as I was acutely sensible of it in my childhood. Before I had reached my tenth year, researching in the realm of acoustic physics had a perfect fascination for me; my whole organism seemed attuned as if it were a harp of a thousand strings; set for the reception of all the conditions associated with sound force as a controlling medium, positive and negative; and with an intensity of enjoyment not to be described. From that time to the present, I have been absorbed in this research, and it has opened up to me the laws that govern the higher workings of nature's sympathetic, hidden forces; leading me gradually on to the solution of the problem relating to the conditions that exist between the celestial and terrestrial outreaches, viz., polar negative attraction." Another question asked by the same editor: "What is the main difficulty to be overcome before completing the system for commercial benefit?" Answer: "The principal difficulty rests in equating the thirds of the thirds of the transmitters (*i.e.*, the gold, silver, and platina sections, of which the transmitting wires are composed) to free them of molecular differentiation. The full control of this force can never be accomplished, until pure molecular equation is established between the nodal interferences (that result in their manufacture) and the chord mass of their sectional parts. When this has been done, the chasm between the alternation of the polar forces, which now exists, preventing the inducing of polar and depolar conditions, will be bridged over and commercial benefits at once established as the result. The devices for inducing these conditions, primarily, are perfect; but the pure, connective link on transmission has to be equated, before continued mechanical rotation and reversion can be attained."

As has already been said, Keely's researches have all been on the line of vibrations; and it was while pursuing them that he "stumbled over," to use his own words, the interatomic subdivision of the molecule, which released the Geni that for years thereafter was his master. Keely's attention not having been turned to molecules and atoms, he was not able, in the earliest years of his discovery of the existence of a "force of nature more powerful and more general even than electricity," to form any opinion as to the origin of the force. He was as one who, in the thick darkness of an underground labyrinth, found himself face to face with a giant, whose form even he could not see to lay hold of in a death grapple; but when a germ of the knowledge that he needed fell on his mind, he was quick to seize it, and the acorn grew into an oak. Here again, to use his own words: "I was as a boulder resting on the summit of a mountain, until an introductory impulse was given to start it on its course; then rushing onwards and carrying all before it, when the goal is reached its concussion will produce the crash that will awaken a sleeping world."

Priestley proclaimed it as his belief that all discoveries are made by chance; but Providence sends chance, and the man of genius is he who is able to improve all opportunities and mould them to his own ends. In a discovery, says Edison, there must be an element of the accidental, and an important one too; discovery is an inspiration, while an invention is purely deductive. The story of the apple dropping from the tree, and Newton starting with a species of "Eureka," he rejects absolutely. Maintaining that an abstract idea or a natural law may, in one sense, be invented, he gives it as his opinion that Newton did not discover the theory of gravitation, but invented it; and that he might have been at work on the problem for years, inventing theory after theory, to which he found it impossible to fit his facts. That Keely claims to have discovered an unknown source of energy has not seemed to disturb the equilibriums of some of the men of science who have witnessed the demonstrations of the force, as much as that he should have invented theories in regard to the operation of the laws that control it. For a man who had lived more than half a century without troubling himself as to the existence of molecules and atoms to suddenly awaken to the knowledge of their existence, and to invent theories as to "what sort of things they are and how they vibrate," was sufficient proof, in their eyes, that he invented his discovery; but men who are, in thought, reaching out into unknown realms, are the very men who are most likely to lay hold of a discovery;—as did Bell, who, speculating upon the nature of sound, filed an invention for his telephone before he discovered that articulate speech could be conveyed along a wire. It was in the same way that Keely, speculating upon the nature of vibration, was led into the field of invention; and while experimenting with one of his inventions, he suddenly stepped into that great unknown territory which lies beyond the horizon of ordinary matter. It took him nearly a score of years to find out where he was. Years of experiment followed before he was able to summon the Geni at will; for when his lever first registered a pressure of 2000 lbs., while subjecting water to the action of multiplied vibrations, he had no idea how to proceed, as far as the number of vibrations were concerned, to repeat the operation. Commencing at a certain point, he increased the vibrations day by day until, six years later, he was able to effect the dissociation at will. But at that time Mr. Keely had too much mechanical work to do to give any of his time to theorizing. He was in the clutches of a speculating Keely Motor Company, whose cry was, "Give us an engine!" and day and night this toiler fought his way in the underground labyrinth, thinking only of a commercial engine. It was not until Macvicar's "Sketch of a Philosophy" fell into Mr. Keely's hands that he realized he had imprisoned the ether. This was in 1884, and, four years later, in 1888, Professor Hertz of Bonn announced that we were using the ether, without knowing it, in all electro-magnetic engines. By this time Keely's researches in vibratory physics had led him well on his way in the construction of hypotheses as to "what sort of things molecules are, and in what way they vibrate." An hypothesis treats a supposed thing as an existing thing, for the purpose of proving, by experimental demonstration, whether the supposition is correct or not. At a critical juncture, Mrs. J. F. Hughes (a grand-niece of Charles Darwin), hearing of Keely's researches, became interested in his work; and her book on "The Evolution of Tones and Colours" was sent to Mr. Keely. An expression used by Mrs. Hughes in that work, brought a suggestion to Mr. Keely. The veil of darkness was rent asunder which had enveloped him in what he called "Egyptian blackness," and from that time he worked no longer in the dark.

Pythagoras taught that the same law which underlies harmonies underlies the motion of the heavenly bodies, or, as Mrs. Hughes has expressed it, "The law which develops and controls harmony, develops and controls the universe." Mr. Keely, nothing daunted by the vast extent, the stupendous "outreach" of the domain, the boundary line of which he had thus crossed, concentrated all his energies upon "the situation;" thinking thereafter, not alone of the interests of commerce as before, but of the developing of a system, which he could give to science in the same hour that he should hand over, to those whose thoughts were only on financial gain, the inventions that our age is demanding, in the interests of humanity, with the stern voice of the master necessity; a voice that never fails to make itself heard in "the voice of the people." Experiment after experiment justified his hypotheses, and converted them into theories. To keep pace with the wants of humanity, invention must now walk side by side with philosophy. It took half a century for the "Principia" of Newton to tread down the contempt and opposition that its publication met with; and now progressive knowledge is overshadowing Newton's vast attainments. Faraday, after discovering electro-magnetic conditions, as related to latent or hidden energy, did not pursue his researches far enough to establish a theory as to the mode of transference of magnetic force, though, in some of his speculations on the line of force, he hit upon truths now advanced in Keely's theories. The physicists of Faraday's time could not reach up to him. They complained of his "obscurity of language," of his "want of mathematical precision," of his "entertaining notions regarding matter and force altogether distinct from the views generally held by men of science." It is not then to be wondered at that modern physicists took up lines of research more in accordance with their own views. The experiences of one age are repeated in another age; and the same charges that were brought against Faraday are now brought against Keely; coupled with shameful attempts to prove him to be "a fraud;" a man "living upon the credulity of his victims;" "a modern Cagliostro;" "an artful pretender." The question is often asked, "Is he not an ignorant man?" Yes, so ignorant, that he knows how ignorant he is; so ignoaant, that he asserts with Anaxagoras, that intelligent will is the disposer and cause of everything; and not satisfied with asserting this great truth, he has devoted the remnant of his days to finding out and demonstrating how this cause operates throughout nature. But ignorant as Keely has always confessed himself to be, he knows more of the mysterious laws of nature which hold the planets in their courses and exert their dynamic effect upon the tides, more of the "shock effect" which, brought to bear upon molecules, causes their disruption and supplies the fine fluid thus liberated, that extends the "shock effect," as Frederick Major has conjectured, to the atoms that compose them. Ignorant as Keely is, he knows that "out of the strife of tremendous forces which is ever going on in nature, is born a creation of law and harmony;" that from atomic recesses to the farthest depth there is naught but "toil co-operant to an end," that "all these atoms march in time, and that it is no blind cause which originates and maintains all." Admitting his ignorance, Keely claims with Dr. Watson that "the many who are compelled to walk should not scoff at those who try to fly." All who agree in believing that "the advance of the modern school of natural philosophy affords no justification for the intolerant and exclusive position taken by certain physicists," will be ready to examine Keely's theories, in the light of his demonstrations, even although they have been stigmatized as fallacies. Science owes large obligations to many fallacious theories.

Canon Moseley has said that the perfecting of the theory of epicycles is due to the astrologers of the middle ages; and that but for them the system of Copernicus would have remained a bare speculation, as did that of Pythagoras for more than two thousand years. In the same way that astrology nurtured astronomy, chemistry was cradled by alchemy.

Keely welcomes criticism of his theories, and is able to answer all who come to him with criticisms in a proper spirit. To quote one of his own expressions, "as far as a physical truth is concerned I never throw up the sponge for any one." Of Professor Crookes, Keely wrote quite recently: "Your friend is wrong in saying that I dabble in chemical heresies. There must be some misunderstanding on his part, for I have never asserted that nitrogen is a necessary constituent of water. I only said that, after a thousand experiments had been conducted, there was a residual deposit, in one of my tubes, of a resinous substance that showed nitrogenous elements, which I could not account for. I consider Professor Crookes one of the greatest of discoverers, and, when he understands my system, he will be one of the first to endorse it."

A philosophical journalist says of the force discovered by Keely, that "it is harder to believe in than either steam or electricity, because it has no visible manifestation in nature. It does not rise in white clouds from every boiling kettle, or flash with vivid light in every thunderstorm. It does not show itself in the fall of every loosened body to the earth, like gravitation, nor can it be discovered, like oxygen, by chemical investigation. If it exists at all, it is in a form entirely passive, giving no hint of its presence until it is brought out by the patient investigator, as the sculptor's chisel brings out the beautiful statue from the shapeless mass of marble.

"Working thus entirely in the dark, with an intangible, imponderable, invisible something whose nature and attributes are all unknown, and whose characteristics differ essentially from those of any other known force, what wonder if the inventor's progress is slow and his disappointments many? Mr. Keely may be deceived, or he may have discovered an actual force which he is unable to harness; but the fact that he is very slow in perfecting whatever discovery he may have made is no proof that he has not made a very great one.

"Far be it from us to say in this age of scientific marvels, that any proposition whatever is impossible of accomplishment; but while we wait for Mr. Keely to make his alleged discovery public, before we become enthusiastic over it, we would not set it down as a fraud and the reputed discovery as a humbug. It is the nature of inventors to be enthusiastic and to think that they are on the eve of success when, in fact, a great deal remains to be done.

"Especially is this the case in the development of a hitherto unknown force. James Watt had a comparatively straight road to travel from his mother's tea-kettle to his first steam-engine, but it took him many years to traverse it. More than a lifetime elapsed after Franklin drew electricity from a cloud before Morse sent it over a telegraph wire, and Morse himself worked for years to make it available for business purposes; while men are still constantly finding new adaptations of the mysterious force of which that was the first practical application."

But, as Frederick Major has said, "Science at present is too full of its own erroneous theories to accept or even notice theories outside of science, until practically proved, and probably not even then unless they can foist them upon the public as partially their own." These words are not applicable to all men of science. There are some, among those most eminent, who, in the spirit of true science, are quite prepared for other roads to knowledge than those of our three hundred years old induction school. The late Professor W. K. Clifford, F.R.S., was one of those men who, in their earnest desire for "truth at any cost," was ready to advance in every direction open to him. No "fear of a false step" held him back. He did not belong to the category of philosophical sceptics whom Dr. Stoney has so well classified as damping all advance, unless it can be carried on, from the beginning, under such conditions of perfection as are impossible in the early stages of every discovery and of almost every inquiry. Professor Stoney has well described Keely's method of work in these remarks: "In the scientific method of investigating the validity of our beliefs, we take our existing beliefs as our starting point, or a careful selection of those which are fitted to enable us to advance. After the legitimate consequences of these have been worked out, the inquirer finds himself in a better position to return and test the validity of the bases on which he proceeded. After these revisions, and such corrections as he finds possible, he makes a step of a like kind farther forward: after which another revision and another advance. Thus real progress is accomplished. Probabilities acquire strength and accumulate; and in the end a state of mind is attained replete with knowledge of the realities within and around us. The sea of knowledge on which man makes his brief voyage is for the most part unfathomable. He cannot hope, except near shore, to measure the *whole* depth, and thus attain philosophical certainty. But the scientific student may diligently use such a sounding line as he possesses—that of probability—and with it explore wide expanses under which there are no rocks nor shoals within the utmost depth that he can plumb, and over which he may securely sail. Compare this with the situation of the philosophical sceptic, groping among rocks along the shore, and not venturing beyond the shallow margin which he can probe with his little pole."

Professor Clifford struck out boldly in this unfathomable ocean of knowledge, when he admitted the infinite divisibility of the atom, which is one of the bases of Keely's theories. And how exquisitely did his penetrating vision pierce the mists of materialism when he wrote :—" Every time that analysis strips from nature the gilding that we prized, she is forging thereat a new picture more glorious than before, to be suddenly revealed by the advent of a new sense whereby we see it—a new creation, at sight of which the sons of God shall have cause to shout for joy. What now shall I say of this new-grown perception of Law, which finds the infinite in a speck of dust, and the act of eternity in every second of time ? Shall I say that it kills our sense of the beautiful, and takes all the romance out of nature ? And, moreover, that it is nothing more than a combining and reorganizing of our old experiences ; that it never can give us anything really new ; that we must progress in the same monotonous way for ever. But wait a moment. What if this combining and organizing is to become first habitual, then organic and unconscious, so that the sense of law becomes a direct perception ? Shall we not then be really seeing something new ? Shall there not be a new revelation of a great and more perfect cosmos, a universe fresh-born, a new heaven and a new earth ? *Mors janua vitæ*, by death to this world we enter upon a new life in the next. Doubtless there shall by-and-by be laws as far transcending those we now know as they do the simplest observation. The new incarnation may need a second passion ; but, evermore, beyond it is the Easter glory."

In these words there is the true ring of divinely inspired prophecy to those who know of the pure philosophy which Keely's system unfolds; teaching the "wondrous ways of Him who is perfect in knowledge." Professor Clifford was one of those whom Ernest Renan has classified as scouts in the great army, who divine beforehand that which becomes ere long patent to all. In their rapid and venturesome advance they catch sight before the others of the smiling plains and lofty peaks. The student of nature has been compared to a hound, wildly running after, and here and there chancing on game, universal exploration, a beating up of the game on all sides, that and that only is the sole possible method. And this is the spirit of those who pursue their researches in a scientific frame of mind : while those who enter the field in a sceptical mood, are indisposed to step out of the beaten track where they feel sure of their footing.

They have no ambitions to meet the fate of the trilobites in Professor Clifford's amusing apologue. "Once upon a time— much longer than six thousand years ago—the Trilobites were the only people that had eyes; and they were only just beginning to have them. Some of the Trilobites, even, had as yet no signs of coming sight. So that the utmost they could know was that they were living in darkness, and that perhaps there was such a thing as light. But at last one of them got so far advanced that when he happened to come to the top of the water in the daytime he saw the sun. So he went down and told the others that in general the world was light, but there was one great light which caused it all. Then they killed him for disturbing the commonwealth; but they considered it impious to doubt that in general the world was light, and that there was one great light which caused it all. And they had great disputes about the manner in which they had come to know this. Afterwards, another of them got so far advanced that when he happened to come to the top of the water, in the night-time, he saw the stars. So he went down and told the others that in general the world was dark, but that, nevertheless, there were a great number of little lights in it. Then they killed him for maintaining false doctrines; but from that time there was a division amongst them, and all the Trilobites were split in two parties, some maintaining one thing and some the other, until such time as so many of them had learned to see that there could be no doubt about the matter that both of the savant Trilobites were right."

Bacon has compared the mind of man to a prisoner in a cave with his back to the light, who sees only shadows of the events passing outside.

Dr. Stoney, in his paper on "Natural Science and Ontology," frames a working hypothesis, which leads up to Keely's theory, that "the laws of the universe are the laws of thought." "This is a very different thing," says Dr. Stoney, "from saying that they are the laws of human thought. The laws of human thought bear to them the same small proportion which the laws of the action of the wheels of a watch upon one another bear to the entire science of dynamics. . . . Natural science is thus, as it were, the study of an ever-changing shadow cast in a special and very indirect way by the mighty march of actual events."

"The history of philosophy," writes Ernest Renan, "should be the history of the thoughts of mankind. Hence we must look upon philology, or the study of ancient literatures, as a *science* having a distinct object, *viz.*, the knowledge of the human intellect."

The philologist and the chemist, because of the results of the researches of the one, and of the nature of the researches of the other, are the students who are best able to comprehend the discoveries of Keely. "It is the characteristic and the pride of modern science to attain its most lofty results only through the most scrupulous methods of experiment, and to arrive at the knowledge of the highest laws of nature, its hands resting on its apparatus. If the highest truths can, as it were, emanate from the alembic and the crucible, why should they not equally be the result of the study of the remains of the past, covered with the dust of ages? Shall the philologist who toils on words and syllables be less honoured than the student of chemistry labouring in his laboratory? It is impossible to guess beforehand what may result from philological researches, any more than one can know in digging a mine, the wealth it may contain. We may be on our way to the discovery of a new world. Science always presents itself to man as an unknown country. The most important discoveries have been brought about in a roundabout way. Very few problems have been deliberately grappled with at the outset, 'taken at the core.' There is nothing more difficult to foretell than the importance with which posterity will invest this or that order of facts; the researches that will be abandoned, the researches that will be continued. In looking for one thing one may stumble upon another; in the pursuit of a mere vision, one may hit upon a magnificent reality."

When a result has been attained, it is difficult to realize the trouble its attainment has cost, says Ernest Renan in "The Future of Science."

Of this nature have been the researches of the present distinguished Professor of Chemistry in the Royal Institution; leading him into a discovery, the great importance of which the future alone can unfold.

Professor Dewar's brilliant success in producing liquid oxygen will be remembered by all who had the privilege of witnessing it last year, on the occasion of the celebration of Faraday's Centenary. Its production is attended with the greatest difficulties; so great that Professor Dewar even felt doubts as to his being successful in his attempt at that time, which made his complete success all the more gratifying to him. When produced, it is difficult to hold and difficult to manipulate; but nothing daunted by these difficulties, Professor Dewar continued his researches, subjecting it to tests which no mind less penetrating than his own would ever have thought of, with the result that, most unexpectedly to himself, he has "hit upon a magnificent reality." The ordeal to which, with consummate skill, he subjected this unstable fluid, disclosed its marvellous affinity for the magnet; and iron is now no longer able to claim the distinction which it has hitherto enjoyed, of monopolizing the affections of the magnet. Sir Robert Ball, LL.D., F.R.S., in commenting upon this important and most interesting addition to our knowledge of the properties of oxygen, says:—" Seeing that water, which is so largely composed of oxygen, is not attracted by a magnet, it might certainly have seemed unlikely that a liquid which was nothing but pure oxygen should be affected to any noteworthy degree. I suspect, however, that Professor Dewar must have had some sagacious reason for anticipating that the magnet would treat liquid oxygen with much more attention than it bestowed on water. At all events, whether he expected it or not, the result as described was of the most extraordinary character. The liquid oxygen was vehemently attracted by the great magnet; it seems to have leaped from the vessel, to have clung round the poles, and continued to adhere to them until it had all evaporated and resumed the form of gas. The appreciation of this discovery will be shared not alone by chemists, but by all who are interested in the great truths of nature."

When Mr. Keely fell upon his discovery of an unknown force, he had not the faintest conception of the infinite extent, nor of the nature, of the territory he had invaded. Step by step he has been led on through years of patient and persistent research, yet even now feeling that he has but lifted one corner of the veil of the goddess of nature, and that a lifetime is too short to do more than this. The physicists whom Keely, in the earlier years of his discovery, invited to confer with him as to the origin of the force which was generated by the disintegration of water, preferred rather to pronounce him an impostor, after witnessing his demonstrations, than to admit that such results should have escaped the penetration of their all-powerful methods. "It indicates," says Dr. Watson, " a mistaken apprehension of the basis of our own so highly valued system of inquiry, that we should arrogate to it absolute exclusiveness, and deride, as though they were searchers after proved impossibilities, all those who choose to make the trial whether truth may be sought by any method besides our own."

History repeats itself, but on new planes. It is not those who are mighty in their own eyes whom Providence chooses as instruments to reveal new truths to the world when the needs of humanity require "a new order of things." The evolution of the human race is slow but sure. If in one century some backward steps are taken, in the next with giant strides all is regained that seemed to have been lost. Each age answers the need of its own time. "The condition of mankind, during the last quarter of the fifteenth century, bore some curious analogies to its state at present," writes Julian Hawthorne, under the heading, " The New Columbus." " A certain stage or epoch of human life seemed to have run its course and come to a stop. The impulses which had started it were exhausted. Once more, it seems, we have reached the limits of a dispensation, and are halted by a blank wall. There is no visible way over it, nor around it. We cannot stand still; still less can we turn back. What is to happen? What happens when an irresistible force encounters an impenetrable barrier? That was the question asked in Columbus' day, and he found an answer to it. Are we to expect the appearance of a new Columbus to answer it again? What Columbus can help us out of our dangers now? The time has come when the spirit of Columbus shall avouch itself, vindicating the patient purpose of Him who brings the flower from the seed. Great discoveries come when they are needed; never too early nor too late. When nothing else will serve the turn, then, and not till then, the rock opens and the spring gushes forth. Who that has considered the philosophy of the infinitely great and of the infinitely minute can doubt the inexhaustibleness of nature? And what is nature but the characteristic echo of the spirit of man? A prophet has arisen, during these latter days, in Philadelphia, who is commonly regarded as a charlatan; but men, cognizant of the latest advances of science, admit themselves unable to explain upon any known principles the effects he produces."

. . . .

"What we are to expect is an awakening of the soul; the rediscovery and rehabilitation of the genuine and indestructible religious instinct. Such a religious revival will be something very different from what we have known under that name. It will be a spontaneous and joyful realization by the soul of its vital relations with its Creator. Nature will be recognized as a language whereby God converses with man. The interpretation of this language, based as it is upon an eternal and living symbolism, containing infinite depths beyond depths of meaning, will be a sufficient study and employment for mankind for ever. Science will become, in truth, the handmaid of religion, in that it will be devoted to reporting the physical analogies of spiritual truths, and following them out in their subtler details. Hitherto the progress of science has been slow, and subject to constant error and revision. But as soon as physical research begins to go hand in hand with moral or psychical research it will advance with a rapidity hitherto unimagined, each assisting and classifying the other.

"The attitude of men towards one another will undergo a corresponding change. It is already become evident that selfishness is a colossal failure. . . . Recent social theorists propose a universal co-operation, to save the waste of personal competition. But competition is a wholesome and vital law; it is only the direction of it that requires alteration. When the cessation of working for one's livelihood takes place, human energy and love of production will not cease with it, but will persist and must find their channels. But competition to outdo each in the service of all is free from collisions, and its range is limitless. Not to support life, but to make life more lovely, will be the effort; and not to make it more lovely for one's self alone but for one's neighbour. Nor is this all.

"The love of the neighbour will be a true act of divine worship, since it will then be acknowledged that mankind, though multiplied to human sense, is in essence one; and that in this universal one, which can have no self-consciousness, God is incarnate.

"The divine humanity is the only real and possible object of mortal adoration, and no genuine sentiment of human brotherhood is conceivable apart from its recognition. But, with it, the stature of our common manhood will grow toward the celestial. Obviously, with thoughts and pursuits of this calibre to engage our attention, we shall be very far from regretting those which harass and enslave us to day. Leaving out of account the extension of psychical faculties, which will enable the antipodes to commune together at will, and even give us the means of communicating with the inhabitants of other planets, and which will so simplify and deepen language that audible speech, other than the musical sounds indicative of emotion, will be regarded as a comic and clumsy archaism,—apart from all this, the fathomless riches of wisdom to be gathered from the commonest daily objects and outwardly most trivial occurrences, will put an end to all craving for merely physical change of place and excitement. Gradually the human race will become stationary, each family occupying its own place, and living in patriarchal simplicity, though endowed with power and wisdom that we should now consider god-like. . . . We have only attempted to indicate what regions await the genius of the new Columbus; nor does the conjecture seem too bold that perhaps they are not so distant from us in time as they appear to be in quality."

If we turn, from this seemingly Utopian forecast, to the matter-of-fact utterances of Ernest Renan, we will find that he anticipates nothing less as the destiny of humanity, than the perfecting of it as a unity. Asserting that the nineteenth century is preparing the way for the enfranchisement of the mind, he proceeds logically to show how this evolution is to be brought about, strong in the faith that Providence will not fail in its design to secure the ultimate happiness of the human race. To quote, at length, from Renan:—"It is the law of science, as of every human undertaking, to draw its plans on a large scale, and with a great deal that is superfluous around them. Mankind finally assimilates only a small number of the elements of food. But the portions that have been eliminated played their part in the act of nutrition. So the countless generations that have appeared and disappeared like a dream, have served to build the great Babel of humanity which uprises toward the sky, each layer of which means a people. In God's vast bosom all that lived will live again, and then it will be true to the very letter that not a glass of water, not a word that has furthered the divine work of progress will be lost. That is the law of humanity; an enormous and lavish expenditure of the individual; for God only sets Himself the large, general plan; and each created being finds subsequently in himself the instincts which make his lot as mild as possible. All help to accelerate the day when the knowledge of the world shall equal the world, when the subject and the object having become identified, God will be complete. Philosophy up till now has scarcely been anything but fancy, *à priori*, and science has only been an insignificant display of learning. As for us, we have shifted the field of the science of man. We want to know what his life is, and life means both the body and the soul; not placed facing one another like clocks that tick in time, not soldered together like two different metals, but united into one two-fronted phenomenon which cannot be divided, without destroying it. It is time to proclaim the fact that one sole Cause has wrought everything in the domain of intellect, operating according to identical laws, but among different surroundings.

"The lofty serenity of science becomes possible only when it handles its imperturbable instrument with the inflexibility of the geometrician, without anger and without pity. True science, the complete and felt science, will be for the future, if civilization is not once again arrested in its march by blind superstition and the invasion of barbarism, in one form or another. But it is contended that the inferiority of the philosophy of science consists in its being accessible to the small minority. This is, on the contrary, its chief title to glory, showing us that we should labour to hasten the advent of the blessed day in which all men will have their place in the sunshine of intelligence, and will live in the true light of the children of God. It is the property of hope to hope against hope, and there is nothing which the past does not justify us in hoping from the future of humanity. Perfect happiness, as I understand it, is that all men should be perfect. I cannot understand how the opulent man can fully enjoy his happiness while he is obliged to veil his face in presence of the misery of a portion of his fellow-creatures. There can only be perfect happiness when all are equal, but *there will only be equality when all are perfect*. Thus we see that it is not a question of being happy; it is a question of being perfect; a question of true religion, the only thing which is serious and sacred. Inequality is legitimate whenever inequality is necessary for the good of humanity. Rights create themselves like other things. The French Revolution is not legitimate because it has taken place, but it took place because it was legitimate; the freeing of the negroes was neither achieved nor deserved by the negroes, but by the progress in civilization of their masters. Right is the progress of humanity; there is no right in opposition to this progress, and, *vice versâ*, progress legitimizes everything. Never, since the origin of things, has human intelligence set itself so terrible a problem as the one which now menaces our age. Upon the one hand, it is necessary to preserve the conquests already secured for civilization; while upon the other, all must have their share in the blessings of this civilization. It took centuries to conceive the possibility of a society without slavery. The traveller who looks only at the horizon of the plain, risks not seeing the precipice or the quagmire at his feet. In the same way, humanity when looking only to the distant object is tempted to make a jump for it, without regard to the intermediate objects against which it may not improbably dash itself to pieces. Socialism is, therefore, right to the extent of discerning the problem, but solves it badly; or rather socialism is not yet possible of solution. Reforms never triumph directly; they triumph by compelling their adversaries to partially adopt them in order to overcome them. It might be said of reforms as of the crusades: 'Not one succeeded: all succeeded.' As one sees the tide bringing the ever-collapsing waves upon the shore, the feeling aroused is one of powerlessness. The wave arrived so proudly, and yet it is dashed to pieces against the sand, and it expires in a feeble career against the shore which it seemed about to devour. But, upon reflection, one finds that this process is not as idle as it seems; for each wave, as it dies away, has its effect; and all the waves combined make the rising tide against which heaven and hell would be powerless. Humanity, when it is fatigued, is willing to pause; but to pause is not to rest. The calm is but an armistice and a breathing space. It is impossible for society to find calm in a state when it is suffering from an open wound such as that of to-day. The age is oppressed by this inevitable and seemingly insoluble problem. We barricade ourselves in one party, in order not to see the reasons of the other side. The conservatives are wrong, for the state of things which they uphold, and which they do right to uphold, is intolerable. The revolutionists are wrong; for it is absurd to destroy when you have nothing to put in place of what you destroy. At these epochs, doubt and indecision are the truth; the man who is not in doubt is either a simpleton or a charlatan. Revolutions must be made for well-ascertained principles, and not for tendencies which have not yet been formulated in a practical manner. They are the upheavals of the everlasting Enceladus turning over when Etna weighs too heavily upon him. It is horrible that one man should be sacrificed to the enjoyment of another. If it were merely a question of self-indulgence, it would be better that all should have Spartan fare, than that some should have luxuries and others go hungry; but, as long as material ease is to a certain extent the indispensable condition of intellectual perfection, the sacrifice is not effected for the enjoyment of another individual, of the luxuries of life, but it is made upon behalf of society as a whole. A society is entitled to what is necessary for its existence, however great may be the apparent injustice resulting for the individual. It is the idea of the ancient sacrifice—the man for the nation. If the object of life were but self-indulgence, it would not be unreasonable that each one should claim his share, and from this point of view any enjoyment which one might procure at the expense of others would be in reality an injustice and a robbery: but the object of life, the aim of society, should be the greatest possible perfecting of all. The State is neither an institution of police, as Smith would have it, nor a charity bureau and a hospital as the Socialists would have it. It is a machine for making progress. In the state of things which I should like to see, manual labour would be the recreation of mental labour. The immense majority of humanity is still at school: to let them out too soon would be to encourage them in idleness. Necessity, says Herder, is the weight of the clock which causes all the wheels to turn. Without the idea of progress, all the ideas of humanity are incomprehensible.

We must keep our machines in order, if we would bring down paradise upon earth; and paradise will be here below when all have their share in light, perfection, beauty, and therefore in happiness.

"It matters little whether the law grants or refuses liberty to new ideas, for they make their way all the same; they come into existence without the law, and they are all the better for this than if they had grown in full legality. When a river which has overflown its banks pours onward, you may erect dykes to arrest its progress, but the flood continues to rise; you may work with eager energy and employ skilful labourers to make good all the fissures, but the flood will continue to rise until the torrent has surmounted the obstacle, or until, by making a circuit of the dyke, it comes back by some other way to inundate the land which you have attempted to protect from it."

These are the advanced views of Ernest Renan, who still sees nothing before us but a fresh cataclysm, a general upheaval and chaos, terrible disturbances when human intelligence will be checkmated, thrown off the rails so to speak, by events as yet unparalleled. We have not yet suffered sufficiently, he says, to see the kingdom of heaven. When a few millions of men have died of hunger, when thousands have devoured one another, when the brains of the others, carried off their balance by these darksome scenes, have plunged into extravagancies of one kind and another, then life will begin anew. Suffering has been for man the mistress and the revealer of great things. Order is an end, not a beginning; but out of respect for the rights of bears and lions are we to open the bars of a menagerie? Are these beasts to be let loose upon men? No, for humanity and civilization must be saved at any cost. But these problems, which make up the capital question of the nineteenth century, are, in a speculative sense, insoluble; they will be solved by brute force, says Renan. The crowd behind is ever pressing forward; those in the foremost ranks are toppled over into the yawning gulf, and when their bodies have filled up the abyss, the last comers pass over on the level."

But let us suppose that what pseudo-science has wrested

from us, true science is ready to restore; ready to offer all that Renan himself tells us is necessary to open the way for the elevation of the people, by giving all men a share in the delights of education; thus widening the basis of the brotherhood of humanity, and making room for all at the banqueting-table of knowledge, enabling men to be "perfect in their measure," for "absolute equality is as impossible in humanity as it would be in the animal reign. Each part is perfect in the hierarchy of the parts when it is all that it can be, and does well all that it ought to do."

Let us suppose that true science offers confirmation of all that revelation has taught of the attributes of the Creator of all things, reiterating the promise of a time when this knowledge shall be spread over the face of the whole earth and made known to all men. Let us imagine that, in addition to the opening of these floodgates of knowledge, the time is drawing near when machinery, unknown now, will be employed to help the workman in his task, and abridge his hours of labour, leaving leisure for the cultivation of his mind. Aristotle has told us what would be the result, "if every instrument could work of its own accord, if the spindles worked of themselves, if the bow played the violin without being held, the contractors could do without workmen and the masters without slaves." Man would so master nature that material requirements would no longer be the supreme motive, and human activity would be directed towards the things of the mind. In such a state of existence men of intelligence would "conquer the infinite."

We are living in a period of wondrous revelations of the power of God, and the crowning discovery of this epoch promises the fulfilment of Scripture prophecy in a dispensation of harmony and peace, that will restore to mankind that measure of faith in God and immortality, which can alone give strength "to endure the evil days without feeling the weight of them" that lie between the present time and the realization of our hopes for the perfection of humanity. With the knowledge that lies in this new revelation of the power of the All-Mighty, no hopes seem chimerical or Utopian. We shall all be as gods, when the fulness of the love of God and the power of God is made known to, and understoood by, all men. Tossing as we are in a seething whirlpool of scepticism, threatened as are the nations with dangers on all sides, if we were bereft of our God, as the leading lights of science would have us believe, there would be no hope for humanity. But though the anchor of ancient faiths has been swept away by materialism, the sheet-anchor of faith by science has been let down from heaven, as it were in our hour of peril, for the saving of the peoples: teaching as often before that the world lies in the bosom of God, like a child in its mother's arms, who with watchful solicitude ministers to its wants as they arise.

Religion as revealed to us by our Holy Master, Jesus Christ, is to know and to love the truth of things. When this religion is understood and practised, then, and not before, will the earth be full of the knowledge that it is God who is, and that all the rest only appears to be. If anarchy and disorder would but wait for this time to arrive, no devastating cataclysms, no destroying whirlwinds, will come as forerunners to prepare the way, as in the past, for progress. The light now dawning will usher in "the new order of things," and we may expect that an era of material prosperity will soon set in, such as the world has never dreamed of; arresting the outbreak of barbarism which seems near at hand. There are some who contend that this revelation of an unknown force will, in the hands of anarchists, put back the progress of civilization and enlightenment for centuries; there are others who proclaim that it will take the bread from the mouths of the hungry and swell the sums amassed by capitalists. But history shows that discovery heralds progress, and walks with it hand in hand. With the costless and unlimited power which will be made available, in every direction where power is required, all works of improvement will be carried out on a far grander scale than has ever been anticipated. The great polar stream, with its exhaustless supply of energy, places at our disposal a force as harmless as the current that draws its keeper to the magnet. We have but to "hook our machinery on to the machinery of nature," and we have a safe and harmless propelling and controlling force, the conditions of which when once set up remain for ever, perpetual molecular action the result. Another step made toward the conquering of the material world which must precede the advent of the reign of the spirit.

Schlegel foresaw that the only hope for a brotherhood of humanity lay in the thorough religious regeneration of the State and of science, and that through these combined powers the underlying purpose of Eternal Mind is to be made known, covering the earth with the knowledge of God as the waters cover the beds of the seas, obtaining a complete triumph for Christianity.

It would fill with despair the hearts of those who are working to bring about this end (so slow, so retrograde at times does the evolution seem to be) did they not know that they have an Invincible Power working with them.

History has again repeated itself, and truth has once more had its birth in a stable. A star has arisen in the West which heralds to all races what the Star of Bethlehem heralded in Judea, viz. the coming of the time when the earth shall be filled with the knowledge of the Lord. There are both Magi and shepherds now, as of old, who have watched for the rising of this star, and who were the first to behold the gold and crimson light of the approaching dawn; in which Faith, which modern science has crucified and laid away in its sepulchre, will have its resurrection and dwell on earth for evermore—the tabernacle of God with men.

THE DAWN.

Dante called his lifetime, " The time of my debt."

I.

Have I not paid my debt, O God,
 What have I left to give?
Yet blest my life in rendering all
 To help the nations live
In harmony, in peace, in love,
 As nations all will be,
When knowledge true shall cover earth
 As waters cover sea.

II.

Nailed to the cross are all my hopes—
  Thou hast not spared me aught:
But raised thereby above the world
  Its treasures count as naught:
Empty its titles and its show,
  Its honours and its fame;
Better the love of God to know
  Than riches, rank, or name.

III.

Two avenues there are, 'tis said,
  From paltry passions vile,
From all calamities of earth,
  From artifice and wile.
Science and Art their votaries lead
  From quicksands and from shoal;
Their guiding torches held aloft
  Will light us to our goal.

IV.

When ended this—my "time of debt"—
  'Tis only Thou canst know;
But when the longed-for quittance comes
  I stay not here below.
Till then give me the torch of Art
  To light my pathway drear,
Let Science lift my thoughts to Thee,
  My lonely hours to cheer.

V.

And when my life-long debt is paid—
  My soul from body free—
No bondage can enslave me more,
  For I shall go to Thee.
Hasten the hour when summons comes,
  To take me to my home;
Here have I lived an exile's life,
  An exile forced to roam.

VI.

The face of love was turned from me
  When most I felt its need,
And in the wilds my feet were set
  To plough and sow the seed.
Ashes and tears to me were given;
  I sat not by the way,
With folded hands to make lament,
  But laboured day by day.

VII.

Thou hast not dealt one useless blow,
    What time I worked in field:
Each tear of blood, each hour of toil,
    Increased the harvest yield;
And now the furrows all are ploughed,
    If I have paid my debt,
By waters still, in paths of peace,
    Thou wilt my footsteps set.

VIII.

Æons may pass before my hopes
    For earth are all fulfilled;
But let " *the dawn* " approach, I pray,
    Before my lips are stilled!
And let true knowledge cover earth
    As waters cover sea—
Knowledge of truth, knowledge of love,
    Knowledge, dear God, of Thee!

IX.

I wait the music of the spheres,
    The rhythmic pulse of earth,
Which, when Death's angelus doth ring,
    Announce immortal birth:
In that blest home beyond the veil
    No discord rends the air
The law of harmony prevails
    And love reigns everywhere.

CONCLUSION.

KEELY'S PHYSICAL PHILOSOPHY.

Mr. Keely begins with sounds whose vibrations can be known and registered. I presume that the laws of ratio, position, duality, and continuity, all the laws which go to mould the plastic air by elastic bodies into the sweetness of music, will also be found ruling and determining all in the high silence of interior vibrations, which hold together or shake asunder the combinations that we call atoms and ultimate elements.—*The Science of Music.* D. C. RAMSAY. *Edited by the* REV. JOHN ANDREW. Marcus Ward & Co.

What Keely has discovered in physics, I am in some measure credited with discovering in metaphysics: this is nothing strange, according to this philosophy, which shows that many people may *divine* the same original truth at the same time by means of the etheric element which connects the Deity, the source of all truth, with all His creatures.—*Preface to Vera Vita; or, the Philosophy of Sympathy.* DAVID SINCLAIR. Author of *A New Creed.* Digby, Long & Co., London.

Abstract of Keely's Physical Philosophy in its main features up to the point of practical application; by PROFESSOR DANIEL G. BRINTON, *of the Pennsylvania University; subject to modifications and additions when Keely has made public his system.*

THE fundamental conception of the Universe is force manifesting itself in rhythmical relations.

This definition is exhaustive, including both thought and extension, matter and mind. The law for the one is the law for the other. The distinction between them is simply relative, i.e. quantitative, not qualitative.

The rhythmic relations in which force acts are everywhere, under all conditions, and at all times, the same. They are found experimentally to be universally expressible by the mathematical relations of thirds.

These threefold relations may be expressed with regard to their results as,—

    I. Assimilative.
    II. Individualizing.
    III. Dominant or Resultant.

From these three actions are derived the three fundamental

LAWS OF BEING.

I. Law of Assimilation : every individualized object assimilates itself to all other objects.

II. Law of Individualization : every such object tends to assimilate all other objects to itself.

III. Law of the Dominant : every such object is such by virtue of the higher or dominant force which controls these two tendencies.

Applying these fundamental laws to an explanation of the universe, as it is brought to human cognition, all manifestations of force may be treated as modes of vibrations.

The essential differences give rise to three modes of vibration :—

I. The Radiating : called also the "Dispersing," the "Propulsive," the "Positive," and the "Enharmonic."

II. The Focalizing : called also the "Negative," the "Negative Attractive," the "Polarizing," and the "Harmonic."

III. The Dominant : called also the "Etheric," or the "Celestial."

These, it will be noted, correspond to the three laws of being. It is not to be understood that any one of these three modes of vibration can exist independently. Each by itself is called a "current," and all three must be present in every "stream" or "flow" of force. The relations of the currents in every flow are expressible in thirds, and it is experimentally demonstrable that the relation of the three are in the order named : as $33\frac{1}{3} : 66\frac{2}{3} : 100$.

The evolution of what is called "matter" from the different

modes of vibration is through the action of the second law, that of focalization, or "negative attraction," or "negative affinity."

Where the vibrations under this mode meet, and are maintained in a state of mutual affinity or equilibrium, there is established what is called a "neutral centre," or, as otherwise expressed, "a centre of sympathetic coincidence."

The terms "neutral attraction," "neutral affinity," "negative attraction," or "polar negative attraction," are employed to express the property of a mode of vibration to direct its components towards such centre.

As no current or flow of force can be composed of one mode of vibration only, but must always be composed of three modes uniting in varying thirds, we have $1 \times 2 \times 3 = 6$ as the total possible forms of sympathetic coincidence, or, to speak in ordinary terms, there can be six; and six only, possible forms of individualized being. These are what Keely calls the six orders of atomic subdivision, or orders of vibratory motion, and he names them as follows:

   I. Molecular.
   II. Inter-molecular.
   III. Atomic.
   IV. Inter-atomic.
   V. Etheric.
   VI. Inter-etheric.

In this list the forms of matter are arranged in the mathematical sequence of the rapidity of the oscillations of their constituent members; the proportion being proved by experiment to be as follows: for the molecular orders:

$$1 : 3 : 9 : 27 : 81 : 243.$$

This arithmetical progression changes in the atomic orders to a geometrical progression as follows:

$$3 : 9 : 81 : 6561 : 43046721, \text{etc.}$$

This same method of progression is believed to hold in all the orders of vibrations above the molecular, and soon passes into mathematical infinity.

Actually, however, all matter of which we are capable of

cognition through the medium of our senses is in one of three forms of aggregation:

    I. Molecular.
    II. Atomic.
    III. Etheric:

in each of which the controlling mode of vibration is respectively,

    I. The Enharmonic.
    II. The Harmonic.
    III. The Dominant.

But it must be understood that each of these modes is a positive and real constituent of every atom and molecule.

It will be seen that as every form of material aggregation is to be considered as a "neutral centre of attraction," where the vibratory force of all three orders are held in "sympathetic coincidence," that is, in balanced activity or harmonized motion, and not by any means cancelled or mutually destroyed, there is no diminution of force, but only temporary suspension of its radiating or propulsive activity or expression.

This is the foundation of Keely's doctrine of "latent force," and of the indefinite power which can be obtained by breaking up the harmonious balance or equation of forces of every mode, which exists in every "neutral centre," that is to say in every mass of matter.

Insomuch as every mass of matter consists thus, in fact, of vibrations in harmonic equilibrium, related by simple proportions of thirds, it follows that every mass of every description stands in harmonic relation to every other mass. This is, in part, what is meant by the sympathy of all forms of matter and of motion; and it is through the study of the methods of increasing or diminishing this sympathy that we reach practical results in this field of research. At present this is best accomplished by resonance; that is, through the harmonic vibrations created by musical instruments, bringing out the acoustic world as the microscope reveals the hidden visual world.

Every visible or tangible mass of matter must be regarded as an aggregation of molecules; the molecules being the true centres of the equated forces of "neutralized attraction."

These molecules have been experimentally proved by Keely to be formed of all three modes of vibration; the proof being that they respond to all three modes when subjected to the tests of compound concordant impulses.

When in that state of neutral aggregation which we know as matter, each molecule is in perpetual oscillation, the range of the oscillation being one-third of the molecule, and its rapidity 20,000 oscillations in a second.

It is through the disturbance of this oscillatory equilibrium, by means of resonant impulses, that Keely alters the relations of the vibratory impulses which constitute matter. This he does by striking the same chord in three octaves, representing the *third, sixth,* and *ninth* of the scale.

Of these, the sixth reduces the range of molecular vibrations or oscillations; and, by thus bringing nearer to each other the neutral centres, increases solidification.

The ninth extends the range of molecular oscillation, and thus tends to give greater tenuity to the mass. It induces "trajectile velocity" from neutral centres, or "neutral radiation." Experiment shows that molecular dissociation does not take place until the molecule attains an oscillation approaching, if not fully reaching two-thirds of its diameter. This can be effected by means of the action of the "enharmonic" or "radiating" current applied to the mass, after its molecules have once been disturbed by an "introductory impulse;" that is, by the musical note above mentioned.

The third represents the "dominant," and when brought under control of a harmonic resonant impulse induces a complete rearrangement of the modes of vibration and oscillation; in other words, will transform the mass either into its component initial forces, or into some other form of matter.

It is the study of the dominant to which Keely has devoted his recent researches. He aims to control the power he evolves by altering the dominant or etheric mode of vibration in the triplicate flows of force.

As all molecules and masses are mere centres of harmonized vibrations, temporarily held in suspension by simple laws identical with those of resonance, it follows that these centres can be broken up or divided by certain orders of vibration impinging upon and disturbing them.

It is a familiar fact that a cord in vibration tends to produce a similar vibration in a cord placed near it. This property belongs to all vibrations, whether resonant or not, and they exert it in proportion to the "order" to which they belong. The distance in space to which this power extends, or can be extended, is what is called "the sympathetic outreach" of the current or flow.

In this manner we have "sympathetic negative attraction," and "sympathetic positive propulsion," with reference to the "outreach" of the third or dominant current of the stream, which is allied to the order of etheric vibrations.

Each molecule of a given mass of matter represents the same harmonic chord or note in its oscillatory motion. The "chord of the mass" is, therefore, the chord of every molecule of the mass.

But as the condition of absolutely stable equilibrium is theoretical only, and does not exist in nature, the chord of the mass is constantly changing. Yet we must learn to control this "chord of the mass" by resonant induction, if we would gain command of the molecular forces.

Keely believes he has solved this problem, by the invention of a mechanical device which brings the chords of all masses within the conditions of a few simple acoustic tests.

The range of molecular oscillation is affected differently in different substances when submitted to the same vibratory impulse, and these ranges can be measured.

In the three metals, silver, gold, and platina, we obtain the proportions——3 : 6 : 9 : — As this is the primary relation of the modes of vibration, a wire made of these three metals is peculiarly adapted to transmit concordant impulses: and nodes made of these substances placed upon a wire, transmitting resonant vibrations, indicate, by the different orders of vibration induced in them, the rate of oscillations of the atomic constituents.

The phenomenon of rotation arises from the harmonic interaction of the dominant and enharmonic elements of the flow: in other words, the first and third, the third and ninth, etc.; those whose vibrations bear the proportions to each other $33\frac{1}{3} : 100$.

A practical example of rotation is a wheel in revolution on its axis. This is force in its commercial or economic aspect. To accomplish this result by molecular vibratory action, we must gain control of the "negative attractive" or "enharmonic" current of the triple flow, and the problem is then solved up to any limit of power.

APPENDIX I.

MORE than four centuries B.C., Leucippus and his disciple Democritus—who expounded the atomic theory of his master—introduced the doctrine of indivisible atoms, *possessing within themselves a principle of energy.* Democritus, it is said, travelling in search of wisdom, visited the Gymnosophists of India (who, by leading ascetic lives, thought they could effect a reunion of the spiritual nature of man, with the divine essence of Deity), and in so doing incurred the risk of being deprived of the rites of sepulture by his "waste of patrimony," there being a law in Abdera to that effect.

Anaxagoras, Heraclitus, Empedocles and other philosophers, had taught that matter was indefinitely divisible, but Leucippus and Democritus were the first to assert that these particles or atoms were originally destitute of all qualities except form and energy; and they are, therefore, called the originators of the atomic philosophy; which is the basis of Keely's system of sympathetic physics.

Sympathetic physics teaches that light is an etheric evolution, propagated by sympathetic conflict between celestial and terrestrial outflows: solar tensions as against terrestrial condensation. True luminosity cannot be induced in any other way. The high order of triple vibration, that induces (progressively) molecular and intermolecular separation, shows luminous results which, when thus mechanically produced, are virtually on a small scale, a fac-simile of nature's operations. "All such experiments that I have made," writes Keely, "resulted in vortex motion invariably, both sympathetically and otherwise. Vortex motion follows nature in all corpuscular action.

"The undulatory theory, regarding light, I have not been

able to reconcile myself to, as anything but hypothetical. The conditions which govern electro-magnetic radiation, disprove the theory in many particulars. The vortex action induced in space, by the differential conflict between the low and high tenuous, shows up results that harmonize with the conditions accompanying the dissociation of hydrogen and oxygen, in disintegrating water: viz., vortex action of the highest order, but peripheral only. If it were not so, the ether could not be held in suspension, neither in the molecular nor atomic envelopes. Undulatory effects are produced by certain conditions of sound; and by other conditions quite opposite effects. In organ pipes, of a certain calibre, very sensitive waves occur at intervals; as according to the character of the sound evolved; but on a combination of resonators composed of brass tubes of more than nine in number, a wave of sound, induced by certain chords passing over them, produces high vortex action of the air enclosed in them. The vibration of tuning forks induces alternate conditions of the air that surrounds them, if in open atmosphere; but quite a different action presents itself when the forks are exercised in resonating tubes, set to thirds of the mass chord they represent. Then high vortex action is the instant result. Vibrators cannot be set promiscuously in tubes, and get such results, any more than a musician can render a musical composition on the violin before tuning it. The conditions under which light is evolved negatize whatever is associated with undulation, as this word is understood by physicists. Aqueous undulations there are, but not etheric undulations.

"The mighty forces latent in corpuscular matter, by which we are surrounded, are all held in oscillating vortex action by the Infinite Designer of workings hidden from us, until the time is ripe for their disclosure. This latent, registered power interchanges sympathetically with the celestial radiating streams, whereby light, heat, electricity, magnetism and galvanic action are propagated in their different orders, vitalizing all nature with their life-giving principles. When this great scientific and religious truth has been made known, and established by demonstration, all controversy as to the source of energy will be for ever silenced. If I am the chosen instrument to develop this knowledge, and to make known the conditions which surround this pure truth, it is only that I may hand the key to those who will use it to enter the doorway that opens into the inaudible, and thus gain an insight into the now invisible region of the operation of Nature's most powerful governing forces, in the control over terrestrial mind by celestial matter."

APPENDIX II.

The flow of electricity, as set down in Keely's system, is governed by triple conditions : 1st. the dominant or high vibratory; 2nd. the sub-dominant or low vibratory; 3rd. the harmonic or undulatory; In combination one flow. Keely writes:—"When electrical experts can construct a mechanical device whereby the low vibratory conditions of the sub-dominant can be assimilated to the harmonic undulatory, by thirds, they will be able to run their dynamos without any extraneous appliances. An introductory impulse, on a certain order of vibration, being all that would be required to give the sub-dominant a concordant relation to the dominant; which would more effectually operate the dynamo than any number of steam-engines; allowing the harmonic stream to be the governor. This concordance, as towards the dominant, would only excite its sympathetic action in a way that would divert the ruling conditions of the two, without being submitted to the destructive effects of the dominant current. I think many lives will be lost before such a position is attained. Tesla has reached out *almost* to the crest of the harmonic wave, leaving all electrical explorers far behind him. It is only when such a condition is reached that the true value of electrical lighting will be understood, and extraneous power dispensed with; but, in my opinion, the present conditions for transferring power will remain unaltered, in the use of electricity, for generations.

"There is but one position to arrive at, that will redeem the many failures of the past decade, in attempts to find an economizing medium for commercial benefit in regard to power; and that position will be attained when the polar sympathetic harness is completed, which will give to the world the control of the polar forces."

In reply to the question, "What do you include in the polar forces?" Keely answers, "Magnetism, electricity, and gravital sympathy; each stream composed of three currents, or triune streams, which make up the governing conditions of the controlling medium of the universe: the infinite ninths that I am now endeavouring to graduate to a sympathetic mechanical combination, will, if I succeed, close my researches in sympathetic physics, and complete my system. These sympathetic streams from celestial space, percussing on the dense atmospheric environment of our earth, by their infinite velocities, wrest from their atomic confinement the latent energies which we call heat and light."

Question.—And where do these sympathetic conditions or streams of force have their origin?

Answer.—'So God created man in His own image, in the image of God created He him: male and female created He them,' Genesis i. 27." All sympathetic conditions, or streams of force, are derived (if we dare to make use of such a term in speaking of Deity) from the cerebral convolutions of the Infinite: from the centre of the vast realm of the compound luminous. From the celestial intermediate, the brain of Deity, proceed the sympathetic flows that vitalize the polar terrestrial forces."—*Keely.*

APPENDIX III.

SOME faint idea of the infinite patience which the nature of Keely's work requires may be gained by a knowledge of his process of converting straight tubes into resonating rings. The tubes, in sections long enough to form a semicircle, are passed between triple rollers, which are set to give them a slight bend. They are then fastened to a bed-plate, and a steel ball, the exact diameter of the interior of the tube, is passed into it and forced through it. It is then passed between the rollers again; which are set so as to slightly increase the curvature, and again the interior of the tube is corrected by the steel ball. This process is intermittently continued until the semicircle is reached. Each process of bending and correcting requires over two hours. Eighty bends are sometimes necessary for the completion of the full circle. When the two semicircles, which form the circle, are finished, they are placed in a steel mould and kept under hydraulic pressure for two or three days, to correct any lateral deflection which has taken place in bending them. They are then taken out of the moulds and screwed rigidly to a face-plate, and joined together by a solder of refined brass and silver. Next they are placed in a hot sand bath of sufficient volume to require seventy-two hours to cool down. This corrects the differentiation in their molecular groupings. They are then submitted to a vibratory flow from the sympathetic negative transmitter, until their intonation, by percussion, represents a pure unmixed chord. The indicator, attached to the rings, denotes when this condition is attained. They are then centred on a steel shaft and rotated at the rate of 2000 revolutions per minute, surrounded by the triple

Appendix III.

circuit ring. If the indicator, on the circuit ring, should vary five degrees on a subdivision of 8000, the process for correcting has to be repeated until the variations are reduced to three; which is near enough to be considered perfect, inasmuch as the circular resonator will then hold the neutral focalization intact during the graduation of the full ninths, or triple triplets, for sympathetic association to polar negative attraction.

Professor Dewar's recent brilliant achievements, in his line of experimental research, not only have an important bearing upon one of the greatest problems of modern science, but upon the science of the future, as forecast by Keely.

Thermal radiation (and its negative, cold), the field of Professor Dewar's researches, in Keely's system comes below the first atomic; while celestial sympathetic radiation comes as the fountain head; the compound inter-etheric, from which all aggregated matter springs, the governing force of all aggregations. If there were no sympathetic radiation from the great celestial centre, space would be void of suspended, or floating, earthy and gaseous matter; consequently, planetary worlds would never have had their birth and growth.

The suggestion of Professor Dewar, that an increase in low temperatures might lead to the liquefying of hydrogen, is an admission that hydrogen may be a compound; for no simple can ever be condensed into a visible form. Keely's experimental researches have proved, to his own satisfaction, that all known gases are compounds, inasmuch as, when the intensity which accompanies sympathetic vibration, in his process, is brought to bear upon any gas, it submits to dissociation.

The low temperatures with which Professor Dewar is dealing cause molecular motion to cease; but the matter thus experimented upon is not "dead matter" after this cessation of motion. Nothing can rob matter of the latent energy which it contains; water is not robbed of it by being frozen. The oxygen and hydrogen still occupy their relative positions and conditions, without depreciation of their vitality. Were water dead matter when frozen, its molecular activity could not be restored by elevating its temperature.

Matter can never be robbed of its soul by any conditions of intensity of heat nor of cold that could be brought to bear upon it.

When Professor Dewar uses the term "dead," in regard to matter, it is purely in reference to the present orthodox theory of heat energy. Take the analogy of a tuning fork or a bell; both are dead, so far as sound is concerned, if they are not in vibration;—they can be examined at rest or in motion, but science has not yet been able to do the same thing with those general motions of a molecular nature called heat. This is what Professor Dewar means by the term "dead," knowing well that the molecular activity can return alike to the fork or the molecule; only the energy must be supplied from some other source. Such are the conditions with which orthodox science is dealing, without acknowledging Deity as the fountain head of all force.

Not until Professor Dewar has witnessed the dissociation of hydrogen will he be able to judge of the truth of the claim, that for nearly twenty years Keely has been researching the nature of the product of this dissociation: leading him to define and classify force and energy very much as Grant Allen has done in his heretical work, on this subject, published by Longmans & Co., in 1887.

James B. Alexander, in his book on "The Dynamic Theory,"[1] makes this distinction between Force and Energy:

"Energy is simply the motion of material bodies, large or small. Force is the measure of energy, its degree or quantity. ... The ether is the universal agent of Energy, and the medium in all motion and phenomena. It may with propriety be called the *Soul of Things*."

---

[1] The Dynamic Theory of Life and Mind." The Housekeeper Press, Minneapolis, Minn.

TO JOHN ERNST WORRELL KEELY.

"*Palmam qui meruit ferat.*"

PRIZED secret of aerial space
  Is thine! Not firmly caught
Without long years of patient toil—
  Of more than giant thought.

Unfaltering thy steadfast faith,
  In all its wise control,
'Mid insults, taunts and sneers, enough
  To crush the bravest soul.

Such the ordeal on the paths
  Of Stephenson, Daguerre,
Of Fulton, Goodyear, Morse, to which
  They gave no heed nor care.

Like them still fearless thou hast toiled
  With heart and will intense,
Until discovery now brings
  Its grandest recompense.

Displaced all powers known, before
  This force of latest birth;
So great no mind can comprehend—
  No being born of earth.

We hail thee, revolutionist
  From every point of view;
For from the marvels thou hast wrought
  Science must start anew.

Longed-for-attainment now is grasped,
  Thy cherished hopes to bless;
And near at hand stands thy reward
  In laurel crowned success!

    ANONYMOUS, in *Cincinnati Illustrated News*

www.ingramcontent.com/pod-product-compliance
Lightning Source LLC
Chambersburg PA
CBHW030733250426
43671CB00034B/87